D1433942

MULTICULTURALISM AND MINORITY RIGHTS IN THE ARAB WORLD

Multiculturalism and Minority Rights in the Arab World

Edited by
WILL KYMLICKA AND
EVA PFÖSTL

Great Clarendon Street, Oxford, OX2 6DP,
United Kingdom

Oxford University Press is a department of the University of Oxford.
It furthers the University's objective of excellence in research, scholarship,
and education by publishing worldwide. Oxford is a registered trade mark of
Oxford University Press in the UK and in certain other countries

© the several contributors 2014

The moral rights of the authors have been asserted

First Edition published in 2014
Impression: 1

All rights reserved. No part of this publication may be reproduced, stored in
a retrieval system, or transmitted, in any form or by any means, without the
prior permission in writing of Oxford University Press, or as expressly permitted
by law, by licence or under terms agreed with the appropriate reprographics
rights organization. Enquiries concerning reproduction outside the scope of the
above should be sent to the Rights Department, Oxford University Press, at the
address above

You must not circulate this work in any other form
and you must impose this same condition on any acquirer

Published in the United States of America by Oxford University Press
198 Madison Avenue, New York, NY 10016, United States of America

British Library Cataloguing in Publication Data
Data available

Library of Congress Control Number: 2013951378

ISBN 978-0-19-967513-5

Printed in Great Britain by
CPI Group (UK) Ltd, Croydon, CR0 4YY

Links to third party websites are provided by Oxford in good faith and
for information only. Oxford disclaims any responsibility for the materials
contained in any third party website referenced in this work.

Acknowledgments

Most of the chapters in this volume were initially presented at a workshop held in Rome on 25–6 March 2011. We would like to thank Queen's University in Kingston, Canada, the Istituto di Studi Politici S. Pio V, Rome, and the Libera Universita Internazionale degli Studi Sociali, Guido Carli, LUISS, Rome, for their financial support and logistical assistance of that workshop. Thanks also to Fahima Charafeddine, Hassan Hanafi, Paola Pizzo, and Giuseppe Scattolin for their helpful contributions to the workshop. We have commissioned a few additional chapters to broaden the focus of the volume. The chapters have been extensively revised and we are grateful to all the authors for their enthusiasm for the project. We would also like to thank Kyle Johannsen for help compiling the manuscript, Dominic Byatt at Oxford University Press for his support, and Benno Simma for designing the wonderful cover image on our behalf.

Contents

Notes on Contributors

Joshua Castellino is Professor of Law and Head of the Law Department, Middlesex University, UK. His books include: *Minority Rights in the Pacific* (Oxford: Oxford University Press, 2009, with David Keane); *Minority Rights in Asia* (Oxford: Oxford University Press, 2006, with Elvira Domínguez Redondo); *The End of the Liberal State and the First Terrorist* (Hendon: Middlesex University Press, 2009); *International Law & Indigenous Peoples* (ed.) (Alphen aan den Rijn: Kluwer, 2004); *Title to Territory in International Law: A Temporal Analysis* (Aldershot: Ashgate, 2003 with S. Allen); and *International Law & Self Determination* (Dordrecht: Martinus Nijhoff, 2000). His most recent book is *Minority Rights in the Middle East* with Kathleen Cavanaugh (OUP, 2013).

Kathleen Cavanaugh is Lecturer of International Law in the Faculty of Law, Irish Centre for Human Rights, National University of Ireland, Galway. She holds a LL M from the Queen's University of Belfast and a Ph.D. in Comparative Politics from the London School of Economics and Political Science. Her research focuses on the study of nationalism, ethnic conflict, political violence, applicable human rights laws in entrenched states of emergency, and the laws of belligerent occupation. Her current projects include *Minority Rights in the Middle East* (Oxford: Oxford University Press), with co-author Joshua Castellino, as well as a monograph entitled *Militant Democracy* which investigates the exclusion radicalization thesis, focusing on the Muslim community in the UK. As a consultant, she has undertaken numerous missions on behalf of Amnesty International including to Northern Ireland, Israel/Palestine, and, more recently, to Iraq.

Francesca Maria Corrao is Professor of Arabic Language and Literature at LUISS University, Rome. Among her books: *Adonis: Nella pietra e nel vento* (Messina: Mesogea, 1999); *Antologia della Poesia Araba* (Rome: La biblioteca di repubblica, 2004); *L'estetica nella poesia del Mediterraneo* (ed.) (Mazara del Vallo: Atti del convegno, 2006); *Les Histoires de Giufà* (Lyons: La fosse aux ours, 2005); *In un mondo senza cielo* (Florence: Giunti, 2007); *Bennis: Il Mediterraneo e la parola* (ed.) (Rome: Donzelli, 2009).

Zaid Eyadat is Associate Professor of Political Science and International Relations at the University of Jordan, where he serves as Chairman of the Human Rights and Human Development Department. His publications include: "Culture and Foreign Policy: An Explanatory Model. American Foreign Policy Post 9/11" and "The Calculus of Consensus: An Alternative Path to Arab Democracy."

Hassan Jabareen is the Founder of Adalah—The Legal Center for Arab Minority Rights in Israel. He has extensive experience in litigating landmark cases before the Israeli Supreme Court on behalf of Palestinians in Israel and in the OPT. He led the legal team in the representation of the thirteen bereaved families of the October 2000 killings before the Or Commission of Inquiry.

Janet Klein is Associate Professor at the Department of History, the University of Akron, Ohio. Her publications include: *The Margins of Empire: Kurdish Militias in the Ottoman Tribal Zone* (Stanford, CA: Stanford University Press, 2011), as well as several journal articles on Kurdish nationalism.

Will Kymlicka is Canada Research Chair in Political Philosophy at Queen's University in Kingston, Canada. He is the author of *Multicultural Citizenship: A Liberal Theory of Minority Rights* (Oxford: Oxford University Press, 1995); and of *Multicultural Odysseys: Navigating the New International Politics of Diversity* (Oxford: Oxford University Press, 2007).

Sebastiano Maffettone is Professor of Political Philosophy at LUISS University, Rome, and Director of the *Centro di Studi e Ricerche sui Diritti Umani* (CERSDU), Rome. Among his books are *Valori comuni* (Milan: il Saggiatore, 1998); *I fondamenti del liberalismo* (Rome: Laterza, 2008, with co-author Ronald Dworkin); *Il valore della vita* (Milan: Mondadori, 1996); *Etica pubblica* (Milan: il Saggiatore, 2001); *La pensabilità del mondo* (Milan: il Saggiatore, 2006); and *Rawls: An Introduction* (Cambridge: Polity, 2010).

Nicholas McGeehan has a PhD from the European University Institute in Florence where his thesis addressed the marginalization of slavery in international law. He is a researcher at Human Rights Watch, covering the Gulf states of Bahrain, Qatar and the United Arab Emirates.

Jacob Mundy is an Assistant Professor of Peace and Conflict Studies at Colgate University. He received his Ph.D. at the Institute of Arab and Islamic Studies, University of Exeter, and is a former fellow with the Center for Maghrib Studies in Algeria. He is co-author with Stephen Zunes of *Western Sahara: War, Nationalism and Conflict Irresolution* (Syracuse: Syracuse University Press, 2010).

Brendan O'Leary is Lauder Professor of Political Science at the University of Pennsylvania, and Director of the University of Pennsylvania Program in Ethnic Conflict. His books include *Understanding Northern Ireland: Colonialism, Control and Consociation* (with co-author John McGarry, forthcoming from Routledge); and *How to Get out of Iraq with Integrity* (University Park: University of Pennsylvania Press, 2009). His paper (with co-authors Paul Mitchell and Geoffrey Evans) on "Extremist Outbidding in Ethnic Party Systems is Not Inevitable: Tribune Parties in Northern Ireland" was awarded the Harrison Prize in 2010.

Eva Pföstl is Director of the Law Department of the Istituto di Studi Politici S. Pio V, Rome. She teaches Minority Rights at LUSPIO University, Rome. Her books include: *La questione tibetana. Autonomia non indipendenza: una proposta realista* (Venice: Marsilio, 2009); and *Società civile e minoranze tra tradizione e trasformazione nell'area del Medio Oriente e del Nord Africa* (ed.) (Rome: Apes, 2011).

Joseph Yacoub is Professor of Political Science at the Institute of Human Rights at the Catholic University of Lyons. His books include *Au nom de Dieu! Les guerres de religions d'aujourd'hui et de demain* (Paris: J.-C. Lattès, 2002); *Christians of Iraq: Menaces sur les Chrétiens d'Irak* (Chambray: CLD, 2003); *Fièvre démocratique et Ferveur fondamentaliste: Dominantes du XXIè siècle* (Paris: Éditions du Cerf, 2008).

1

Introduction

Will Kymlicka and Eva Pföstl

Around the world, the question of how states address the claims of ethnic minorities and indigenous peoples is an important and sensitive issue. We are often said to be living in an age of "identity politics" or the "politics of recognition," in which minorities are more likely to demand forms of official recognition and accommodation, such as language rights, cultural or religious autonomy, regional self-government, or increased political representation. Yet the nature both of these minority demands and of state responses to them varies considerably from region to region. The goal of this volume is to explore the way these issues are understood and debated within the Arab world. What concepts do people use to describe issues of ethnic diversity, and what models or historic precedents do they invoke as examples of success or failure? What hopes or fears drive their response to minority claims? What criteria do they use to distinguish fair from unfair accommodations, or progressive from regressive claims, or deserving from undeserving minorities? The goal is not simply to catalog the various laws and policies that have been adopted in relation to minorities in different Arab countries—that has already been done by others[1]—but rather to understand better the cultural frames and normative

---

[1] Surveys of this kind include Ofra Bengio and Gabriel Ben-Dor (eds.), *Minorities and the State in the Arab World* (Boulder, CO: Lynne Rienner, 1999); Moshe Ma'oz and Gabriel Sheffer (eds.), *Middle Eastern Minorities and Diasporas* (Brighton: Sussex Academic Press, 2002); Mordechai Nisan, *Minorities in the Middle East: A History of Struggle and Self-Expression* (Jefferson, NC: McFarland, 2002); Maya Shatzmiller (ed.), *Nationalism and Minority Identities in Islamic Societies* (Montreal: McGill-Queen's University Press, 2005); Milton Esman and Itamar Rabinovich (eds.), *The Study of Ethnic Politics in the Middle East* (Ithaca, NY: Cornell University Press, 1988); Kirsten E. Schulze, Martin Stokes, and Colm Campbell (eds.), *Nationalism, Minorities and Diasporas: Identities and Rights in the Middle East* (London: Tauris Academic Studies, 1996); and Ronald D. McLaurin (ed.), *The Political Role of Minority Groups in the Middle East* (New York: Praeger, 1979). From a more anthropological perspective, Philip Khoury and Joseph Kostiner (eds.), *Tribes and State Formation in the Middle East* (London: Tauris, 1991) and Faleh Abdul-Jabar and Hosham Dawod (eds.), *Tribes and Power, Nationalism and Ethnicity in the Middle East* (London: Saqi, 2004); and from a more legal perspective,

assumptions that shape how state–minority relations are debated, and to identify which options are thereby opened up or foreclosed.

Since the vast majority of the people living in the twenty-two countries of the Arab League are Arabic-speaking and Sunni Muslim, it is common in the literature to think of "minorities" in the Arab world as those who differ in one or both respects from that demographic majority. Based on this logic, Ma'oz and Sheffer offer the following threefold typology of "minorities":

(1) Arab but not Muslim: religious groups that are ethnically/linguistically Arab but not Sunni Muslim, including several Arab Christian communities—Greek Orthodox, Greek Catholic, Copts, Maronites, Latins, and Protestants—as well as various Muslim sects, notably Shi'ites, 'Alawis, Druze, and Isma'ilis;

(2) Muslim but not Arab: ethnic/national groups that are Sunni Muslim but not Arab, such as the Kurds, Amazigh/Berbers, Turkomans, and Circassians;

(3) Groups that are neither Arab nor Muslim: the Jews, Armenians, Assyrians, and Southern Sudanese tribes.[2]

Needless to say, such typologies need to be viewed with caution. Not only are they schematic, but also potentially reifying, ignoring the ways these identities and their boundaries have changed over time.[3] Moreover, they tell us nothing about the significance or salience of these distinctions to people's lives or to a society's politics. That the members of any of these groups self-identify and politically mobilize as a "minority" is something to be explained, not taken as a given.

Nonetheless, these categories provide at least a provisional sense of the universe of possible cases to explore, and as we will see, both the ethnic and the religious axes of differentiation are important to keep in mind. Our focus in this volume is primarily on the second and third of these categories—that is, on groups that express (or to whom are attributed) an ethnic and national identity distinct from that of the Arab majority. However, since the debate on the status of ethnic/national groups in the Arab world is heavily shaped by the historical treatment of religious diversity, we shall inevitably cover the first category as well.

Gianluca Parolin, *Citizenship in the Arab World: Kin, Religion and Nation-State* (Amsterdam: Amsterdam University Press, 2009).

    [2] Ma'oz and Sheffer, *Middle Eastern Minorities and Diasporas*, 8–9.

    [3] For a critique of the "mosaic" conception of the Arab world, which sees Arab societies as composed of a fixed and unchanging set of component ethnic, linguistic, religious, sectarian, and other groups, see Seteney Shami and Nefissa Naguib, "Occluding Difference: Ethnic Identity and the Shifting Zones of Theory on the Middle East and North Africa," in Sherine Hafez and Susan Slyomovics (eds.), *Anthropology of the Middle East and North Africa* (Bloomington, IN: Indiana University Press, forthcoming).

In today's world, in every region of the globe, debates on issues of ethnic minorities have both a local and a global dimension, and draw upon both global discourses and local vernaculars. On the one hand, there is a global discourse of multiculturalism, which is championed by various international organizations such as the European Union and the United Nations, and which is formulated in recent international declarations on minority and indigenous rights. A few of the more prominent statements of this global discourse would include:

- UN Declaration on the Rights of Persons Belonging to National or Ethnic, Religious and Linguistic Minorities (1992);
- UN Declaration on the Rights of Indigenous Peoples (2007);
- Council of Europe's European Charter for Regional or Minority Languages (1992);
- Council of Europe Framework Convention for the Protection of National Minorities (1995);
- UNESCO's Universal Declaration on Cultural Diversity (2001).

This discourse, which is strongly shaped by Western liberal-democratic experiences of multiculturalism, frames minority rights as a natural and appropriate extension of existing human rights principles, and hence a matter of universal principle. This reflects a significant shift for these international organizations, which in earlier decades often supported strongly assimilationist models of nation-building. While international organizations continue to insist on respect for the sovereignty and territorial integrity of existing states, and while echoes of that earlier assimilationist approach remain, respect for minority rights is now often seen as one of the requirements of a decent and modern state.[4] These normative expectations are increasingly applied to Arab states. Indeed, some commentators have argued that "for every state of the Middle East, respect for minority rights has become—together with women's rights—the barometer of its successful transition to democracy."[5]

On the other hand, every region of the world has its own traditions of ethnic and religious coexistence, often with its own distinctive vocabularies and concepts which may differ from Western or international approaches. These

[4] For an overview of this shift, and its uneven nature, see Will Kymlicka, *Multicultural Odysseys: Navigating the New International Politics of Diversity* (Oxford: Oxford University Press, 2007). For the view that international organizations still instinctively privilege state unity over minority accommodation, see John McGarry, Brendan O'Leary, and Richard Simeon, "Integration or Accommodation? The Enduring Debate in Conflict Regulation," in Sujit Choudhry (ed.), *Constitutional Design for Divided Societies: Integration or Accommodation?* (Oxford: Oxford University Press, 2008).

[5] Elizabeth Picard, "Nation-Building and Minority Rights in the Middle East," in Anh Nga Longva and Anne Sofie Roald (eds.), *Religious Minorities in the Middle East: Domination, Self-Empowerment, Accommodation* (Leiden: Brill, 2012), 67.

traditions continue strongly to shape people's expectations about what constitute legitimate and appropriate forms of state–minority relations. In the Arab world, this would include Islamic ideas of the *dhimmi*, and Ottoman models of the millet system, and experiences such as the long and painful history of Western interference in and manipulation of minority issues, dating back to the capitulation agreements between Western powers and the Ottoman Empire, as well as memories of ethnic cooperation and conflict during national liberation struggles.

A central question, therefore, is how citizens understand the relationship between the global and local discourses around ethnic diversity. We should not automatically assume that the two are contradictory or incompatible. It is worth noting, for example, that Arab states voted unanimously at the UN for both the 1992 Declaration on Minority Rights and the 2007 Declaration on Indigenous Rights, as well as the 2001 UNESCO Declaration on Cultural Diversity. Yet it remains true that appeal to the new global discourse of minority rights is politically sensitive. Research from other regions suggests that minority activists often appeal to this global discourse as a way of legitimating their claims, yet also seek to show that such claims are compatible with existing local discourses, while other actors may insist that the two discourses are more radically at odds, or that the global discourse is discredited by its Eurocentric or colonialist origins. These dynamics are already well known in the broader field of human rights more generally—witness the vibrant debates about the relation between Islam and international human rights norms[6]—and our volume examines this dynamic in the specific context of minority rights in the Arab world.

In some times and places, international norms and local discourses work together to help motivate sustainable improvement in the legal and political status of minorities. The most prominent example is Latin America, which has proven to be a receptive ground for ideas of multiculturalism (or "interculturalism," as is more common in the Spanish-language debates), particularly

---

[6] There is a vast literature on how Western liberal-democratic theories of democracy and international human rights norms relate to local philosophies and traditions in the Arab world, such as Masudal Alam Choudhury, *Reforming the Muslim World* (London: Kegan Paul, 1998); Abdullahi An-Na'im, *Islam and the Secular State: Negotiating the Future of Shari'a* (Cambridge, MA: Harvard University Press, 2008); Abdulaziz Sachedina, *Islam and Human Rights* (Oxford: Oxford University Press, 2009); Hamid Haidar, *Liberalism and Islam: Practical Reconciliation between the Liberal State and Shiite Muslims* (New York: Palgrave, 2008); Andrew March, *Islam and Liberal Citizenship: The Search for an Overlapping Consensus* (Oxford: Oxford University Press, 2009); and Nader Hashemi, *Islam, Secularism, and Liberal Democracy: Toward a Democratic Theory for Muslim Societies* (Oxford: Oxford University Press, 2009). All these works focus on the need to build plausible and compelling cultural foundations for liberal democracy, connecting (and where necessary adapting) liberal principles to Arab and Islamic cultural sources. Yet there is no comparable volume that examines how liberal theories and practices of *minority rights* relate to the Arab world.

in relation to indigenous peoples. A commitment to indigenous rights has become a well-established component of the idiom of democratization in the region, not just amongst Western-trained elites, but in civil society more generally. This is reflected in the dramatic rise of what Donna Lee Van Cott calls "multicultural constitutionalism" throughout Latin America.[7] The shift from military dictatorships to democracy has been accompanied by constitutional recognition of the distinct legal status of indigenous groups, including rights to self-government, land claims, and recognition of customary law in many countries.

Moreover, international organizations (IOs) have played a vital role in enabling and encouraging this shift towards the recognition of indigenous rights in Latin America, through their support for indigenous advocacy groups, and their diffusion of best practices and standards. Alison Brysk's book *From Tribal Village to Global Village* traces the dense web of connections linking local struggles for indigenous rights with IOs and their affiliated "global policy networks," and many other commentators have also highlighted the crucial role that IOs and international NGOs have played.[8]

Latin America, therefore, represents the clearest case where international efforts to diffuse multiculturalism have had local resonance, and effectively supported domestic reforms. Indeed, these ideas have taken root to such an extent that Latin American countries as a group have become more vocal and active proponents of international norms of indigenous rights than the established Western democracies.[9]

There are vibrant and unresolved debates in Latin America about how well these models of multiculturalism are actually working in practice. Some critics argue that they involve merely symbolic changes. Indeed some argue that these policies were designed by neo-liberal elites precisely to deflect political attention away from underlying power structures.[10] Others argue that while perhaps providing tangible benefits to indigenous peoples, multicultural reforms are creating new ethnic hierarchies in the process—for example, by excluding

---

[7] Donna Lee Van Cott, *The Friendly Liquidation of the Past: The Politics of Diversity in Latin America* (Pittsburgh, PA: University of Pittsburgh Press, 2000), ch. 9.

[8] Alison Brysk, *From Tribal Village to Global Village: Indian Rights and International Relations in Latin America* (Stanford, CA: Stanford University Press, 2000). See also Van Cott, *The Friendly Liquidation*; Deborah Yashar, *Contesting Citizenship in Latin America: The Rise of Indigenous Movements and the PostLiberal Challenge* (Cambridge: Cambridge University Press, 2005); Rachel Sieder (ed.), *Multiculturalism in Latin America: Indigenous Rights, Diversity and Democracy* (London: Palgrave, 2002); Virginia Tilley, "New Help or New Hegemony? The Transnational Indigenous Peoples' Movement and 'Being Indian' in El Salvador," *Journal of Latin American Studies* 34 (2002): 525–54.

[9] For example, when the UN's Declaration on indigenous rights was put up for a vote at the General Assembly in 2007, the main opposition came from British settler states (Canada, USA, Australia, New Zealand), not from Latin American states.

[10] Charles Hale, "Does Multiculturalism Menace? Governance, Cultural Rights, and the Politics of Identity in Guatemala," *Journal of Latin American Studies* 34 (2002): 485–524.

Black (Afro-Latino) groups who are not typically considered as "indigenous peoples."[11] Yet others argue that they are imprisoning people in cultural scripts, and jeopardizing individual freedom. In order to qualify for new multicultural rights, members of indigenous communities are expected to "act Indian"[12]—i.e. to follow "authentic" cultural practices—an expectation that strengthens the hand of conservative or patriarchal leaders within the community who assert the authority to determine what is "authentic."[13] As we will see, similar concerns have been raised about the risks of adopting multiculturalism in the Arab world.

Most commentators, however, while acknowledging these risks, argue that the shift to multicultural constitutionalism in Latin America has been a positive force, and not just for indigenous peoples, but for society generally. It has helped to enhance democratic participation amongst previously excluded groups, to reduce the danger of a return to authoritarian rule, to build legitimacy for the process of democratic consolidation, and indeed to serve as a laboratory for innovative experiments in democratic citizenship.[14] While inspired by international norms, local actors have moved beyond them to develop new conceptions of inclusive citizenship not found elsewhere. In this sense, at its best, the new minority politics has been truly transformative, not just in the sense of transforming the lives of minorities, but more generally in transforming national politics in a more progressive, inclusive, democratic, tolerant, and peaceful direction.

Can we imagine a comparable story in the Arab world? Do international norms have local resonance, and if so, can they underpin effective and sustainable improvement in the status of minorities? Can minority politics serve as a vehicle for a more general transformative politics, supporting a broader culture of democracy and human rights, and challenging older authoritarian, clientelistic, or patriarchal political tendencies?

It is too early to make definitive pronouncements, and the essays collected in this volume come to different conclusions. However, it is safe to say that the evidence to date is not particularly encouraging. Throughout the Arab world, minorities remain "marked citizens" whose political mobilization is viewed with distrust if not outright repression.[15] Indeed, the minority issue remains

---

[11] Juliet Hooker, "Indigenous Inclusion/Black Exclusion: Race, Ethnicity and Multicultural Citizenship in Contemporary Latin America," *Journal of Latin American Studies* 37/2 (2005): 285–310.

[12] Tilley, "New Help or New Hegemony?"

[13] Rachel Sieder, "Advancing Indigenous Claims Through the Law," in Jane Cowan et al. (eds.), *Culture and Rights: Anthropological Perspectives* (Cambridge: Cambridge University Press, 2001): 201–25.

[14] Yashar, *Contesting Citizenship.*

[15] The term "marked citizens" comes from Gyanendra Pandey, *Routine Violence: Nations, Fragments, Histories* (Stanford, CA: Stanford University Press, 2006), who was applying it

a taboo topic in many countries. We can recall here the now (in)famous case of the aborted 1994 "Conference on the International Declaration on the Rights of Minorities in the Arab World and the Middle East," co-organized by an Egyptian NGO, the Ibn Khaldun Center for Development Studies, and the UK-based international NGO, Minority Rights Group. The conference was intended to explore the implications of the recently passed UN Declaration on the Rights of Persons Belonging to National or Ethnic, Religious and Linguistic Minorities (which, as noted already, was supported by Arab states), and was one of many such conferences organized around the world at the time by similar coalitions of local and international NGOs. However, announcement of the conference unleashed a storm of protest, leading to its relocation to Cyprus.[16] This made clear that the ritual support of Arab states for international minority rights norms was not intended to encourage, or even permit, public debate or political mobilization to actually claim those rights. From that point forward, the Arab world was effectively absent from the global policy networks working on minority and indigenous rights. The dense web of connections that Brysk identified in the Latin American context, linking local minority struggles with international NGOs and intergovernmental organizations, is missing in most of the Arab world. As a result, Arab voices have largely been absent from the international debate.[17]

We can see a similar dynamic at the level of regional organizations. In response to the UN's Declarations on minority and indigenous rights, several regional organizations have developed their own declarations, such as the two Council of Europe conventions already listed on minority languages (1992) and the protection of national minorities (1995), or the Organization of American States' draft declaration on indigenous rights (1997), or the African Commission's Working Group on Indigenous Peoples/Communities (2003). This is a common pattern in the field of international human rights: global declarations at the UN are followed by declarations and strategic plans at the

---

primarily to minorities in the Indian subcontinent. For its relevance to the Arab world, see the chapter by Klein in this volume.

[16] On this event, see Peter Makari, *Conflict and Cooperation: Christian and Muslim Relations in Contemporary Egypt* (Syracuse, NY: Syracuse University Press, 2007), 162–9 and 146–51; Seteney Shami, "'Aqalliyya/Minority in Modern Egyptian Discourse," in Carol Gluck and Ana Tsing (eds.), *Words in Motion: Towards a Global Lexicon* (Durham, NC: Duke University Press, 2009), 167; Saba Mahmood, "Religious Freedom, The Minority Question, and Geopolitics in the Middle East," *Comparative Studies in Society and History* 54/2 (2012): 418–46. The head of the Ibn Khaldun Center (Saad Eddin Ibrahim) was later jailed for defaming the state, which many commentators view as a result of his too-vocal concern for minorities.

[17] Or more exactly, since minority voices from within Arab states are absent, it has often been left to exile/diaspora groups to speak on their behalf in international settings. It is Coptic groups in the US, or Amazigh groups in France, who have been most vocal internationally.

regional level. However, neither the Arab League[18] nor the Organization of the Islamic Conference[19] has attempted to develop regionally specific interpretations or action plans for minority rights.

This is not to deny the existence of a range of minority accommodations in various Arab countries—think of the historic forms of power-sharing in Lebanon, for example, or recent moves to provide greater cultural space for Amazigh language and culture in Algeria. Yet these accommodations have rarely, if ever, had the transformative and democratizing effects that advocates of minority rights aspire to. On the contrary, they are widely seen as essentially bribes offered by authoritarian regimes to minority elites precisely on the condition that they do not challenge the basic authoritarian and undemocratic structures of the state. They are viewed, not as harbingers or tools of broader democratic and human rights reforms, but as part of the architecture of authoritarian rule. Even where minority elites have initially framed their demands in more transformative terms, Arab states have managed to divorce minority accommodations from broader social change.[20] As a result, even democratic reformers in the Arab world have not made minority rights a priority.

What explains this skepticism of, and resistance to, the new minority politics? There are obviously many factors at work, and each of our contributors offers his or her own diagnosis. But we can identify at least three common

---

[18] For a discussion of the potential role of the Arab League, see Omar Dajani, "Responding to Ethnic and Religious Conflict in the Emerging Arab Order: The Promise and Limits of Rights," *UCLA Journal for International Law & Foreign Affairs* (forthcoming), who concludes "an attempt to develop a detailed minority rights treaty for the Middle East seems neither feasible nor advisable at this juncture," and that "transforming the League into a forum in which the rights of minorities within the states of the region can be debated, negotiated and promoted will take considerable time and, perhaps also, a re-imagination of its mission." See Yacoub's chapter in this volume for a more optimistic account of the potential role of the Arab League.

[19] Interestingly, the Organization of the Islamic Conference has a Department on Minority Affairs, but its formal resolutions focus exclusively on the rights of Muslim minorities living in non-Muslim majority countries (see Saad Khan, "The Organization of the Islamic Conference (OIC) and Muslim Minorities," *Journal of Muslim Minority Affairs* 22/2 (2002): 351–67). It is a vociferous champion of the rights of Muslim minorities in India or the Philippines or the West, sensitive to any forms of discrimination or exclusion they suffer. Yet the OIC has never attempted to formulate norms, or to establish monitoring mechanisms, regarding the mistreatment of ethnic minorities within Muslim-majority countries, such as the Kurds in Syria, the Ahwaz in Iran, the Hazars in Afghanistan, the Baluchs in Pakistan, the "Al-Akhdam" in Yemen, or the Berbers in Algeria.

[20] For the "failure of transformative minority politics" in Algeria, see Jacob Mundy, "The Failure of Transformative Minority Politics in Algeria: The Kabyli Citizens' Movement and the State," in Michael Mbanaso and Chima Korieh (eds.), *Minorities and the State in Africa* (Amherst, MA: Cambria, 2010), and Pföstl's chapter in this volume. For the comparable failure in Egypt, see Gregoire Delhaye, "Contemporary Muslim–Christian Relations in Egypt: Local Dynamics and Foreign Influences," in Longva and Roald (eds.), *Religious Minorities in the Middle East.* For other examples, see the special issue on "Representation(s) in the Middle East," *Representation* 48/3 (2012), discussing cases where deals cut to increase minority representation came at the expense of women's representation and broader democratic forces.

themes: (1) the legacy of the millet system; (2) the legacy of colonial rule; and (3) the imperatives of postcolonial state-building. We will briefly discuss each in turn.

The Millet Legacy: First, any discussion of minorities in the Arab world is immediately interpreted in the light of the long history of Ottoman policy towards minorities, known as the millet system. Indeed, many commentators have argued that the term "minority" in the Arab world is simply the modern secular replacement for the term "millet," and hence minority rights are assumed to be "neo-millet" claims. To understand resistance to minority rights, therefore, we need to understand the ambivalent views regarding the millet system.

The Arab world was ruled for 500 years by the Ottoman Empire, and the basic framework of Ottoman policy was maintained by the European colonial powers who replaced the Ottomans at the end of the World War I. Under the millet system, the Ottoman Empire recognized that the other monotheistic "peoples of the Book"—particularly Christians and Jews—were entitled not only to tolerance, but to a degree of self-government and internal autonomy. This millet system served a number of instrumental purposes for the Ottomans, but it was also seen as a requirement of Islam, since the Qur'an mandates that Muslim rulers protect these religious minorities so long as they in turn accept Muslim rule. Ottoman millets are, in that sense, an interpretation of the Qur'anic principle of "*dhimmi*," or protected religious minorities.[21]

When compared with the fratricidal religious wars that engulfed Europe for much of this 500-year history, the Ottoman millet system is widely and rightly seen as an impressive example of religious toleration and coexistence. And some commentators have argued that this tradition provides a firm and clear foundation for contemporary ideas of minority and indigenous rights. (See e.g. the chapter by Castellino and Cavanaugh in this volume.)

Others, however, view the millet legacy not as a constructive resource to be built upon, but as a stigma that burdens minority claims. While impressive as a historic scheme of tolerance, the millets also had a number of troubling features. The millet system—and its underlying Qur'anic idea of *dhimmi*—is premised on the assumption that the state belongs exclusively to Muslims, who then extend protection and toleration to subordinate and submissive groups. As a result, the status of *dhimmi* is seen as a second-class status—what critics call "dhimmitude"—based on a "bond of submission," reflected for example in restrictions on the size of churches, and in asymmetrical rules about conversion (Muslims can proselytize amongst Christians but not the reverse; Muslims who convert to Christianity lose their property but not the

---

[21] For a classic discussion of the millets, see B. Braude and B. Lewis (eds.), *Christians and Jews in the Ottoman Empire: The Functioning of a Plural Society* (New York: Holmes & Meier, 1982).

reverse, etc.).[22] Moreover, it has the implication that such minorities are not part of the larger society in whose name the state governs: the state belongs to Muslims, and minorities are excluded from certain high offices in the state. Thus the millet system is said to ghettoize minorities. And finally, critics argue that the millets sustain illiberal and undemocratic politics. The millet system accords power to patriarchal elites within minority groups, who in return help to prop up undemocratic rulers in the state. The millets thereby represent a form of clientelistic politics.[23]

In so far as minority claims are interpreted as claims to maintain or re-establish a millet-type order, they are widely seen in the Arab world as inconsistent with modern conceptions of equal citizenship, national unity, and democratic accountability. It is worth noting that these features of the millet system are in no sense an entailment of the concept of "minority" as it is used in the broader international debate. On the contrary, both the UN and regional bodies such as the Council of Europe emphasize that minorities must be seen as full citizens of the state, that minority rights are intended as a way of facilitating their contribution to society, and that minority rights must them-selves comply with fundamental principles of gender equality, democratic accountability, and personal freedom. Contemporary international norms of minority and indigenous rights have little if anything in common with historic ideas of dhimmitude. Yet this association is so strong in many Arab countries that even minorities themselves resist appealing to international norms of minority rights, for fear that it will consign them to dhimmitude.[24]

For example, when the Ibn Khaldun Center proposed its 1994 conference on the implication of the UN minority rights declaration in the Arab world, some high-profile Coptic intellectuals accused him of downgrading the status of Copts from "full citizenship" to "isolated minorities."[25] When the Copts fought together with Muslims against the British colonizers in Egypt, they were fighting for a future in which they would be full citizens, and the label "minority" is seen as returning them to the sidelines of political life as a

---

[22] The Qur'anic injunction that minorities must be fought against until they are "brought low" (Q 9: 29) "marks the beginning of the idea that non-Muslims—even if excluded from the Islamic community and organized in separate groups—can be connected to the ummah by a bond of submission" (Parolin, *Citizenship in the Arab World*, 46).

[23] Gregoire Delhaye, "Contemporary Muslim–Christian Relations in Egypt: Local Dynamics and Foreign Influences," in Longva and Roald (eds.), *Religious Minorities in the Middle East*; Paul Rowe, "Neo-Millet Systems and Transnational Religious Movements: The *Humayun* Decrees and Church Construction in Egypt," *Journal of Church and State* 49/2 (2002): 329–50. Paul Sedra describes the "millet partnership" as one that is "characterized by conservatism and quiescence" (Paul Sedra, "Class Cleavage and Ethnic Conflict: Coptic Christian Communities in Modern Egyptian Politics," *Islam and Christian–Muslim Relations* 10/2 (1999): 219–35 at 227).

[24] See the discussion in Mahmood, "Religious Freedom." She quotes a leading Coptic intellectual, Samir Murqus, saying "there is a fundamental contradiction" between the concept of citizenship and minority, a claim that seems to rest on equating minority with millet.

[25] Shami, "'Aqalliyya/Minority in Modern Egyptian Discourse," 167.

protected but submissive and isolated *dhimmi*. As the Ibn Khaldun Center tried to explain, the modern UN conception of minority does not have the implication of either isolation or submission, and the dozens of minority groups and indigenous peoples around the world who appeal to these international norms clearly do not see themselves as renouncing citizenship for dhimmitude. Yet millets remain the most salient image of minority political status in the region. As a result, minority politics is associated not with empowerment, participation, and contribution, but rather is "associated with legal vulnerability, political marginality, and social inferiority."[26]

The Colonial Legacy: Minority politics is burdened with the legacy not only of dhimmitude, but also with that of colonial manipulation and divide-and-rule strategies. Indeed, "protection of minorities" was one of the central justifications given for colonial rule, on the assumption that local majorities could not be trusted to govern fairly. This was the alleged justification for European powers to claim extra-territorial jurisdiction over Christian minorities in the Ottoman Empire, and then for full-blown colonial rule as Ottoman rule retreated. Having relied upon this justification, colonial rulers naturally had an incentive not only to identify the minorities needing protection, but also to exaggerate their need for that protection, in part by inflating the alleged cultural differences and levels of distrust or animosity between groups. One needn't go as far as to say that the colonial powers "invented" the minorities, but they certainly worked diligently to harden the boundaries between ethnic and religious groups, and to discourage the formation of any unified national liberation movement against colonial rule.[27] Colonial rulers not only "protected" certain minorities, but also privileged some of them, both materially (e.g. by giving them easier access to schooling, and hence greater access to civil service jobs), and symbolically (e.g. by describing the minorities as more civilized or more freedom-loving), while denigrating majorities.[28] In short,

---

[26] Anh Nga Longva, "From the Dhimma to the Capitulations," in Longva and Roald (eds.), *Religious Minorities in the Middle East*, 67. As Picard puts it, millet "is a controversial concept, as some analysts consider it a source of inspiration for liberalising the status of minority groups, while others denounce its fragmenting role and the subsequent paralysis of the nation-building process in the Middle East" ("Nation-Building and Minority Rights in the Middle East," 328).

[27] The literature on the colonial manipulation of minority issues is immense. For two recent studies of the Levant, see Benjamin White, *The Emergence of Minorities in the Middle East: The Politics of Community in French Mandate Syria* (Edinburgh: Edinburgh University Press, 2011); Kais Firro, *Metamorphosis of the Nation (al-Umma): The Rise of Arabism and Minorities in Syria and Lebanon, 1850–1940* (Brighton: Sussex Academic Press, 2009). For the Maghreb, see Jonathan Wyrtzen, "Colonial Legacies, National Identity and Challenges for Multiculturalism in the Contemporary Maghreb," in Moha Ennaji (ed.), *Multiculturalism and Democracy in North Africa* (New York: Routledge, 2014).

[28] On the role of education in facilitating minority advancement under colonial rule, see Catherine Le Thomas, "Education and Minority Empowerment in the Middle East," in Longva and Roald (eds.), *Religious Minorities in the Middle East*; on the French colonial propagation of the "Berber myth" (of the Berbers as a freedom-loving minority who need French protection

"the figure of the 'minority' in Middle Eastern history has served as a site for the articulation and exercise of European power."[29]

Nor is this just ancient history. Foreign powers continue to exploit the minority issue in Arab states, and minorities are widely perceived as collaborating with foreign powers to weaken state rule.[30] In the past, it was primarily Christians who "have been persistently suspected of having strong allegiance to outsiders and lacking in patriotism," but since the Iranian revolution, now Shi'ites too are seen as a fifth-column for Iran.[31] Rumours abound about CIA support for the Copts, or about Israeli support for the Kurds, all intended to keep Arab states weak and divided.[32] As Picard puts it, "In the past, communal groups opposed to the government were suspected of collusion with European powers; now they are accused of being 'agents' of Israel and the United States. Instead of being part of the legitimate political game, protestation by minorities became stigmatised as manipulation by the West and Israel, and repressed through land confiscation, restriction of public expression, and heavy security rules."[33] As a result, the very idea of "protection of minorities," particularly where it involves potential appeal to international actors, is seen not as a legitimate and normal form of domestic political contestation, but as a geopolitical threat to state security. In this sense, minority politics in the Arab world remains highly "securitized," and as such, subject to harsh forms of control.[34] Relations between states and minorities are seen, not as a matter of normal democratic politics to be negotiated and debated, but as a matter of state security, in which political discussion and mobilization has to be limited in order to protect the state. Under these conditions, the prospects for multicultural citizenship are remote.[35]

---

against Arab rule), see Wyrtzen, "Colonial Legacies"; Paul Silverman, "The Kabyle Myth: Colonization and the Production of Ethnicity," in Brian Axel (ed.), *From the Margins: Historical Anthropology and its Futures* (Durham, NC: Duke University Press, 2002), 122–55.

[29] Mahmood, "Religious Freedom, the Minority Question," 419.

[30] L. Binder (ed.), *Ethnic Conflict and International Politics in the Middle East* (Gainesville, FL: University of Florida Press, 1999).

[31] On Shias as Iranian agents, see Longva, "Domination, Self-Empowerment," 15; Laurence Louer, "Shi'i Identity Politics in Saudi Arabia," in Longva and Roald (eds.), *Religious Minorities in the Middle East*, 229; Madawi Al-Rasheed, "Sectarianism as Counter-Revolution: Saudi Responses to the Arab Spring," *Studies in Ethnicity and Nationalism* 11/3 (2011).

[32] Saad Eddin Ibrahim, "Management and Mismanagement of Diversity: The Case of Ethnic Conflict and State-Building in the Arab World" (MOST Discussion Paper 10, UNESCO, 1995), 9 (posted at: <http://www.unesco.org/most/ibraeng.htm>, accessed August 2013). See also P. R. Kumaraswamy, "Problems of Studying Minorities in the Middle East," *Alternatives: Turkish Journal of International Relations* 2/2 (2003).

[33] Picard, "Nation-Building and Minority Rights," 339.

[34] See Ole Waever, "Securitization and Desecuritization," in Ronnie Lipschutz (ed.), *On Security* (New York: Columbia University Press, 1995), 46–86, for a classic discussion of the general phenomenon of "securitization."

[35] For a more extensive discussion of the securitization of ethnic relations, and how a viable form of multiculturalism requires "desecuritization," see Kymlicka, *Multicultural Odysseys*.

In order to avoid accusations of disloyalty and collaboration, minorities have not only to vocally and visibly swear their loyalty, but they may even have to renounce appeal to the very idea of minority rights. As Saba Mahmood puts it, "because the principle of minority rights was the vehicle for the subjugation of national sovereignty to foreign rule it cannot now serve as the instrument for Coptic salvation. Any embrace of this principle necessarily entails the inscription of Copts in this longstanding colonialist project." Indeed she describes this as "the impossible paradox that haunts the discourse of minority rights in the Middle East."[36]

Postcolonial Nation-Building: Given these legacies of Ottoman millets and colonial divide-and-rule, postcolonial Arab states were faced with a delicate and difficult task in building up a sense of national unity while managing ethnic and religious diversity. It is important to remember that the borders of Arab states were not drawn to facilitate self-determination for the peoples of the region, but were often the arbitrary result of colonial rule, combining disparate groups into a new polity while simultaneously splitting historic communities across borders.[37] In most cases, therefore, there was little pre-existing sense of nationhood to draw upon. The citizens of these new Arab states often had a sense of pan-Arab or pan-Islamic allegiance, as well as more local ethnic, sectarian or regional identities (some of which cut across state borders), but may have had little sense of being, say, "Tunisian" or "Iraqi."[38] Nor were there usable traditions of political sovereignty or national citizenship that were ethnically and religiously inclusive.

Given these conditions, one might ask whether the very idea of a "nation-state"—which was after all exported to the region under Western imperialism—was really suitable to the Arab world. However, no less than elsewhere, the nationalist ideal of "one nation one state" has been widely embraced in the Arab world, and the leaders of postcolonial states have been expected and encouraged, both by their own citizens and by the international community, to engage in "nation-building."[39]

It would have taken particularly inspired leadership to address the challenge of building an inclusive and solidaristic sense of nationhood under these

---

[36] Mahmood, "Religious Freedom," 440.

[37] David Fromkin, *A Peace to End all Peace: The Fall of the Ottoman Empire and the Creation of the Modern Middle East* (New York: Holt, 2009).

[38] S. Amin, *The Arab Nation: Nationalism and Class Struggles* (London: Zed, 1978); J. Piscatori, *Islam in a World of Nation States* (Cambridge: Cambridge University Press, 1986); M. Hudson (ed.), *Middle East Dilemma: The Politics and Economics of Arab Integration* (London: I. B. Tauris, 1998); R. Hinnenbusch, *The International Politics of the Middle East* (Manchester: Manchester University Press, 2003).

[39] "If the progress of multiculturalism has made the exclusivist nationalist ideology somehow less legitimate, especially in the west, the 'one nation, one state' motto remains very much influential everywhere, including in the Middle East" (Delhaye, "Contemporary Muslim–Christian Relations in Egypt," 80).

conditions, and it's safe to say that postcolonial Arab states have rarely enjoyed such leadership. On the contrary, postcolonial Arab states have, by and large, gravitated towards heavy-handed forms of nation-building that over time have exacerbated feelings of marginalization and exclusion.

Much has been written on the evolution of Arab nationalisms, and the way authoritarian leaders of Arab states have manipulated ideologies of Arab nationalism to legitimate their rule. According to one familiar narrative, postcolonial Arab states initially embraced a secular conception of nationhood that privileged the Arab language and culture and pan-Arab ties. This secular conception had the virtue of including Arab-speaking Christians as full members of the Arab nation, although at the cost of excluding ethno-linguistic minorities such as the Kurds or Berbers. Since the 1967 war, this secular conception of Arab nationalism has been challenged by a more (Sunni) Islamic definition of nationhood, privileging pan-Islamic ties, which has the virtue of including Kurds and Berbers as fellow Muslims, although at the cost of excluding Christians and heterodox Muslims such as Shi'ites.

There is some truth in this familiar narrative about Arab nationalisms. All Arab states did initially adopt Arabization policies that privileged the Arab language and pan-Arab ties to the detriment of other components of the local society, stigmatizing other local dialects, vernaculars, and cultures as backward and divisive.[40] And this secular focus on Arabization has partly given way to a focus on Islam as the source of political unity and identity. Whereas after independence the legal systems of most Arab states turned away from Islamic-based law, or limited its jurisdiction to family affairs or religious matters, in the 1970s and 1980s several states introduced constitutional amendments requiring that state law conform to Islamic norms.[41] And this departure from secular politics combined with legally imposed inequalities and official claims for theocratic universalism has been perceived as detrimental by religious minorities.[42] So the source of national identity in the Arab world, and the sorts of inclusions and exclusions it entails, have changed over time.

---

[40] Heather Sharkey, "Language and Conflict: The Political History of Arabisation in Sudan and Algeria," *Studies in Ethnicity and Nationalism* 12/3 (2012): 427–49; Y. Suleiman (ed.), *Language and Identity in the Middle East and North Africa* (London: Curzon, 1996); B. Tibi, *Arab Nationalism: A Critical Enquiry* (London: Macmillan, 1981); C. Miller, "Linguistic Policies and the Issue of Ethno-linguistic Minorities in the Middle East," in A. Usuki and H. Kato (eds.), *Islam in the Middle Eastern Studies: Muslims and Minorities*, JCAS Symposium Series 7 (Osaka: Japan Centre for Area Studies, 2003), 149–74.

[41] For a discussion see Robert W. Hefner, *Shari'a Politics: Islamic Law and Society in the Modern World* (Bloomington, IN: Indiana University Press, 2011).

[42] We can trace these forms of inclusion and exclusion in citizenship policies. In his recent study of citizenship laws in the Arab world, Parolin shows that citizenship in each Arab country combines, to a varying degree, elements of pre-Islamic structures of kinship, the ideal of *ummah* as a religious community, the idea of pan-Arabism as a national community, and the idea of a territorially bounded popular sovereignty. As a result, Muslims or Arabs living outside the state may have privileged access to citizenship, while non-Muslims, non-Arabs, or Muslim

But some commentators argue that the contrast between secular and Islamist conceptions of nationhood is overdrawn. Although nominally secular, Arab nationalism was always in fact linked to Islam, since Islam was widely seen as the "crowning glory" of Arabs' history, and the Arabic language was precious because it was the language of the Qur'an.[43] More generally, "few Islamists have followed the logic of Islamic community as against the nation, and few nationalists have not accorded religion a place of honour in the attributes of the nation."[44] As a result, non-Arab and non-Muslim minorities have always had, at best, a fragile and conditional inclusion in the nation, before or after 1967.

A more relevant contrast, perhaps, is Khaddar's distinction between "anti-colonial nationalism" and "state nationalism." According to Khaddar, anti-colonial nationalism in the Arab world was "diverse and inclusive in the movements of resistance to colonial oppression," whereas state nationalism (in either its secular or Islamic version) has been authoritarian and homogenizing, treating all forms of dissent as anti-national and a security threat.[45] Forms of multicultural citizenship that were imaginable in the moment of anti-colonial nationalism have been snuffed out by the imperatives of state nationalism. Authoritarian Arab states, like Communist states, made claims to "national unanimity," claims that could only be sustained by suppressing diversity and dissent, and which therefore involved a "forced consensus."[46]

These "unanimist" conceptions of nationhood are now broadly discredited, but they have left a legacy in which the political mobilization of communal groups is seen as a threat and a problem. In any event, the original problem remains. Postcolonial Arab states are still confronted with the task of nation-building, sixty or more years after independence. Many Arab countries remain

nonconformists living within the country may be denied citizenship or face loss of citizenship. See Parolin, *Citizenship in the Arab World*.

[43] Longva, "Domination," 11. See also Sharkey's observation that "Arabisation and Islamisation frequently developed hand-in-hand, while the staunchest and most ideologically committed Islamists tended to be the firmest supporters of Arabisation" ("Language and Conflict," 431).

[44] Sami Zubaida, "Islam and Nationalism: Continuities and Contradictions," *Nations and Nationalism* 10/4 (2004): 407–20 at 408. By "the logic of Islamic community," Zubaida refers to the traditional Islamic doctrine that the Muslim community constitutes a single "nation" or *ummah*, undivided by ethno-linguistic or sectarian divisions, which ideally should be politically united, and which therefore views ethno-nationalism as un-Islamic. See Firro, *Metamorphosis of the Nation*, 146–7.

[45] M. Moncef Khaddar, "Nationalist Ruling Parties, National Governments Ideologies, Partisans and Statesmen: Human Rights Offenders and Human Rights Defenders in the North African Postcolonial States and Societies," *Journal of North African Studies* 17/1 (2012): 67–96.

[46] For a description of Arab states as "unanimist," see Picard, "Nation-Building and Minority Rights," 332; for the politics of "forced consensus," see Etienne Copeaux, "Le consensus obligatoire," in Isabelle Rigoni (ed.), *Turquie: les milles visages* (Paris: Syllepse, 2000).

examples of "weak states and strong societies,"[47] where the state struggles to assert its legitimacy against competing identities at the sub-state and trans-state level, and so presents itself as "defender of the (Arab) nation" and/or "defender of the (Muslim) faith" to legitimate its fragile rule. In practice, defending the nation and the faith all too often means not only resisting aggression from external powers, but also oppressing minorities within. Put another way, the failure to respect minorities is in large part due to the state's fragile legitimacy amongst the majority,[48] and any sustainable progress on minority rights requires that the state also be a more effective representative of the interests and identities of the ordinary mass of its citizens. The hope, in the Arab world as elsewhere, has to be that "nation-building and minority rights might improve dialectically,"[49] and this virtuous dialectic requires new conceptions of Arab nationhood and nation-building as much as new conceptions of minority rights.[50]

These three factors—the legacies of the millet system; colonial and neo-colonial manipulation; and the perceived imperatives of postcolonial nation-building—are obviously interconnected. The fact that the millet system deprives minorities of an effective political voice helps to explain why minorities look to external powers for protection, which in turn helps to explain why minority rights are seen as incompatible with nation-building. Taken together, these factors go at least part of the way to explaining the hostility to minority politics in the Arab world. Each, in its own way, helps to explain why there is opposition not only to this or that specific minority rights claim, but to the very idea of minority rights, or indeed to the very idea of a "minority." As Shami puts it, there remains debate about whether the term "minority" applies in Arab societies, and "whether acknowledging the word 'minority' necessarily

---

[47] For the classic analysis of "weak states and strong societies," see Joel Migdal, *Strong Societies and Weak States: State–Society Relations and State Capabilities in the Third World* (Princeton, NJ: Princeton University Press, 1988).

[48] Ibrahim quotes Lebanese political scientist Antoine Messara's observation that "no political Arab regime has had a serious problem with an ethnic minority without also having a serious problem with the majority in the same country" (quoted in Ibrahim, "Management and Mismanagement of Diversity," 10).

[49] Picard, "Nation Building and Minority Rights," 346. For a similar diagnosis about the dialectic of nation-building and minority rights, see Kymlicka, *Multicultural Odysseys*, 83–4.

[50] This is one reason for being skeptical about the idea that the solution to diversity in the Middle East is to promote a post-national "cosmopolitanism"—an idea that is often associated with nostalgia for the alleged cosmopolitanism of such cities as Beirut or Alexandria in the Ottoman or colonial period, prior to the rise of Arab nationalism. As Will Hanley has shown, this "grieving cosmopolitanism" is almost always elitist, indifferent to the plight of the Arab masses who were effectively excluded from power (see Will Hanley, "Grieving Cosmopolitanism in Middle East Studies," *History Compass* 6/5 (2008): 1346–67). A viable approach to empowering minorities must simultaneously recognize the legitimacy of Arab nation-building.

implies a political and social 'problem'," and whether the term inappropriately imposes Western concepts and preoccupations on Arab societies.[51]

Given these factors, it might seem that resistance to minority rights in the Arab world is overdetermined, and that this explains the apparent "Arab exceptionalism" to the general global trends towards multiculturalism.[52] But this is too simple and too quick. Many of the factors we have discussed are equally present outside the Arab world. Legacies of colonial divide and rule, for example, as well the imperatives of postcolonial nation-building, are omnipresent throughout Asia and Africa, not just the Middle East. And many regions have their own historic versions of precolonial "dhimmitude" that burden contemporary minority politics.[53] And so, as one would expect, resistance to minority and indigenous rights is also widespread. If the Arab resistance to contemporary minority politics seems to stand in stark contrast to the embrace of ethnic politics in the democratization of Latin America, the contrast is much smaller with other parts of the postcolonial world, such as southeast Asia or sub-Saharan Africa.

Here as elsewhere, therefore, we should be wary of claims to "exceptionalism," not least because of the way such claims play into Orientalist perceptions of the Arab or Muslim world.[54] Benjamin White has rightly emphasized the

---

[51] Shami, "'Aqalliyya/Minority in Modern Egyptian Discourse," 151. She goes on to note that, given the unhappy baggage that accompanies the term "minority," "For this reason, contestations in Arab intellectual discourse over who is and is not a 'minority' should not be read as denial, repression or ethnic cleansing, although there are instances of these practices" (p. 152).

[52] In his study of "regimes of ethnicity," Şener Aktürk places Arab states into the "anti-ethnic" category. See Şener Aktürk, "Regimes of Ethnicity: Comparing East, West, and South" (paper presented at the American Political Science Association annual meeting, 2011). His analysis examines countries for the presence of fifteen distinct policies of ethnic recognition, from the use of ethnic categories in the census to minority language rights to territorial autonomy.

[53] For a discussion of these factors in the Asian context, see Baogang He and Will Kymlicka, "Introduction," in *Multiculturalism in Asia* (Oxford: Oxford University Press, 1996), 7–12.

[54] It is important here not to conflate the Arab world with the Muslim world. Several Muslim states outside the Arab region seem to be following the general global trends towards multiculturalism. Consider Indonesia or Malaysia, with their complex systems of minority and indigenous rights. There is indeed a vibrant literature on multiculturalism in Muslim-majority societies outside the Arab world, particularly in Indonesia, Malaysia, and the subcontinent, such as Robert Hefner, *The Politics of Multiculturalism: Pluralism and Citizenship in Malaysia, Singapore, and Indonesia* (Honolulu, HI: University of Hawaii Press, 2001); John Bowen, *Islam, Law and Equality in Indonesia* (Cambridge: Cambridge University Press, 2003); Abdou Filali-Ansary and Sikeena Karmali Ahmed (eds.), *The Challenge of Pluralism: Paradigms from Muslim Contexts* (Edinburgh: Edinburgh University Press, 2009); or Katharine Adeney, *Federalism and Ethnic Conflict Regulation in India and Pakistan* (Basingstoke: Palgrave, 2007), all of which tackle some of the underlying theoretical and normative issues regarding the prospects for multicultural citizenship in these countries. This suggests that the travails of multiculturalism in the Arab world have less to do with Islam per se, and more to do with the specificities of the Ottoman and colonial legacies, and of current regional geopolitics. Similar issues have been raised in the well-known debate about "Muslim exceptionalism" versus "Arab exceptionalism" in relation to democracy. Stepan and Robertson argue that the travails of democracy in the Arab world cannot be explained by Islam, given the relative success of democracy in Muslim-majority states outside

need to avoid "the notion that the Middle East is an exception in the number, treatment, or sensitivity of its minorities."[55] Indeed, viewed through a broader lens, rather than seeing the Arab world as an exception to the generally positive reception and transformative effects of multiculturalist politics in most regions of the world, we might instead see Latin America as an exception to the generally hostile reaction and ambivalent effects of multiculturalist politics in most regions.

Taking this broader lens also helps avoid overly deterministic claims about the prospects for multiculturalism. While resistance to minority and indigenous rights is widespread in the postcolonial world, it is clear that countries can overcome these legacies. History is not destiny, and there are striking differences even between neighboring countries with similar demographics and historical legacies. We are very far from knowing the necessary or sufficient conditions for the adoption of minority and indigenous rights. Nor do we have well-established theories about when such rights will be effective in practice, or transformative in their impact. Several commentators have argued, for example, that the rise of "indigenous" or "autochthonous" politics in sub-Saharan Africa has fostered undemocratic, exclusionary, and even violent politics,[56] rather than building more inclusive and peaceful relations of democratic citizenship as in Latin America.

We must firmly reject therefore both exceptionalism and fatalism regarding minority politics in the Arab world. Rather than trying to identify some alleged Arab exceptionalism or some predetermined Arab response to minority claims, our aim in this volume is to examine the Arab world as one important context for exploring what are in fact genuinely universal questions about the prospects for multiculturalism. What are the conditions under which we can envisage a mutually supportive dialectic of nation-building and minority rights? Under what conditions can struggles for minority rights have a transformative effect? Under what conditions can international norms play a constructive role in this process? If these questions are difficult and unsettled in the Arab world, for the reasons discussed earlier, they are far from easy or resolved in any other region, and it is our hope that studying the Arab world can shed light on global debates about diversity and democracy.

One final introductory comment about the "minorities" we are primarily focused on. As noted earlier, the Ottoman millet system defined minorities along religious lines, and there is already a vast literature on the status of Christians and Jews as protected minorities in the Arab and Muslim worlds.

---

the Arab world (Alfred Stepan and Graeme Robertson, "Arab, not Muslim, Exceptionalism," *Journal of Democracy* 15/4 (2004): 140–6).

[55] White, *The Emergence of Minorities in the Middle East*, 5.

[56] Peter Geschiere, *The Perils of Belonging: Autochthony, Citizenship, and Exclusion in Africa and Europe* (Chicago, IL: University of Chicago Press, 2009).

While the legacy of the Ottoman millets is of crucial importance for our issue, for reasons explained earlier, our aim is not to duplicate existing studies of religious minorities. Rather, our focus is on how ethno-national diversity is conceptualized and debated within the Arab world, and how this connects to emerging global discourses on minority and indigenous rights. These new global discourses are focused less on religious groups, and more on groups such as the Sahrawis in Morocco, the Kurds in Iraq or Syria, the Amazigh in Algeria, or the Southerners in Sudan. Just as Palestinians in Israel or Arabs in Iran do not wish to be seen as simply a religious minority but rather as a distinct national group or indigenous people (with its associated claims to land, autonomy, language rights, etc.), so too various groups within Arab countries make claims not only for religious accommodation, but also for the status of national minority or indigenous people. Other ethnic groups face caste discrimination (e.g. the Al-Akhdam in Yemen) or exclusion (e.g. migrant workers in the Gulf). It is these types of ethnic and national groups that are the main focus of recent international discourses on minority and indigenous rights, yet the potential relevance or appropriateness of these international norms for the Arab world remains largely unstudied.[57] Our volume aims to fill this important gap.

OVERVIEW OF THE VOLUME

The volume is organized in two Parts: Part I examines the issues from broad historical and theoretical perspectives, Part II provides a number of detailed case studies. We begin in Chapter 2 with Janet Klein's historical overview of discourses on minorities in the Arab world, particularly in relation to the Kurdish "periphery." She explores the construction of minorities in the late-Ottoman period, and how foreign intervention in the late-Ottoman and post-Ottoman periods of nation-building not only helped to construct certain groups as "minorities," but also fed the process through which these "marked citizens" (to use Pandey's term) came to be branded as threats to the nation

[57] We should also clarify the term "Arab world." In the first instance, we use this term in its conventional geographic sense to refer to Arab-majority countries, all of whom belong to the Arab League. (The League also includes a few countries such as Comoros, Djibouti, Mauritania, and Somalia where Arabic is an official language but not a majority language, but our focus is on Arab-majority countries.) However, we also consider the case of Arab minorities in neighboring countries, such as that in Israel. These Arab minorities have their own distinctive ways of connecting their Arab/Islamic traditions and local realities with more global discourses and institutions. And we also include relevant comparisons with neighboring countries: for example, comparing the way Kurds are viewed within Arab-majority countries (such as Syria and Iraq) with their treatment in Iran or Turkey. These sorts of comparisons help shed light on what (if anything) is distinctive about minority issues within Arab-majority states.

and national unity, leaving a lasting legacy that continues to play out to this day. In approaching the issue of minority rights today, she argues, it is essential to understand this background so that we avoid strategies—including well-intentioned international strategies—that will simply reinforce their status as marked citizens.

If Klein reminds us how the burdens of history complicate efforts to address the minority issue, Joshua Castellino and Kathleen Cavanaugh in Chapter 3 emphasize instead the potentially positive contributions that the legacy of the millet system can offer. They argue that the millet legacy has important lessons not only for protecting minorities, but also for building a more inclusive national identity, and more representative public institutions. They also argue that international minority and human rights norms, suitably interpreted, can play a constructive role in building the positive dialectic of nation-building and minority rights.

These first two chapters give some indication of the complexity of identifying what Will Harvey calls the "materials for the credible histories of diversity so needed in the present day."[58] In Chapter 4, Zaid Eyadat turns our attention to the contemporary situation minorities face in the Arab world, and the models or methods that are on offer for managing diversity. After mapping the landscape of minorities in the Arab world, Eyadat discusses a range of approaches including traditional and modern Islamic theorizing, liberal multiculturalism, and consociationalism. While each has its limits, he defends a model that combines the strengths of each, offering not only firm protection for minorities, but also their incorporation into the construction of an overlapping and cross-cutting national identity in the Arab states.

In Chapter 5, Francesca Maria Corrao and Sebastiano Maffettone focus specifically on the relevance of liberal multiculturalism for minorities in the Arab world. Corrao and Maffettone argue that if liberal multiculturalism is to be relevant and helpful, the relationship between liberalism and multiculturalism must be reformulated to make clear that liberalism is prior to multiculturalism, and that securing the basic structure of liberal-democracy is prior to pursuing a specifically multicultural version of liberal-democracy. Upholding this priority is essential, they argue, not just for the Arab world, but also in the West. If multiculturalism in the Arab world cannot take root until a minimal threshold of liberal democracy is in place, it is equally true that multiculturalism in the West faces backlash and retreat when it is seen as departing from core liberal principles. More generally, liberal-democracy is a precondition for a sustainable multiculturalism.

Following these more theoretical chapters, we then turn in Part II to a number of detailed case studies, moving across the Arab world from west to east.

---

[58] Harvey, "Grieving Cosmopolitanism," 1348.

In Chapter 6, Jacob Mundy explores the Western Sahara dispute, as a case study of how ethnic disputes have been "imagineered" in the Arab world. The Western Sahara conflict is one of the most protracted territorial disputes in Africa and the Middle East today. While ethnic Sahrawi nationalists continue their forty-year struggle to create an independent Republic in Western Sahara, the Kingdom of Morocco's occupation of the territory is stronger than ever. Meanwhile, the twenty-year-old UN mission in Western Sahara seems no closer to obtaining a final status agreement between Morocco and the independence movement that will deliver the long-promised self-determination referendum. This chapter seeks to understand the nature of this impasse in local, regional, and international frames. While some commentators have defended territorial power-sharing as the appropriate solution for Western Sahara, based on European models of federalism or territorial autonomy, others have argued that such models have little sociopolitical saliency in Arab cultural and historical contexts, and that Arab problems require Arab solutions. Through an analysis of the politics of representing the Western Sahara conflict by both the Moroccan government and Sahrawi nationalists, Mundy argues that both sides of this problematization—"Arab solutions" and "Arab problems"—are untenable, and indeed dangerously reifying. Furthermore, this problematization fails to elucidate the ways in which the structures of global politics today are largely at fault for the prolongation of suffering that surrounds issues such as Western Sahara. Since ethnic conflicts in the Arab world are already deeply penetrated by global power structures, the solution must also span both local and global levels.

In Chapter 7, Eva Pföstl moves to neighboring Algeria, and examines the increasing political salience of Amazigh (Berber) identity. When Algerian nationalists adopted the slogan "Islam is my religion, Arabic is my language, and Algeria is my country," the result was to render invisible the Amazigh, even though they had played an important role in the struggle for national liberation, and they have repeatedly fought for recognition since independence. As noted earlier, the Algerian state has, in the past, been able to confine Amazigh demands to a narrowly cultural domain, leaving largely untouched the broader political structures and imperatives of state nationalism. But this strategy has depended on a structure of state–society relations that is arguably unstable, and which is being challenged by the liberalization and democratization processes of the Arab Spring. Pföstl explores the potential of the Amazigh movement to be truly transformative *vis-à-vis* the Algerian state. She considers in particular the potential for a process of transitional justice to improve both nation-building and minority rights. Transitional justice in Algeria, like territorial autonomy in Western Sahara, is sometimes viewed as a "foreign" model being imported into the Arab world, but Pföstl argues that it has the potential to help consolidate more inclusive relations of democratic citizenship.[59]

In Chapter 8, Nicholas McGeehan turns to the Arab Gulf, and to one of the most striking examples of exclusion in the Arab world—namely, the treatment of migrant workers in the United Arab Emirates and neighboring states. In many countries the exploitation of minorities occurs despite paper guarantees in the law of fair treatment. In the UAE, however, the exploitation of migrant workers occurs not despite the labor laws and the protection afforded them by the justice system, but precisely because of the labor laws and the justice system. That is to say that their mistreatment is the direct result of an official system of exploitation, which McGeehan argues can even be characterized as facilitating their enslavement. He provides an overview and legal analysis of the country's labor system, and outlines the extent of the ruling elite's resistance to reform. His analysis casts doubt on the applicability of notions of citizenship or multiculturalism in a society as polarized as the UAE,[60] and argues that it is the persistence and significance of domestic slavery in the region that explains the serious exploitation of workers in labor-intensive sectors such as construction.

In Chapter 9, Hassan Jabareen turns to the most prominent example in the region, not of a minority in an Arab-majority state, but rather of an Arab minority in a non-Arab-majority state—namely, the case of Arab-Israelis. Arabs within Israel became a national minority in 1948, although many were exiled or internally displaced. Since there is no history or tradition of Arabs being national minorities, they have had to invent a framework and terminology for articulating their claims, including group rights such as recognition of their "national" (not just religious) status; claims for bilingualism; cultural autonomy; and restitution of land. In developing this new vocabulary, they have drawn upon international discourses of minority and indigenous rights, and have participated in UN forums on minority rights, while also adapting this international discourse to their local context. Were these claims accepted, Israel might provide an important model for the region of genuinely multicultural citizenship. In reality, however, Jabareen argues, relations between Jews and Arabs in Israel remain defined by a

---

[59] For broader debates about transitional justice in the region, see the Chatham House report on "Transitional Justice and the Arab Spring" (February 2012): <www.chathamhouse.org/publications/papers/view/182300>, accessed August 2013.

[60] See also the Chatham House report on "Identity, Citizenship and Sectarianism in the GCC," (February 2012), which opens by noting that "Gulf states—particularly the port cities—have strong historical traditions of diversity and multiculturalism that could be drawn upon to develop more inclusive notions of national identity," but which then discusses how this legacy has been set aside by ruling families who privilege a narrow religious and tribal identity, uphold restrictive citizenship laws, and equate diversity with disloyalty (<www.chathamhouse.org/publications/papers/view/183415>, accessed August 2013).

"friend–enemy" polarity that undermines not only the national rights of the Arab minority, but even their basic individual citizenship rights.

In Chapter 10, Brendan O'Leary compares the federalization of Iraq with the break-up of Sudan. Both Sudan and Iraq can be seen as the creations of British colonialism, in which sizeable and territorially concentrated non-Arab minorities were involuntarily included in a larger Arab-dominated state, and both have witnessed prolonged periods of ethnic conflict. Why has Sudan broken up while Iraq has held together? In 2005 after the making of the Constitution of Iraq and the making of Sudan's Comprehensive Peace Agreement, many analysts expected the reverse outcome—i.e. that Iraq would break up, and that the South Sudanese would eventually opt for federalism and power-sharing. While some analyses point to differences between the two minorities (e.g. that Kurds are Muslim whereas South Sudanese are predominantly Christian), O'Leary argues that the fundamental factor lies in differences between the two Arab majorities. The internal divisions amongst Arabs in Iraq created political possibilities for minorities that were not present in Sudan. This analysis helps us to avoid deterministic assumptions that Arab states are inherently anti-pluralistic, while also helping us to identify the preconditions for a successful multination state.

Finally, in Chapter 11, Joseph Yacoub explores the Assyrian-Chaldeans in Iraq as a case study for changing ideas about minorities in the Arab world. Although united by many social and historical factors, the Arab world is composed of a plurality of ethnic, national, cultural, linguistic, and confessional affiliations of long-standing origins and complex entanglements. Achieving multicultural recognition of this plurality has proved very difficult and conflictual, not least within Iraq. However, Yacoub argues that there has been a change in Arab perceptions of multiculturalism and minorities, reflected in recent revisions to the Arab Charter of Human Rights. Despite its theoretical inadequacies and practical deficiencies, the revised Arab Charter of Human Rights may prove to be a useful starting point for remedying this gap. The Charter contains several provisions regarding cultural pluralism and the rights of minorities that could guide the Arab Spring in a more diversity-friendly direction. He then applies these ideas to the case of the Assyrian-Chaldean minority in Iraq.

CONCLUSION

Needless to say, the set of arguments and cases explored in this volume represent just a small sample of the universe of state–minority issues in the Arab world, and much work remains to be done in mapping the possible trajectories of multiculturalism and minority rights across the region. We hope our volume will help stimulate such work.

Even based on the small sample represented here, however, it is already clear that we are very far from achieving any sort of consensus or convergence on appropriate models for managing diversity in the Arab world. If some of our contributors are generally optimistic about the trajectory of multicultur-alism, others are much more skeptical about its feasibility, or even its desir-ability. We do not even have an agreed vocabulary to discuss the issues. The very terms "minority rights," "indigenous rights," or "multiculturalism" may not always be appropriate or helpful in the Arab world. Yet we need to find a way to talk about these issues. A global discourse on multiculturalism has emerged with little input from Arab voices, and we need not only to under-stand better the relevance and impact of that discourse within Arab-majority countries, but also to understand how that global discourse must be better adapted to reflect the needs and experiences of the Arab world. As with the broader debate on human rights, if the interaction between global and local discourses is to be constructive, it must be bi-directional. Our aim in this volume is to take some modest and exploratory first steps in this direction.

Part I

Theoretical and Historical Perspectives

2

The Minority Question: A View from History and the Kurdish Periphery

Janet Klein

After the start of the most recent Gulf War in Iraq, the Kurdistan Regional Government (KRG) launched a novel kind of marketing campaign—to "sell" Kurdistan to the outside world. This was not a mere insert in the *New York Times* or *International Herald Tribune*, where states sometimes try to market themselves to tourists or investors. Rather, this unique advertising campaign, which was carried out on television and especially via the internet, sought to market the quasi-state's image as "civilized" and sovereign with the goal of attracting widespread international support for its bid for independence should Iraq fall or be torn apart. And if, along the way, it succeeded in bringing investors and tourists, even better!

Although I have examined this marketing campaign in the context of the performative aspect of nation-building elsewhere[1] and do not intend to dwell on it at length here, I would like to highlight its relevance to the topic I am treating here—minority rights and multiculturalism in the periphery of the Arab world from a historical perspective. The key points articulated in—if we can use them as an example here—what I call the KRG's "nationalist info-mercials" were: The KRG is stately (i.e. has state capacity), and under the KRG the Kurds as a people value democracy, the rule of law, and especially human rights (particularly the rights of women and minorities). All of this aims for what McAdam, Tarrow, and Tilly call the "certification" of that potential state by the international community; after all, for a state to be a state it must be "recognized in international law as governing a defined population and territory."[2] The process of "certification" is, as McAdam, Tarrow, and Tilly

---

[1] Janet Klein, *A Potential Kurdistan: The Quest for Statehood*, Occasional Paper (Abu Dhabi: Emirates Center for Strategic Studies and Research, 2009).

[2] Arthur A. Goldsmith, "Foreign Aid and Statehood in Africa," *International Organization* 55/1 (Winter 2001): 123–48 at 124.

put it, a "political version of a very general phenomenon" that involves "the validation of actors, their performances, and their claims by external author-ities,"[3] and that validation may indeed, according to the Montevideo Conven-tion on the Rights and Duties of States, be tacit.[4] In its state-building venture the KRG seeks to demonstrate that it has not only state capacity (which "refers to states' ability to carry out sovereign functions"[5]), but that it embodies all the qualities that the international community (the West, in particular) looks for in a state—democracy, women's rights, minority rights, and economic and political stability. It is also handy to highlight ethnic distinctiveness and the "nation's" history of oppression under "foreign" rule, and to make the most of the notion of statelessness. Although the architects of this campaign tread carefully through the potential minefield of launching accusations against others—particularly the states and peoples who have incorporated the Kurds and dominated them—the campaign does hint that Kurds are better equipped to uphold international standards of human rights than their Turkish, Persian, and especially Arab neighbors. While my aim here is not to analyze the veracity of these subtle claims, I raise this point to draw attention to the *discourse* that the KRG campaign is employing, for if we can unpack and historicize this discourse we can better grasp how minority rights and multi-culturalism have been viewed and contested in the Arab world and beyond. This chapter will trace the roots of this discourse and will demonstrate how, by understanding how the framework of current debates on minority rights and status emerged in the nineteenth century and has continued to evolve to the present, we can be supportive of the many voices in the Arab world and its neighbors who seek democracy, the rule of law, and social justice by working together to establish a new—and more helpful—framework for discussion of minorities (and wider human rights issues). This chapter will also consider how the historical construction of Kurds as minorities and Arabs, Turks, and Persians as majorities left a lasting legacy that continues to play out today.

The Kurdistani marketing campaign that I've just cited was not the first of its kind for the Kurds, although it is certainly true that the media used to wage the campaign are novel and appropriate to the early twenty-first century. A similar campaign of sorts was launched by Kurdish-Ottoman intellectuals a century earlier when—amidst the confusing and unsettling experience of watching their empire crumble around them—some Kurdish thinkers sought to create or insert themselves in a new political structure should the empire fall apart. And they did this using the language of nationalism, which was being

---

[3] Doug McAdam, Sidney Tarrow, and Charles Tilly, *Dynamics of Contention* (Cambridge: Cambridge University Press, 2001), 145.

[4] Montevideo Convention on the Rights and Duties of States, <http://www.jus.uio.no/treaties/01/1-02/rights-duties-states.xml>, accessed August 2013.

[5] Goldsmith, "Foreign Aid and Statehood in Africa," 124.

established as the dominant and most legitimizing idiom through which actors could agitate for political and social power. As one Kurdish-Ottoman intellectual wrote in 1913 in a *Rojî Kurd*, a Kurdish-Ottoman gazette, "We are in a period in which the nationalities are being decided and recognized."[6] Kurdish intellectuals grew more aware of the new world order in which the discourse of nationalism and nation-statehood was emerging as hegemonic, and as they participated in larger power struggles they used the newly legitimate vocabulary of nationalism to verbalize their political debates and agitate for empire-wide changes as well as local power. It was in the discourse of nationhood that all the issues surrounding modernity and progress converged. Kurdish intellectuals deemed that they needed to enter modernity as a nation, since nationhood was the key to political representation in the modern world. Yet at the same time, in order for the Kurds to be recognized as a nation and to obtain their "national rights," their intellectuals needed to instill in Kurds themselves nationalist sentiments and prove to the world powers that Kurdish nationhood was an "objective" reality and that the Kurds, as a nation, possessed all the "requirements" of modern progress. The numerous nationalist projects and reforms conceived by Kurdish intellectuals and disseminated to their reading public through their presses reflected, then, the efforts of a segment of the Kurdish elite to both create and reform their own Kurdish nation along modern lines and to earn recognition from the world powers that Kurds comprised a distinct nation, deserving of its nationhood by virtue of its conforming to "the requirements of the age," a point upon which I will elaborate further.

Embedded in this discourse was the budding suggestion (yet a hint at this point)—very novel at the time—that the Kurds were *minorities* in the Ottoman context, and were not only minorities but a people whose relatively "backward" situation vis-à-vis the majority Turkish group derived from their minority status. Indeed as early as 1898, Abdurrahman Bedir Khan wrote in the journal, *Kurdistan*, which he founded with his brother Mikdad Midhat, "Rum [Istanbul] establishes the great schools in regions populated by Turks. The government takes money from the Kurds and spends it on the Turks. The poor Kurds are slaves to this government."[7] And later in 1901 he asserted,

After serving the Turks for so many years, what good has come of it? . . . This state has killed many Kurds in its wars, but to this day not a single Kurd has fought for his fatherland. It is as if we were created to serve foreigners. Five hundred years ago there

---

[6] Doctor Abdullah Cevdet, "Bir Hitab" [An Address], *Rojî Kurd* 1 (2 Haziran, 1329/15 June 1913), 3.

[7] Abdurrahman Bedir Khan [Untitled], *Kurdistan*, No. 6 (28 Eylül 1314/October 10, 1898).

was not a single Turk in our country. These Turks came from Turan [and settled] in our country, and [now] they rule us in our own land.[8]

I should also note here another point that I will elaborate on further, and that is the concept of the ruling group as *foreigners*. Just as the concept of minority emerged in the nation-state context (as I will illustrate), so did the concept of foreigner shift in the nation-state context.

By reading the Kurdish-Ottoman journals to which Kurdish intellectuals contributed beginning in 1898 with the founding of *Kurdistan*—the first of its kind—it is possible to follow the evolution of a new discourse on identity in which the key themes of nation, nationality, and minority featured prominently. We can also see how terms such as "modernity" and "progress" came to take center stage at the same time. However, at this point it is perhaps more important to examine the wider context in which a new framework was being established on a global level and in which new debates emerged so that we can better situate the specificities of the discourse treated in this chapter.

While the aforementioned quotes by Abdurrahman Bedir Khan illustrate that the concept of the Kurds as a minority was beginning to be articulated by the late nineteenth century, even if the term "minority" was not used, it is essential that we do not exaggerate the significance of these particular quotes, or others like them. After all, it is perhaps more important to emphasize that most Kurds, along with other Muslim Ottomans, did not regard their ethnic identity as being of primary significance in constructing social and political loyalties and allegiances even during the last years of the empire's existence, and the concept of the Turks as "foreigners" for Kurds, Arabs, and others was only just beginning to be articulated. Indeed it was the policies of the new post-Ottoman states that emerged after the empire's demise that caused Kurds (and other groups) to view themselves as minorities, and particularly as persecuted minorities who were ruled over by a "foreign" people. Nonetheless, the discourse in which these concepts featured prominently was in the making during the years we've reviewed to this point. Therefore, it is in order at this point to examine the roots of this discourse and to problematize and historicize the concept of "minority."

"Minorities are not automatically minorities," as Pandey notes; "minorities, like communities, are historically constituted."[9] Indeed the term, "minority," which was used in reference to a group that was "distinguished by common ties of descent, physical appearance, language, culture or religion, in virtue of which they feel or are regarded as different from the majority of the population

---

[8] Abdurrahman Bedir Khan [Untitled], *Kurdistan*, No. 27, (28 Şubat-ı Evvel [*sic*: Kanun-i Sani] 1316/10 February 1901).

[9] Gyanendra Pandey, *Routine Violence: Nations, Fragments, Histories* (Stanford: Stanford University Press, 2006), 171.

in a society,"[10] only emerged in the mid-nineteenth century, and here was restricted to religious groups. Although the concept of minority quickly came to identify numerically inferior "national" and "ethnic" groups (which this chapter will treat in more detail presently), as Ben White notes, "[i]t is not surprising that *religious* minorities were identified first: before the emergence of secular nationalism, the politically salient form of identity was religious." And "[n]or," he continues, "is it surprising that religious minorities were not identified as *minorities* until quite recently (c. 1850). Previously, it was their status as subordinate *religious* groups that was important. Only when modern states appeared did the numerical inferiority of these groups become more salient than the religious cleavages separating them from the majority."[11]

In the Ottoman context (which is worth exploring here since much of the Arab world and its periphery were incorporated—even if sometimes loosely—into this vast and long-lasting empire), religious communities were organized into the millet system, and while it is certainly true that non-Muslims were a subordinate group, they "were not subordinated because they were a *minority* (often they were not), but because they were non-Muslims."[12] Even before the Ottomans achieved regional dominance, earlier Islamic states ruled over non-Muslims and developed doctrines and practices for this rule. Although non-Muslims were subordinate, Islamic law and imperial practice guaranteed them specified rights and status that the state upheld and recognized.[13] Furthermore, when we wish to consider how this "subordinate" status affected people in practice we must consider other factors, and when we do we find that a person's religion determined relatively little about their quality of life. One's religion might determine *which* paths were available for accumulating wealth and acquiring social status but not *if* paths were open at all.

The literature on Christians and Jews in the Ottoman Empire and on relationships between the various groups is vast and has grown particularly in recent decades, but there remain two key problems with the literature. The first is the tendency to treat the concept of "minority" ahistorically and without problematizing the term itself. As such, a plethora of works has emerged on "minorities" in the Ottoman Empire, and while some rightly use the term in their studies of the modern period when the concept of minority was being articulated, too many others use the term when referring to studies of Christians and Jews (or even ethnic groups) in earlier periods when the concept was rather meaningless. Another problem lies in the

---

[10] Alan Bullock et al. (eds.), *Harper Dictionary of Modern Thought*, new and rev. edn. (New York: Harper, 1988), cited in Benjamin White, "The Nation-State Form and the Emergence of 'Minorities' in Syria," *Studies in Ethnicity and Nationalism* 7/1 (2007): 64–85 at 65.

[11] White, "The Nation-State Form and the Emergence of 'Minorities' in Syria," 65–6 (italics in original).

[12] White, "The Nation-State and the Emergence of 'Minorities' in Syria," 66.

[13] Again, see White on this point (66).

treatment of inter-group relations. Scholars of late have found many flaws
with previous mainstream portrayals of inter-religious group interactions as
inherently—even primordially—one of discord, and have rightly opened our
eyes to the complexities of these relationships and how they were often much
more positive and fluid than mainstream literature has portrayed them.
However, in their attempts to overturn ahistorical presentations of age-old
religious hatreds or rigid group boundaries, some of these scholars have swung
to the other extreme and have painted a much rosier picture of group relations
than the historical record warrants. In other words, while it is good to
recognize that these relations were much better and more nuanced than
previous portraits have shown them to be, the "kumbaya" approach leaves
us without the means to consider conflict when it did arise—for indeed it did.
Thankfully, the more recent work of scholars such as Ussama Makdisi and
Christine Philliou, for two recent examples, have brought us highly nuanced
studies that capture the complexities of these relationships and the contingencies that converged to promote strife when it did occur.[14] What is important to
point out here is that enmity between religious groups took on a dangerously
different dimension with the evolution of the modern state and the development of a set of uneven power relations between European powers and the
Ottomans in which a discourse surrounding minorities (which, as I will
illustrate further, began to extend to "ethnic" and "cultural" groups) and
new concepts of rights became elements in a wider global discourse on
modernity, civilization, sovereignty, identity, and power.

Mainstream literature on the development of nationalism—for indeed the
concept of minorities is intimately linked to nationalism—has often regarded
"national thinking" as originating in the West and emanating outwards to the
rest of the world. In this view, "national" institutions and discourse were
adopted by intellectuals in non-Western lands, often in lands that had been
colonized or otherwise subject to an imperialist relationship. Even Benedict
Anderson's contribution to the subject, which was so important for decenter-
ing Europe and demonstrating that nationalism originated and spread on a
global (instead of insular European) scale, could not move beyond the idea,
which he articulated through his concept of "Creole pioneers," that Western-
ish figures in the Americas carved out the models, and the rest of the world
emulated them by following the blueprints they had created.[15] In response to

---

[14] Ussama Makdisi, *Culture of Sectarianism* (Berkeley and Los Angeles, CA: University of
California Press, 2000); Christine Philliou, "Communities on the Verge: Unraveling the Phan-
ariot Ascendancy in Ottoman Governance," *Comparative Studies in Society and History* 51/1
(2009), and *Biography of an Empire: Governing Ottomans in an Age of Revolution* (Berkeley and
Los Angeles, CA: University of California Press, 2010). See also my *Margins of Empire: Kurdish
Militias in the Ottoman Tribal Zone* (Stanford, CA: Stanford University Press, 2011).

[15] Benedict Anderson, *Imagined Communities: Reflections on the Origins and Spread of
Nationalism* (London: Verso, 1991).

Anderson's work, Partha Chatterjee asked, "If nationalisms in the rest of the world have to choose their imagined community from certain 'modular' forms already made available to them by Europe and the Americas, what do they have left to imagine?" Dealing specifically with anti-colonial nationalisms, Chatterjee suggested that "the most powerful as well as the most creative results of the nationalist imagination in Asia and Africa are posited not on an identity but rather on a *difference* with the 'modular' forms of the national society propagated by the West."[16] For Chatterjee, nationalist elites created their "own domain of sovereignty within colonial society" before they initiated their political struggle with the imperial power, and they did this through "dividing the world of social institutions and practices into two domains—the material and the spiritual," or the outer and inner. While nationalists acknowledged Western superiority in the outer domain of science and technology, and acquiesced to studying and emulating Western achievements there, they launched their most creative project in the "inner" domain: "to fashion a 'modern' national culture that [was] nevertheless not Western."[17] Although Chatterjee also aims to decenter Europe in his theory on the development of nationalism and to demonstrate the intellectual creativity of nationalists in non-Western settings, he still notes that these thinkers took European ideas and passed them through their own "ideological sieve."[18] And indeed they did, for a global hegemonic discourse that was based on European (orientalist) depictions of the peoples they colonized did emerge (a point I will develop further) and is arguably still active today, albeit with new catchphrases. This is an essential point to keep in mind when looking at the origins and development of discourses and policies on minorities in the Arab world and its periphery because they were developed by agents on the ground engaging with this hegemonic discourse. However, we must keep in mind that it was not *all* borrowing. There were historical circumstances and contingencies that came together to allow Ottomans (and others) to begin "thinking" like "nationals" in a nation-state while still in an empire, and this was an element that contributed to the emergence of "minorities" that was not simply handed down from European thinking. While I do not have the space to develop this idea fully here, I would like to touch on it briefly before considering the role of the global discourse on minorities and some specificities on how this discourse played out in parts of the Arab world and its periphery.

A significant part of the development of the modern state—indeed the modern *nation*-state—was the process through which the "edges" and

---

[16] Partha Chatterjee, *The Nation and its Fragments: Colonial and Postcolonial Histories* (Princeton, NJ: Princeton University Press, 1993), 5.

[17] Chatterjee, *The Nation and its Fragments*, 6.

[18] Partha Chatterjee, "The Nationalist Resolution of the Women's Question," in Kumkum Sangari and Sudesh Vaid (eds.), *Recasting Women: Essays in Indian Colonial History* (New Brunswick, NJ: Rutgers University Press, 1990), 236.

boundaries of states transitioned from frontiers to borderlands to bordered lands. In the Ottoman case, and elsewhere, there were many people who may have been under the control of the state, but only nominally. It was important for modern state-crafters to carve out and expand state spaces and to incorporate or at least neutralize the nonstate spaces that were within the boundaries of the state (however fuzzy they may have been) but that the state could not yet *govern*,[19] as "these stateless zones . . . played a potentially subversive role, both symbolically and practically."[20] Initially this most often took place in the borderland regions, as it was here that the state perceived the greatest threats. But it would also come to include all parts of the state's territory. It was a larger process that involved not only delimiting the area to be governed but also mapping the peoples who lived within them. For Mary Douglas, this involved "making up people," and in this "dynamic process . . . new names [were] uttered and forthwith new creatures corresponding to them emerge[d]."[21] While a good part of these new identities was ascriptive, i.e. assigned from outside the group in question, Douglas also points out that "individual persons [made] choices within the classifications," which I would add then helped to shape the ascriptive character of these identities as the two "sides" emerged in conversation with each other. Nonetheless, the question that gradually entered the minds of many Ottomans even before the empire's demise was that nation-state question, "whose country is this anyway?"[22] In the context of an Ottoman state that was witnessing what many perceived to be a collusion between the forces of Europe and the empire's Christians to weaken or dismantle the empire, Christians became a "minority" (as they had been identified as such by their self-appointed European "protectors"), and not only a minority but what Pandey calls "marked citizens." Muslims, as Pandey puts it, became the "we" that needed no articulation,[23] and while there may have been Muslim groups that the state viewed with suspicion, the burden was placed overwhelmingly on Christians—now viewed as a minority—to demonstrate their loyalty to the state and, in Pandey's words, "the sincerity of their choice" to remain Ottoman citizens.[24] This feature of "marked" citizenry would gradually swing to include ethnic groups and to bring people to view ethnic groups as minorities as well. Indeed, as we shall see below, this concept of the "marked citizen" continues to apply today, in even stronger terms. In

[19] See Anthony Giddens on the distinction between ruling and governing (*The Nation-State and Violence: Volume Two of a Contemporary Critique of Historical Materialism* (Berkeley, CA: University of California Press, 1985), 57).

[20] James C. Scott, *Seeing Like a State: How Certain Schemes to Improve the Human Condition Have Failed* (New Haven, CT: Yale University Press, 1998), 186–7.

[21] Mary Douglas, *How Institutions Think* (Syracuse: Syracuse University Press, 1986), 100, after Ian Hacking.

[22] Pandey, *Routine Violence*, 84.

[23] Pandey, *Routine Violence*, 146.   [24] Pandey, *Routine Violence*, 132.

the Ottoman case this shift really took place only in the twentieth century, but the wider global discourse, which I will discuss presently, was such that all states began to view minorities in ethnic as well as religious terms. Since World War I, the focus has been on ethnic identity and "national" self-determination, a point that was most vociferously articulated in Woodrow Wilson's Fourteen Points, the twelfth point of which called for the self-determination of the various Ottoman (ethnic) groups.[25] The discourse and policies of the new post-Ottoman states that emerged from the wake of World War I cannot be viewed without considering this historical context.

But there is a further element to the global discourse on minorities that I would like to explore here, and if the reader will permit me, I would like to illustrate how the work of gender historians in particular can help us to understand better how a larger discourse on modernity, progress, and civil-ization was developed in the nineteenth and twentieth centuries (and indeed continues to be elaborated and debated today) and became hegemonic, and how some of the rhetoric and policies on minorities in the Arab world emerged through a history of engaging with this global hegemonic discourse. I hope to demonstrate that because this discourse was largely European, and because the actors in the Arab (and neighboring) worlds who were forced to engage with it were either colonized or subject to imperialist influence, they generally took two approaches: one was to accept (often implicitly) the terms of the debates and the other was to reject the terms of the debates by actively engaging in policies that appeared to counter the ideals articulated by Euro-peans in this discourse, but which nonetheless implicitly recognized the European framework of the debates. This would have lasting consequences for debates on human rights, of which minority rights came to be a part, indeed to the present day.

In brief, this larger discourse on "rights" surrounded the veil in particular, and women's rights in general. Debates on the veil, women's segregation, and women's rights in general arose in the context of a wider colonial/imperialist discourse that at heart was about civilization, modernity, and progress, and who was "fit" to rule others and who, due to their backwardness, needed to be ruled over and reformed. As Leila Ahmed shows, "that the Victorian colonial

---

[25] The relevant portion reads: "The Turkish portion of the present Ottoman Empire should be assured a secure sovereignty, but the other nationalities which are now under Turkish rule should be assured an undoubted security of life and an absolutely unmolested opportunity of autonomous development . . ." White also points out that the "11th edition of the *Encyclopaedia Britannica*, published in 1910–1911, contains no entry for 'minorities,'" but that by the 14th edition in 1929, "the entry on minorities runs to eleven pages, mostly discussing the post-World War One peace settlements and the League of Nations" (White, "The Nation-State and the Emergence of 'Minorities' in Syria," 64). The *Oxford English Dictionary* began to cite "national" and "ethnic" minorities only in the 1918 and 1945 editions respectively (White, "The Nation-State and the Emergence of 'Minorities' in Syria," 65).

paternalistic establishment appropriated the language of feminism in the service of its assault on the religions and cultures of Other men, and in particular on Islam, in order to give an aura of moral justification to that assault at the very same time as it combated feminism within its own society— can be easily substantiated by reference to the conduct and rhetoric of the colonizers." In her analysis of the development of a particular discourse on the veil and Muslim women, Ahmed shows how Cromer, in his rule over Egypt, believed that "Islamic religion and society were inferior to the European ones and bred inferior men."[26] He advocated policies that were supposedly aimed to raise the position of women, but in fact these policies were "detrimental to Egyptian women." This was not surprising, for after all Cromer had clear "paternalistic convictions" in relation to women in his own country. As Ahmed puts it, "Feminism on the home front and feminism directed against white men was to be resisted and suppressed; but taken abroad and directed against the cultures of colonized peoples, it could be promoted in ways that admirably served and furthered the project of the dominance of the white man."[27] I would add that although not as powerful symbolically as a crusade to reform Muslim society by abolishing the veil, the discourse on minorities was similar, and indeed of the very same family. European societies saw the emergence of "minority questions" in their midst, and as the Jewish case, for one, demonstrates, responded to Jewish attempts to either assimilate or assert their rights as minorities with violence and other tactics of suppression. But in the Ottoman Empire, as elsewhere, the same European powers that suppressed their own minorities became the "protectors" of the Christians, and championed their "minority rights." And they used the plight of "minorities" here to justify occupation and intervention in these lands.

The irony in all of this was not lost on Ottoman and Egyptian observers, who drew frequent attention to these paradoxes in their writings. But the further irony rested in their own proposed social and political reforms with regard to women, and eventually minorities as well. The idea was, as Chatterjee has shown, that in order to throw off the yoke of the colonizer, reformers needed to fashion an "authentic" and modern culture within the most private domain of the family and social life that the colonizer could not touch before taking on the political, or indeed even military, battle with the colonial or imperial power. The reforms advocated by Qasim Amin's book, *The Liberation of Women* (1899), for one, attempted to do just this. However, as Ahmed points out, Amin's assault on the veil and gender segregation "represented not the result of reasoned reflection and analysis but rather the

---

[26] Leila Ahmed, *Women and Gender in Islam* (New Haven, CT: Yale University Press, 1992), 152.

[27] Ahmed, *Women and Gender in Islam*, 153.

internalization and replication of the colonialist perception."[28] Amin's tract, in other words, "conducted an attack that in its fundamentals reproduced the colonizer's attack on native culture and society." What is perhaps a further irony is that "For Amin as for Cromer, women and their dress were important counters in the discourse concerning the relative merits of the societies and civilizations of men and their different styles of male domination; women themselves and their liberation were no more important to Amin than to Cromer."[29] And the rebuttals to Amin and others like him came "in the form of an affirmation of the customs that he had attacked—veiling and segregation. In a way that was to become typical of the Arabic narrative of resistance, the opposition appropriated, in order to negate them, the terms set in the first place by the colonial discourse."[30] A hegemonic global discourse thus took root, and although I have highlighted elements of the "woman question" that was a significant part of this discourse, we should note that at heart it was much larger—it was part of a wider discourse on modernity, progress, and civilization, and ultimately sovereignty. The issue of how a state or society should treat its minorities was not yet fully articulated in the late Ottoman period simply because the question of minorities, particularly when referring to ethnic minorities, was quite new and still taking shape. But as it took shape it was worked into the larger discourse—which was becoming hegemonic—on what constituted a civilized, modern society. Although the treatment of women in the Islamic world became one of the most powerful and potent symbols of—in European terms—the *lack* of civilization and modernity there, the perceived persecution of Christians became another, and indeed turned into a new kind of crusade. Soon, after the creation of post-Ottoman states, these states' policies vis-à-vis minorities would become another crusade, and again, one that imperialist powers would use to justify their direct rule over these new countries or their influence in these states' internal affairs.

My point here is that it is very important to understand the discursive element of this battle, for even today it continues to play out. We have today what is widely considered to be universal(ist) standards and norms for human rights, of which minority rights are a part. It is certainly not the intention of this chapter to promote a relativist argument for upholding human rights or for excusing their violation when violations occur. Rather, in the interest of more *successfully* promoting human rights on global and local levels we must recognize that the historical development of the *discourse* surrounding human (here, minority) rights took place in a non-neutral setting and amidst unequal power relations between "the West," whose agents articulated the concepts in a manner that would become hegemonic, and "the rest," who were deemed to

---

[28] Ahmed, *Women and Gender in Islam*, 160.
[29] Ahmed, *Women and Gender in Islam*, 161–2.
[30] Ahmed, *Women and Gender in Islam*, 162.

be less civilized and less modern, and therefore in need of European intervention to ensure that they conformed with the "requirements of the age"; as such, the foundations of this discourse continue to matter in regions of the world where people feel that their societies, cultures, and religions remain under attack. Human rights violations—then and now—have been called out in *cultural* terms, with Western powers and media blaming Arab or Islamic *culture* for failing to conform to international standards. As a result, the response by Arabs and Muslims has sometimes been to reframe the practices that are called into question in cultural terms and to draft them into the discourse of cultural authenticity. Just as George Bush's "axis of evil" speech was so very unhelpful to the democratization process in Iran as it spurred Iran president Mahmoud Ahmadinejad to reassert oppressive practices in the name of an Iranian/Islamic culture that was publicly insulted, the international community needs to reexamine the genealogical roots of this discourse and its impact when engaging with discussions on human rights—minority rights in particular here—in the Arab world and elsewhere. At the same time (to return to a point I made just now), the story of minorities in the Arab world does not just take place on the discursive plane, although we certainly need to keep in mind our excursion into the discursive to view the full picture. We also need to recall our earlier discussion of borders, nation-state identities, and marked citizens, and how concrete political developments have shaped the discourses and practices affecting minorities and wider human rights issues in these regions.

It is beyond the scope of this chapter to consider the whole Arab world, but I would like briefly to consider those parts that have significant minorities, who can serve as an example for what I'd like to suggest, and since I'm most familiar with those states that house Kurds, I will deal with the "Arab" states of Iraq and Syria, as well as the states across their borders—Turkey and (to a lesser extent) Iran. Here we will find that while the discourse on minorities inspired and empowered several groups to seek their "own" state, it also contributed to concrete fears on the part of the new post-Ottoman regimes that their newly constructed states could be destabilized by separatist (sometimes irredentist) movements. Thus, for those in power a tension emerged between the need to pay lip-service, at the very minimum, to the global discourses on human rights (of which minority rights is a part) and the other perceived need to control—indeed squash—minority movements (and often the minorities themselves). Because these policies have often been very brutal, states have had to justify them by portraying the minority group in question as being either the one who is actually violating international norms (by being backwards, extremist, or anti-modern) or the group who is collaborating with the "imperialists," both options implicitly working within the global discourse that I've described above. Not frequently acknowledged in the middle are the more democratic elements in society that unself-consciously adopt a much more nuanced view of minorities (perhaps, indeed, by *not* problematizing the concept) as they have agitated for social and economic justice and democratic, transparent rule in more general terms. By briefly tracing how discourses and practices on minorities evolved in the early years of statehood in Iraq, Syria, and Turkey, and in the newly configured state of Iran starting in the 1920s as well, I hope to illustrate some of the factors that played a role in the development of some shared and state-specific discourses and practices regarding minority populations in the borders of these new states—dynamics that continue to play out today.

A series of questions should be asked: to what extent did Syria and Iraq as *Arab* states evolve a particular set of policies and discourse on minorities, i.e. is it even valid in this sense to view the Arabness of the states as significant in determining these things? To what extent did the *manner* in which each state came into existence impact these things? To what extent did the demographic make-up of each state influence these policies and discourses? And to what extent can we identify the nation-state form and the politics of state-building in general as generating similar processes in all these states? It might be more fruitful to pursue these questions thematically rather than submit the case of each state to separate scrutiny. As all of these states—Iraq, Turkey, Syria, and Iran—have significant Kurdish populations, I will focus on the "Kurdish question" in each as a lens through which to examine these larger questions.

Although the break-up of the Ottoman Empire was long chalked up to nationalist, separatist movements—some of which succeeded in breaking away before the empire fell and others of which would have broken away had the empire remained intact after World War I—recent scholarship has cast shadows on this assumption. For the mostly Muslim regions that remained in the empire at the end of World War I (a region comprised mainly of Turks, Kurds, and Arabs), the vocabulary of nationalism and self-determination was certainly current, as we've seen in the case of Kurdish intellectuals, whose writings I cited above. However, it was by no means *sui generis* and uncomplicated. As I've shown elsewhere in the case of the Kurds, "nationalist" expression did not necessarily mean *separatist* desires.[31] Rather, for most Kurds and Arabs in the early twentieth century, remaining within the Ottoman framework was a given; rather, the debates surrounded the *terms* of that incorporation. Kurdish and Arab intellectuals and notables were often resistant to the centralizing policies that the state had pursued throughout the nineteenth century and sought a return of their *local*, decentralized power.

---

[31] Janet Klein, "Kurdish Nationalists and Non-Nationalist Kurdists: Rethinking Minority Nationalism and the Dissolution of the Ottoman Empire, 1908–1909," *Nations and Nationalism* 13/1 (January 2007); and see also Hasan Kayalı, *Arabs and Young Turks: Ottomanism, Arabism, and Islamism in the Ottoman Empire, 1908–1913* (Berkeley, CA: University of California Press, 1997), for the Arab case.

Many notables, after all, had their interests intimately bound up with those of the continued existence of the state. The vocabulary of nationalism was, however, becoming hegemonic and was deployed often in the interests of more local power. It could also serve as a means of bet-hedging in case the fragmenting empire did fall.

In the aftermath of World War I the Empire was occupied and the people within found that plans for its territories had been drawn up by the victors before the war had even concluded. Seeing the writing on the wall, prominent figures from each ethno-linguistic community came forth to the peace conference in 1919 to press for their own state. "Arabs" demanded the Arab kingdom that had been promised to them in return for their assistance to the British war effort; "Kurds," represented by Şerif Pasha, used the twelfth of Woodrow Wilson's Fourteen Points to press for an independent Kurdistan, and indeed in 1920 saw provisional plans for such a state in the Treaty of Sevres; and although (or perhaps because) there was no "Turkish," but rather Ottoman, representation at the peace conference, a separate Turkish nationalist movement began to percolate in Anatolia, which would result in the rejection of empire and the foundation of the Turkish Republic. The unified Arab kingdom was not to materialize, but with the mandate system set up in 1920 the new Arab states of Syria and Iraq (among others) were established with the British and French overseeing their construction.

The manner in which these states (and also Iran, which was never part of the Ottoman Empire) came into being would certainly impact politics in each state, and would also influence—to a certain extent—the framework in which the question of minorities arose and played out. As James Gelvin points out, "The states that emerged in the Middle East in the wake of World War I were created in two ways: In the Levant and Mesopotamia . . . France and Britain constructed states. Guided by their own interests and preconceptions, the great powers partitioned what had once been the Ottoman Empire and created states where states had never before existed. The wishes of the inhabitants of those territories counted for little when it came to deciding their political future." Syria and Iraq were two such states. Turkey and Iran, however, emerged as independent states in different manners—Turkey as the result of an anti-imperialist struggle (often called the Turkish War of Independence) and Iran through a coup d'état.[32]

Although Syria and Iraq were not colonies per se, there existed in them "a particular pattern of control known as the 'colonial state,'" which Owens believes "can be used to highlight a number of general features that shaped the exercise of power and defined the political arena in most of the countries

---

[32] James L. Gelvin, *The Modern Middle East: A History* (New York: Oxford University Press, 2005), 175.

created or dominated by Europeans."[33] A major problem was that in these mandates social forces were really not able to engage with the state, and political organizations did not care to, or were not able to, obtain a broad-based national constituency. As a result, the state was very vulnerable when its colonial protectors left and, not being rooted in society, was "'up for grabs' to the highest or, more relevantly, the most militarily effective, bidder."[34] The mandates left a distinct legacy in Syria and Iraq. As Peter Sluglett points out, the state structures were constructed too rapidly, and were pushed on a population that had little involvement in their formation. Whatever liberal economic or political structures the mandates seemed to offer "were little more than a façade." Political freedoms were actually "glorified cronyism," and were enjoyed by very few. And lastly, "The foundations of the institutional structures...were too fragile to be capable of peaceful reproduction or renewal, which meant that it was relatively easy for the state to be captured by well-organised or even fortuitously positioned armed groups, generally from lower middle class rural or urban backgrounds, acting on their own initiative." Soon, "loyalty to the regime...became more important than competence (both military and civil), which led to the gradual depoliticisation of the middle classes (and indeed of most of society) and to their general alienation from the state. The result, *pace* Migdal (1988), was both a weak state and a weak society, with the forces of coercion and repression taking charge and acting largely on their own behalf."[35]

Turkey and Iran, by contrast, emerged under different conditions, and while the regimes that installed themselves were certainly coercive as well, a much greater link between state and society became possible in both countries. One reason that both states started out with a "firmer foundation for nation-building than that enjoyed by the states created in the Levant and Mesopotamia" was that there evolved a "national myth recounting the deeds of a heroic leader or founding generation."[36] They also did not have the same legacy of colonialism. Both Mustafa Kemal and Reza Khan (who crowned himself Reza Shah Pahlavi in 1926) pursued a distinctly Westernized model, and worked to centralize and "modernize" their respective countries, in the process forging a stronger link between state and society (a connection, it should be noted, that was coercive and certainly not uncontested) than seen in much of the semi-colonized Arab world. Although Reza Khan certainly had British support, he was not seen as a colonial plant in the same way that the early rulers of Iraq and Syria were.

---

[33] Roger Owens, *State, Power and Politics in the Making of the Modern Middle East*, 3rd edn. (London: Routledge, 2004), 9.

[34] Peter Sluglett, *Britain in Iraq: Contriving King and Country* (New York: Columbia University Press, 2007), 215.

[35] Sluglett, *Britain in Iraq: Contriving King and Country*, 215–16.

[36] Gelvin, *The Modern Middle East: A History*, 175.

The manner in which each of these states came into being impacted the policies and discourses on minorities that developed mostly in Syria and Iraq, where the mandatory powers worked to impose *their own* visions of who was a minority, what kinds of minorities there were, and what their status should be in each state—policies based on an increasingly hegemonic European model of minority-hood and also on the needs of the mandatory powers to create divisions and alliances that would secure their own rule. In the case of Iraq, as Toby Dodge explains, "British understandings of Iraqi society were heavily dependent upon the rigid boundaries of its different ethnic, religious and social groupings. Orientalism determined the way in which Islam was conceived. The religious divide was a major category through which British personnel understood the urban communities of Iraq. These groupings were ranked according to overlapping criteria at the heart of an Orientalist discourse: how rational and hardworking were they and how favorably disposed towards the British."[37] As a result, Jews and Christians, although noted to be only 7 percent of the population at the time, were seen to be progressive allies while the majority Muslim population was viewed as backward, and largely dismissed. The British regarded the Shia, in particular, with suspicion, and saw them as "aliens, Persians, who owed neither loyalty nor commitment to Iraq."[38] Indeed, for those like Gertrude Bell, who pressed for the inclusion of the Mosul province in the new mandate, it was essential to balance out the Shi'ite population with Sunnis, and to leave final authority with them. Otherwise, as she said, "Iraq would exist as 'a mujtahid run, theocratic state, which is the very devil.'"[39] The Mosul province had as its majority, however, the Kurds (and also a number of Turcomans and Assyrians), which complicated things further. The British had initially found allies in some Kurdish tribal leaders and courted them with promises of possible Kurdish independence so that they would not join forces with Mustafa Kemal's independence movement in Anatolia. These promises were whittled down to guarantees for minority protections in subsequent treaties, but when the British "left" Iraq (and I put this in scare quotes as they did not really leave Iraq for some time to come), their interest in minority rights was abandoned in favor of creating a stable and reliable regime.

In Syria, French interests also impacted the construction of minority-hood. There, the French were somewhat less concerned with exploiting ethno-linguistic divisions and focused more on reifying *religious* divisions (as *they* understood them, not necessarily as the Syrian population saw them). As White puts it, "This policy of extending, rather than reducing, the religious divisions of Ottoman law derived from the French authorities' religious

---

[37] Toby Dodge, *Inventing Iraq: The Failure of Nation Building and a History Denied* (New York: Columbia University Press, 2003), 67.
[38] Dodge, *Inventing Iraq*, 68.   [39] Dodge, *Inventing Iraq*, 69.

understanding of Syrian society, which was itself influenced by France's historical links with the Christian communities. Maintaining these communities as client groups and justifying the separation of a Lebanese state dominated by Maronite Christians from the rest of the mandate territories required a system of political organisation that kept them distinct from the rest of the population."[40] The Kurds, whose representatives had petitioned for administrative autonomy for Kurdish areas in 1929, were dismissed by the French because they were not a religious minority, and also because their demographic distribution was uneven.[41] Sunni Arabs emerged as a "majority," albeit an uncertain one, just as in Iraq (we might instead call them the dominant group). What is important to note here is White's point that in spite of the visions and policies the mandatory powers embraced vis-à-vis the different ethno-linguistic and religious groups in Syria (and, I would add, Iraq as well), these "minorities" did not always act as planned. It became easier, then, in some regards, for Arabic-speaking Christians to join Arab nationalist movements than to remain in the categories in which the mandatory powers placed them.[42]

This brings together two of the questions I asked earlier: to what extent did Syria and Iraq as *Arab* states evolve a particular set of policies and discourse on minorities; i.e. is it even valid in this sense to view the Arabness of the states as significant in determining these things? To what extent did the *manner* in which each state came into existence impact these things? To these I would tentatively suggest that both played *some*, but not the most significant, role. Arab nationalism certainly emerged among a small group of educated, mostly urban, elites before these states were even conceived, but distinct political movements actually grew in response to the imperialist policies that created the states of Syria and Iraq along with the other mandates and divided up the "Arab kingdom" that had been promised during World War I. Arab nationalism became a movement of resistance to "colonial" rule and was quickly exploited by rulers and power-seekers in these states to legitimize their rule or claims to power. In this scheme, however, certain religious groups were marginalized (the Shia, for example, as they would be a minority in a wider Sunni-Arab entity, and they were further viewed as "Persianate," having suspect links to Iran), but most particularly ethno-linguistic groups were shut out and severely repressed. The Kurds, as the most populous and vocal in their demands for recognition and autonomy, stand out here, and their story will be treated presently in more detail.

---

[40] White, "The Nation-State and the Emergence of 'Minorities' in Syria," 71.

[41] Nelida Fuccaro, "Kurds and Kurdish Nationalism in Mandatory Syria: Politics, Culture and Identity," in Abbas Vali (ed.), *Essays on the Origins of Kurdish Nationalism* (Costa Mesa: Mazda, 2003), 210.

[42] White, "The Nation-State and the Emergence of 'Minorities' in Syria," 72.

The most salient feature of the policies that emerged in all these states was their similarity on discursive grounds and the fact that they were all in the nation-state form, and in this sense it mattered little whether or not they were "Arab" states or had been carved out by imperial powers. As modern states, indeed nation-states, it was imperative that the new rulers could create and disseminate a powerful nation-state identity around which they could construct their regimes of power. In all cases, nationalist leaders constructed founding myths, invented or reappropriated traditions, and made selective use of the historical past to establish and disseminate new nation-state identities with the goal of building a homogenous, loyal community within the new borders and to justify (or sometimes dispute) these borders. As mentioned above, that nation-state question, "whose country is this anyway?" arose, and now took on a new level of urgency as each state was engaged in a vigorous process of asserting its existence and legitimacy vis-à-vis neighboring states, and as the regimes within attempted to legitimize their rule to their respective populations. Within this context, as we have seen, those groups who asserted a different agency in the process of "making up people," one that set them apart from the dominant group (now often regarded as a *foreign* culture)[43] and that *resisted* the dominant group's nation-state identity, were viewed as "marked citizens" (again, to use Pandey's term), and the burden was placed overwhelmingly on *their* shoulders to prove their loyalty to the new nation-state. This was particularly the case for those groups who were "homeland" minorities,[44] and who threatened the territorial integrity of these new states. These were generally not Christian groups, as they most often did not form a concentrated population in an area that could potentially be carved out as autonomous or independent, but the case of the Assyrians in Iraq was certainly a major exception. The brutality with which the newly "independent" Iraqi state suppressed an Assyrian revolt in 1933 showed that the new state would not accept challenges to its territorial integrity, and also that minorities could be pegged as stooges of British rule. Crushing the Assyrians further demonstrated the state's military awe and its monopoly on the use of violence, here in particular where rebellious minorities (as they were now construed) were concerned.[45] The most significant challenge to all these states—particularly Iraq and Turkey—however, was the Kurds.

---

[43] On the concept of dominant ("majority") culture as "foreign culture" see Janusz Mucha, "Dominant Culture as a Foreign Culture: Dominant Groups in the Eyes of Cultural Minorities—Introduction," in Janusz Mucha (ed.), *Dominant Culture as a Foreign Culture: Dominant Groups in the Eyes of Minorities* (n.p.: East European Monographs, distributed by Columbia University Press, 1999).

[44] Kymlicka, *Multicultural Odysseys* (Oxford: Oxford University Press, 2007).

[45] See Eric Davis, *Memories of State: Politics, History, and Collective Identity in Modern Iraq* (Berkeley, CA: University of California Press, 2005), 60–2.

I should state at the outset that it was not inevitable that the Kurds would become a minority per se, or at least not "marked citizens," and I do not say this only in reference to the possibility that there could have existed an independent Kurdistan in which Kurds would then have been a dominant "majority." Such an entity certainly *could* have been created had it been as much in the interests of the relevant imperial powers to create it as it was for them to carve out states such as Syria and Iraq. Rather, what I would like to suggest is that we must historicize the construction of the Kurds as a minority, and particularly as a transnational minority, in order to account for the contingencies that came together to create the circular process through which they were perceived and regarded themselves as minorities. Such a process certainly did involve all the dynamics laid out earlier in this chapter— modern nation-state "thinking," which involved the transformation of bor- derlands to bordered lands and the accompanying shift in identities within and beyond those borders, and also the global hegemonic discourse on modernity, progress, and civilization (intimately connected with ideas about who deserved sovereignty) in which discussions of minorities and self- determination came into play. However, the nation-state identities that evolved *after* the creation of these states were not inevitable either, and the Kurds initially—as others—could have been open to incorporation into any of these states (at least with less resistance) had the dominant identities chosen by the new regimes, along with the accompanying policies of enforcement, evolved differently in a manner that did not construct Kurds (and others) as "minorities," or "marked citizens."

I've pointed out already how the colonial policies of the British and French in Iraq and Syria respectively impacted the construction and subsequent status of minorities in each state. While the British recognized the Kurds as a minority and initially offered rights to them, they failed to ensure that these protections were actually observed and put into practice. In Syria, as we have seen, the French preferred to recognize religious groups as minorities, and largely ignored the arguments of such groups as Circassians and Kurds that they, too, deserved minority status. In both of these states, however, it was the development of Arab nationalism as a resistance movement to imperialist control that would come to impact the status of the Kurds most significantly. As a non-arabophone group, the Kurds found there was no space for them within the dominant nation-state identity that was evolving. As one headline in a Syrian nationalist gazette put it as early as 1927, "There are no *peoples* in Syria: there is one Arab people."[46] There was even less space for them in the pan-Arab discourse that would evolve in later decades. To add to that, Kurdish activists quickly picked up on the global hegemonic discourse on minority

---

[46] Cited in White, "The Nation-State and the Emergence of 'Minorities' in Syria," 81.

rights and used these standards to demonstrate their minority-hood and their repression to the world, and to try to gain the support of European powers for their cause (which was sometimes an independent Kurdistan, but most often a demand for cultural rights and local autonomy within their respective states). Nationalists in Iraq and Syria saw this as treachery, particularly since they regarded themselves as being in a battle against the same powers to whom the Kurds were reaching out. The Kurds in Syria were a proportionally smaller minority than they were in Iraq (about 10 percent vs. 20–25 percent), and they engaged in fewer armed uprisings. But the Kurds in Iraq were able to mount significant challenges to state authority through their armed insurgencies, and this was something that neither the "colonial" state nor "independent" Iraqi authorities would tolerate; brutal repression was henceforth the norm in dealing with Kurdish demands. In Syria, when Arab nationalism became an official ideology of the state, many Kurds were stripped of their citizenship, becoming truly stateless individuals. Today there are nearly 300,000 Kurds in Syria (of a total of around 1.5 million) who are undocumented.[47]

While the identity of Kurds *as Kurds* was never denied per se in Syria, Iraq, and Iran, in Turkey the Kurds were, until recently, systematically denied a non-Turkish identity. It was not inevitable that this would be the case during the Turkish anti-imperialist struggle that would result in an independent Turkish republic. After all, Mustafa Kemal appealed to the Kurds *as Muslims* and framed the struggle in those terms. For their part, many Kurds saw the movement as one to retain what was left of the empire that housed both peoples and did not expect a chauvinist Turkish nationalist state to take its place. Although the Turkish state quickly moved to sever its links to the empire and also to the caliphate—both steps that worked at the same time to rupture ties between Turks and Kurds—it continued to view minorities only in religious terms despite the fact that it was now a secular state. With the Armenian population now decimated and dispersed and most "Greeks" having been "repatriated" to Greece in the population exchange, the Kurds were now the only significant group that remained to pose a challenge to the Turkish nationalist identity of the state. But this threat was in fact manufactured to a large extent by the new Turkish state and its policies. Indeed, it was only *after* the state engaged in a systematic policy of denying a separate Kurdish identity, which included practices such as changing place names, outlawing Kurdish names, persecuting those who asserted their Kurdish identity, and deliberately keeping the Kurdish regions underdeveloped, that Kurdish nationalism as a form of resistance to Turkish state oppression spread beyond the intellectual and notable classes where it had originated.

---

[47] See Radwan Ziadeh, "The Kurds in Syria: Fueling Separatism in the Region?" *United States Institute of Peace Special Report* 220 (April 2009).

While it is true that the existence of the Kurds as a cross-border, "home-land" minority has posed what appears to be an inevitable threat to the territorial integrity and sovereignty of each of these states simply because all have been operating within the nation-state framework in which borders are sacred and governing technologies have been intimately bound up with the imposition of unifying nationalist identities, it has really been the policies of these states that have created the *actual*, as opposed to *potential*, threat, even if these real threats have been much smaller in reality than perceived by para-noid state agents. And since there is nothing primordial or inevitable about strife between Arabs, Turks, Persians, and Kurds, policy changes in these states can go far in alleviating these "majority/minority" tensions. After all, a significant part of the story that too often flies under the radar of outside observers is the fact that in all these countries there have been many move-ments in society in which ethnic and religious identity took a back seat to larger issues, namely movements for social and economic justice and democ-racy. In all these states, Kurds have been attracted to leftist (socialist and communist) movements as well as other organizations that have both focused on the nation-state framework (without explicitly privileging the dominant group within) and also looked beyond the nation-state framework in their attempts to fight for social and economic justice. Indeed, communist parties in all these states were particularly successful in Kurdish areas. In Iraq after World War II, for example, although Kurdish nationalism was being embraced by more and more Kurds, "a powerful critique of the inequalities and injustices of Kurdish society was also emerging. As in the Arab regions of Iraq, there was much to criticise in terms of the distribution of wealth and the power which unequal land ownership gave a small minority over the lives of the vast majority of Kurds."[48]

In Syria, as Robert Lowe points out, the Syrian Communist Party had significant Kurdish affiliation and "was a strong competitor with Kurdish parties for Kurdish support in the cities, especially among the young."[49] In these movements the common bond was not between minorities and major-ities as they came to be constructed, but between individuals and groups working together in the common interest of better living conditions, more humane working conditions, and more equal distribution of wealth and resources, and against censorship and other forms of repression. As such, these groups rejected the concept of "marked citizen" in favor of class struggle.

Where elements in society have been stirred up to collaborate with state forces in the repression (sometimes genocidal) of another group it has gener-ally been because of an alarmist state-sponsored discourse that has worked to

[48] Tripp, *A History of Iraq* (rev. edn. Cambridge: Cambridge University Press, 2007), 115.
[49] Robert Lowe, "Kurdish Nationalism in Syria," in Mohammed M. A. Ahmed and Michael M. Gunter (eds.), *The Evolution of Kurdish Nationalism* (Costa Mesa: Mazda, 2007), 294.

spread the idea that if "we" don't take steps to stop "them" first, "they" (i.e. the "marked citizens") will harm us. As A. Dirk Moses puts it, "the genocidal impulse and national liberation impulse are effectively the same: to preserve the endangered genus or ethnos against an Other that supposedly threatens its existence."[50] Support from the "majority" public for oppressive or violent measures against a minority has typically been worse when that minority has been seen as acting in collaboration with colonial or imperial powers. In some regions, in fact, as Kymlicka has shown, it is sometimes the "*majority* that feels that it has been the victim of oppression, often at the hands of minorities acting in collaboration with foreign enemies."[51] Although Kurds in all these states have suffered clear oppression from the dominant majority group in power, the majority in power has worked to "justify" the often violent repressive measures it has taken against the Kurds by pointing to moments when the Kurds in its borders have sought or gained support from an enemy, whether that enemy was an imperial(ist) power or a neighboring state. Kurds as "marked citizens" have also been the targets of a regional *mission civiliza-trice* discourse in which urban elites continued attacks on the "backwardness" of Kurdish tribes begun by Ottoman intellectuals early in the new state-building era. King Faysal in Iraq, for example, perceived the Kurds (and the Shia and Assyrians as well) as "national problems," to be managed and controlled.[52] In Turkey, while Kurdish identity is now recognized, it has been often demonized in official circles and in popular culture as backward, violent, and in need of civilization. Indeed there has been a recent obsession with "Kurdish" honor crimes in the Turkish media, where news reports and television series portray Kurds as challenging now not just the territorial integrity of the state but also its secular and modern character.[53]

It is fairly clear today that, with the possible exception of the Kurds in Iraq, the Kurds in these states have generally accepted—for better or worse—the nation-state framework in which they exist, and would be relatively content with cultural and educational rights, a measure of local autonomy, economic opportunities and development, and an overall commitment to democratic freedoms at large. Indeed while Kurds in Turkey, Syria, and Iran have participated in national politics using the political discourses at play in these

---

[50] A. Dirk Moses, "Empire, Colony, Genocide: Keywords and the Philosophy of History," in A. Dirk Moses (ed.), *Empire, Colony, Genocide: Conquest, Occupation, and Subaltern Resistance in World History* (New York: Berghahn, 2008), 31.

[51] Will Kymlicka, "The Internationalization of Minority Rights," *International Journal of Constitutional Law* 6/1 (2008): 1–32 at 29. The author notes these regions to be post-communist countries, but I would suggest that this also applies in many parts of the Middle East.

[52] Orit Bashkin, *The Other Iraq* (Stanford, MA: Stanford University Press, 2009), 198.

[53] Sevin Gallo, "Modernity and Honor Violence: The Case of Turkey and the Kurds," unpublished paper presented at the Middle East Studies Association Annual Meeting (San Diego, CA, November 2010).

states, one trend to follow may be the one in Turkey, where Marlies Casier has shown that Kurdish activists have begun to focus on effecting *local* change at the municipal and regional level and have also been drawing upon more global social-justice movements and discourses. While they continue to work within the nation-state framework to a large extent, their activities appear to veer toward the post-national and transnational.[54] Iraqi Kurds, having lived in the largely autonomous Kurdistan Region for some two decades, are unlikely to relinquish their level of independence and to be reintegrated into an Iraq in which they have little local control. They are also likely—should the opportunity present itself—to press for further sovereignty if not full independence (but only if there is clear support for this by major powers). As of now that possibility appears slim, even to Iraqi Kurds themselves, but their "marketing" campaign that I cited at the opening of this chapter can be seen as one tool that they are using to achieve those ends. The campaign can be effective, for after all it uses all the catchphrases in the globally hegemonic discourse on minority rights as they exist today.

It is my tentative suggestion here, in lieu of a conclusion, that when addressing the issue of minority (and wider human) rights in the Arab world or anywhere else we need to understand the historical circumstances that created majorities and minorities and particularly the discourse surrounding this process. Because this discourse emerged against a backdrop of unequal power relations, it left a particular legacy that continues to play out today. Too often, diplomats and public figures continue to use "civilizing mission" terminology (although in more "politically correct" terms) when addressing the issue of minority rights (and wider human rights) in the Arab world, for one. The parties under attack are not just defending whatever dismal record they have in the realm of minority rights in particular or human rights in general but are defending their sovereignty. Recognizing the history and power relations behind these dynamics might help us to formulate a more helpful global discussion on minority and other rights in the Arab world and elsewhere.

Lessons from history can also help us contextualize the range of options that is available to citizens of these states as they continue to struggle to work out identities and power-sharing arrangements that might be more palatable to the minorities within their borders and also more in touch with international human rights standards that have been articulated by international bodies and

---

[54] Marlies Casier, "'Another Middle East is Possible': Turkey's Kurdish Movement's Capitalization on the Social Forum Instrument for Internal Change or Internationalization of the Cause," paper presented at the panel, "Leftists After All? The Kurdish Movement in Turkey and the Left from the 1960s to the 2000s," Middle East Studies Association Annual meeting (San Diego, CA, November 2010).

NGOs.[55] While the nation-state form was not inevitable,[56] and while there are certainly alternative political arrangements that can appear in the future, we are simply not in a post-national world. Therefore, it is likely that citizens within all these states will continue to work within the nation-state frameworks handed down to them, as they have largely been doing for decades now. One can hope, however, that groups in all these states can strive for a "post-national" version of this identity (even within the confines of the nation-state form, which demands a specific kind of identity and allegiance) in which ethnicity and sect take a back seat to non-ethnicized political, economic, and civic concerns, and in which Arabness, Kurdishness, etc. become less politicized identities. There are trends from history that would support this shift, but there are equally salient—if not more powerful—historical memories and continued cross-border relationships that also make it unlikely that ethnicity will simply cease to be so important, particularly for minorities such as the Kurds as well as Arab majorities. On the one hand, the power of the nation-state institutions that have governed and incorporated the peoples within these states has resulted in a situation in which all of the actors—whether they are Kurds, Arabs, or other groups—have come to see their field of discourse and activity within the larger discourses and politics of the individual states of Turkey, Iran, Syria, or Iraq—in whichever of these states they find their home. While many Kurds have focused on specifically *Kurdish* concerns within these contexts, they have also engaged with other groups—from the time that these states came into existence to the present—over issues that all citizens have faced, namely, social- and economic-justice causes and movements for increased political freedoms. In this sense, there is common ground among citizens in these states for movement in the direction of civic identities and politics that might help ethnic identities play a less significant role. (However, in Turkey it is less possible to emphasize a nation-state identity for all citizens than it is in Iraq, Syria, or Iran partly because while all citizens can be Syrians, Iraqis, or Iranians, as the name of the state does not privilege a particular ethnic group, in Turkey the only civic identity that has been available has also been that of the dominant group—Turks (although some have begun to use the term "Türkiyeli" (one who is from Turkey), rather than "Türk" (Turk) to achieve a less nationalist and slightly more inclusive nation-state identity).) At the same time, there are regional dynamics underway that continue to play a role in pan-Arab identities (although pan-Arabism itself is no longer a powerful discourse) simply because of the institutions of print capitalism and popular culture outlets that easily cross borders. The

---

[55] I thank Will Kymlicka for suggesting that I adopt this line of thinking in this paper. I hope to develop these thought further in future work.

[56] Etienne Balibar, "The Nation Form: History and Ideology," *Review (Fernand Braudel Center)* 13/3 (1990): 329–61.

recent revolutions and popular protests in the Arab world have shown how institutionalized each state has become (as actors within are acting as Egyptians, Tunisians, Libyans, Syrians, etc.), but also how much movements in one state have inspired those in others, and how widespread the conversation is among Arabs across borders. While this has been a long-standing trend in the Arab world, it is a slightly newer phenomenon in the Kurdish world, or rather, perhaps, it is taking a different shape than it has in the past. While there have always been cross-border connections between Kurds, there have also been linguistic barriers to developing a press, literature, and other popular culture media; after all, not only did they use different alphabets in the post-Ottoman era (not to mention different, non-standardized dialects), but Kurdish was also repressed in all these countries, and this has affected media output. Now, however, expanded communications—particularly internet access—and efforts of the Kurdish diaspora to create standardized dialects have brought Kurds across borders closer than ever before. Furthermore, the kinds of "stately" institutions that have been under construction in Iraqi Kurdistan for two decades have begun to attract more cross-border movement. No longer confined to family visits and smuggling activities, the Kurdistan Region is serving as a magnet for many Kurds beyond its borders (particularly in Turkey), who are now coming to work or attend one of the Kurdish universities there. And cross-border trade between Kurds in the region continues. In spite of the fact that nation-state borders are less porous than before, many Kurds appear to be constructing a wider Kurdistan Region as a field of activity in spite of these borders. In this sense, they are moving in a different kind of post-national direction—one that views Kurdish regions in these states as one of their many fields of focus, trade, and cultural exchange but without constructing any pan-state-like institutions.

The question, "whose country is this anyway?", continues to be as pressing as ever in all these states. Although Iraq has received the most attention (and correspondingly the most proposals) here, I would argue that the question continues to be just as salient in Syria, Turkey, and Iran. From the perspective of many Kurds (without essentializing or reifying such a perspective, for indeed there are many of them), this question remains as important as it was when these nation-states were under construction. Kurds have—in all the states examined in this chapter—been shut out of the dominant nation-state identity and have suffered unique persecution as a result. It is unlikely that they will drop their Kurdish identities as such, after such a struggle to have them recognized. It is more likely—at least in Syria, Turkey, and Iran—that they can *depoliticize* their Kurdish identity in so far as that identity has demanded a separate state. Of course this can take place only with a concomitant depoliticization of the dominant Arab identity in Syria, Turkish identity in Turkey, and Persian/Shi'ite identity in Iran. Given that the latter is unlikely to happen, however, the general proposal on the table for Iraq—the

non-ethnic, regional, federal model, delineated by Liam Anderson, for one[57]—
might be a more palatable and workable option for all these states. Of course it
might take shape differently in each one; Anderson's proposal for a regional
model in Iraq will still be ethnicized, as the Kurds are unlikely to relinquish
claims to a separate Kurdistani identity for the region they control, and as they
are also likely to continue to press for the inclusion of Kirkuk and other
Kurdish-majority areas in the Kurdistan Region. In Syria and Iran, where
Kurds form about 10 percent of each country's population, the threat posed by
regional autonomy is less, but in Turkey, where Kurds are at least 20 percent of
the total population, matters are more complicated. Kurds comprise about a
quarter of the population of Istanbul (and significant numbers in other "non-
Kurdish" cities) and the majority population in historic Kurdistan. In Turkey,
a measure of regional autonomy would have to be accompanied by "multinational" thinking—that Turks and Kurds together can forge a new nation-
state identity in Turkey. Problematic as it is, the "Kurdish opening" in Turkey
may be one step in that direction.[58]

The question, "whose country is this anyway?" continues to be important
for those—like Kurds—who are "marked citizens" in the countries they
inhabit. At the same time, however, we need to make note of other trends
that *all* groups in these countries are exploring, and this—as evidenced by the
recent revolutions in the Arab world—is "*what kind* of country are we?" By
focusing on the *what kind* over the *whose* it may be possible to reinvigorate
shared historical memories of movements in the past in which various elements from society came together in opposition to undemocratic and authoritarian regimes to create a more hopeful, democratic future for all.

---

[57] Liam Anderson, "The Non-Ethnic Regional Model of Federalism: Some Comparative
Perspectives," in R. Visser and G. Stansfield (eds.), *An Iraq of its Regions: Cornerstones of a
Federal Democracy?* (New York: Columbia University Press, 2008), 205–55.

[58] For a critical approach to this "democratic opening" or "Kurdish initiative" and its
continued problems see Marlies Casier, Andy Hilton, and Joost Jongerden, "'Roadmaps and
Roadblocks' in Turkey's Southeast," *MERIP* (30 October 2009) (<http://www.merip.org/mero/
mero103009.html>); and Kerem Öktem, "Suriçi, Diyarbakır," *MERIP* (30 October 2009)
(<http://www.merip.org/mero/mero103009_sidebar.html>), both accessed August 2013.

3

Transformations in the Middle East: The Importance of the Minority Question

Joshua Castellino and Kathleen Cavanaugh

INTRODUCTION

Although the revolutionary projects that are underway in Egypt, Tunisia, Bahrain, Yemen, and Syria are far from complete, they have given rise to a multiplicity of narratives (historical, political and ideological) that contest the meaning of the Arab Spring. Debates over how to classify and assess the political and ideological transformations reflect a broader hegemonic contestation over how we are to understand the Middle East, often situated between the goalposts of secularism and sectarianism.

The debate on the secular, that is, the political and ethical questions of religion in the public square, are not unique to the Middle East. Similarly sectarianism, within or outside the region, is understood as "a neologism born in the age of nationalism to signify the antithesis of nation; its meaning is predicated on and constructed against a territorially-bounded liberal nation-state."[1] When applied to the "Middle East" however, these concepts take on specific meanings and the accompanying discourses take on a specific function.

We use the term "function" with purpose; the hegemonic contestation to which we refer signals not solely competing intellectual or analytical readings, but political ones. Nationalist projects—past and present—often posit sectarianism as an obstacle to "a tolerant and secular modernity,"[2] and secularism as a way toward it. The secular state that emerged in the late Ottoman period has competed for space and influence with "Islamism" and Arab nationalism. The

---

[1] U. Makdisi, "The Modernity of Sectarianism in Lebanon," *Middle East Report* 200, Minorities in the Middle East: Power and the Politics of Difference (July–September, 1996), 23–6 and 30 at 24.

[2] U. Makdisi, *The Culture of Sectarianism: Community, History, and Violence in Nineteenth-Century Ottoman Lebanon* (Berkeley, CA: University of California Press, 2000), 6.

so-called Islamic revival has placed the emphasis back on Arab secularism. Yet in this context "secularlism" is understood as something more than just the absence of religion; in more recent time it has come to be framed—particularly in Western discourse—as fundamental to rooting democracy.

The status of minorities, or more accurately, questions concerning how to engage with minority rights protection in the Middle East, have often been framed within these much larger contests. Thus, the rise of faith-based (Muslim) regimes has often been scripted as a threat to non-Muslim religious communities in the Middle East. In turn, this argument has been carefully woven into a militant secularist approach to minority rights protection. Whilst colonial projects were built on divide-and-rule policies and externally driven sectarian entrepreneurs, nationalist projects (past and present) have, on the one hand, endeavored to extinguish difference in order to build a collective identity (something all "nation states" must possess) whilst on the other, systematically promoting sectarian identities as a means of establishing economic and political power.

The recent political ground captured by moderate Islamist parties in Egypt and Tunisia and the singular lens through which sectarian violence (especially in Iraq) has been filtered, suggest sharp divisions that ignore the messy realities that these transformations clearly display. The uprisings that have occurred and the civil society movements that underpin them cannot be ascribed to fixed and stable sets of norms and principles—Islamism, secularist, liberal, or left, as these sharp divisions "fail to account for the many individuals and groups who borrow from each other, and who converge on particular ideological core beliefs such as social justice, individual freedom and—of course—the need for political reform."[3] These cross-cutting cleavages require a reassessment of how the minority rights discourse in the Middle East is understood and, in particular how notions of "secularity" and "sectarianism" are engaged in transformations of the political and ideological landscapes in the region.

In providing such a reassessment, pointed questions that must be asked include the nature of emerging national identities and the potential future of the states. Yet, we suggest that in addressing minority rights in the Middle East, we need to rethink some of the existing theoretical and conceptual toolkits, as so much of the framing of the discourse on minorities is reductionist; often explained through an ethno-confessional lens. Failure to take into account the diversity of communities in the Middle East risks creating new structures that are equally unrepresentative as the ones being deposed. Much has been made in the Western media about the rise of Islamist parties and the threat of sectarianism. Both are real elements in the context of the

---

[3] S. Haugbolle, "Reflections on Ideology After the Arab Uprisings" (*Jadaliyya*, 21 March 2012) <http://www.jadaliyya.com/pages/index/4764/reflections-on-ideology-after-the-arab-uprisings>, accessed August 2013.

future matrix of power relations: yet painting them in stark light and justifying various interventions risks destroying the ethos of those who struggled long and hard to arrive at this point in their histories. For scholars interested in issues concerning minorities in the region, the twin issues highlighted undoubtedly pose significant threats: yet the approach we advocate is, first and foremost, to respect the democratic rights of the populations; second, to be willing to work with the results of any fair democratic process; and third, to insist on minimum safeguards concerning human rights and the rights of minorities. Such an approach is likely to ensure that the transitions in the Middle East remain genuinely evolutionary: a tentative step toward, and not a last chance for, democracy.

In order to elaborate our hypothesis we advocate the importance of minority rights as a key indicator of human rights compliance. To nuance this further the opening section identifies three key challenges that need to be overcome in securing longer-term peace, stability, and democracy for the region. The second section seeks to offer an insight into the legacy of the millet system through Ottoman and European colonization, in order to explain the segmented and politicized identities that have subsequently emerged. While not advocating a system that relies on a reification of this practice (as in Lebanon), we believe that either ignoring this legacy or pretending it can be subsumed under the banner of national identity may nourish existing suspicions, contributing to a longer-term threat from this quarter that can destroy existing states. The conclusion to this chapter seeks to reflect on the implications of minority rights issues in the future politico-legal contexts of the region, focusing on how the challenges highlighted in the opening section might be overcome.

Engaging the troubled legacy of the millet system and its contribution to the contours of identity ought to be deemed central to the reengineering of national identities, as states strive to become representative. While it remains early to comment on the extent to which contemporary events could bring about consolidated change, this chapter offers insights into these questions by, first, highlighting three general issues that need to be borne in mind to understand questions concerning national identity; second, by highlighting the historical legacy of minority rights and its contemporary impact; and third, by substantiating the strategy indicated above in the context of international involvement in the processes unfolding in the region.

READING EXCEPTIONALISM IN THE MIDDLE EAST

The history, politics, and ideological landscapes of the Middle East have preoccupied academic and other writings, and often engage contested theoretical and conceptual terrain. As noted elsewhere,

[c]oming closer to an understanding of what we refer to as the contemporary Middle East will challenge, often confuse, and most certainly demand that we unpack existing narratives. The meta-narrative aspect of the Middle East is captured in discourse which endeavours to define the political, territorial and cultural contours of this space.[4]

Before tackling the question of minority rights in the "Middle East," it is important to recognize that the "contours" to which we refer are constantly changing. Rather than suggesting a fixed and immovable space, the Middle East ought to be viewed as comprising multiple geographies. Rather than suggesting that the overt identification of religion in the public sphere is definitive of the region and key to understanding all that transpires within the Muslim world, we argue that ideologies of social movements in the Middle East have fluid, not fixed, boundaries. Therefore any interpretation of the status of minorities in the region must avoid such limited and reductionist views.

That the Middle East comprises multiple geographies disrupts any singular analysis of minority rights. Rather than thinking of the Middle East as one common region with shared problems, our approach focuses on three distinct sub-regional classifications. The first, the oil-rich heartlands, or the Gulf Cooperation Countries, include Saudi Arabia, Bahrain, Kuwait, Oman, Qatar, and the United Arab Emirates.[5] Yemen may fit within this grouping, though it probably bears greater similarity to states further west.[6] This second sub-group of states includes Lebanon, Syria, Iraq, Iran, Jordan, and Egypt.[7] While Israel could fit into this group geographically, it remains in a *sui generis* category, while its Palestinian population and territories fit within the sub-regional grouping. Turkey may fit into this group through its historical role in the region, and further afield, in the Central Asian States.[8] The third sub-regional grouping includes states of the Maghreb: Morocco, Tunisia, Libya, Algeria and Mauritania who have a shared history and the fact that the Sultan of the Sherifian state (precursor to modern Morocco) was considered the spiritual head of the entire region.[9]

---

[4] See J. Castellino and K. Cavanaugh, *Minority Rights in the Middle East: A Comparative Legal Analysis* (Oxford: Oxford University Press, 2013).

[5] From an economic perspective these states on the Arabian peninsula are characterized by their reliance on oil. For more see U. Fasano and Z. Iqbal, *GCC Countries: From Oil Dependence to Diversification* (Washington, DC: IMF, 2003).

[6] For more on Yemen see P. Dresch, *A History of Modern Yemen* (Cambridge: Cambridge University Press, 2000).

[7] Our reason for grouping these states is the nature of their minority populations in conjunction with their experience under Ottoman rule. For more see Castellino and Cavanaugh, *Minority Rights in the Middle East.*

[8] For a commentary on how Central Asian States are coming to terms with their own transitions see S. N. Cummings (ed.), *Oil, Transition and Security in Central Asia* (London: Routledge Curzon, 2003).

[9] For more, see generally, E. Gellner and C. A. Micaud (eds.), *Arabs and Berbers: From Tribe to Nation in North Africa* (London: Duckworth, 1973).

The minority and governance questions posed in each sub-region are distinct, with dangers inherent in the adoption of a uniform analysis likely to neglect the varied histories of human identity that have developed through the different influences brought to bear on each sub-region.[10] Since this is detailed elsewhere, we will not revisit the status of minorities for each of these sub-groupings here. However, it is important to note that the experiences of minorities within these sub-regional groupings, and indeed in each state, are not attributed to inter-religious or ethnic/tribal divisions, but rather to the relationship of these groups (historically and contemporaneously) to sites of power which vary not only within these sub-groupings but from state to state. Reducing these relationships to the "exceptionalism"[11] of the Middle East, that is, the forces of "sectarianism" or "fundamentalism" that are viewed as constant, masks a more complicated reality. Threads of narratives are often ignored in favor of a singular interpretation of events scripted to a particular ideological lens. Here, instead of the blurring of lines between secular, religious, liberal, and left (certainly part of the more recent events in the region), we are given the sharp edges of ideological divisions.

A second preliminary issue that needs to be tackled at the outset is the importance of questions concerning minority rights. Many question the efficacy of such classifications, arguing that they reify division contrary to received notions of nation-building devoted to articulating a single unifying "national" narrative. Common objections to focusing on minority questions raised in the literature include challenging the parameters of what (or whom) such identities might encompass[12] and the dismissal of identity groupings as parochial historical divisions of less resonance than urban and rural divides or, at the least, the questioning of the extent to which identification of groups and their inclusion on this basis in the political process may fragment and segment emerging states.[13] While taking these objections seriously, their potency needs to be balanced against the risk attendant upon ignoring identity-based claims in the belief that these can be subsumed at the altar of "national-identity" politics. Sixty years of postcolonial "nation-building"[14] in the UN era reflect that such projects generate "national identities" that cater exclusively to

---

[10] This is discussed in greater detail in Castellino and Cavanaugh. *Minority Rights in the Middle East*.

[11] Contemporary accounts of conflict, religion and human rights in the Middle East have been shaped by a perceived "exceptionalism" of the region. Whilst we have, in our larger examination of minorities in the Middle East, challenged such an approach, the idea of a violent and conflict-ridden landscape characterized by primordial and fundamentalist leanings remains a strong thread.

[12] See E. Kedourie, "Minorities and Majorities in the Middle East," *European Journal of Sociology* 25/2 (1984): 276–82.

[13] B. White, "The Nation-State Form and the Emergence of 'Minorities' in Syria," *Studies in Ethnicity and Nationalism* 7/1 (2007): 64–85.

[14] K. Deutsche and W. Foltz, *Nation Building* (New York: Atherton, 1963).

dominant majorities, and in excluding non-dominant groups, often create legacies that are easily stoked by those seeking to undermine the emerging state later in its political life. Acknowledging the pluralist identity tendencies in states where they exist, and including a wider range of stakeholders in political rights discourses, may forestall and dampen antagonisms, longings, and desires of submerged nations where they exist.

Any discussion concerning questions of the democratization and political futures of the states needs to account for three factors that could be deemed fundamental to engaging questions of "national identity": (1) the issue of territoriality and state boundaries; (2) the nature of conflict; and (3) the question of faith in democracy.

The issue of territoriality and state boundaries

The boundaries of postcolonial states show significant signs of colonial intervention. In the *Western Sahara Case* the late Judge Harry Dillard famously stated: "It is for the people to determine the fate of a territory, and not vice versa."[15] The aspirational value of such a statement is at odds with postcolonial history in the region and elsewhere, which suggests the reverse: it is the dimension of the territory that determines the fate of the people within it.[16] In the first two sub-regions discussed above, the Sykes Picot Agreement[17] and the Balfour Declaration[18] have been fundamental to determining state boundaries. These agreements dissipated for instance, the aspirations for an independent Kurdistan promised by the colonial powers at various stages of the region's colonial history.[19] The creation of Israel in the heart of Arab-occupied lands is one of the most significant events in terms of territoriality in the sub-region.[20] Such a creation could be viewed as the ultimate form of minority protection: provided in the aftermath of genocide, it rehabilitates the historical dispossession of Jews in the region. Against this, the creation of Israel has displaced

---

[15] "Western Saraha—Advisory Opinion of October 16, 1975," General List No. 61 (1974–1975) *ICJ Reports* (1975), p. 116.

[16] See R. Higgins, "Judge Dillard and the Principle of Self-Determination," *Virginia Journal of International Law* 23 (1983): 387–94.

[17] The Sykes Picot Agreement was signed on 9 May 1916 as a secret pact during World War I, with the main parties being the United Kingdom and France, with the assent of Russia. See L. M. Surhone, M. T. Timpledon, and S. F. Marseken, *Sykes Picot Agreement* (Saarbrücken: VDM Betascript, 2009).

[18] The Balfour Declaration takes the form of a letter between Arthur James, Lord Balfour and Lord Rothschild and was written on 2 November 1917. It is reproduced in W. Laqueur and B. Rubin (eds.), *The Israel–Arab Reader: A Documentary History of the Middle East Conflict* (New York: Facts on File, 1984, 4th edition), 17.

[19] See D. Natali, *The Kurds and the State: Evolving National Identity in Iraq, Turkey and Iran* (New York: Syracuse University Press, 2005).

[20] For a rich source of documents see Laqueur and Rubin, *The Israel–Arab Reader*, 18.

Palestinians as a direct consequence, and the failure to respect *their* legitimate claims to self-determination has cast Israel as a pariah state. The security paradigm underlying the ethos of the state and its building of settlements on dispossessed Arab lands continues to undermine its legitimacy in the eyes of many Arabs, and has locked identity politics into a two-dimensional struggle of Arab versus Jew, masking the myriad sub-national identities that exist from external purview.[21]

The nature of conflict

Although the Middle East is often characterized in terms of conflict and violence, the region is rather unexceptional in this regard—no more or less conflict-ridden than other parts of the world. Whilst not exceptional, the region has experienced conflict—internationally, regionally, and internally. In recent history alone there have been significant armed conflicts in 1948, 1967, and 2007 (concerning Israel); from 1972 to 1989 (Iran–Iraq war); from 1975 to 1982 (the Lebanese Civil War); 1990 (concerning Iraq and Kuwait); in 1991, 2003 to 2011 (over Iraq); and in 2011 (over Libya).[22] Events in Syria, at the time of writing, are akin to a state of internal armed conflict, and the violent suppression of the 2011 Shi'ite uprising in Bahrain and similar movements in previous years in Iran indicate a level of tension in society that may or may not ignite to full-scale inter-state or intra-state war. Conflicts in the Middle East generally take one of two forms:

(1) Inter-state disputes resulting in wars and/or boundary tensions notoriously difficult to contain within states, with potential destabilizing impact on the region (e.g. Israel v. Lebanon, Iraq v. Iran, Iraq v. Kuwait, Saudi Arabia v. Yemen, Bahrain v. Qatar, Egypt v. Libya, Morocco v. Mauritania, and Jordan v. Syria); and

(2) Intra-state disputes inevitably drawing implicit support from regional and external powers (Lebanon, Iraq, Syria, Algeria, Jordan, Yemen, and Oman).

Closer analyses reveal that inter-state rivalries manifest in colonialism and failed statecraft, and disputes over natural resources underpin many of the conflicts. The intersection of colonization and conflict also recurs in ethno-nationalist conflicts. The strategic objectives of colonial powers—most significantly Britain and France—left an indelible impact on communities

---

[21] Also see "Legal Consequences of the Construction of Wall in the Occupied Palestinian Territory," Advisory Opinion ICJ, *ICJ Reports* (2004): 136.

[22] For a general source examining conflict in the Middle East see G. Ben-Dor, *State and Conflict in the Middle East: Emergence of the Post-Colonial State* (New York: Praeger, 1983).

within artificially created borders. The Balfour legacy in particular remains a potent reminder of catastrophic British intervention in the region. The multiple and contested geographies of the region and borders that remain less than fixed lie at the heart of the Arab–Israeli dispute and Palestinian and Kurdish struggles for self-determination.[23]

The modern uprisings have been instigated by a desire for equal treatment and a thirst for democracy. Franck argued for the "emergence" of a "right to democratic governance" in 1992, premised on twin norms drawn from the American Declaration of Independence: the notion of the consent of the governed, and the external legitimacy that followed for any government elected by the people.[24] His analysis seemed premature at the time: framed against the context of unraveling authoritarian regimes in eastern and central Europe, the Arab world appeared a black spot resistant to change, where long-serving dictators and oppressive measures were standard forms of governance. The recent upheavals give Franck's prophecy legitimacy, but highlight the importance, from a minority perspective, of a need to focus on democracy as a process concerned with values, as much as accommodating majoritarian ambitions. Any other interpretation is unlikely to deliver social good to small and medium-sized minorities in the range of countries that make up the region.

Faith in democracy?

One of the most important determinant factors in "national" or "other" identity in the wider region is the consolidation of Islam as the major faith among different communities. The conception of "minority status" therefore needs to be viewed through the lens of how group cohesion came about more generally. The early expansion of Islam was accompanied by political, theological, and jurisprudential struggles that impacted the formation of religious identities and established fault-lines along which entitlement systems based on identity later emerged. The recent past had seen a secularist identity emerge in the guise of a supervening pan-Arab identity that submerged myriads of ethno-linguistic and religious dividing lines.[25] The extent to which these relatively secularist approaches, fostered under the dictatorial regimes that

---

[23] For more on this issue see Castellino and Cavanaugh, *Minority Rights in the Middle East*, ch. 1.

[24] T. Franck, "The Emerging Right to Democratic Governance," *American Journal of International Law* 86 (1992): 1–46.

[25] For an early critique of emerging processes of Arab nationalism see C. E. Farah, "The Dilemma of Arab Nationalism," *Die Welt des Islams*, ns 8/3 (1963): 140–64. For how this was manifested in Syria see P. Khoury, *Syria and the French Mandate: The Politics of Arab Nationalism 1920–1945* (Princeton, NJ: Princeton University Press, 1987).

are currently becoming undermined, have succeeded is contentious in light of recent events.

From a historical perspective there have already been two major governance transitions in the Middle East in the last century: from Ottoman to European rule, and then through decolonization from European rule. The first transition appeared greater than the second, wherein the minority rights discourse adopted by European powers "became associated with hypocrisy and selfish political ambitions" as they were "notably lacking in sympathy for the aspirations for freedom on the part of the Muslim Middle Easterners,"[26] but monitored the treatment of the non-Muslim communities in the Middle East and engaged anti-discrimination discourses when profitable. Rather than aiding state formation and bureaucratic development, these practices probably contributed to its "discontinuity." As Anderson notes:

> Repeated changes in administration policies, indeed in the very borders of the mandates in the Fertile Crescent and frequent efforts to isolate, aid, and protect favoured communities, from the Christians in Lebanon to the Berbers in Morocco, contributed to administrative instability and exacerbated the discontinuity and lack of legitimacy that characterized European rule in the region during the interwar period.[27]

There remains, unsurprisingly, a "historical Muslim ambivalence"[28] to the concept of state. The resurgence of Islam in the public sphere, especially in demands for the restoration of shariah as public law, have reopened questions related to the status of non-Muslims, including a call in some countries for the reintroduction of the *dhimmi* status, discussed further. Yet early shariah discourse on minorities, legal and theological, sits uneasily with the notion of a secularist public law and related international human rights legal obligations of states. However, despite this resurgence and its historical baggage, "the institution [of the state] is now firmly and irrevocably established throughout the Muslim world" and as a consequence "historical" shariah must adapt and adjust to "the reality of the modern nation-state."[29] Yet conflicts and "the ambiguities of loyalty and legitimacy characteristic of Middle Eastern politics may indicate the fragility of the present-day states."[30] The fluidity and conditionality of "state" is, in some ways, mirrored when questions concerning minorities are addressed. As Martin observed, whereas the historical distinction of "self" for non-Muslims from the Other (e.g. Muslim majority) would

---

[26] E. A. Mayer, *Islam and Human Rights: Tradition and Politics* (Boulder, CO: Westview Press, 1999), 148.

[27] L. Anderson, "The State in the Middle East and North Africa," in *A Political History of the Middle East* (Boulder, CO: Westview Press, 1999), 5.

[28] A. An-Na'im, *Islam and the Secular State: Negotiating the Future of Shari'a* (Cambridge, MA: Harvard University Press, 2008), 8.

[29] An-Na'im, *Islam and the Secular State*, 72.

[30] Anderson, "The State in the Middle East and North Africa," 2.

have been based on features that fall under a cultural umbrella (language, religion, custom), minority identities in recent decades have taken on "distinctive political roles or outlooks."[31] Whether or not a particular minority group remains a "cultural and/or an intellectual force" or assumes a greater role in the public square and becomes "politically mobilized when faced with a particular brand of state nationalism is crucial for understanding current conflicts."[32] A brief study of the millet system, its genesis, contribution to the creation of cohesive communities, and politicization is vital to understanding the role identity is poised to play if democratization is to become sustainable. The next section of this chapter is devoted to addressing these issues.

THE HISTORICAL LEGACY OF THE MILLET SYSTEM

The "sectarian divide" in the Middle East is often attributed by commentators to narrow parochialism. This hypothesis appears to portray peoples in the region as somehow similar (i.e. either Arabs or Jews) but who, due to disagreements over inconsequential detail fail to get along and build sustainable communities. A study of the history of communitarian identity reveals that such a reading is Orientalist, deeply flawed, and consequentially extremely superficial. This section aims to engage with three specific aspects to challenge this misconception, to: (1) explain the foundation for the *dhimmi* system which differentiated Muslim from non-Muslim; (2) provide insights into the development of the system through centuries of Ottoman rule; and (3) explain its politicization, transformation, and widening under colonial rule.

The foundation of the millet system

Discussion of minority questions or, framed in its historical context, the treatment of non-Muslim groups living in Muslim lands in the Middle East, can be traced to the formative period in Islam when *ahl al-kitab* (Peoples of the Book) were conferred political privileges and status as *dhimmi*: a legacy that persists in many Middle Eastern states. This status was traditionally extended to Christians and Jews, but history documents that others such as Zoroastrians, the Sabi'ans of Harran, and Hindus also came under such

---

[31] M. Shatzmiller, "Introduction," in *Nationalism and Minority Identities in Islamic Societies* (Montreal: McGill-Queen's University Press, 2005), p. vii.
[32] Shatzmiller, "Introduction," p. vii.

protection.[33] One view of the granting of *dhimmi* status was that it was a necessary strategy that would allow the expansion and consolidation of state-building processes. From a contemporary human rights perspective it is difficult to attribute *dhimmi* status as it developed under Ottoman rule as akin to human rights, since it was not based on principles of equality and non-discrimination, nor on equal dignity and worth. There were clear distinctions between ordinary citizens and the *dhimmi*:[34] the latter were not allowed to serve in the military or in official public positions. *Dhimmi* were also liable for additional taxes (*jizya* and *kharaj*). However, what makes it appropriate to label this probably the first organized system of minority rights in the world is that while the *dhimmi* were subject to the rules of shariah, they had autonomy in terms of their social and religious affairs, including the freedom to worship. Any critique of the distinctions made between subjects and the *dhimmi* would be unjustified in the context of the principle of inter-temporal law,[35] namely, that affairs in any given time period have to be judged in the appropriate period and not against more modern standards. There are legitimate questions as to whether the *dhimmi* system can be equated with a system of "minority" protection. For a start it only favored religious groups along the lines identified above. Second, it did not seek to deliver equality and non-discrimination as characteristic of other affirmative action remedies synonymous with such protection. Third, the *raison d'être* for such classification was not to ensure a framework of equal rights across society, but rather lay in an attempt to recognize and attribute value to a particular set of groups on the grounds of religion. Thus heterodox Muslim groups were not given special status and were treated with suspicion, even though there would be equally compelling religious grounds for considering them adherents to the same Book that merited protection for Christians and Jews. Rather than seeking to challenge the wisdom of equating *dhimmi* systems with minority rights directly, our assertion that the system be considered the foundation for contemporary minority rights is pragmatically driven. First, as a process for the identification of a particular type of difference in society it gained salience, and created the basis for the institutionalization of such difference that persists to this day. Second, as we shall see, the attempt to replicate the system through colonial rule simply widened its application and contributed to the deepening of other schisms that existed within the body politic. It could thus be argued, as White and Kedourie do, that the use of "minority" reifies the troubled

---

[33] U. Makdisi, "After 1860: Debating Religion, Reform and Nationalism in the Ottoman Empire," *International Journal of Middle Eastern Studies* 34 (2002): 601–17 at 601.

[34] See generally, B. Aral, "The Idea of Human Rights as Perceived in the Ottoman Empire," *Human Rights Quarterly* 26 (2004): 454–82.

[35] See T. O. Elias, "The Doctrine of Intertemporal Law," *American Journal of International Law* 74/2 (April 1980): 285–307.

colonial heritage of identity.[36] On the other hand, there is clearly an unequal distribution and access to human rights based on identity, which reflects a legacy of identity politics that ought not to be ignored in any analysis that is forward-looking. We believe that the traditional discourse of minority rights seeks to remedy such structural deficiencies in rights by: (1) identifying target groups; (2) highlighting the discrimination they face; (3) revealing the structural nature of such discrimination; and (4) advocating the design of specific social policies, legislative, administrative, and judicial measures aimed at remedying such discrimination. However, for such policies to be precisely targeted the identification of groups is crucial, especially in a context where equality and non-discrimination edifices remain *de jure* processes that fail to tackle de facto realities.

In line with such historical analyses contemporary identity in the Middle East could be broken down on grounds of religion with a focus on People of the Book, namely adherents to Islam, Christianity, and Judaism with others, including the Baha'i, falling outside these parameters and struggling for recognition. Such a broad-brush picture fails to reflect the richness of identity and the historical processes that have shaped distinctions between the different sects of Islam and Christianity, rendering obsolete several sectarian identity groupings within the religions. A purely religion-based analysis of the different communities in the Middle East would also gloss over the historical distinctions in society between monotheist communities and tribal polytheists (*mushrikun*), perceived as problematic since they stand accused of denying a fundamental premise of Islam: the belief in one God. Such an approach also excludes questions of heterodox communities, and converts to Islam. Ignoring underlying ethnic concerns within religious communities would also fail to allow distinction for major identity groupings such as the Kurds.

History may suggest that the Middle East ought to have been the model for multiculturalism, not least because the brand of multiculturalism that flourished there was not tinged by the secularist flavor that laces the currency in states such as the United Kingdom and Canada. Rather Greater Syria, with its contribution to three of the world's prominent religions, has been a place where groups have come to the fore on the basis of real religious bonds that sought to differentiate them from their neighbors.[37] One Ottoman scholar argued that "the secret behind the long endurance of the Ottoman Empire must be seen in the efficiency of its justice system."[38] The development of strong local identities, usually referred to in the literature as "clans," signified three important

[36] Kedourie, "Minorities and Majorities in the Middle East"; and White, "The Nation-State Form."

[37] See A. H. Hourani, *Syria and Lebanon: A Political Essay* (Oxford: Oxford University Press, 1946); also see F. Zachs, *The Making of a Syrian Identity: Intellectuals and Merchants in Nineteenth Century Beirut* (Leiden: Brill, 2005).

[38] Aral, "The Idea of Human Rights," 466.

developments: (1) the emphasis on religion as well as ethnicity as a basis for group cohesion; (2) the growth of strong leaders who were mandated by the community with the role of securing autonomy for the community; (3) inter-group rivalry that, over time, came to regard other groups with a degree of suspicion.[39] Even in contemporary Syria, ruled by the minority 'Alawite community, the group ethos has remained, with many sources describing the rise of the Asads to power as indicative of strong communitarian bonds within.[40]

The Ottomans and the millet system

Aral argues that the Ottoman system contained vestiges of human rights, but that these privileged collective rights and emphasized justice rather than freedom.[41] Also the Ottoman state was significantly *laissez-faire*, with attempts to control the public sphere only commencing with the Tanzimat reforms.[42] One version of Ottoman history could highlight its role as an upholder of minority rights: as early as 1492 it provided refuge and sanctuary to the Jews of Spain when they were expelled en masse.[43] Indeed various snapshots of history reveal plenty of agreements on *Hukm Thati* or self-government, concluded between authoritarian minority regimes such as the Baathist movement (Iraq) the 'Alawites (Syria), and in Sudan, seeking autonomy within federal states.[44] However, these agreements did not hold sway for long and collapsed as ruling elite realized the inherent dangers in raising aspirations of well-established communities such as the Shi'ites and the Kurds.

From the perspective of those interested in minority rights it is clear that the aspect of Ottoman history of most interest is the development of the millet system that allows clans, sects, and other groups to maintain their autonomy. The system has been described as "a sophisticated and comprehensive system of protection."[45] However, an important point that requires emphasis is that the Ottomans did not consider ethnicity or language to be the basis of separate identity, relying instead on religious difference, with Muslims treated as a

---

[39] This is most clearly demonstrated in Lebanon. For more see S. Khalaf, *Civil and Uncivil Violence in Lebanon: A History of the Internationalization of Communal Conflict* (New York: Columbia University Press, 2002).

[40] E. Zisser, "The 'Alawites, Lords of Syria: From Ethnic Minority to Ruling Sect," in Bengio and Ben-Dor (eds.), *Minorities and the State in the Arab World* (London: Lynne Rienner, 1999), 129–45. Please note that while the surname of the Syrian rulers is often spelt "Assad" we use "Asad" since it is closer to its Arabic pronunciation.

[41] Aral, "The Idea of Human Rights." [42] Aral, "The Idea of Human Rights."

[43] Aral, "The Idea of Human Rights," 455.

[44] M. Ma'oz, "Middle Eastern Minorities: Between Integration and Conflict—An Overview," in M. Ma'oz and G. Sheffer (eds.), *Middle Eastern Minorities and Diasporas* (Brighton: Sussex Academic Press, 2002), 29–40 at 38.

[45] Aral, "The Idea of Human Rights," 475.

single category irrespective of ethnicity or language.[46] The underlying basis for the protection of religious minorities in a state lay in the fact that Christian and Jewish millets, as "People of the Book," gained special protection as *dhimmi.*[47] This status afforded them protection by the state of their lives, honor, and property, and the autonomy to conduct their lives according to their own customs and traditions. *Dhimmis* paid special taxes as indicated above, and were guaranteed a range of rights: " . . . to communicate in their own language, to regulate their civic matters according to their own (mostly religious) law, to enjoy freedom of religion and conscience, the right to set up foundations, and to arrange for their own education."[48] The millet system could, at first sight, seem particularly unfair and unjust. In the words of Aral:

sharp distinction [was] drawn between adherents of different religions [which] may be seen as oppressive when looked at from the perspective of modern human rights doctrine. Equally, a number of impositions designed to facilitate the recognition of non-Muslims by those outside of their own community may be perceived as insulting: the house of a non-Muslim could not be higher than that of a Muslim; non-Muslims were banned from living in certain neighbourhoods; they were not allowed to dress like Muslims; they could not carry arms without special permission; they could not serve in the army; a non-Muslim man could not marry a Muslim woman; non-Muslims could not take up employment in the public sector; they could not witness against a Muslim in a court of law; and it was forbidden to toll the church bell loud enough to be heard from the outside. All these examples indicate that difference of status between Muslim and non-Muslims was institutionalized under Ottoman rule in favour of Muslims. For that reason, the intermingling of different *millets* with Muslims was almost impossible.[49]

Against this, community leaders were recognized by the Sultan as Pasha and had complete autonomy over their (usually his) community. They played a role in the collection of taxes, acted as arbitrators in disputes, and were key instigators of the establishment of community schools. Also, despite the differentiations just listed, Aral stresses that the Ottoman Empire was recognized as particularly respectful of minorities who chose to live under its protection.[50] This would seem an appropriate conclusion in a temporal context where minorities were either seen as a threat elsewhere or willfully disregarded as subjects of international law, denied any rights, and colonized.[51]

---

[46] Aral, "The Idea of Human Rights," 475.

[47] For a concerted explanation of the *dhimmi* see K. Hashemi, "The Right of Minorities to Identity and the Challenge of Non-discrimination: A Study on the Effects of Traditional Muslims' Dhimmah on Current State Practices," *Int'l Journal on Minority & Group Rights* 13/1 (2006): 1–26.

[48] Aral, "The Idea of Human Rights," 475.   [49] Aral, "The Idea of Human Rights," 476.

[50] Aral, "The Idea of Human Rights," 477.

[51] Russell Barsh engages in an interesting analysis of subjects and objects in the context of indigenous peoples that could easily be considered applicable in the Middle East. See R. L. Barsh, "Indigenous Peoples in the 1990s: From Object to Subject in International Law?" *Harvard Human Rights Journal* 7 (1994): 33–62.

Attempts were made to replace the millet system with a notion of uniform citizenship as part of the Tanzimat Reforms, specifically the Imperial Rescript of Gülhane, 1839.[52] However, while this legislation seemed intent on destroying the fabric of the millet system and creating cohesion in the face of fragmentation, the deep-rooted grounding of the system within communities diluted its impact. Instead, another edict was passed, the Imperial Reform Edict of 1856, which removed the points of inequality between Muslims and non-Muslims, while leaving the system relatively intact.[53] Aral implies that the attempt to dilute the millet system, rather than engendering empire-wide solidarity and unity, was a mitigating circumstance in the decline of the empire as various groups sought to assert political independence, and as the Muslim community became disillusioned with their own perceived loss of status.[54]

"From millet to minority"[55] and beyond

In his examination of the Ottoman millet system, White notes that religion was its main identity marker; that religious law was paramount to its operation; and that religious hierarchies were wielded over non-Muslim communities on behalf of the Sultan.[56] Attempts to secularize religious law and foster secular governance that commenced toward the end of Ottoman rule had long-lasting consequences. Growing European power, backing one or other community, contributed to the emergence of assertive versions of ethno-nationalist identities. European misunderstanding of the millet system—viewing millets as mutually suspicious groups—was a clear mitigating factor in the proliferation of sectarian identities.[57] This process proved politically useful in creating a bulwark against pan-Arab solidarity, and with inter-group rivalry heating up, constructed territorial demarcations became an easy way to foster divide-and-rule policies under colonial rule.

While contemporaneous attention remains focused on questions of sectarianism, understanding how to address notions of vulnerability in the context of the current transitions in the Middle East requires that we understand

---

[52] Aral, "The Idea of Human Rights," 477. [53] Aral, "The Idea of Human Rights," 478.

[54] Aral, "The Idea of Human Rights," 478.

[55] This phrase has been used in several of the literatures, though we draw from Benjamin White's work in this section. See also A. Rodrigue, "From Millet to Minority, Turkish Jews," in P. Birnbaum and I. Katznelson (eds.), *Paths of Emancipation: Jews, States, and Citizenship* (Princeton, NJ: Princeton University Press, 1995); also B. White, *The Emergence of Minorities in the Middle East: The Politics of Community in French Mandate Syria* (Edinburgh: Edinburgh University Press, 2011), 45.

[56] White, "The Nation-State Form," 69. [57] White, "The Nation-State Form," 70.

fundamental aspects of the historical social formation of minority communities, and the relationships of these groups to state authorities, which have shifted regularly over time. A modern overview of minorities reveals three specific categories of vulnerable groups: religious minorities, Muslim ethnic groups, and "Others." In our larger work on minorities in the Middle East, these categories are analyzed with a view to explaining groups' minority status within a society.[58]

The first category, non-Muslim communities, consists of historically well-established groups that were prominent during the Ottoman Empire, namely, Christians and Jews. The relationship between Muslim and non-Muslim societies in the Middle East is complex. The traditional "order" that *dhimmi* status conferred upon this relationship, expressed through "hierarchically organized religious bodies with a decidedly political function,"[59] changed with European influence. European favoritism of non-Muslims over Muslims "allowed indigenous Christians, as well as Jews, to achieve positions of power and wealth,"[60] subverting traditional relationships. For Jews, this relationship was recalibrated with the rise of Zionist discourse and the establishment of Israel in 1948. While global Jewish immigration to Israel in 1948 and since has swelled Jewish numbers in the region, many once-prominent Jewish communities elsewhere in the Middle East have all but disappeared.[61] Christian groups, traditionally diverse, are differentiable by sect and include Chaldeans, Assyrians, Nestorians, Copts, Greek Orthodox, Catholic, Protestants, and others.[62] Though traditional *dhimmi*, Christian communities are in differing positions in states across the region. They remain prominent in Lebanon where Maronites have traditionally dominated governance structures and have held positions of power in other states including Syria. The shifting kaleidoscope of identity politics has exposed them to existential threats, no more so than in modern Iraq, where sectarian violence has caused many to flee in large numbers.[63]

[58] See Castellino and Cavanaugh, *Minority Rights in the Middle East*, Introduction.

[59] B. Masters, *Christians and Jews in the Ottoman Arab World* (Cambridge: Cambridge University Press, 2001), 61.

[60] D. E. Arzt, "Religious Human Rights in Muslim States of the Middle East and North Africa," *Emory International Law Review* 10 (1996): 139–61 at 139 and 156.

[61] See M. M. Laskier, *Northern African Jewry in the Twentieth Century: The Jews of Morocco, Algeria and Tunisia* (New York: New York University Press, 1994).

[62] Masters, *Christians and Jews in the Ottoman Arab World*, 59.

[63] There are a number of sources that document the situation of religious minorities worldwide. Most prominent is the United States Commission on International Religious Freedom, USCIRF, which publishes an annual report. Also see Minority Rights Group Internationals, *World Directory of Minorities and Indigenous Peoples*, although it is worth noting that some of the information in these reports is derived from a variety of secondary and at times tertiary sources. Finally, Amnesty International and Human Rights Watch publish country and thematic reports that often include sections on minority groups. For the situation in Iraq, in particular, see UN High Commissioner for Refugees, *Statistical Report on UNHCR Registered Iraqis and Non-Iraqis*, 30 September 2011.

While religion may signal difference, there have been considerable historical trends differentiating the *umma* or Muslim community by sect. The sectarian affiliations within Muslim communities are primarily, though not exclusively, reflected in the Shia–Sunni divide rooted in theological and political conflict. With a majority adhering to Sunni schools of thought, the teachings from the Shia schools have been viewed by some from within Sunni schools and in the West as "heterodox."[64] While the Shia–Sunni divide can generally be described in terms of States (Iraq, Iran, and Bahrain are majority Shia states), these distinctions become meaningless since the divide exists within Sunni-dominated states. Communities such as the Kurds, who argue with some historical justification that they are a "nation," straddle this divide.[65] In their case the internal religious divide is less salient than their collective ethnic identity. A second fault-line exists between Muslim minorities and others such as Druze, 'Alawis, and Yazidis, considered heretics by some, for violating what are considered sacred founding notions of Islam.[66] Historically prominent, Druze power in Lebanon has become undermined by growing Sunni influence, and the 'Alawis are currently under pressure as the Asad regime begins to crumble in Syria. Undifferentiated from other Muslims under the Ottoman Empire, some of these sects gained prominence through colonial policies, and are now key identity groupings in the contemporary Middle East with genuine concerns over the survival of some, and ambitious political aspirations among others.

The third category of communities, labeled "Other," is diverse: from significant "national minorities"[67] such as the Palestinians,[68] to growing numbers of migrant workers attracted to the region to low-skilled jobs. Many Palestinian communities were displaced from what is now Israel and the Occupied Territories and became refugees in the aftermath of the 1948 and 1967 wars.[69]

---

[64] We do not adopt this contested term, but use it here drawing on literature that denotes an approach within Islam to teachings that are contrary to the dominant position within a given state.

[65] See D. Romano, *The Kurdish National Movement: Opportunity, Mobilization and Identity* (Cambridge: Cambridge University Press, 2006).

[66] See Castellino and Cavanaugh, *Minority Rights in the Middle East*, ch. 2.

[67] One definition of this term is "a group numerically inferior to the rest of the population of a State whose members—being nationals of the State—possess ethnic, religious or linguistic characteristics differing from the rest of the population and who, if only implicitly, maintain a sense of solidarity, directed towards preserving their culture, traditions, religion or language." See Francesco Capotorti, *Étude des droits des personnes appartenant aux minorités ethniques, religieuses et linguistiques*, UN Doc. E/CN. 4/Sub. 2/1979/384 (Geneva: Publications des Nations Unies, 1979). However, in his work on Multicultural Citizenship, Kymlicka draws a distinction between national minorities—as autochthonous groups that were forcibly assimilated—and immigrant ethnic minorities who have chosen to adopt a new language and culture. See W. Kymlicka, *Multicultural Citizenship: A Liberal Theory of Minority Rights* (Oxford: Oxford University Press, 1995), 61.

[68] We have referred to Palestinians (and indeed Kurds) elsewhere as "trapped minorities." See Castellino and Cavanaugh, *Minority Rights in the Middle East,* ch. 3.

[69] See B. Morris, *Righteous Victims: A History of the Zionist Arab Conflict 1881–2001* (New York: Vintage Books, 2001).

There are prominent communities of Palestinian refugees outside the Occupied Territories, primarily in Jordan, Lebanon, Egypt, Syria, and Iraq. With the exception of some Palestinians living in Jordan, most Palestinians remain stateless.[70] The region also hosts a number of other refugees fleeing from war, most recently as a consequence of the illegal American and British intervention and occupation of Iraq.[71] The oil-producing states also have significant nomadic communities of Bedouin, often stateless, alongside migrant workers, who are usually beyond the reach of global standards of international human rights law. One clear measure of the extent to which "democracy" takes root in the governance of Middle Eastern and North African states is whether previously marginalized communities such as these gain access to the promised socioeconomic and political rights in existing mechanisms of international human rights law.

CONCLUSION

Many well-informed commentators seek to question the legitimacy and value of the legacy of communitarian identity in the region. Part of this questioning is based on a scientific reading of the history of community rights. This seam of argument suggests that what were essentially decentralized masses of communities under loose Ottoman governance were turned into politico-legal entities through concocted colonial divide-and-rule policies engineered for the maximum benefit of the colonizers. Thus for commentators such as White, Kedourie, and others, to engage in minority rights discourse based on a reading of the millet system is to succumb to externally enhanced divisions. Yet it is equally salient that ever since the proverbial genie has been let out of the box, such identities have gained a life of their own, and do not easily retract into where they emerged from. Our engagement with minority rights in the region is driven by an attempt to understand the extent to which a rights discourse will be available to *all*: including rights to speak into political communities and strive for greater political participation, even if that process

---

[70] Jordan has conferred citizenship on some Palestinians, although more recent legislation appears to be aimed at rescinding that citizenship. Syria had, historically, endeavored to integrate Palestinians into civil society (short of conferring citizenship) whilst in other states, such as Egypt and Lebanon, the relationship has been much more complex. Ostensibly, citizenship has been withheld so as to strengthen the right to return but, in reality, this has also reflected the degree to which Palestinians are (were) seen as a threat to state authority.

[71] Palestinian refugees living in Iraq have been especially vulnerable as they have been perceived, with some justification, as having been favored by Saddam Hussein's regime. See T. Charles, "An Ongoing Nakba, The Plight of Palestinian Refugees in Iraq," *Jadaliyya*, 6 February 2012. Available at: <http://www.jadaliyya.com/pages/index/4264/an-ongoing-nakba_the-plight-of-palestinian-refugee>, accessed August 2013.

ultimately stems from colonially induced readings of difference. Thus while there is no doubt that such communitarian identity derives from European influence, we believe that engagement with the *dhimmi* legacy and its discontents is central to the context of building sustainable robust democracies.

A second strand of equally well-founded critique concerns the extent to which the engagement of sectarian identities reifies sub-national identities, and ultimately creates fragmentary societies that are likely to undermine existing states at a time of transition. This sentiment has engaged many minds throughout international legal history and has led to the celebration of such doctrine as *uti possidetis juris* and firm principles concerning the inviolability of boundaries. It is clear that at times of uncertainty, entertaining any possibility of the fragmentation of states is risky, and as events have unfolded in Iraq and Afghanistan, the message concerning power vacuums and the extent to which these can be exploited has been reiterated. Similar fears were central to the decolonization of Africa and Asia through the United Nations era of decolonization, and more recently in the 1990s as the Soviet Union and Yugoslavia unraveled. Engaging with identity politics at times such as these is clearly dangerous and many well-informed commentators prefer to stress messages of "national" unity, even if a few accept the problematic nature of such unity. We accept and respect this position, but posit that this does not justify the submergence of sub-national identities, especially in circumstances where such sub-national groupings have faced historical and contemporary discrimination and existential threats. While it is probably true that one way of guaranteeing stability is to subjugate sectarianism, it remains in doubt that such identity politics can be subsumed by the use of force, the creation of exclusive strong modern national identities, or artificial attempts to affect an agenda of unity. For this reason we recommend engagement with the legacy of identity in the region, in a bid to formulate dialog and inclusion.

Finally, it often appears that analyses of the events of 2011 and 2012 highlight sectarianism as an *orientalist* tendency that privileges parochialism. This position is ill founded: sectarianism, or the assertion of difference, is clearly not an exclusive characteristic of the Middle East, and its revival is probably symptomatic of any great change of the nature being imagined. Thus while the specter of sectarianism is real and the possibility of ethnic strife a distinct possibility, such forces, whether deemed "post-modern tribalism"[72] or genuine, may be quests for inclusion, and ought to be viewed as synonymous with transitions that involve a rearticulation of new identities, rather than a symptom of parochialism.

---

[72] See T. Franck, "Post-Modern Tribalism and the Right to Secession," in Catherine Bröl-mann, Rene Lefeber, and Marjolene Zieck (eds.), *Peoples and Minorities in International Law* (Dordecht: Martinus Nijhoff, 1993), 3.

In the final analysis the only route toward building sustainable democracies is through concerted dialog at a national level between the various communities that constitute the state. This dialog needs to be premised on the need to build inclusive societies where the rights available to every individual will accrue irrespective of their religious, linguistic, or ethnic identity. Getting the modalities of engagement of such a dialog is intrinsically difficult and fraught with numerous obstacles. However, without a genuine effort at seeking such engagement, true multicultural states cannot emerge. In the context of minorities that have faced the wrath of the state in the past, this dialog may need to be prefaced by a sincere apology for rights violations accompanied by a welcome to the negotiating table.

The holding of free and fair elections is a crucial element to this equation, with a range of candidates chosen from as wide a range as possible. Elections by their nature favor majoritarian communities, so efforts need to be made to ensure that the voices of minorities are heeded, whether by encouraging/running candidates from such backgrounds or through campaigning on such issues by mainstream candidates. It is fundamental to any change of this nature that the elections are free and fair, and conducted in an ambience that guarantees the security of candidates and those seeking to exercise their franchise. We believe that the Arab League would probably be ideal interlocutors in this process and would caution against European and Western involvement in this quest, due to the unsavory history of such actors in the region.

There has been much critique recently about the extent to which elections may be "hijacked" by Islamist forces. Many have raised fears about such a scenario, painting the transitions as black days for women, minorities, and human rights. However, it is fundamental to appreciate the nuances of a democratic process. It is for the individuals and communities within the country to elect their representatives: undue interference in the nature of the candidates or the election itself to engineer a result seen as positive, even on human rights grounds, sends out the wrong message. The people in the region have earned the right, through their incessant struggle under externally imposed and supported dictators, to be trusted to make their own choices, and also have the right to get the exercise of this choice wrong. Attempts to influence the process, particularly by Western European states or the United States of America, would be justifiably seen as interference in a process that has already been badly affected by such interference in the past. Rather, if the international community of states is committed to assisting in the building of robust democracies, it is imperative that willingness is shown to work with whatever regime emerges from the exercise of the franchise by the people.

Once such a regime has emerged and taken its place in the pantheon, others need to engage human rights mechanisms and cooperative processes between states as a means to raise the level of human rights. Such a role is in keeping with how other states are treated at present, and this needs to be offered to the new ones that emerge. This necessarily requires the adoption of a long-term vision for the states in the region, based on aspirations expressed in the Uprisings, and must defeat short-term gains that were sought for reasons of national interest. This is particularly so since, as we have demonstrated in this chapter, the pursuit of the short-term national interests of outsiders has been crucial to the state of unrest in the region over the past few centuries.

4

Minorities in the Arab World: Faults, Fault-lines, and Coexistence

Zaid Eyadat

As the Arab Spring spreads through the Arab world, many previously ignored and taboo political and social issues are being raised and debated. Perhaps one of the most contested issues being discussed amid the spreading discontent is the thorny matter of minorities. In societies such as Tunisia and Egypt, where the Jewish and Coptic minorities are easily identified and defined because of cultural separation and alienation, which they were forced to maintain over the years, the minority issue may seem straightforward enough. However, what appears to be fairly simple and clear-cut in this instance is hardly so in reality. The complexities of majority/minority relations in socially plural societies are often obscured by the ambiguity of the terms themselves. For instance, often the fluidity of cultural identity renders one both part of the mainstream culture and a minority at the same time. Many a regime's failure or refusal to realize and acknowledge the complexities and intersections of cultural identity has proven to be its undoing and a threat to the state's stability and security, such as in Sudan, Lebanon, Syria, and Iraq.

It is a fact that the Arab world, particularly the Middle East and North Africa (MENA) region, is no stranger to conflict and warfare; however, according to Moshe Ma'oz and Gabriel Sheffer, while the Arab–Israeli conflict has long occupied center-stage in Arab history and politics, internal conflicts between minorities and majorities are just as crucial.[1] The Arab revolutions attest to the failure of Arab governments to deal creatively with the issue of minorities and the overall problem of societal pluralism. The same divisions that these regimes have fostered and promoted in order to maintain their hegemony have fueled pro-reform movements and the recent sociopolitical

---

[1] Moshe Ma'oz and Gabriel Sheffer, "Introduction," in *Middle Eastern Minorities and Diasporas* (Brighton: Sussex Academic Press, 2002), 1–29 at 2.

unrest. For instance, the power divide in Syria where the numerical minority has ruled the silent majority for more than forty years is finally being challenged by the majority. It is no surprise that the violence in Syria is mostly sectarian between the Sunni and 'Alawi, corresponding to the identity divide along which power divisions have been imposed by the regime. A similar example is the revolutionary movement in Bahrain. After years of partial disenfranchisement, the Shia majority has started to demand its share of power from the ruling Sunni monarchy. Also, the Coptic minority in Egypt has voiced its demands for civil rights and power-sharing in the new state after years of marginalization and repression.

However, the failure of these regimes to approach wisely the general issue of ethno-religious pluralism may be due to the lack of authentically Arab models and paradigms as well as the relative novelty of the concept of minority in Arab politics. The concept, in its political sense, is linked to the emergence of the nation-state, which is also a relatively novel form of political organization in the Arab context.

Even with the emergence of the Arab nation-state during the first half of the twentieth century, the Arab public discourse on minorities has remained almost non-existent. The Arab regimes adamantly refused to acknowledge the reality of societal segmentation and its importance, while vehemently asserting the homogeneity of the societies over which they ruled. This failure can be explained by these regimes' quest for hegemony and legitimacy which would be threatened by any confrontation or discussion of the pluralism issue and bring dissenting voices to the surface and disturb the image of a cohesive nation-state.[2] Meanwhile, processes of either integration or alienation are at work resulting from the state's efforts to define the identity of the majority as opposed to that of the minority, a part of larger efforts at national-state building and loyalty-forging.[3] Two main examples are the Sudanese and Jordanian diversity of identities. For decades, the regimes in both countries tacitly institutionalized and condoned the identity divides amongst their peoples. In Sudan, the regime's marginalization and exclusionist policies of Southern Sudanese and non-Arab tribes served to ingrain the Arab/African and North/South identity divides. This same divide has been the basis upon which the anti-regime independence movements in southern and western Sudan took root and mobilized supporters. In Jordan, within the larger division between the loyalists and protesters, there are several significant cross-cutting identity segmentations, the most prominent of which is between Jordanians of Jordanian origin and Jordanians with Palestinian roots. The former is then fragmented into regional and tribal identities, from the north, the south, and the center. These identity divides are considered a taboo subject

---

[2] Ma'oz and Sheffer, *Middle Eastern Minorities and Diasporas*, 2.
[3] Ma'oz and Sheffer, *Middle Eastern Minorities and Diasporas*, 5.

but are ingrained in the very political culture of the country. Loyalists question the agenda of the opposition, predominantly of Palestinian origin, and accuse them of supporting the alternative homeland project. Dissenting voices question the motives of certain opposition actors, especially the Islamists, undermining the reform movement and strengthening the regime's tacit claim to its position as mediator and peacemaker between the different factions and sections of society.

However, if the Arab Spring and the ethnic and sectarian conflicts are any indication, this traditional manner of approaching the issue of minorities cannot continue much longer, and Arab regimes must rethink their discourse and abandon their top-down methods of building their nation-states.

In this chapter, I examine the general topic of sociocultural diversity in the Arab world with emphasis on the pressing issues of minority–majority relations, and strategies employed in treating these issues in traditional Islamic and contemporary theorizing in the Arab context. After reviewing and examining the general landscape of minorities, I will describe the main competing paradigms that have dealt with the problem of minorities and impacted the minority-related experiences in the region. I present a brief assessment of each paradigm and maintain that each of the existing models, alone, is inadequate, inapplicable, and incapable of granting minorities their rights and preserving stability and coexistence among the diverse social groups constituting the individual Arab polities. Instead, I propose an alternative paradigm that draws on and combines constructive elements from three models of state–minority relations. It is a combination that would go beyond mere tolerance and protected subordination offered by other paradigms, but will facilitate the recognition and validation of minorities' right to equality, protection of their interests, and their incorporation into the construction of an overlapping and cross-cutting national identity in the Arab states.

DEBATING MINORITIES: CONCEPTUAL AND THEORETICAL

It is almost impossible to discuss minorities without referring to and mentioning cultural identity. Although embarking on a full dissection of cultural identity and its intricacies is well beyond the scope of this chapter, it is crucial to recognize the impact certain anomalies of identity have on minority issues and the way fault-lines separating and defining certain groups in society and state at the sociopolitical level are constantly arranged and rearranged. One of the notable anomalies of identity is its fluidity, the way it is perceived and lived in a context-reliant manner that defies all molds and constraints. In other words, identity is in a perpetual state of negotiation. It is often that a Sunni Arab finds herself belonging to the majority in one instant and to the minority in another, or even in both mainstream and minority culture simultaneously. In a context where the majority are Sunni men, a Sunni Arab woman finds herself firmly in the minority, while a Sunni Kurd is firmly in the majority, but not for long. If the highlight of a certain context is ethnic rather than sectarian, the positions are reversed and the woman is back in the majority while the Sunni Kurd is in the minority. Similarly, if a woman elects to emphasize her gender identity over her religious identity, she might very well find herself with the rest of her gender, regardless of her religion, categorized with the minority.

However, with the emergence of the nation-state system in mid-seventeenth-century Westphalia, the need to establish loyalties and affiliations, ethnic, religious, or otherwise, to secure allegiances and legitimacy and reduce power struggles became more and more imperative. Forging such loyalties entailed the construction of corresponding barriers and fault-lines that identified certain identities as a prototype of majorities and "others" as quintessentially minorities and defined, or "imagined," as Benedict Anderson would assert, the center as opposed to the periphery. Despite such states' ceaseless constructionist efforts, the ambiguity of identity and the majority–minority binary have rendered most regimes and systems vulnerable to massive discontent and have made many existing models of governance in socially plural societies inadequate to manage "minorities" in a way conducive to their societies' happiness, stability, and legitimacy, especially as noted in the Arab world.

The relatively recent emergence of the nation-state in the Arab world, and by extension the concept of minority, is inexorably linked to the history of colonization by which the region has been shaped. Not until Arab states could gain their independence and autonomy could they establish their sovereignty and right to self-governance and legitimacy. Nationalistic struggles, inspired by the colonizers' nationalism, came to overthrow the colonizer and establish the nation-state as the order of the day. Once independent, leaders sought to establish coherence and homogeneity in order to preserve their power and lend themselves legitimacy; minorities were clumsily identified and silenced and the majority was given free rein as long as it could reinforce the regime's legitimacy and control. Failure to recognize the importance of the role of minorities in ensuring the new regime's ascendant position could easily be attributed to the leaders' inexperience. However, after years of independence and autonomy, this pretext has lost its plausibility and the deliberate manner with which minorities were defined and then ignored has become more questionable and has elicited much discontent.

Unfortunately, the models and strategies from which Arab countries could select to perceive their internal diversity and handle their minorities have proven to be limited and manifested little probability of success if implemented in Arab states. The oldest model was the Islamic traditional one that focused on minorities and drew on the shariah to define their rights, duties, and status in the "Islamic state," or the Muslim-majority state, led by Arab rulers. This model provided the basis for the millet system under the Turkish sultans of the Ottoman Empire who, as Sunni monarchs, ruled over an ever-growing ethnically and religiously diverse population. I will explore the modern Islamic model that attempted to revolutionize Muslim thinking by focusing more on contemporary liberal and human rights values. I argue that the shortcomings of each of these competing models have rendered them inapplicable in the Arab world and inadequate for reasons analyzed later in the chapter.

MINORITIES IN THE ARAB WORLD: MAPPING THE ARAB SOCIAL FABRIC AND EMERGENCE OF NATION-STATES

In order to appreciate and understand the sociopolitical situation of minorities in the Arab world, we must look at the big picture first and determine who we mean by "minorities" and how they are perceived. We need to identify the pieces that make up the Arab demographic, ethnic, and religious mosaic and how they fit together into one larger picture, however incongruously.

Given the size of the Arab world, which stretches through 14 million square kilometers (8.6 million square miles) across North Africa and parts of Northeast Africa and Southwest Asia, it is only to be expected that the demographic landscape will be correspondingly diverse. According to the UN Economic and Social Commission for Western Asia (UN-ESCWA)'s 2009 Demographic Profile of the Arab Countries, the total population of the Arab world had reached 352.2 million that year.[4] The majority of the population in the Arab world, from the Atlantic Ocean to the Persian Gulf, is Sunni Arab, defining the mainstream religious, sectarian, ethnic, and ultimately sociopolitical landscape of the region.[5] However, as explained above, the definition of "majority" is not as unambiguous as the previous statement might suggest. This overwhelming majority and the resulting groupings are often shaped and reshaped by external contextual imperatives that sometimes enable "unorthodox" members to join the elite by privileging particular identity variables rather than others. Perhaps the Lebanon example is most evident as majorities and minorities are less determined by the ethnic variable and more by the

---

[4] ESCWA, "The Demographic Profile of the Arab Countries," Economic and Social Commission for Western Asia (ESCWA), <www.escwa.un.org/information/publications/edit/upload/sdd-09-TP9.pdf>, accessed August 2013, 2.

[5] Ma'oz and Sheffer, *Middle Eastern Minorities and Diasporas*, 8.

sectarian or denominational one. This is easily accounted for by looking at the political and ideological context in Lebanon.

In addition to the contextual factors from without, there are certain factors from within that might also influence the shaping of individual and group identity. For example, it has been argued that many Shia Muslim and Christian Arabs perceive their "Arabism" as the primary axis of their identity, superseding their religious or denominational orientation and leanings; their self-identity highlights the "linguistic-cultural" or "ethnic" variables as the more outstanding ethnic divide in a certain context.[6] In other words, it is important to recognize the significance of one's self-identity as well as the situational factors in shaping one's group identity.

Be that as it may, the very fact that one is compelled to explain the constant shift in the borders framing the different groupings in the Arab world is an acknowledgment of an original set of borders defining the prototype identity of each of the groups. Recognizing this, without discounting the previously mentioned context-specific identity conception, is very important in any practical analysis of the current minority situation in the Arab world; otherwise one risks falling into the trap of obscuring the issue and ignoring the marginalized and vulnerable groups and minorities in the Arab world region, and thereby failing to protect their rights, just as many regimes have done in the past.

Therefore, in order for us to understand the previously mentioned mosaic, it is crucial to recognize the main cultural fault-lines along which groups in the Arab world are constructed and communities are imagined: language, religion, denomination, and ethnicity. The linguistic minorities consist of Kurds, Armenians, Aramites, Turkmens, Turks, Persians, Western Jews, African Tribes, Nubians, and Berbers. Religious minorities include Christians, Jews, and those adherents of heterodox religions such as Sabeans, Yazidies, and Baha'is. As for non-Sunni Islamic sects, they consist of Twelvers, Zaidies, Ismaelies, Druz, 'Alawites, and Abadhi Kharajites.[7]

As for the ethnic heterogeneity, it is evident in most Arab countries. It has translated into acute ethnic tensions and even intermittent, and sometimes constant, conflicts in Sudan, Lebanon, Iraq, Syria, Algeria, Morocco, Mauritania, Bahrain, and Yemen. This sociopolitical unrest is from time to time exacerbated by the double, and sometimes treble, burden these ethnic minorities carry; ethnic differences often entail linguistic and/or religious/denominational ones. Some Kurds, especially those who are most alienated from mainstream culture both in Iraq and Syria, present a good example of this case, as do some

---

[6] Saad Eddin Ibrahim, "Ethnic Conflict and State-Building in the Arab World," *International Social Science Journal* 50/156 (1998): 229–42.

[7] Albert Habib Hourani, *Minorities in the Arab World* (London: Oxford University Press, 1947).

Berber tribes in North Africa. Such minorities suffer compound conditions of alienation and antagonism and are forced to relinquish their own authenticity to the imposed national identity.

Similar conceptualizations and categorizations of minorities in the Arab world were made more briefly and succinctly by Albert Hourani, as cited by Ma'oz and Sheffer, as "those communities that differ from the Sunni Arab majority in their religious affiliation and/or their ethnic-cultural identity." Ma'oz and Sheffer then subdivide this definition and grouping further and introduce the following categories:

[R]eligious communities that are non-Sunni Muslim, but are ethnically or culturally Arab, namely, most Christian communities—Greek Orthodox, Greek Catholic, Copts, Maronites, Latins, and Protestants; the various Muslim heterodox sects, notably Shi'is, Alawis, Druze, and Isma'ilis. The second category includes ethnic or national groups which are non-Arab but Sunni Muslim: the Kurds, Turkomans, and Circassians; and groups that are neither Arab nor Muslim: the Jews, Armenians, Assyrians, and Southern Sudanese tribes.[8]

As mentioned earlier, with such a diverse landscape Arab regimes have opted not to address the issue of heterogeneity lest they threaten their own legitimacy; in fact, in order to strengthen their hegemony, they have deemed it taboo to even recognize the heterogeneity that characterizes their nations, which, by extension, makes it equally inconceivable to address the concept of power-sharing and to achieve a balance of powers in their states. Bahrain would serve as a perfect example of this. The issue has been ignored for so long that the minority has become the more powerful group and the majority has been effectively silenced. The Sunni regime in Bahrain is one example amongst several, including the Syrian regime which represents a minority of 'Alawi amongst the Sunni majority. Such imbalances of power add a rather unsettling dimension to the minority landscape in some Arab states, and have been a catalyst of the Arab Spring.

This heterogeneity and its resulting complexities are perhaps better understood through social science approaches developed to explain minority politics in the Middle East. Esman and Rabinovich describe the emergence of minorities and minority politics in the region historically and correlate it to the formation of Arab nation-states. The history of the gradual development and emergence of national identity in the contemporary Arab world can be traced to the nineteenth century, which brought the slow disintegration of the Ottoman Empire and its traditional Sunni Islamic policies and order. The Ottoman state had successfully employed the millet system to regulate the relationship between itself and its non-mainstream (Sunni) citizens, which

---

[8] Ma'oz and Sheffer, *Middle Eastern Minorities and Diasporas*, 8–9.

strengthened intra-millet affiliations and religious solidarity and identity.[9] Ethnic identity emerged as a new variable in Ottoman politics in the late nineteenth century; ethno-religious identities became so important as to form the foundations upon which national identities would be organized.[10] Arab, Turkish, and Persian nationalisms emerged among others.[11] Arab nationalism was initially characterized by its secularism but soon became predominantly Sunni Muslim.[12]

The second phase of shaping the Arab national identity and nation-state did not begin until the collapse of the Ottoman Empire in the early 1920s. This stage in Arab nation-state formation was associated with subsequent Western colonialism based on the Mandate system, which led to the establishment of a new state system built on Arab nationalism and modern territorial states. The "search for political community" that accompanied the development of Arab territorial nationalisms played a major role in determining future minority politics.[13] Egypt's search for identity and its dilemma as to whether it is an Arab Muslim country or a monolithic nation with pre-Islamic origins impacted the status of Copts as a group in the Egyptian state.[14] The Fertile Crescent nascent states were drawn arbitrarily by the colonizer, rendering the quest for the definition of the "relationship between geographic entity, state, and political community" much harder.[15] The fragmentation and division of the population of these states and the dominance of the Sunni doctrine in Arab nationalism, in addition to the colonizers' policies, affected intercommunal relations negatively—the Shi'ite and Kurdish problem in Iraq is an example of such difficulties.[16]

In this sense, as Esman argues, the problems associated with minorities in the Arab world can be considered "within the same conceptual framework that has evolved from the recent experience of other postcolonial states in Asia and Africa."[17] The similarities extend to the minorities' quests for a greater share in power, wealth, and status in their countries. Esman argues that the postcolonial state could not initially accommodate the emerging minorities (formerly millets) due to their increasing numbers and diversity, the challenge of modernization and economic development, the limited resources and capabilities of the postcolonial state, and its susceptibility to external influence and

---

[9] Milton J. Esman and Itamar Rabinovich, "The Study of Ethnic Politics in the Middle East," in Milton J. Esman and Itamar Rabinovich (eds.), *Ethnicity, Pluralism, and the State in the Middle East* (Ithaca, NY: Cornell University Press, 1988), 3–28.

[10] Esman and Rabinovich, "The Study of Ethnic Politics."

[11] Esman and Rabinovich, "The Study of Ethnic Politics."

[12] Esman and Rabinovich, "The Study of Ethnic Politics."

[13] Esman and Rabinovich, "The Study of Ethnic Politics."

[14] Esman and Rabinovich, "The Study of Ethnic Politics."

[15] Esman and Rabinovich, "The Study of Ethnic Politics."

[16] Esman and Rabinovich, "The Study of Ethnic Politics."

[17] Esman and Rabinovich, "The Study of Ethnic Politics."

intervention. What makes the Arab world different, despite the general similarity between it and other regions is, according to Esman, its geography, its
Islamic and Ottoman heritage, and the presence of the large number of trans-
border cultural, religious, and ethnic communities and minorities.[18] The
implementation of the European model of the sovereign state by the colonial
powers and afterwards by the Arab postcolonial state posed a threat to the
diverse ethno-religious minority groups who enjoyed a degree of autonomy
under the Ottoman Empire. Esman explains that although the Ottoman Empire's official religion was Sunni Islam and the hegemonic people were the
Ottoman Turks, minorities, especially ethnic groups and communities, were
granted protection, and even some cultural autonomy, as long as they complied
with the state's authority and paid tribute.[19]

The third phase brought Arab states' political independence, and along
with it more complications and ethno-religious politics. In the 1940s to
1960s, Arab countries had inherited populations characterized by heterogeneity and fragmentation, ethnic, religious, and denominational. This period saw
the appearance of minorities as a decisive factor in the process of defining
boundaries between geographic entities, nation-state building, and "imagining" communities. After a brief decline in the importance of minority politics
in the late 1940s, their importance rose rapidly in the 1950s and 1960s; ethnic
conflicts were rampant in Iraq, Lebanon, Sudan, and Syria especially.[20]
The quest for unity against Israel gave rise to pan-Arabism and to the
dominance of Nasserite and Ba'thist nationalisms, overshadowing to a degree
the problem of the minorities and giving the region a more secular character.[21]
Affected by the Cold War and its ideological and geopolitical conflict, the
political Arab identity in this phase was based on the secular concept of Arab
nationalism which highlighted Arabic culture and language as the cornerstones of the state, society, and citizenship.[22] In this sense Arab nationalism
has been a secular ideology—any citizen who belongs to the Arab culture
and is a native Arabic speaker is considered as a member of the Arab
nation and enjoys full citizenship rights despite ethnic or religious affiliations.
Although non-Arabs would be treated as equal to Arab citizens by the law,
they were perceived as minorities and were not considered autonomous
communities or independent entities.[23]

The last and most recent phase of national and cultural identity formation in
the Arab world can be traced back to the 1970s, which has been characterized

---

[18] Esman and Rabinovich, "The Study of Ethnic Politics."
[19] Esman and Rabinovich, "The Study of Ethnic Politics," 4.
[20] Esman and Rabinovich, "The Study of Ethnic Politics."
[21] Esman and Rabinovich, "The Study of Ethnic Politics."
[22] Saad Eddin Ibrahim, "Ethnic Conflict and State-Building in the Arab World," in G. Kemp
and J. G. Stein, *Powder Keg in the Middle East* (Lanham, MD: Rowman & Littlefield, 1995).
[23] Ibrahim, "Ethnic Conflict and State-Building."

by a strong movement towards asserting minorities' identities and differences. This period witnessed many examples of aggressive resurgence of minority movements, especially in Lebanon, Iraq, and Syria. Many political and social factors contributed to shaping this phase, including domestic politics, regional forces, the political role of Islam after the Islamic revolution in Iran, and the dynamics of competing ideologies such as Arab nationalism and socialism, the emergence of new ones, and the decline of secular and more equalizing ones such as pan-Arabism.[24] Most importantly, this phase witnessed the emergence of regimes much more powerful and hegemonic than the ones they replaced—regimes that were able to survive through coercion (i.e. the Iraqi and the Syrian regimes that were able to stifle the majority and other regimes that emerged to stifle the minorities).[25] Such, often violent, insurgencies indicate a serious problem and flaw in the way Arab regimes have since approached the issue of minorities and the way minorities have been redefined and identified.

Esman and Rabinovich argue that whether theorists apply primordialist and instrumentalist theories of integration and conflict models to the problem of minorities in the Arab world, all scholars agree that at the core of minorities' conflicts lies the quest for power, wealth, hegemony, security, and status.[26] They assert that the Middle East consists of many diverse ethnic minorities and groups who are destined to coexist under the same political authorities, all of which have mobilized to further and defend their groups' interests especially in the aftermath of the withdrawal of the colonial powers from the newborn and artificial states they left behind.[27] The goals these ethnic communities have advanced differ and change depending on the overall local and regional situation and variables and the ideologies of their changing leaderships.[28] The authors give the Kurds in Iraq and Black Muslims in Sudan as examples of those minorities who sought self-determination and self-governance; the Maronites in Lebanon as examples of those who struggled to maintain and protect their threatened hegemony; and the Copts in Egypt and Druze in Syria as examples of those who demanded equality and recognition of their rights as minorities.[29] All these numerical minorities have had different degrees of power in their states and have accordingly applied different strategies to achieve their rights and goals. The Shi'ites in Lebanon only started to become militarized after the Islamic revolution in Iran for instance, indicating a certain shift in power relations regionally and locally.[30]

[24] Esman and Rabinovich, "The Study of Ethnic Politics."
[25] Esman and Rabinovich, "The Study of Ethnic Politics."
[26] Esman and Rabinovich, "The Study of Ethnic Politics."
[27] Esman and Rabinovich, "The Study of Ethnic Politics."
[28] Esman and Rabinovich, "The Study of Ethnic Politics."
[29] Esman and Rabinovich, "The Study of Ethnic Politics."
[30] Esman and Rabinovich, "The Study of Ethnic Politics."

Esman and Rabinovich argue that the diversity of the demographic and
ethno-religious landscape of the Arab world prevents the social scientist from
applying any single theory or approach to explain minority politics and/or
ethnic pluralism and conflict in the Middle East.[31] They assert that in order to
understand ethnic conflict, one must at least consider minority collectivities
and solidarities as self-defined as political actors and agents that affect and are
affected by the larger state politics, and that one has the pitfall of imposing
certain theories and conceptions on minorities in order to understand their
behavior (e.g. applying a Marxist approach to certain ethnic collectivities and
framing them in terms of class instead of ethnicity, even though they might
pursue economic goals as an ethnic community).[32]

In the complementary account he offers, Kedourie expands on Esman and
Rabinovich's analysis and explains the process through which millets were
turned into national majorities and minorities in the postcolonial state's
search for political legitimacy and the emergence of nationalism. He explains
that the concept of minorities was part of the "nation-state" package Arab
states had imported from the West upon the disintegration of the Ottoman
Empire; with the state and sovereignty concepts came the need for legitimizing
the government by popular suffrage.[33] Previously drawn from "conquest,
traditional prescription, and religious warrant," the authority to rule came to
find its source in the citizens.[34] Suffrage was deemed the mechanism through
which citizens give legitimacy to governments and the millets, which enjoyed
relative autonomy and the right to administer their own communal affairs
under the authority of the state, were morphed into minorities.[35]

If political legitimacy is conferred by the suffrage system of the citizens, and if the
majority of the citizens in a state are members of 'one' nation among two or more
inhabiting the state, the majority becomes a national majority—that is, a permanent
and fixed quantity—which is pitted against other, smaller, permanent and fixed
quantities, namely of national minorities. Nationalism, then, radically changes the
concept of majority and minority. This is not only because majority and minority
become permanent and fixed quantities, but also because the notion of consensus,
without which the major pars cannot be accepted as the senior pars, is subverted and in
the end destroyed. With the nationalist idea of the nation, and the existence of a
permanent majority, majority comes simply to mean force, the force of number, and
force gives no legitimacy.... The transformation of majority and minority into national majority and national minority is fatal to the idea of government by consent.
It is transformed in this way, and divorced from its conciliar and representative

---

[31] Esman and Rabinovich, "The Study of Ethnic Politics."
[32] Esman and Rabinovich, "The Study of Ethnic Politics."
[33] Elie Kedourie, "Ethnicity, Majority, and Minority in the Middle East," in Esman and
Rabinovich (eds.), *Ethnicity, Pluralism, and the State.*
[34] Kedourie, "Ethnicity, Majority, and Minority."
[35] Kedourie, "Ethnicity, Majority, and Minority."

matrix—as a free-floating idea endowed with great dynamism—that the notion of majority and minority came to the Middle East.[36]

The suspicion and animosity increased between millets (now minorities) which had been autonomous and self-contained and subject only to the ruler's power instead of the majority of the people.[37] As the notion of nationalism spread among the different millets, as well as later among mainstream ruling Muslims, each ethno-religious group started to conceive of itself as a separate nation; unfortunately it was not feasible to give each "nation" its own territorial unit and/or nation-state.[38] Millets became national minorities who often strived to separate themselves from the majority in their own state (i.e. ethnic mobilization).[39]

In his competing account, social scientist P. J. Vatikiotis blames Islam's aversion to pluralism and the exclusiveness of the Islamic tradition entrenched in the Arab world for the minorities' problems, especially sectarianism. He argues that Islam is characterized by an ideological faith that is tied to temporal power that cannot be shared with others who are not of the same faith and that, contrary to Islamic protestations, the Islamic system is a total system that can only accommodate "separatism" rather than "pluralism."[40] This explains the non-Muslim minorities' preference for "secular solutions for the national community" and the increase in integration of non-Muslim minorities during the pan-Arabism era when Islamists and Islamism took a back seat to secularism (i.e. during the Nasserite era).[41] With the proliferation of Islamism and political Islam and militarism, which dealt the final death-blow to any systems that allowed for at least a semblance of pluralism, minorities were pushed to ask for their own separate states.[42] The Islamic order has rendered the Islamic state incapable of accommodating minorities because to give people, both Muslims and, especially, non-Muslim minorities, the right to participate in according power and legitimacy to the ruler would be in conflict with Divine Law which, according to the doctrine of Islam, is the exclusive source of legitimacy and authority. Kedourie, however, introduces the example of Lebanon to undermine Vatikiotis' argument; he maintains that the conflict with minorities in the Arab world is an intertribal problem, and believes that even the modern European concept of the state cannot

---

[36] Kedourie, "Ethnicity, Majority, and Minority," 29.

[37] Kedourie, "Ethnicity, Majority, and Minority."

[38] Kedourie, "Ethnicity, Majority, and Minority."

[39] Kedourie, "Ethnicity, Majority, and Minority."

[40] P. J. Vatikiotis, "Non-Muslims in Muslim Society: A Preliminary Consideration of the Problem on the Basis of Recent Published Works by Muslim Authors," in Esman and Rabinovich (eds.), *Ethnicity, Pluralism, and the State.*

[41] Vatikiotis, "Non-Muslims in Muslim Society."

[42] Vatikiotis, "Non-Muslims in Muslim Society."

save it.[43] According to Kedourie, Lebanon was the typical secular political order, and that did not lead to greater welfare and security but rather to insecurity and conflict.[44]

As illustrated above, it is almost impossible to deny the role religion and traditional conceptions of religion have played in shaping many identities across the Arab world. Islam was the dominant ideology in the Ottoman Empire to ensure the Muslim majority's allegiance and loyalty. Perhaps taking a look at the traditional systems that have been employed to manage the heterogenic Arab and Muslim societies over the course of history will give us access to a better comprehension of the way minorities are conceptualized today and how they could be approached and their rights secured.

COMPETING PARADIGMS

Islamic theorizing on minorities

Traditional theorizing in Islam is political in that it has advanced, for centuries, the idea of the Islamic state, and sometimes divine rule, and presented a corresponding model that designated shariah law as the only effective system and decreed that it should be employed to govern and organize the affairs of the state. Such affairs include the relationship between the subject and the ruler and between the non-Muslim minority and the state.

Although this model might secure the majority's allegiance and strengthen the state's legitimacy, one of its limitations and flaws is that it deprives religious minorities of their right to power-sharing and equal treatment and is therefore liable to cause resentment and conflict between the minorities and the state and/or the majority, undermining stability and peace. According to Megezil, as cited by Ibrahim, this model stipulates the exclusion of religious minorities from power and prevents them from assuming state or governmental roles, perceiving them as "protected communities" (*Ahl al-dhimma*) who are to run their own communal affairs and pay the *jizyah* (poll tax) without being eligible for top commanding offices (e.g. heads of state, governors, and the judiciary).[45] They are required to respect the Muslim majority and recognize the sovereignty of the Islamic state in order to be treated with reciprocal respect and compassion and shown religious tolerance.[46] All Muslims, however, are considered equal regardless of their ethnic origins or cultural background.

---

[43] Esman and Rabinovich, "The Study of Ethnic Politics."
[44] Esman and Rabinovich, "The Study of Ethnic Politics."
[45] Ibrahim, "Ethnic Conflict and State-Building."
[46] Ibrahim, "Ethnic Conflict and State-Building."

What is most noteworthy about this model is that it conceives of only religious minorities and fails to recognize ethnic and cultural minorities, which is an inadequate response to the contemporary realities of the Arab nation-states and, moreover, dangerous and subversive at both the national and international levels. While, according to this type of Islamic theorizing, Muslim Kurds, Berbers, and Black Muslims are not considered "minorities," Christian Arabs are, and are sociopolitically alienated. In the contemporary Arab nation-state, however, Christians prove to be one of the most integrated minorities in the Arab world, unlike Muslim Kurds.

The very term "*Ahl al-dhimma*" is well documented in Islamic history and jurisprudence as referring to minorities. The term finds its roots in the pact that a believer agrees to respect, the violation of which makes him liable to *dham* (blame)[47] (another meaning of *Ahl al-dhimma* is the guarantee of safety, *aman*).[48] Legally, the term connotes and refers to certain rights which must be protected by the state. The people whose rights are protected are known as *dhimmis*, or protected subjects. The shariah, or Islamic law, governs the relations of the *dhimmis* with both individual Muslims and the Islamic state on the basis of religious distinction,[49] and regards *dhimmis* as religious groups and not individuals.[50]

It is crucial to note the development in the status of minorities in the Islamic tradition, however, which fails to conceive of people as citizens but insists on treating them as subjects. The earliest usage of the term *dhimmah* was in the Constitution of Madinah, which states that "The *dhimmah* [the pact guaranteeing security and protection] of God is one." This implies that all the people of Madinah—Jews and Muslims alike—were protected by the new Muslim rulers of the city. The pact also acknowledges that Jews and Muslims each have their own religion and the right to practice it.[51] Later, most jurists and interpreters chose to consider a particular sura as the basis for the legal regulation of the status of non-Muslims in the Islamic state. In Sura Al-Tawbah (9: 29) it is stated that Muslims should fight the People of the Book—a term used to refer to Christians, Jews, Zoroastrians, and Sabi'ans—until they willingly consent to paying a special tax or tribute (*jizyah*). It is these early regulations that paved the way for the later legalization of non-Muslims' status

---

[47] Majid Khaddouri, *War and Peace in the Law of Islam* (Baltimore, MD: Johns Hopkins University Press, 1955), 198.

[48] Yusuf Al-Qaradawi, *ghayar al-muslimin fi al-mujtama'al-islami* (Cairo: Maktabatwahbah, 1977); and Abdullah An-Na'im, "Religious Minorities under Islamic Law and the Limits of Cultural Relativism," *Human Rights Quarterly* 9/1 (1987): 1–18.

[49] Sa'id Ramadan, *Islamic Law: its Scope and Equity* (London: P. R. Macmillan, 1961).

[50] Abdul Rahman Doi, *Non-Muslims under Shari'ah (Islamic Law)* (Lahore: Kazi, 1981), 73–4.

[51] Dr. Jamal Badawi (undated), "Muslim/Non-Muslim Relations," Fiqh Council of North America, available online at: http://www.fiqhcouncil.org/node/24.

in the shariah, a process that reached its peak during the Abbasid period (750–1258 CE).[52]

Along with their protection by the Islamic state, minorities, in this model, are given a set of "rights" or freedoms, such as freedom of religious practice, judicial autonomy, and freedom of internal affairs, but are deprived of the most basic right to equality. Even the rights that they are granted are conditioned by networks of social obligation and duty, which according to Dalaoura, renders them privileges rather than rights or claims, and designates minorities second-class citizens.[53]

The Ottoman millet system

The millet system of the Ottoman Empire was directly based on the traditional Islamic theorizing and practices going back to the early years of Islamic history as described already. The Ottoman sultans utilized the millet system to regulate the relationship between the government and minority groups that formed the bulk of their population. The millet system recognized religious differences as the only important factor in shaping both individual and group identity. This system was based mainly on the separation of different religious groups from each other and a legal status was granted to each religious and denominational community with specific communal rights and privileges. This provided some degree of autonomy to non-Muslim groups within the Ottoman Empire. The system constituted one of the basic administrative units of the empire in which Orthodox, Armenian, and Jewish communities carried out their administrative affairs with the state through their community organizations, and maintained their own culture, customs, language, and religion. The system was based on religious faith, not ethnic and/or national identity, and all members of the millets were the political subjects of the Sultan, who was the central pillar of the political order. While the basis for religious identity was the millet organization, the state authority determined the common political identity. In other words, the status of non-Muslims was determined not by the "minority" status of the millet members, but by their loyalty to the state and their subservient position below the Muslim majority led by a Sunni Muslim Ottoman ruling dynasty.

---

[52] Sayed Khatab, "Citizenship Rights of Non-Muslims in the Islamic State of Hakimiyya Espoused by Sayyid Qutb," *Islam and Christian–Muslim Relations* 13/2 (2002): 163–87.

[53] Katarina Dalacoura, *Engagement or Coercion: Weighing Western Human Rights Policies on Turkey, Iran and Egypt* (London: Royal Institute of International Affairs, 2003).

Modern Islamic theorizing on minorities

Change, however, was destined to come from within, for a new scholarship emerged from the Arab world aimed at reforming and reconstructing the shariah and the Islamic paradigm focused on, amongst many things, the status of minorities in the Muslim-majority state. Scholars such as Abdullahi An-Na'im and others have taken it upon themselves to develop a new line of Islamic thinking that is compatible with liberalism and the international human rights discourse and which is founded on reason rather than dogma.

Modern scholars stress the theme of the possibility and importance of new interpretations of Islamic traditions that better fit in the modern context of the contemporary world. Scholars working within this approach criticize the idea that only one true traditional meaning of the holy texts is valid in all historical and social contexts. They argue that the shariah system is historically contingent and represents one expression of one possible interpretation of Islamic sources, and that it is necessarily fallible and far from divine. The need for new hermeneutics of the Qur'an and Sunna, they argue, springs from the need to accommodate and respond to the modern circumstances amidst which the Arab and Muslim nations find themselves and which necessitate a systematic and rational reconciliation between Islam and Islamic thought and universal human rights.

Some of the attempts to debunk traditional shariah and its approach to minorities in general start with conducting a discourse analysis of the shariah and its development over history in an attempt to reveal the way it has been shaped by contextual factors rather than textual evidence, undermining the divine status it has gained, and highlighting its dogmatic status. Modern scholars maintain that a careful reading of Islamic history reveals that there was no uniform practice toward non-Muslims and that the status of non-Muslims varied from one caliph to another. For instance, while the first Islamic constitution in Medina and Abu Bakr's approach both gave Muslims and non-Muslims equal rights and duties and established a pluralistic society, Umar's approach was different in that he created restrictions upon non-Muslims (Pact of Umar) in terms of religious institutions, symbols, and the sale of certain goods such as wine. This "pact" came to be the basis for the later juristic debate on the rights of non-Muslims and influenced the attitudes of Muslims towards non-Muslims.[54]

The traditional Islamic political thought about citizenship and the rights it entails are based on jurists' readings and interpretations of the Qur'anic texts and the traditions (Hadith), which were often governed by their own experience, the

---

[54] Abdullah Saeed, "Rethinking Citizenship Rights of Non-Muslims in an Islamic State: Rashid Al-Ghannūshī's Contribution to the Evolving Debate," *Islam and Christian–Muslim Relations* 10/3 (1999): 307–23.

type of political establishment they encountered, and the mindset and attitude of the Muslim community toward the non-Muslims in their context.[55] The reality of the nation-state with unified national identity in both the Muslim and the international communities has significantly changed the physical and mental composition of society; thus, the contemporary debate among modern Islamic scholars goes beyond the traditional binary Muslim/*Ahl al-dhimma*. In fact, Fahmi Howaidi, one of the modern Islamic scholars, suggests that the juristic formulations should be revised, including the concept of *Ahl al-dhimma*, which he considers as a historical value that is not in any way binding, while advocating the renunciation of the concept of *Ahl al-dhimma* and replacing it with citizenship in terms of terminology and substance.[56] Most modern Islamic scholars declare that their priority is the implementation of the fundamental principles of the Qur'an, and the authentic Sunna, and the details of Islamic jurisprudence are subject to change, requiring a new methodology to deal with the new problems in the modern Muslim society.[57]

I focus on two main approaches that dominate modern Islamic thought on the issues of minority and citizenship rights as advocated by two important thinkers—Abdullahi An-Na'im and Rashid Al-Ghannūshī.

An-Na'im has argued strongly for the rethinking of key aspects of Islamic law, including the concept of citizenship. He maintains that the "personal" concept of citizenship dominant in traditional Islamic law should be replaced with a "territorial" concept of citizenship:

Whereas the personal concept of citizenship would confer this status on the basis of some personal attribute or quality such as religion or ethnicity, the territorial conception of citizenship, which has now become the norm, confers the benefits and burdens of citizenship on all those born and permanently resident within the territory of the state, as well as those naturalized under the relevant provisions of the law of the land. It is morally repugnant and politically inexpedient, I submit, to deny a full citizenship to any person who was born and permanently resident within the territory of the state unless such person opts for and requires the citizenship of another state.[58]

An-Na'im stresses that although most constitutions of modern Islamic states guarantee protection against religious discrimination, most of these constitutions authorize the application of traditional shariah laws; as such, they sanction discrimination against religious minorities. He states that the existence of

---

[55] Saeed, "Rethinking Citizenship Rights of Non-Muslims."

[56] Fahmi Houwaidi, *Muwatinoun la dhimmiyyoun* (Cairo: Dar al-shorouq, 1999).

[57] Saeed, "Rethinking Citizenship Rights of Non-Muslims."

[58] Abdullah An-Na'im, *Toward an Islamic Reformation: Civil Liberties, Human Rights, and International Law* (Syracuse, NY: Syracuse University Press, 1996), 84.

such contradictions and the underlying tensions they reflect call for an urgent and candid discussion of this problem.[59]

Moreover, An-Na'im diligently attempts to debunk the validity of the concept of "Islamic state" and advances an Islamic post-secular liberal model instead. He argues that the concept of an "Islamic state" is a nascent one that is based on European ideas of state and law, and not Islamic sources, and that the ideas of human rights and citizenship are more consistent with Islamic principles than with claims of a supposedly Islamic state whose task is to be the keeper of shariah.[60] He further claims that the only way to achieve consensus on human rights is to work toward a natural formation, because any ideology including the religious value system will always have the criterion of inclusion and exclusion.[61]

An-Na'im's important theory about Islam and the secular state paves the way for the total equality between Muslims and non-Muslims in all rights and duties. He confirms that the need for a secular state springs from the pragmatic necessity to maintain freedom and security; he maintains that in order to have that, every citizen must act from conviction and choice instead of compulsion. Unlike the traditional approach, An Na'im's model opens the door to all persons in the state, irrespective of their religious or cultural affiliations, to contribute to the public sphere and have equal sociopolitical and legal status.[62]

The second approach that I focus on here is the one advanced by many scholars, such as Rashid al-Ghannūshī, Muhammed al-Awwah, Muhammad Amarah, and Hasan al-Turabi, as particularly discussed in detail in al-Ghannūshī's two key works on citizenship rights: *Al-hurriyyat al-amma fi addawla al-islamiyya,* and *Huquq al-muwtanana: huquqghayr al-muslimin fi- al-mujtama' al-islami.* He makes no claims to having a formal solution to the problem in either book; he emphasizes the relativity of the subject and his fallibility as a theorist and scholar while highlighting the most relevant and important aspects of the question of citizenship in relation to twentieth-century Islamic thought. In order to understand the issue from a modern perspective and to give meaningful answers to the problems raised by the nation-state, al-Ghannūshī stresses the need to return to the authoritative texts, the Qur'an and the Hadith, and to examine the practices of the Prophet's Companions, alongside jurisprudential and historical developments.[63] The main idea in al-Ghannūshī's modern theorizing on the issue of minority rights is that the reexamination of the sacred texts of the Qur'an and Hadith should

[59] Abdullah An-Na'im, *Islam and the Secular State: Negotiating the Future of Shari'a* (Cambridge, MA: Harvard University Press, 2008).

[60] An-Na'im, *Islam and the Secular State.*

[61] An-Na'im, *Islam and the Secular State.*

[62] An-Na'im, *Islam and the Secular State.*

[63] Saeed, "Rethinking Citizenship Rights of Non-Muslims."

be governed by the principle of justice (*adl*). For al-Ghannūshī, it is the principle of "just dealing" or "right action," the interpretation of which must be based on the Prophet's instruction: "Wish for your brother what you wish for yourself." It is in the light of this principle, according to al-Ghannūshī, that the authoritative texts, the Qur'an and Sunna, should be read because this fundamental Islamic principle is embodied in the Qur'anic verse that says: "God commands justice, the doing of good, and liberality to kith and kin, and He forbids all shameful deeds, and injustice and rebellion: He instructs you, that you may receive admonition" (16: 90).[64]

Al-Ghannūshī emphasizes this verse as the central imperative in all religious rulings, which will ensure that all shariah would revolve around the justice axis; additionally, he stresses that one of the main objectives of Islam from the beginning was to establish a just order. To support this argument, he points out that the term *adl* and its derivatives appear more than twenty times in the Qur'an, along with a number of similar terms denoting "justice." Al-Ghannūshī views this as a command to rulers and judges to deal with people with justice and equality, regardless of whether the subjects are Muslims or non-Muslims, because the focus in all these verses is justice toward all people, not just among Muslims, so all people should be treated on an equal basis in all affairs of the state.[65]

The difference in citizens' belief systems should not be used as a pretext for depriving them of some of their rights, for Islam has guaranteed the right to practice one's religion freely. Al-Ghannūshī describes the freedoms that all citizens, whether Muslims or non-Muslims, would enjoy in an Islamic state by referring to the Qur'anic verse that advises the Prophet not to be overly concerned to convert people: "You are not one to manage people's affairs" (88: 22); "We know best what they say; and you [Muhammad] are not a tyrant over them [to force them to believe]" (50: 45). He demonstrates that the Qur'anic position on the issue of freedom of belief is clear: religion is acceptable only if people believe in it of their own free will as this is stated in the verse: "There is no compulsion in religion" (2: 256).

In his discourse, al-Ghannūshī argues that all faiths have the right to exist and have their place in society. He criticizes the traditional Muslim scholars who denied non-Muslims their right to build and maintain churches, and asserts non-Muslims' and Muslims' right to freely express and preach their religion. Indeed, al-Ghannūshī believes in absolute equality between Muslims and non-Muslims in the matter of religious practices and he draws attention to the fact that non-Muslims are also entitled to defend their religious beliefs, and there should be a rational debate between Muslims and non-Muslims on

---

[64] Rashid Al-Ghannūshī, *Al-hurriyyat al-amma fi addawla al-islamiyya* (Beirut: Markazderasat al-wehda al arabiyya, 1993).

[65] Al-Ghannūshī, *Al-hurriyyat al-amma fi addawla al-islamiyya*.

the comparative differences and strengths of their respective systems. He maintains that there is nothing in the shariah that prevents non-Muslims from exercising their equal rights within the limits of the law, as long as they show their allegiance to the state and abide by its laws.[66]

Another thorny issue that al-Ghannūshī discusses, although in a manner less compatible with liberalism and equality, is the issue of minority members holding critical state positions. His conclusion is that such positions should be given through equal competition for all citizens on the basis of expertise and qualifications, the only exceptions being the most senior positions of Imam and Commander-in-Chief of the armed forces, traditionally known as *Amir al-Mu'minin* or Caliph. These positions, in al-Ghannūshī's view, are very closely related to "religious" positions and, hence, should be reserved for Muslims. They should, however, be the only such reserved positions.[67] He also argues that historically, many critical government positions have been filled by non-Muslims, and that the Prophet himself assigned a number of men to such positions, including an ambassador to Ethiopia; he also entrusted various responsibilities to non-Muslims during war.[68]

Here, however, scholar Tariq al-Bishri counters the argument by explaining that the *fuqaha*, or Muslim jurists, had previously viewed the issue of public office from a politicized and hegemonic perspective, where power was in the hands of the ruler or caliph or king. The system of government has changed over the years, becoming more institutionalized and democratic. Because sovereignty is, ideally, in the hands of the people who elect whomever they desire, there is no position in the modern state that is the repository of absolute power, and hence, all the positions of the modern Islamic state are open to non-Muslim citizens. Under this system, the rulers adhere to the constitution and the laws which are approved by the people through their constitutional institutions. Thus, rulers are considered more accountable than institutions, and the sovereign in this context is the constitution and the law. Accordingly, there is no fear from individuals so long as it is in our power to elect or reject them, and so long as the individuals are powerless to affect anything in the public order except through our will and desire.[69]

Al-Ghannūshī, however, ends up undermining some of his enlightened theorizing by emphasizing the importance of the ethos of the Islamic state, and that it can only be assured by making the legislative and statutory bodies subject to Islamic law, so that non-Muslims cause no threat. Taking Iran as a model, al-Ghannūshī argues that a safeguard could be a Constitutional

[66] Al-Ghannūshī, *Al-hurriyyat al-amma fi addawla al-islamiyya*.
[67] Al-Ghannūshī, *Al-hurriyyat al-amma fi addawla al-islamiyya*.
[68] Al-Ghannūshī, *Al-hurriyyat al-amma fi addawla al-islamiyya*.
[69] Tariq Al-Bishri, *Al-Muslimunwalaqbat fi itar al-jama'a al-wataniyyah* (Cairo: Dar al-Shorouq, 1981); and Tariq Al-Bishri, *Al-Jama'a al-wataniyyah: al-'ozlawalindimaj* (Cairo: Dar al-Shorouq, 2005).

Council, which would determine that laws passed are in accordance with Islamic law and the constitution. Under these conditions, the existence of non-Muslim representatives could be of benefit to the nation without there being any possibility of conflict.[70]

Despite his good intentions, al-Ghannūshī advances a model of limited rights for minorities and seems unaware of it. The need to protect the state's ethos from potential non-Muslim dissidents speaks of his inherent suspicion of minorities and the need to stay on guard lest they corrupt the Islamic state. The mere need for the Constitutional Council is threatening to his model in that it poses the possibility of eventually turning Islamic law, no matter how initially liberal it is, into a dogma and ideology. This system admits no fallibility on the part of Constitutional Court members, and gives them power that is almost divine.

AN ALTERNATIVE MODEL

Finally, in light of the previously mentioned systems of "minority management," and their limitations and shortcomings, and taking into account the intricacies of minority politics expounded in the social science literature mentioned earlier, I propose an alternative model that could possibly accommodate minorities in the Arab world, especially after the Arab Spring. It is an eclectic power-sharing model that is based mainly on consociationalism, and draws on constructive elements from the modern Islamic models as well as writings on multiculturalism. This model seeks to develop a new approach to religious minorities that ensures equality rather than their protected subservience and subordination, and it must address ethnic minorities as well—something neglected by the aforementioned Islamic models.

First, however, I shall attempt to examine Arend Lijphart's consociationalism theory, the main grounding upon which my suggested model is founded. The consociational model was developed in the late 1960s by Lijphart when examining the political systems of the Netherlands, Belgium, and other countries both European and Asian. This is a conflict management system aiming at maintaining political stability in states characterized by severe social segmentation and diversity. Lijphart sought to explain why Belgium, the Netherlands, and Switzerland were stable and democratic despite the lack of structurally endogenous bases for national unity and deep cultural and societal segmentation. He attributed this stability partly to the role played by the elite and the "politics of accommodation" whereby elites in each of the political

---

[70] Al-Ghannūshī, *Al-hurriyyat al-amma fi addawla al-islamiyya.*

blocs would agree to follow a particular set of "rules of engagement" and political interaction.[71] Consociationalism is a political system that is results-oriented, where disparate ideological commitments are tolerated, and critical political decisions are made by elite consensus; in this system, no bloc receives political or economic preference, culturally contentious issues are depoliticized, and the secrecy of the bargaining process within the elite, as well as the overriding right of the government to govern, are important and respected.[72] In order for consociationalism to be capable of facilitating power-sharing in deeply divided and heterogeneous societies, it is necessary to meet certain criteria and standards. Lijphart identifies four main conditions/components of such a system: (1) the heterogeneous autonomy of the social and demographic fabric of the state, (2) a grand coalition government representing the different social segments, (3) proportionality, and (4) the minority veto.[73] These represent the main features shared among consociationalist systems across the world.

Lijphart explains the "grand coalition" criteria where, instead of pursuing a "minimum winning coalition", parliamentary parties should pursue a "grand coalition" that will allow for all groups in society to be represented, approximately based on the group's proportion within the country's overall population.[74] Thus, a grand coalition constitutes a form of an "executive" authority encompassing all leaders of all parties representing all the country's community segments.[75] This represents a form of power-sharing and a participatory approach to decision-making, to which representatives of all groups and minorities contribute. In its most unorthodox form, which happens to be in one of the most ethnically and religiously divided countries in the Arab world—Lebanon—consociation is implemented through the allocation of top governmental offices, including the presidency, prime ministership, and assembly speakership, to leaders from specific ethnic or religious groupings.[76]

Lijphart stresses the idea of proportionality in representation in both the grand coalition and electoral system, yet he warns against exaggerating it and using it as a political tool to the detriment of the smaller minority groups.[77] Such misuse of this tool will undermine democracy and give the majority more power through the use of the force of numbers. In fact, this emphasis on proportionality has already tempted many a minority in Lebanon to tamper

---

[71] Arend Lijphart, "Consociational Democracy, World Politics," *World Politics* 21 (1969): 205–25.

[72] Lijphart, "Consociational Democracy, World Politics."

[73] Stefan Wolff, "Liberal Consociationalism in Theory and Practice," talk given at King's College London, 2011.

[74] Lijphart, "Consociational Democracy, World Politics."

[75] Lijphart, "Consociational Democracy, World Politics."

[76] Lijphart, "Consociational Democracy, World Politics."

[77] Lijphart, "Consociational Democracy, World Politics."

with the demographic structure of the country and artificially enlarge its numbers, either through questionable naturalizations or through encouraging procreation. Rae has cautioned against such "manufactured majorities," which obviously undermine the very spirit of power-sharing and democratic governance.[78]

A significant right that consociationalism affords minority elites is the veto power. Lijphart points out that all groups have the right to apply the brakes to a decision process, and that any minority can veto a policy change.[79] This "mutual veto" could lead to political immobility, although Lijphart thinks that it will not, because each party will want to protect the system's stability in order to promote inter-group peace. Consequently, the elites will make concessions occasionally to prevent constitutional change or conflict.[80] This has long since been proven inaccurate in failed models of consociationalism that include Cyprus and Lebanon.

Most importantly, Lijphart emphasizes the role of politicians in shaping minorities and therefore the corresponding system of management. He asserts the instrumental-situational notion that societal differences defining minorities are only mobilized when politicians appeal to them.[81] This means that democratic politicians have the option either to appeal or not to appeal to such societal fault-lines. From a rational perspective, Lijphart concludes that although it might not be the most selfless or moral act, politicians would appeal to such differences as ethnicity and religion because even if they did not, other, more opportunistic politicians would.[82] Those who fail to highlight these differences do so at their own risk and peril.[83]

The fluidity and intersection of allegiances should be acknowledged and respected, in part by giving minorities the means to flexible self-determination, or what Lijphart calls "predetermination". This includes "(1) elections by means of proportional representation and (2) the right of voluntary associations to organize their own, autonomous but state-funded, schools and cultural organizations ... Proportional representation permits the emergence and political representation of any group, ethnic or non-ethnic, and is not biased for or against ethnic parties."[84] Other advantages of this are that it facilitates power adjustment to accommodate any changes or shifts in the

---

[78] Douglas Rae, *The Political Consequences of Electoral Laws* (New Haven, CT: Yale University Press, 1967), 74–7.

[79] Lijphart, "Consociational Democracy, World Politics."

[80] Lijphart, "Consociational Democracy, World Politics."

[81] Arend Lijphart, "Power-Sharing, Ethnic Agnosticism, and Political Pragmatism," *Transformation* 21 (1993): 94–9.

[82] Lijphart, "Power-Sharing, Ethnic Agnosticism, and Political Pragmatism."

[83] Lijphart, "Power-Sharing, Ethnic Agnosticism, and Political Pragmatism."

[84] Lijphart, "Power-Sharing, Ethnic Agnosticism, and Political Pragmatism."

boundaries of minorities and groups and allows for the representation of new interest groups such as environmental groups and political advocacy movements.[85]

However, it is very important to note that the individual inadequacies of these approaches to managing minorities does not mean their total failure as concepts. Right now, the Arab world is in urgent need of a system that will combine the positive elements of the consociational, modern Islamic, and multicultural approaches. It would be beneficial to look at and consider the merits of each of these paradigms and create a hybrid framework that would integrate all the necessary and positive components of those models while shedding problematic ones.

Components of the consociational system in Lebanon are very advantageous when one considers its relevance to the country's diversity and sectarian divisions. Its liberal pluralism is in line with the heterogeneity one finds in the Arab world in general. This system transcends mere acceptance and tolerance, advanced by traditional Islamic theorizing. A "coalition of elites" based on proportional representation of each confessional segment or faction of the population guarantees the protection and advancement of each interest group and therefore mitigates inter-confessional and inter-elite conflict and power struggle.[86] The constant conflict in Lebanon can be attributed to the inequality in representation of the different confessional groups, which is based on a census conducted back in 1932. However, the demographics of the population have changed and have been manipulated since that time.[87] This has exacerbated and worsened the inter-confessional conflict, overrepresented the interests of a few groups at the expense of others, and generated resentment between the factions and their elites on the one hand and between the different factions on the other. However, the flawed implementation of the consociational system in Lebanon does not detract from its viability in principle.

Nevertheless, one of the flaws of the Lebanese model is that it only recognizes identity division along the lines of confessional cleavages. This is why one needs to incorporate some components of the multicultural model that would provide the modified consociationalism model with the needed pluralistic shell and value system based on tolerance and recognition. This model would recognize more fully intersecting affiliations and forms of identification in order to forge correspondingly cross-cutting instead of mutually exclusive allegiances, religious as well as ethnic. This will represent a significant yet crucial modification to the aforementioned consociational model and its limiting pluralistic political processes. It will also contribute to the construction of

[85] Lijphart, "Power-Sharing, Ethnic Agnosticism, and Political Pragmatism."
[86] Richard Hrair Dekmejian, "Consociational Democracy in Crisis: The Case of Lebanon," *Comparative Politics* 10/2 (1978): 251–65 at 253–54.
[87] Dekmejian, "Consociational Democracy in Crisis," 254.

a cross-cutting, harmonious, and overlapping national identity through pinpointing ethnic minorities and acknowledging their autonomy by incorporating their elites into the government's consociational coalition. Chechens in Jordan, for example, would be represented as such and not just as Muslims, in acknowledgment of their status as an ethnic minority despite their belonging to the religious majority. Similarly, in Lebanon, the main non-Muslim group is the Armenian community, which is recognized as a religious minority as well as an ethnically distinct grouping.

Additionally, in a society where Islam is the dominant religion, it is vital to recognize the compatibility between such a model and Islam and its compliance with Islamic principles of equality and justice. Incorporating elements from the modern Islamic models is important to provide solutions for religious and other types of minority that would transcend the protection provided by the millet system. A modified consociational system would not work in an Islamic state. This is only feasible in a religiously neutral state that would allow the representation of religious and ethno-religious groups, which is a major component of the Islamic enlightenment thinking that posits a post-secular or religiously neutral state as justified within an Islamic framework. This alternative model achieves tolerance and acceptance, respect and harmony, the construction of a cross-cutting national identity along community lines, and protection of minority rights.

In constructing an alternative model, additional guidance can be gained from the consociational systems of Canada, India, Russia, and Switzerland, where federalism is used to decentralize and democratize these multicultural societies. The federal consociational model could be particularly relevant to the North African Arab states of Libya, Algeria, Morocco, and Sudan. The present Iraqi regime represents an unstable and badly conceived variant of federal consociationalism.

Finally, for any consociational system to succeed, the economic dimension requires priority attention, particularly in the distribution of wealth among the constituent ethnic and religious communities and within each community. A key factor in Lebanon's consociational failings is the substantial income and wealth inequalities among its diverse sectarian groups, whereby inter-group segmentation is reinforced by class bifurcations, as some minorities are richer than the others, a factor leading to class conflict.

CONCLUSION

The model I suggest takes from contemporary Islamic theorizing the idea of the religion-neutral state and territorial citizenship—with special emphasis on the compatibility between Islam and these principles; from the multicultural approach, the acknowledgment of the different intersecting instead of mutually exclusive affiliations and forms of identification, such as religious and ethnic ones among others; and from the consociationalist model, its grand coalition and proportionality principles.

The alternative model I have suggested is a transformational one that would require much work in the future to begin to take practical and achievable concrete shape. It is equally important to realize that this is a model of a process of accommodation and conflict management rather than a "resolution." It could provide a much-needed medium to facilitate the political transformation toward more democratic pluralistic systems in the Middle East region.

5

Arab Minorities, Liberalism, and Multiculturalism

Francesca Maria Corrao and Sebastiano Maffettone

"I am not . . .
What shall I do, Muslims?
I don't recognize myself anymore . . .
I am not Christian nor Hebrew,
neither Magus nor Muslim.
I am not from the East nor from the West,
neither from the earth nor from the sea."[1]

These verses of the famous fifteenth-century Islamic Sufi master, Jalaluddin Rumi, are a beautiful example of the Islamic attitude toward multiculturalism. The poet affirms to be a human being regardless of his religious or regional affiliation: he is a lover of God no matter if he is Hebrew or Christian or Muslim. Islamic society was multicultural from its very beginning and has been so for a long period of its history. In order to maintain a peaceful coexistence the Prophet Muhammad issued the Medina Constitution (or Charter of Medina) to grant freedom of religion and political and cultural rights to religious minorities.[2] Later these rights were extended in the Covenant of the caliph Omar (635) with further modification until the institution of the millet system under the Ottoman Empire.[3]

---

[1] Jalal al-Din Rumi, *The Masnavi: Book One*, trans. Jawid Mojaddedi (Oxford: Oxford University Press, 2004).

[2] M. Watt, *Muhammad at Medina* (Oxford: Oxford University Press, 1956). For an analysis of the text see R. B. Serjeant, "The Constitution of Medina," *Islamic Quarterly* 8 (1964): 3–16 at 4; and R. B. Serjeant, "The *Sunnah Jāmi'ah*, Pacts with the Yathrib Jews, and the *Taḥrīm* of Yathrib: Analysis and Translation of the Documents Comprised in the So-called 'Constitution of Medina'," *Bulletin of the School of Oriental and African Studies* 41 (1978): 1–42.

[3] C. E. Bosworth, "The Concept of Dhimma in Early Islam," in B. Braude and B. Lewis (eds.), *Christians and Jews in the Ottoman Empire: The Functioning of a Plural Society*, 2 vols. (New York: Holmes & Meier, 1982).

The spread of Islam in medieval Europe introduced important innovations in this direction. In Sicily, the chancellery at the court of the Emperor Frederick II adopted significant elements of customary law in order to protect minorities introduced when the Arabs ruled the island. The Islamic system at that time was rather advanced and thus granted minority groups a decent status. In medieval al-Andalus, the harmonious coexistence between Muslim and minority groups became a model for the Arab poets fighting for political freedom and justice in the last century under colonial rule. Influential poets and intellectuals such as the Egyptian Ahmad Shawqi (1868–1932) with his play entitled *The Andalusian Princess*, or the Syrian Adonis (1930) in his long poem *Prolegomenon to the History of the Petty Kings*, echoed the mythical unity of the Andalusian experience. Intellectuals and scholars believed the Andalusian multicultural experience had been the ideal model for Arab modern society. As we read in Adonis's poem dedicated to Granada:

> A single house for earth and sky
> Here between the Mediterranean and the Sierra Nevada.
> The mountain puts the hand in the wave's hand,
> the sea climbs the windows of the trees.[4]

Some scholars have shown that this model was advanced for the standards of the Middle Ages, and that Andalusian coexistence was in fact more successful than anywhere else, even if from time to time it did not protect minorities from repression and abuse, and even if minorities were always considered second class compared to Muslims.[5]

In the Ottoman Empire, the condition of minorities was tied up with the attempt by Western powers to extend their protection over them, formalized in the "capitulations." After Bonaparte's campaign in Egypt, Muhammad Ali Pasha (1868–1932) relied heavily on European and local minority experts to promote military and economic reforms.[6]

By the end of the nineteenth century, in response to colonial aggression, Muhammad 'Abduh (1849–1905) launched a reform of Islamic thought. The reformer of Al-Azhar revived *ijtihad* (reinterpretation of the texts in the light

---

[4] Sh. M. Toorawa, "Introduction to the History of the Petty Kings by Adonis," *Journal of Arabic Literature* 23 (March 1992): 27–35. Also the Iraqi 'W. Al-Bayyātī wrote *Andalus in Love, Death, and Exile*, trans. Bassam K. Frangieh (Washington, DC: Georgetown University Press, 1990). See also the Palestinian poet M. Darwīsh, *The Adam of Two Edens: Selected Poems*, ed. Munir Akash and Carolyn Forche (Syracuse, NY: Syracuse University Press and Jusoor, 2000).

[5] S. Fanjul, *Al-Andalus contra España; la forja del mito* (Madrid: Siglo XXI de España, 2000); A. Garcia Sanjuan, "¿Fue al-Andalus un paraíso de tolerancia religiosa?," in Rosa García Gutiérrez, Eloy Navarro Domínguez, and Valentín Núñez Rivera (eds.), *Utopía: los espacios imposibles* (Frankfurt am Main: Peter Lang, 2003), 273; and P. Chalmeta, *Invasión e islamización: la sumisión de Hispania y la formación de al-Andalus* (Jaén: Universidad de Jaén, 2003), 209.

[6] J. Beinin and Z. Lockman, *Workers on the Nile: Nationalism, Communism, Islam, and the Egyptian Working Class, 1882–1954* (Cairo: American University Press, 1988), 8.

of the changed historical necessities) and, while also taking inspiration from the principles of the French Revolution, restored Islam to the original spirit of justice. Muslim, Christian, and Jewish intellectuals participated in the more general debate on the guiding principles of the national state. An important liberal trend, supported first by the Umma party and later by the Wafd, promoted more liberal ideals open to a secular concept of citizenship, guaranteeing the principle of equal rights for minorities. This position was contested first by Hasan al-Banna (1906–49) and later by Sayyid Qutb (1906–66), the founder and ideologue of the Muslim Brotherhood, who developed a more conservative interpretation of Islam, closer to an idealized model of the Community's early days. Both the religious movements and the secular parties played their part in the liberation of the Arab countries, united with the local minorities by a common national spirit.

In this light, our thesis is that the most radical change with respect to minorities was not connected with the Muslim tradition. This change happened at the end of colonial rule, when nationalist leaders sacrificed pluralism for a one-party system, geared to promote the development of the country. Various minority movements were outlawed and persecuted in the name of that nationalist spirit which should have defended their rights. This led the political system toward authoritarianism and corruption. In Egypt the violent repression following the defeat of June 1967 drove some of the more extremist fringes of the Muslim Brotherhood to more radical positions, but at the same time it fostered among others a new phase of democratic openness. In opposition to this repressive nationalist policy, in the 1980s various authoritative scholars, such as Hassan Hanafi in Egypt, took a new look at the role played by the Prophet, stressing the revolutionary aspect of the call for justice, equality, and freedom contained in his message.[7] Emphasis was placed on the Islamic attribute of tolerance and the relative freedom granted to minorities, who had favored its propagation.

To give a comprehensive overview of the most significant aspects of the Arab tradition toward minorities across history is beyond our scope here. It is enough to understand that for a long period this tradition has been liberal—at least if compared with others—and that when this liberal attitude changed it was for reasons that were not religious but rather political, connected with the postcolonial unification of many Arab countries. In this chapter our intention is different and more abstract. We want to discuss some theoretical questions concerning minorities and the Arab world starting with the following premises:

---

[7] H. Hanafi, *Al-Islàm wa'l-thawra, From Dogma to Revolution* (Cairo: Madbuli, 1985); and A. R. Al-Sharqawī, *Muhammad Rasūl al-hurriya* (Cairo: al-Hay'a al-Misriyya al-'Amma li 'l-Kitāb 1978). In the same years, the famous Egyptian intellectuals Tāhā Husayn (1889–1973) and 'Abbās Mahmūd al-'Aqqād (1889–1964) also wrote on this subject.

- In an age of "identity politics," minorities demand forms of recognition, such as language rights, cultural or religious autonomy, regional self-government, or increased political representation.

- The nature of these minority demands and of responses to them vary considerably from culture to culture.

- Our concern is with the way these issues are understood and debated in the relations between the Western and the Arab world.

- By "minorities in the Arab world" we mean here both minorities in Arab-majority countries and Arab minorities in the Western world.

The discussion between the Western and the Arab world on minority rights can be considered part of a larger discussion on multiculturalism. And, no doubt, the global discourse on multiculturalism is shaped by Western liberal-democratic multiculturalism. Nevertheless, every significant area of the world has its own traditions of ethnic and religious coexistence, which may differ from Western approaches. The Arab region is no exception. In particular, Islamic civilization has been multicultural since its very beginning, as we have seen from the first lines of our chapter.

In exploring the interaction between local and global discourses, it is interesting to examine it in both directions. That is, we should examine not only whether or how global discourses are being used or contested within the Arab world, but also how Arab voices and Arab experiences are shaping global discourses. In discussing the issue with our Arab colleagues, we have seen that it is not easy to locate Arab voices within a preformulated Western schema of liberal multiculturalism. Indeed, perhaps the basic motivation behind our chapter consists in trying to understand the reasons for such difficulty.

We believe that there are two main reasons. First, we cannot consider Arab minorities independently from where they are located. Arab minorities in the West confront different challenges than do minorities within the Arab world. In the West, there is a recent history of liberal multiculturalism to be discussed and possibly reexamined in the light of the recent past. Second, the difficulties some Arab scholars and activists find in applying or adapting the Western model of liberal multiculturalism in the Arab world are substantial, and depend on the way in which the relationship between liberalism and multiculturalism is formulated. We believe that this relationship must be rethought and rephrased; even if we do not believe that this revision requires abandoning the basic logic and vocabulary of democracy and human rights (as many postcolonial scholars seem to believe). In addressing this topic, we also face difficult questions of terminology. To talk about "minorities" let alone "minority rights" might already conflict with the way these issues are understood or debated in Arab countries.

We have made an attempt to respond to these fundamental interrogatives by adopting a three-step strategy. First, we present—in the next section—a general framework into which the problem is set. This framework shapes our investigation by separating three levels of liberal-democracy and two contexts through which we will pursue our theoretical objectives (the Arab and the Western). We argue that we cannot discuss multiculturalism coherently until we first get a clearer picture of the possible levels of liberal-democracy.

Second, we explore why the discourse on minority rights is so difficult in the Arab world. Our central claim here is that many Arab countries have not yet achieved the minimal liberal-democratic threshold needed for a discourse on multiculturalism to make sense. For example, in some Arab countries (e.g. Saudi Arabia) women do not yet have the right to be elected or have the full right to vote (e.g. in Algeria), and some minorities are not even citizens (as with many Kurds in Syria). If one accepts the thesis according to which one cannot have proper multiculturalism if there is no prior liberal-democratic citizenship, then it is clear why many Arab scholars are not ready to accept the standard discourse on minority rights. Their claim is that we need liberal-democratic citizenship before we can obtain a proper account of minority rights.

Finally, we discuss the ways in which contemporary multiculturalism has gone into retreat in many Western countries. This fact serves as a motivation to deepen our understanding of multiculturalism from a theoretical point of view. In our view, the retreat from multiculturalism shows that we must go from the classic "liberal multiculturalism" (hereafter LM) to what we call a new "multicultural liberalism" (or ML). This latter model insists on minimal liberal-democracy as a precondition and premise to any multicultural commitments. It is worth noting in this regard that the timing of the supposed crisis of multiculturalism in the West is surely linked to the growth of Islamophobia after the 9/11 terrorist attacks. Denunciations of multiculturalism are now as popular as celebrations of multiculturalism were fifteen years ago. Still, it is unclear what it properly means to be multicultural. There are many ways to be multicultural and correspondingly many ways to deny the very possibility.

To conclude, we will argue that to be multicultural in a sensible and right way—when discussing minorities in the Arab World—one must first be liberal in the sense of pluralist. More generally, liberal-democracy is a precondition for sound multiculturalism. This is so in both the contexts we discuss, the Western and the Arab, albeit in different ways.

ARAB MINORITIES AND LIBERAL-DEMOCRACY

The problem of Arab minorities can be investigated from different points of view:

1. The perspective of a Western observer concerning an Arab minority within a liberal-democratic Western country;

2. The perspective of an Arab observer concerning an Arab minority within a liberal-democratic Western country;

3. The perspective of a Western observer concerning an Arab minority within an Arab country;

4. The perspective of an Arab observer concerning an Arab minority within an Arab country;

5. The perspective of a Western observer concerning a non-Arab minority in an Arab country; and

6. The perspective of an Arab observer concerning a non-Arab minority in an Arab country.

For the sake of simplicity, we only consider Arab and Western observers, taking Arabs as our test-case instead of a more general focus on Muslims that would also include important perspectives such as those of Asian Muslims. We also—and for the same reason—assume that all Arab observers are Muslim (or at least seriously influenced by a generic Islamic doctrine), and that all Western observers are not Muslim. Moreover, even more unrealistically, we draw no distinction between Sunni and Shia, and the Arab Muslim doctrine here considered is a vague and generic Islamic form of background culture. Finally, the fact that we put "liberal-democratic" before "Western country" in the above list must not be taken to be saying that all Western countries are liberal-democratic and that all Arab countries are not so, but is rather a simplification strategy.

Under these simplifying assumptions, it is appropriate to split the analysis into two parts: what happens in the liberal-democratic West, say Europe (which is the core of this first part of the chapter); and what happens in the Arab world (which is the core of the second part). Given this binary framework, we imagine from a normative vantage point that liberal-democracy offers a privileged position that we are universally invited to accept. Of course, we all know there is not only one liberal-democracy but several, and that many people—especially outside the West—would endorse forms of liberal-democracy different from the traditional Western one. Still, normatively, we will pivot our pluralistic approach around a fixed point that consists in approving an ideal form of liberal-democracy. In other words, we take as our starting point that generic liberal-democracy is a precondition for pluralism and consequently for multiculturalism. Of course, this form of liberal-democracy will be thin. We have in mind under the universal acceptance of liberal-democracy only the general agreement on the fact that we prefer a society in which some basic human rights are respected and some consultation procedures are observed.[8]

---

[8] A society that is "decent" in the Rawlsian sense.

If we assume the normative priority of liberal-democracy in this minimal form, then it follows that there are limits to admissible pluralism and that these limits are oriented by the prior legitimation that the common liberal-democratic viewpoint offers.[9] In our interpretation, there are many different ways of justifying this legitimation of liberal democracy, including a wide range of both secular and religious justifications, and these different approaches can coexist. This coexistence of various justifications is possible so long as they are rooted in what Rawls calls "reasonable comprehensive doctrines," the required reasonableness being provided by the fact that all accept the common normative standpoint of liberal-democracy (albeit in a partial and limited way). Continuing with the Rawlsian terminology, in these conditions a fusion of horizons based on an "overlapping consensus" becomes now plausible. Different people, with different beliefs anchored in alternative worldviews, can nevertheless converge on limited political pre-conditions concerning liberal-democracy.

The normative approach, so conceived, provides a transparent vantage point: one assumes that all the participants in this ideal dialog share a common interest in liberal-democracy. This shared political commitment trumps or transcends several distinctions originating in background culture, such as differences in religion, permitting a limited, overlapping consensus. For the same reason, we can imagine that Arab and Western observers of minority rights can converge and constrain the differences coming from their alternative background cultures when fundamental political items are at stake.

The next step consists in assuming that minimal liberal-democracy is part of the shared political culture. Both the observers, the Arab and the Western, share the minimal liberal-democratic political part, whereas they are divided by their respective general comprehensive doctrines. On such a basis, it is possible to conceive of some basic rights that both observers, the Arab and the Western, would like to be respected everywhere when they think of multiculturalism. This means that these rights are conceived of as a priori constraints with respect to the policies that Western and Arab states are authorized to implement. The implication for the discussion of minority rights is that both observers, the Arab and the Muslim, should endorse treatment of minorities that respects basic rights and favors consultation procedures.

This much we assume can be shared across Western and Arab contexts and observers. But now important differences will start to emerge, because under our assumptions Western states are more robustly liberal-democratic. This implies that in the Western context, there will be a stronger claim to protect liberal rights and democratic procedures than in the Arab context. To recognize this fact does not put in doubt the shared minimal liberal-democratic

---

[9] See S. Maffettone, *Rawls* (Cambridge: Polity, 2010).

perspective of the observers, or the form of the overlapping consensus, but does affect the content of this overlapping consensus. In particular, it affects the role of *public reason*.

According to Rawls, public reason does not concern a specific or determinate object, but rather defines the nature and limits of public debate when fundamental questions are at stake within a liberal-democratic society. Public reason concerns the constraints upon the way we address each other in a liberal democracy.[10]

Public reason helps to keep citizens united over fundamental issues of justice under conditions of substantial pluralism, and as such is a virtue of liberal-democratic citizenship that emerges when diversity is at stake. However, there are two ways in which this role can be understood. In the first, more robust, interpretation, public reason depends on a strong point of view from which controversial issues concerning basic justice must be evaluated. In the second, less robust interpretation, public reason depends on the mere convergence of different points of view. From a historical and interpretative perspective, one can maintain that countries with long-standing and firm traditions of liberal-democracy tend to adopt the first, more robust interpretation of public reason, whereas other countries adopt the second, less robust interpretation. Thus Western countries typically adopt the stronger conception of public reason, whereas Arab countries aim to reach the weaker conception of public reason.

To grasp the difference and the similarity between these two contexts, we can think of a situation such as the following. We assume that both the Arab and the Western observer share a political culture in which—from a normative point of view—basic rights and minimal democracy are embedded. Both can achieve this level of what we called the convergence view of public reason. However, a Western liberal-democratic institutional background provides a unifying framework that does not exist in most of the contemporary Arab world. This unifying framework coincides with the adoption of a stronger form of public reason.[11]

In relation to the treatment of minorities, this means that we can presuppose similar attitudes of both Arab and Western observers regarding the general respect of basic rights and minimal democracy. This level coincides with the acceptance of a weak view of public reason. Within the context of Western

---

[10] In Rawls's own account, these constraints apply primarily (a) to arguments regarding "constitutional essentials" and "matters of basic justice"; and (b) to persons occupying certain roles, including most obviously public officials. This leaves considerable space for persons in their private lives to engage in various forms of "non-public" reason.

[11] For the meaning of this distinction see Stephen Macedo, "Why Public Reason? Citizens' Reasons and the Constitution of the Public Sphere" (23 August 2010). Available at SSRN: <http://ssrn.com/abstract=1664085>, accessed September 2013.

liberal-democracy, however, we can advance stronger liberal-democratic claims aligned with a more robust view of public reason.

What are the consequences of this dual system? Note that we have imagined an inclusive duality. Western societies are assumed to possess the protections provided by both weak and strong public reason, whereas Arab societies are assumed to share weak public reason.[12] What difference in protection does this make? Basically, the difference we see is that Arab societies share a more restricted normative plateau. This normative plateau may be seen as similar to the content of basic human rights. In Western societies, by contrast, we purport to adhere to much more.

If true, this distinction would be of paramount importance. The minimalist human rights-like normative plateau that is the concern of the Arab societies as here imagined is a matter of international concern. The violation of its main rules is not solely an internal affair of each state, but rather is something the international community will monitor and criticize, and potentially will even intervene in ways to be decided case by case. By contrast, the more ambitious Western platform of rights is—in standard cases—defended by states in their capacity as representatives of their citizens. The crisis of multiculturalism in the West, we would argue, depends precisely on the fears Western populations nourish that migrants (in particular Muslims) will violate their ambitious system of rights. This system is connected with a robust view of public reason.

We can model the conflict between respect for pluralism and fear of its related risks in the West in roughly game-theoretical terms. We can imagine a tit-for-tat situation, in which Western societies are ready to accept pluralism for migrants but only if migrants themselves are inclined to accept prior basic liberal rules of conduct. As a consequence, states will propose to the representatives of migrants an offer including some liberty rights on the understanding that they will respect some preliminary conditions with respect to the rules of the game as seen by a Western liberal-democratic society. This strategy exemplifies the main difference between what we earlier defined as "liberal multiculturalism" (LM) and "multicultural liberalism" (ML). As we shall see, LM is ready to give rights to minorities first, while hoping for adaptation by the migrant (minority) population later. ML, by contrast, implies that the state bargains in the name of its citizens: migrants will not get multicultural rights except through a prior commitment to respect of public reason.

---

[12] Of course, some societies may not yet have even a weak sense of public reason. In this case they are "before" justice, and the claims of minority cultures are not seen at all.

MINORITIES IN THE ARAB WORLD:
EXAMPLES AND PROBLEMS

There is a standard way in the West to criticize the Arab treatment of minority rights. Arabs, it is said, fail to separate civitas and religion properly mainly because Islamic religious culture has not yet undergone its own critical revision or Reformation. Therefore it is difficult to respect the limits of public reason as we conceive it in Western culture. A fair consideration of Arab history shows that this standard critique is flawed. If there is sometimes a powerful convergence of political and religious authorities within the Arab world, it is due to political motivations, and more particularly with a conception of the "national interest." National interest so interpreted has nothing to do with the impossibility of respecting the limits of public reason in the light of Islam. On the contrary, national interest is often invoked by government forces to resist the demands of all opposition forces, this opposition being voiced together by secular civil society and movements of Muslim inspiration. In this way, national-interest-based power can exercise repressive coercion against the opposition, weakening the status of public reason. In so far as minorities play a role in the camp of the oppositions, as is often the case, they are repressed like other forces of the opposition.

In some countries minorities have been given special political space both in government and opposition. Actually, the old role of the translator and mediator of the Ottoman dragoman has been revived, attributing diplomatic functions to Christians, too, as in the case of the appointment to vice minister for foreign affairs of Boutros-Ghali in Egypt, or Tāriq ʿAzīz's privileged position in Iraq. The situation is rather different in Syria, where a Shi'ite minority, the ʿAlawites, are in power and guarantee a fair degree of autonomy for Christian minorities, but not for ethnic minorities, such as the Armenians and Kurds.[13]

In some geographical areas, as a result of particular historical conditions each country developed its own peculiar characteristics, influenced also by cultural conditions. Algeria, for example, is a particular case since, first, French colonial rule, and then civil conflict, have dramatically penalized the aspirations to self-government and linguistic autonomy of the autochthonous population of the Imazighen. Institutional emergency was the occasion to postpone a response to their demands and claims, blocking the natural

---

[13] The Kurds took part in the Syrian national liberation struggles, but after the United Arab Republic was implemented in 1958, the Syrian government started attacking their rights, and even stripped many of them of citizenship. Since 1962, many Kurds living in Syria have no citizenship, and so cannot officially get married or frequent the public schools or hospitals. See G. Endress, *Islam: An Historical Introduction* (New York: Columbia University Press, 2002); and M. Galletti, *I Curdi nella storia* (Chieti: Vecchio Faggio, 1990), 213–14.

evolution of the movement in favor of linguistic autonomy and the constitution of a party to defend the rights of that important minority. More or less the
same situation arose in Morocco, where, however, at the cultural level greater
scope has recently been granted to the representatives of Imazighen culture.

Lebanon presents a particular political and social fragmentation, so it was
provided with a special constitution that represents a peculiar application of
minority rights law in the Middle East. The Lebanese Constitution is an
exogenous novelty in the emblematic case of the region, where a rigidly secular
mandatory nation, France, backed the creation of a constitution geared to the
protection of the local Christian community. Developed by the mandatory
power in 1922, at the level of the legislative assembly this constitution guaranteed representation of all faiths, in practice defining a system of power based on
the proportions of the communities, with a ratio that favored Maronite Christians. This principle was subsequently confirmed with the Constitution of 1926
and the National Pact of 1943. Suad Joseph observes that reconstruction from
effect to cause of a national community consisting of various ethnic and
religious groups is a myth serving to legitimize relations between state and
groups of citizens.[14] The citizen is guaranteed rights as a member of the group,
and not as an individual; suffice it to recall that full voting rights for women were
achieved only in 1957. We can argue that in Lebanon minority rights are
granted but this does not mean that women enjoy the same rights as men at
work or at school. Culturally, as recent research by Fahima Charafeddine shows,
when economic difficulties arise the girl in a Lebanese family (Muslim or
Christian) will often leave school because the parents will invest in the boy's
school career.[15] Recently the Shi'ite community has been asking for a change in
the constitution because they believe that the voting booth does not respect the
will of the citizen but rather the choice of the leaders of minority groups. The
Lebanese case makes clear that minority rights dealing with all groups in an
egalitarian way may not protect the freedom of individuals within the group.

All this goes to show that the problem of minority rights is not confined to
Islam, but is rather a problem of the political strategies of postcolonial states.
In this respect the Egyptian intellectual Fahmī Huwaydī remarks that if a
citizen does not enjoy rights, it is due to political choices. In fact, in many
Muslim countries non-residents do not enjoy rights, as is the case with Gypsies
and the stateless.[16] It is a situation that shows a whole series of endemic
conflicts arising from migrations amongst the Arab countries themselves; we

---

[14] S. Joseph, *Gender and Citizenship in the Middle East* (Syracuse, NY: Syracuse University Press, 2000), 110–14.

[15] F. Sharaf al-Din, "Al-Mar'a wa 'l-tanmiyya al-mustadāma fī zurūf lubnān," in *al-Mar'ah al-'arabiyya bayna thiql al-waqi'a wa tatalla'āt al-taharrur* (Beirut: Markaz al-Dirasāt al-Wahda al-'Arabiyyah), 239–55.

[16] R. Al-Ghannūshī, *Al-Hurriyyāt al-'ammā fī 'l-dawla 'l-Islāmiyyā* (Beirut: Markaz al-Dirāsāt al-Wahda al-'Arabiyya, 1993), 290–1.

may cite, for example, the expulsion of the Egyptians from Iraq and of the Palestinians from Kuwait at the time of the war in 1991. Another emblematic case is that of the workers from Bangladesh in Dubai and other Gulf Emirates, who have practically no civil rights at all.

REVISING IDEAS ABOUT COMMUNITY
AND INDIVIDUALS WITHIN ISLAM

Legislative shortcomings in defense of the rights and duties of the citizen, regardless of religious creed or ethnic group, inevitably lead to unfair treatment of minorities—not only religious but also ethnic and gender minorities. In order to understand the causes of the problem we will examine three aspects of it: the mandate between governor and subject, the debate on human rights, and, finally, minority rights.

According to the Sudanese historian Abdelwahab El-Effendi, what was missing in the transition from the Ottoman state to the modern national state was the possibility of developing the conscience of a modern citizen. The elites that took over power in the aftermath of the nationalist postcolonial revolutions—generally military—organized themselves in the form of a single dominant party, often at the expense of other existing political groupings, as we have seen. In so doing, however, they did not receive any mandate on the part of the citizens. While ostensibly asserting rights and duties for the citizen, in practice the new order did not comply with the traditional Islamic mandate (*walā'*) holding between governor and subject. According to El-Effendi, there was a transition from *dawla/umma* (state/community) to *dawla/watan* (state/nation), with no room for any emergence of the figure of the citizen in the sense of *mawtin* (citizen in the modern sense of the term).[17] In the absence of a mandate, or of the traditional agreement between governor and subject, there is neither protection for the (minority) *dhimmi* nor respect for the (individual) citizen. The former is no longer recognized by the postcolonial state, and the latter did not have the time and the social conditions to develop meaningful relations or practices of citizenship.

Various other studies dealing with the formation of the Arab national state have pointed out that the birth of the state was not accompanied by any recognition of the rights and duties for the citizens to fulfill *vis-à-vis* the state

---

[17] See Abdelwahab El-Effendi (ed.), *Islam and its Modernity: Essays in Honour of Fathi Osman*, forthcoming; Abdelwahab El-Effendi, "I'adat al-Nazar fi 'l-Mafhūm al-Taqlīdī li 'l-Gāmā'at al-Siyāsiya fi 'l-Islām: Muslim au Muwātin?," in *Al-Muwātina wa 'l-Dimūqrātiyya fī 'l-Buldān al-'Arabiyya, Citizenship and Democracy in Arab Countries* (Beirut: Markaz Dirāsāt al-Wahda al-'Arabiyya, 2001), 55–75.

and vice versa.[18] In relation to this serious shortcoming, the scholar Shaltūt points out that according to the Qur'an diversities were created for mutual awareness and respect, rights and duties therefore, according to the author, being given equally for all: "We created you from a single (pair) of a male and a female, and made you into nations and tribes, that you may know each other (not that you may despise each other). Verily the most honored of you in the sight of God is (he who is) the most righteous of you" (Sura hujurāt: 13).[19]

HUMAN RIGHTS AND MINORITY RIGHTS: THE DEBATE IN ARAB COUNTRIES

Muslim scholars tend to refuse exogenous principles and ideas, but there are still numerous examples of the positive reception of Western theories in Arab countries, both for principles and for practical application, as for example we see with the Lebanese Constitution. We have said that the minimal platform of public reason includes some respect for human rights. Let us consider how their specific content is understood within the Arab debate.

The authority of human rights, and the purposes they serve, have been called into question ever since the proclamation of the Universal Declaration of Human Rights in 1948. Suffice it to consider, for example, Saudi Arabia's refusal to embrace the Declaration as not being based on Islamic principles.[20] The effective status of the Declaration in the Arab world is somewhat controversial. Formally it is a United Nations Charter subscribed to by many Islamic states, but in practice not all of them apply it. And the applicability of the Declaration of Human Rights varies, as does the formal institutionalization of these rights, given difficulties of jurisdiction, lack of appropriate protection, and interpretative doubts about their global or specific meaning in relation to the persons (individuals or groups) to whom they refer. Eventually Islamic organizations issued their own Universal Islamic Declaration on Human Rights, and even if it is addressed to Muslims it declares that in principle one has the right to profess another faith.[21]

However, the last few decades have seen an important development: a great many NGOs, both secular and religious,[22] have adopted a human rights

---

[18] Abdelwahab El-Effendi "I'adat al-Nazar fi 'l-Mafhūm al-Taqlīdī li 'l-Gāmā'at al-Siyāsiya fī 'l-Islām: Muslim au Muwātin?"

[19] M. Shaltūt, *Al-Islām 'aqīda wa shar'iyya, Islam and Legal Reason* (Cairo: Dār al-Shurūq, 1992), 452. Shaltūt was the Shaikh of Al-Azhar during the Nasser government.

[20] F. M. Corrao, "Human Rights in Islam," *Journal of Oriental Studies* 9 (1999): 78–95.

[21] A Muslim Commentary on the Universal Declaration of Human Rights is in Ann E. Mayer, *Islam and Human Rights, Tradition and Politics* (Oxford: Westview, 1999), 23 and 159–60.

[22] Campanini e Mezran, *I Fratelli Musulmani* (Torino: Utet, 2010); see also the Muslim Brotherhood website, <http://www.ikhwanweb.com>, accessed September 2013.

culture and struggle to obtain respect for it, as was evident during Arab Spring revolutions. Reflecting on the phenomenon, we have elsewhere argued the need to start thinking rights anew, comparing various ethical and juridical conceptions in order to formulate a more widely accepted view of human rights.[23]

Secular—or, better, military—powers have shown scant concern for minorities, apart from Lebanon and Syria. Nevertheless, the crisis in relations between religious and political minorities on the one hand, and dominant powers on the other, has led to some further hard thinking. Some moderate Muslim jurists and scholars have expressed a new approach to the issue.

Let us recall first that the four major schools of Islamic law converge on respect for religious minorities, although at the present state of debate certain points of discrimination persist, including the tax system, access to positions of power, military service, and, in some cases, citizenship. In the broader debate on our subject, we can note at least four major trends: one essentially secular, open to modernization; one based on a religious conception, proposing a modern, liberal reinterpretation of Islam; another one, more conservative at the religious level, but liberal in economic terms; and, finally, an intransigent faction currently associated with a conservative approach to the message of the Qur'an. We will briefly review these four trends.

Tariq al-Bishri, of Al-Azhar University, has written an important study on minorities from a religious point of view but open to a more secular approach, where he considers minorities within the frame of the modern national Muslim state.[24] Today, perusing the writings of authoritative experts in religious education such as the popular Imām Yūsuf al-Qarḍāwī and 'Abd al-Hamid Kishk, we still find a great number of limitations to their concept of the legally constituted state.[25] According to al-Qarḍāwī, within a more conservative position, it is logical to hold that Qur'anic law should prevail in a country where the majority is Muslim, just as in democracies minorities bow to the decisions of the majority.[26] Moreover, he points out, at this level Islam offers Christians greater guarantees than the secular system. Kishk argues that

---

[23] S. Maffettone, *La pensabilità del Mondo, World Thinkability* (Milan: Il Saggiatore, 2006).

[24] According to Tarik al Bishri, non-Muslims can participate in government in Muslim societies, see El-Effendi (ed.), *Islam and its Modernity*; and El-Effendi, "I'adat al-Nazar fī 'l-Mafhūm al-Taqlīdī li 'l-Gāmā'at al-Siyāsiya fī 'l-Islām," in *Al-Muwātina wa 'l-Dimūqrātiyya fī 'l-Buldān al-'Arabiyya, Citizenship and Democracy in Arab Countries* (Beirut: Markaz Dirāsāt al-Wahda al-'Arabiyya, 2001), 55–75.

[25] M. G. Kisk, "Les Minorités dans l'état islamique," in F. Huwaydī, "Des Citoyans, pas des dimmīs," in *Al-Dimma l'Islam et les minorités religieuses*, Études Arabes. Dossiers 80–1 (Rome: PISAI, 1991/1–2), 191–201, 233–55. Today applications of these principles differ in the various Islamic states. Even those who refer back to the Constitution of Medina give a modern interpretation of them. In the course of history some happy cases and times are recorded during the Abbasid Caliphate (750–1258), but also episodes of persecution, for example the cases mentioned by the Christian poet Ibn Rūmī (836–96).

[26] al-Qarḍāwī, "Un Islam évolué... ou une évolution musulmane?" *Islam et laïcité* 91/2 (1996–7): 112–27.

as Christians theorize separation between state and church, they cannot have access to the centers of political power.

Moroccan ʿAbbās al-Ḡarrārī theorizes that minorities are to be exempt from military service, while Huwaydī holds that they can play their part in defending the country.[27] However, these positions do not take into account the rights of the single individual, regardless of religious faith or ethnic origins. Tariq Ramadan, the Muslim scholar nephew of Hasan al-Banna, believes that non-Muslim minorities in Arab countries must be respected according to the pact of protection as it is the will of God.[28]

Hassan Hanafi has developed a new current of thought open to comparison with the UN Human Rights Declaration and developments in liberation theology. The Egyptian philosopher has taken a positive approach to traditional texts, pointing up the principles of social solidarity, human rights, respect, and tolerance to be found there. Hanafi believes that minorities are respected in the Islamic state, and to prove it he quotes the example of the Andalusian symbiosis, writing that it was not an isolated case. He affirms that this was the perfect example for "high respect and cooperation [that] shows one multidimensional community, a common citizenship irrespective of religion or ethnicity, in which religious denomination is a free individual choice, while citizenship is a common denominator."[29]

Many of these opinions frame the question in a group-oriented way, in terms of the relation between the Muslim community and minority groups. In traditional Islamic culture the community has priority over the individual, the latter being defined as believer.[30] In this connection the Syrian philosopher and poet Adonis, commenting on Islamic culture in terms of the current Salafite interpretation, writes "we find in this religious culture no room for the individual personality to be able to move about freely, to confirm or deny, refuse or accept, doubt or believe. Subjectivity is dissolved in the nation community."[31] This is the major point of the discussion for Adonis: respect for the rights of the individual comes before any abstract rights of minorities.

---

[27] ʿA. al-Ḡarrārī, "Pour une vision cohérente des non-musulmans en pays d'Islam, aujourd'-hui," in *Al-Dimma l'Islam et les minorités religieuses*, 205–13.

[28] Yusuf Qaradhawi, *Il lecito e l'illecito nell'Islam* (Massafra: pub. n.k., 2005), 322–3; and T. Ramadan, *Islam, le face à face de la civilization* (Amman: Tawhid, 1996), 158–61, 164–5.

[29] H. Hanafi, *Islam in the Modern World* (Cairo: Dar Kebaa Bookshop, 2000), ii. 288–9.

[30] C. Wagley and M. Harris, *Minorities in the New World: Six Case Studies* (New York: Columbia University Press, 1958), 10.

[31] Adonis, *Beirut. La non-città*, trans. A. Celli (Milan: Medusa, 2007), 88; Adonis, *The Black Ocean* (Beirut: Dar Al Saqi, 2005). The emergence of the Salafiyya current is dated to the times of Ibn Taymiyya (14th century); it was eventually taken up again with the work on the modernization of Islam by Muhammad Abduh, advocating, at the end of the 19th century, a return to the purity of the original Islam of the times of the Prophet. What marks out Abduh's approach is its openness to renewal, developed with some of his disciples. See H. Lauzière, "The Construction of Salafiyya: Reconsidering Salafism from the Perspective of Conceptual History," *International Journal of Middle East Studies* 42 (2010): 369–89; and Endress, *Islam*.

According to another influential Syrian philosopher, Sadik al-Azm, the very concept of rules based on the rights of the "citizen" is, in essence, alien to Islamic law. Reacting against this practice, al-Azm urges the need to found a secular state guaranteeing freedom of opinion for every single citizen. This principle would give equal rights to the minorities, with an approach undreamt of even within the most advanced system of the Ottoman millet.[32]

If we consider the perspective of Arab observers in Europe, we find opposite positions. For the Syrian philosopher Bassam Tibi, it is necessary to implement both citizens' rights and human rights, because Islam can accept Western values.[33] Tariq Ramadan asserts that Arab minorities in liberal democratic Western countries suffer because corrupt governments violate human rights both in secular Europe and in Islamic countries. He believes that different concepts of human rights must be confronted in order to find a convergence, because to impose one opinion over the other is not a solution because it can create reciprocal rejection.[34] On this specific point also, the Moroccan philosopher al-Jabri wrote that adopting exogenous theories is doomed to fail, and therefore it is more appropriate to study Islamic sources and create a proper response to modern needs within its tradition.[35]

Artists denounce the political exploitation of rivalries between the various religious communities. Recently the Egyptian poet and philosopher Hasan Teleb dedicated a poem to the tensions between Muslims and Christians in Egypt.[36] The Copts protested the limitations imposed on the building of new churches. Teleb offers his body on which to display a cross, because he wants to build bridges between people and bring harmony with the environment: "If you want to draw a cross, just do it on my body. I would create a temple for each religion of my country."[37] The poet also warns against the risks arising from the widespread tendency to distinguish and separate, bringing out only the negative aspects in contrasting positions. This warning is also presented in the writings of another eastern philosopher, Daisaku Ikeda, who underlines

---

[32] From the eighteenth century the Ottoman Empire accorded special privileges (or "capitulations") to foreign powers that were extended to the Christian communities; these acquired fiscal privileges in trade gaining advantage over the Muslims; see F. M. Corrao, *La Rinascita Islamica: Il nazionalismo di Muhammad Farīd* (Palermo: Quaderni del Laboratorio Antropologico Universitario, 1985), 10–15; E. D. Akarli, *The Problem of External Pressures, Power Struggles and Budgetary Deficits in Ottoman Politics under Abdulhamid II, 1876–1909: Origins and Solutions* (Princeton, NJ: Princeton University Press, 1979).

[33] B. Tibi, *EuroIslam: l'integrazione mancata* (Venice: Marsilio, 2003).

[34] Ramadan, *Islam, le face à face de la civilization*, 164–5.

[35] al-Jabri, *Al-'Aql al-siyasi al-arabi, The Arab Political Reason* (Beirut: Markaz al-Dirāsāt al-Wahda al-'Arabiyya, 2004), 34–5.

[36] On the conditions of minorities in the Middle East, see B. Heyberger, "Eastern Christians, Islam and West: A Connected History," *International Journal of Middle East Studies* 42 (2010): 475–8.

[37] The poem "Draw a cross in the shape of a crescent" is part of a collection of poems in print; a partial French translation was published in *Ahram Ebdo*, 23 April 2008.

that nothing can exist in isolation, cut off from other relationships. The concept of common origin, which extends to the concept of inseparability between life and environment, makes eloquently clear the essential dynamics of life and environment: they are two distinct things, and at the same time always combined. It is a view that leads us to see the issue of relations with minorities from the perspective of interconnection, not of contraposition. An indication not dissimilar from this is to be found in the Qur'an, where it is stated: "Those to whom the Scriptures were given disagreed among themselves through jealousy only after knowledge had been given them" (3: 19). As Muhammad Shaltūt sees it, equality of rights and duties of Muslims, Christians, and Jews is implicit in this verse, and in various other verses of the sacred text.[38] Fahmī Huwaydī, too, asserts that the fact of belonging to the modern state makes all citizens equal before the law, regardless of faith, a principle already upheld in Islam.[39]

Clearly, then, the principle of respect for the citizen and for minorities emerges in both religious and secular discussions. The problem of conflict, as Teleb warns, arises elsewhere, and it is in this further dimension that the causes are to be sought. Why, we ask, is respect for minorities neglected, and how are we to remedy the exclusion of an element present at both the religious and institutional levels? What are the mechanisms through which in the modern Arab state human rights are distorted or neglected to give precedence now to one interest, now to another?

In the last few decades the findings of Arab sociologists have shown that the issue of rights is connected with that of citizenship, the social contract, and the systematic violation of the rights of man. In a recent conference the Bishop of Algiers suggested the possibility that the crisis in relations between religious communities arose from an underlying political cause, pointing out that in any case, in order to overcome conflict between various religious communities and between West and East, it is indispensable to start from the level of information and education, changing the sectarian contents of schoolbooks in both the cultural areas.[40]

As a basis for the reform of rules and regulations and the definition of a social pact there must be the conviction that every human being is, as such, worthy of respect. In fact, human rights are also a matter of protecting the

---

[38] M. Shaltūt, *Al-Islām 'aqīda wa shara'iyyah* (Cairo: Dār al-Shurūq, 1992), 452.

[39] Fahmī Huwaydī believes that in Islam rights and duties are equal for everybody: quoted by Abdelwahab El-Effendi in *Al-Muwātina wa 'l-Dimūqrātiyya fī 'l-Buldān al-'Arabiyya, Citizenship and Democracy in Arab Countries* (Beirut: Markaz Dirāsāt al-Wahda al-'Arabiyya, 2001), 55–75.

[40] The topic was discussed at the conference organized by the Community of S. Egidio, "Agenda of Living Together: Christians and Muslims for a Future Together," Rome, 23 February 2011; see also *Un destino comune: Cristiani e Musulmani in Medio Oriente*, introd. Andrea Riccardi, I Libri di S. Egidio (Rome: Leonardo International, 2010).

weak from the overwhelming power of the majority. With the emergence of a more liberal, individualistic temperament the very nature of social life will be transformed. In reconciling the positions of people holding creeds, who see in religion the possibility for the development of an individual's spiritual nature, secularism has failed to develop the third fundamental value emerging with the French Revolution, namely, brotherhood. The problem facing a culture that defends the rights of the group, as Islamic culture tends to do in the Salafite tradition, is to tackle the isolation of the individual which leads to the development of that excessive selfishness that emerges in Western society characterized by economic liberalism. Again, from the Eastern point of view, as Ikeda observes, the worry is that ethnic and religious differences are so readily distinguished that they may eventually be approached in absolute terms, with the fundamental error of attributing all the problems to these differences.[41] From Bosnia to the Western Sahara, and as far as Sudan, we see how exaggerated nationalism can lead to the outbreak of violent episodes of xenophobia and racism, as indeed can an excessive stretching of the concept of self-determination.

Growing attention is being paid to these issues and the ongoing debate cannot be simplified or reduced to commonplaces. Awareness of the phenomena, their complexity, and the forms they take is to be cultivated, constituting the necessary basis for future development. In the MENA region, as a result of the recent revolutions, there is a new trend in the relations between governments and citizens. As an example, the King of Morocco, Muhammad VI, has promoted a new Constitution approved by a referendum, where the Sahrawi are accorded more autonomy. The Egyptian al-Wasat party platform, expressing the political wing of the Muslim Brotherhood, declares among its political issues: "Guaranteeing equal citizenship rights to all Egyptians, regardless of religion, sex, race, status or wealth."[42]

In sum, the secular plea is for granting individual rights, needed in a communitarian society such as the Islamic cultural context where the freedom of individuals is not always protected within the group. As for the religious plea, the priority is for defending the rights of the community. For non-Muslim religious minorities in Arab-majority countries, their rights have long been recognized by Islamic law, and so can draw upon historic precedents and religious sources. For Arab minorities living in the Western context, however, as Tariq Ramadan notes, the situation is more difficult. Fearing the disruptive model of extreme individualism in liberal societies, Muslims in the West ask for

---

[41] D. Ikeda, "Toward a World of Dignity for All: The Triumph of Creative Life," <http://www.daisakuikeda.org/main/peacebuild/peace-proposals/pp2011.html>, accessed September 2013.

[42] <http://egyptelections.carnegieendowment.org/2010/09/16/center-al-wasat-party>, accessed September 2013.

special measures to protect the identity of the community, a request that is often seen as contradicting the traditions and core values of the host society.

It should be clear that the treatment of minorities is deeply contested, and deeply contextual. The few examples mentioned so far demonstrate that minority groups in some Arab countries are the elite in power (Sunni in Bahrain), and in others do not even enjoy civil rights (Kurds in Syria). In Europe Muslims are a minority and claim for rights that some Muslim countries do not extend to Christian minorities (Saudi Arabia, for instance). It is evident that each situation needs specific study, and no one formula will work for all. However, we would argue that in all these different contexts, respect for basic liberal rights is essential to promote a peaceful, multicultural society.

It is worth mentioning that in a study on violence against women in Lebanon, Fahima Charafeddine writes that women are vulnerable in every community, regardless of faith. Muslims, Christians, and Druze all have their share of the same cultural behavior.[43] An example is given in the prose of the Lebanese poet Etel Adnan: "They teach to the kids that the boys are superior to the girls. Yes. When Hasan beats Negma, Negma is beaten by her father because she has been beaten by Hasan, and so on...."[44]

These cases show that, contrary to standard postcolonial claims, liberalism is essential to multiculturalism because it fights the logic of power and oppression. In order to create an overlapping consensus in a diverse society, citizens must converge on limited preconditions concerning liberal democracy. Within this perspective we should consider the proposal made by Muhammad Arkoun to create in Europe an institution to educate Muslim scholars, prepared in both Islamic and European law, to be the teachers of a new generation of liberal and Muslim citizens.[45]

A debate on basic rights is required to bring the Islamic point of view into dialog with liberal-democratic concepts. There is on the one hand the need to study Islamic sources in order to give appropriate solutions to the emergence of modernity, and on the other these solutions can be confronted with Western liberal-democratic laws. A discussion can bring about a new culture, secular and religious, open to accepting basic rights and minimal democracy, adopting a weaker form of public reason in Arab countries and a stronger one in the West.

---

[43] F. Sharaf al-Dīn, *Asl wāhid wa suwar kathīrah: Thaqāfatu 'l-'ūnf diddah al-mar'ah fī lubnān* (Beirut: Dār al-Farābī, 2002).

[44] E. Adnan, *Ai confini della luna*, first published in an Italian trans. by Toni Maraini (Rome: Jouvence, 1994), 23; in English, *Master of the Eclipse* (Northampton, MA: Interlink, 2009).

[45] M. Arkoun, "Conclusions du Rapporteur General," in *La Contribution de la civilisation islamique à la culture européenne* (Strasbourg: Council of Europe, 1992), 146–7.

TOWARD MULTICULTURAL LIBERALISM

The case of Arab minorities in Europe raises an interesting confrontation with the Islamic tradition on minority rights and presents problems for traditional Western multiculturalism. The recent retreat from multiculturalism suggests that the traditional reconciliation between the claims of liberalism and the claims of multiculturalism does not work well when Arab minority rights are at stake in Europe. We have identified such traditional reconciliation as "liberal multiculturalism" or LM. To many Europeans, it appears that LM is not able to address Western fears of losing too much of their level of liberal-democracy—and of their strong notion of public reason—when confronted with significant Muslim minorities. While this fear is sometimes dismissed as mere prejudice, it is worth remembering that within Arab countries themselves it is often argued that liberal-democratic citizenship and public reason are necessary premises for accepting multiculturalism. On this basis, we propose multicultural liberalism or ML as an approach that better fits these needs.

The argument in favor of ML is not difficult to understand if we have in mind the case of Muslim migrants in the West and in Europe in particular. Here, we interpret public reason in the light of a Rawlsian view of political liberalism. This view requires not only that the state cannot be used to impose any version of the good life connected with a comprehensive doctrine, but also that citizens cannot force others to act in agreement with any one conception of what is the good life. This requirement is particularly important in relation to those groups that might wish to impose compliance with a comprehensive doctrine on their own members. In the past, there were many examples of Christian sects that had such illiberal ambitions, but today liberals tend to assume that it is Muslim minorities that pose the greatest threat of violating liberal norms. For liberals, these norms set limits on what minorities can and cannot do within a liberal-democratic Western environment. Minorities must, for example, guarantee free exit and liberty of religion to their members; they have to educate children to pluralism; they cannot punish their members in a cruel and unusual way; and cannot impose harmful practices (such as genital mutilation); and so on.

If these requirements are easy to accept for liberals, often they are not so for members of Muslim minorities.[46] Members of Arab minorities in Europe may even feel offended by the imposition of a liberal outlook obliging them to respect rules they do not agree with. Liberals themselves can understand what is at stake here: public reason is after all intended to permit people more independence and autonomy, not less. And this general predicament is

---

[46] Andrew March argues that Muslims can be part of an overlapping consensus on liberalism, but he acknowledges these difficulties; see Andrew March, *Islam and Liberal Citizenship: The Search for an Overlapping Consensus* (Oxford: Oxford University Press, 2009), 97ff.

supposed to be valid also for Muslim citizens and residents in Western states. Still, liberals fear that permitting too much autonomy and independence to members of cultural minorities—in particular if Muslim—can undermine the public-reason-oriented bases of their liberal-democratic regime.

At this point, we can imagine a kind of bargaining situation that we can conceptualize in terms of an assurance game: liberal citizens of Western states want to be assured that the liberties that are quintessential to their political regimes will not be used by cultural minorities to implement illiberal strategies and forms of behavior. In particular, within the framework we have presented, liberal majorities in the West, when confronted with Muslim minorities, are afraid of eroding the strong conception of public reason that is at the centre of their liberal-democratic system. It is here that ML and LM differ. For ML requires a more stringent acceptance of the basic liberal framework before including minority differences within the community. The more stringent acceptance we have in mind coincides with the acceptance by the cultural minorities of a strong conception of public reason.

To reframe the thesis within the terminology of public reason, one could argue that the challenge of multiculturalism can be reframed in the West—and in Europe as a sub-case within the West—as a challenge to a more robust form of public reason. Western countries are afraid of the multicultural challenge because they fear that the differences it introduces in society can be too violent to keep alive the strong conception of public reason they normally adopt in their liberal-democratic citizenization. LM does not give a sufficient response to this perceived danger, whereas ML can.

RECONCILIATION STRATEGY

There is a sort of natural mismatch between "liberalism" and "multicultural-ism." Reconciliation strategies, in this light, try to make multiculturalism compatible with liberalism. The best-known liberal view of liberal multicul-turalism has probably been proposed by Will Kymlicka in numerous and important writings.[47] Liberal multiculturalists claim that states should not only endorse traditional civil, social, and political rights but also recognize the identities and aspirations of ethno-cultural groups.[48] This particular

---

[47] For other influential defenses of multiculturalism, see Charles Taylor, "The Politics of Recognition," in Amy Gutmann (ed.), *Multiculturalism and the "Politics of Recognition"* (Prince-ton, NJ: Princeton University Press, 1992), 25–73; and Nancy Fraser, "Social Justice in the Age of Identity Politics: Redistribution, Recognition and Participation," in Grethe Peterson (ed.), *The Tanner Lectures on Human Values* (Salt Lake City, UT: University of Utah Press, 1998), 1–67.

[48] W. Kymlicka, *Multicultural Citizenship* (Oxford: Oxford University Press, 1995).

reconciliation strategy is based on the idea of recognition. We will mainly allude to Kymlicka's view when we speak of "liberal multiculturalism" or LM.

In general terms, to reconcile liberalism and multiculturalism LM aims to provide a connection between individual autonomy and minority rights. The central idea within this project of reconciliation consists in the "context of choice" view. According to this view, freedom of choice—which is the standard liberal starting point—cannot be context-independent. Freedom of choice, and consequently the possibility to form and revise conceptions of the good life, is, on the contrary, shaped by the cultural milieu in which we are necessarily embedded. In this view, in sum, one cannot reach full autonomy without going through an original cultural context.

The corollary is that often minority groups are deprived of this choice or are at risk of being so. Traditionally these groups were silenced when attempting to exit this marginalized status. LM reasonably argues that this discriminatory situation is not acceptable any more and that traditional liberal "benign neglect" is not enough to protect endangered cultural minorities. This is why we need a normative theory that protects minorities from cultural repression and erosion. Directly protecting the cultural environment of groups and assuming the context-of-choice view, LM also claims indirectly to protect autonomy in the traditional liberal sense. To universalize: if we are all embedded in groups and if true autonomous choice depends on this contextualization, then there is no way to guarantee autonomy but by protecting group rights.

However, multiculturalism often seems to endanger the very possibility of taking liberalism seriously. This mainly depends on two factors: (1) liberalism is based on individual rights and within a multicultural agenda we speak of group rights; (2) these group rights are not part of the traditional liberal agenda that focuses instead on individual civil and political rights. Does the reconciliation strategy of LM avoid this risk? From this point of view LM has been critically discussed at length. In particular, LM has been challenged by (at least) four different alternative approaches: (1) reactionary liberalism, championed by authors such as Brian Barry and Giovanni Sartori, according to which liberalism and multiculturalism inherently promote inconsistent values, and liberalism must resist any multicultural infections or corruptions; (2) the multiculturalism of fear, proposed by Jacob Levy, which criticizes LM for pursuing an ideal justice when it should be more attentive to a kind of negative consequentialism (first: avoid dangers!); (3) anti-essentialist liberal-democracy, championed by authors such as Anne Phillips, Nancy Fraser, Anthony Appiah, and Seyla Benhabib, according to which the legitimate interest of members of minorities can be protected without adopting group-based measures that risk reifying and essentializing cultural differences; (4) postcolonial thought, championed by authors such as Edward Said and Ra-najit Guha, according to which liberalism is intrinsically unable to capture basic features of multiculturalism because it uses a logic of power and oppression to evaluate the situation (e.g. the logic of the colonialists). Postcolonial critics maintain that it is this logic that must be changed.

To these objections, Kymlicka provides a response from the reconciliation strategy standpoint.[49] In order to defend LM, Kymlicka maintains among other things that:

- for LM minority rights are part of a larger human rights revolution and more generally of an enlargement of democratic citizenship;

- LM's defence of minority rights, far from relying on essentialism and a static view of cultures and groups, is in fact transformative of both majority and minority identities;

- LM recognizes the priority of basic liberal-democratic rights (e.g. forced marriage or clitoridectomy are not admitted). For a sound LM not all cultural particularities must be celebrated;

- While LM cannot work in every context, and in particular where ethnic relations are highly securitized and the rule of law is not upheld, these preconditions do exist in the West today.

Whether critics will be persuaded by this reconciliation strategy is open to question: Kymlica's response seems more compelling on some issues than others. The essential doubt concerning LM, however, focuses on the context-of-choice view itself. Within its framework, the reconciliation strategy is based on inserting (independent) communitarian arguments into a liberal-demo-cratic platform. From the contemporary political theory point of view, this implies adopting a perfectionist account of liberalism.[50] This move has sig-nificant consequences in terms of the strategy of public reason we are discuss-ing. In substance, the more you move toward a liberal perfectionist vision, the less you are inclined to accept a strong view of public reason. As a matter of fact, liberal-perfectionist visions—here read in terms of insertions of commu-nitarianism into liberal-democracy—nourish a thick conception of the good. As a consequence, they emphasize respect for diversities and conceive of public reason as a thin umbrella permitting a decent compromise. In other words, liberal-perfectionists tend to be in agreement with a weak view of public reason, rejecting a strong conception. LM is based on such a strategy.

---

[49] See his "Multiculturalism: Success, Failure, and the Future," in Migration Policy Institute (ed.), *Rethinking National Identity in the Age of Migration* (Berlin: Bertelsmann Stiftung, 2012), 33–78.

[50] For the classic statement of perfectionist liberalism, see Joseph Raz, "Autonomy, Toler-ation, and the Harm Principle," in *Issues in Contemporary Legal Philosophy*, ed. Ruth Gavison (Oxford: Oxford University Press, 1987), 313–33. For an overview of the perfectionism vs. neutrality debate within liberal theory, see George Klosko and Stephen Wall, *Perfectionism and Neutrality: Essays in Liberal Theory* (Lanham, MD: Rowman & Littlefield, 2003).

If we reflect upon this conclusion, we can argue that these limits of LM are connected with two perplexities. Cultural pluralism is different from moral-political or ideological pluralism. The latter primarily concerns the conceptions of the good of individuals, whereas the former concerns primarily the comprehensive cultures of groups. The second is eminently private whereas the first is typically public. These differences make cultural pluralism much more problematic in terms of public reason and its associated ideals of state neutrality and the duty of civility.

Authors in favor of LM are natural critics of the serious restraints imposed by public reason. But in renouncing these restraints, LM does not satisfy the assurance problem raised by liberal-democratic majorities in the West. It is here that the ML strategy differs from LM. If those in favor of LM have a propensity to defend a weak view of public reason as contingent convergence, those in favor of ML have instead a propensity to defend a stronger view of public reason. Authors in favor of ML are for a strong common center which for them also permits more peripheral freedoms. In other words, if you want plural jurisdictions or valid religious marriages—inspired by minority traditions—for ML you have to accept a strong common core of liberal-democratic precepts. Communitarian bonds are easily acceptable if and only if you assume pre-given and safe liberal-democratic restraints.

CONCLUSION

We have discussed the situation of cultural minorities—in particular Muslims—within a Western state. ML has been presented as a better strategy than LM to assure Western majorities worried about the ways in which minorities can jeopardize their strong view of public reason. The same kind of argument can be extended to cover different situations, however. In fact, ML seems to be sensible not only where Western majorities fear a weakening of their strong conception of public reason, but also where there is not yet a basic liberal-democratic tradition. If, for example, you take a Confucian universe, it does not make sense to enforce more communitarianism before assuring you have enough liberal-democracy.[51]

The same argument can be used for minorities within the Arab world. As we have seen, many Muslim thinkers find it difficult to even speak of minority rights because they think that liberal-democratic citizenship is a premise for cultural pluralism. There is—according to them—clear evidence that minority

---

[51] In fact, defenders of LM are likely to agree on this point. To give more power to communal authorities in a world without liberal democracy would not go in the direction of more individual autonomy, as the context-of-choice view claims to do.

rights must be preceded by individual liberal rights. Consequently, here too, ML can work better than LM.

What does all this mean in practice? Basically to adopt ML means that there are many liberal-democratic prerequisites for making multiculturalism acceptable. In recent years, LM has offered a reasonable platform of rights that minorities should have been entitled to within the protective umbrella of a liberal-democratic state. These rights include non-discrimination, administrative autonomy, protection of the language of the minority, liberty of religion, alternative education, permission to adopt different dressing styles, and more generally the adoption of a (partial) legal pluralism. ML just says that all these rights are intrinsically acceptable provided that we a priori respect some basic liberal-democratic principles. These principles include securitization, relative secularization, respect for individual autonomy, pluralism in education, and constitutional loyalty. Respect of these principles can be taken as an instrumental good, providing a platform that reinforces and makes stable public reason when significant cultural minorities are present.

Part II

Case Studies

6

Bringing the Tribe Back In? The Western Sahara Dispute, Ethno-history, and the Imagineering of Minority Conflicts in the Arab World

Jacob Mundy

Efforts to ameliorate conflicts between peoples often prescribe various forms of territorial power-sharing: asymmetrically devolved government, special regional status, autonomy statutes, federalist arrangements, interstate confederation—to name the most popular.[1] This is particularly the case with conflicts whose geography seems to have a sub-state or sub-regional character. In so far as state-making is never finished (the state is never definitively "right-sized"[2]), the track record for each and all of these approaches is unproven. Even in the world's most wealthy and militarily powerful countries, centrifugal and centripetal state dynamics are still in play centuries after Westphalia ostensibly ushered in the modern international system or even decades after the United Nations allegedly fixed the parameters of the international system.[3] The 2008 global economic crisis has not only brought EU expansion to a grinding halt, it has also led serious commentators to speculate as to whether or not the confederation will survive the test of financial strain. While politicians in the United Kingdom continuously debate withdrawal from the European Union, Scottish independence and Northern Ireland's secession remain

---

[1] For background on these approaches and their application to "ethnic" conflicts, see John McGarry and Brendan O'Leary, "Territorial Approaches to Ethnic Conflict Settlement," in Karl Cordell and Stefan Wolff (eds.), *Routledge Handbook of Ethnic Conflict* (New York: Routledge, 2010).

[2] Brendan O'Leary, Ian Lustick, and Thomas M. Callaghy (eds.), *Rightsizing the State: The Politics of Moving Borders* (Oxford: Oxford University Press, 2001).

[3] For a critique of the mythology of Westphalia, see Stephen D. Krasner, *Sovereignty: Organized Hypocrisy* (Princeton, NJ: Princeton University Press, 1999).

vivid possibilities. The recent blunting of Catalonian efforts to seek maximal autonomy by Spain's supreme court might only have convinced many in the region to seek definitive independence. Belgium, host of the European Union, is likewise facing a crisis stemming from its bilateral federalism, which has only helped nourish the polity's divisions. Central characters on the national political stage in the United States now proudly boast prior involvement in state-based secessionist movements, notably the larger states of Texas and Alaska.

Elsewhere, the picture is just as undecided. As much as the implosion of Yugoslavia problematized the relationship between weak states and failed states, the "Dutch disease" oil curse similarly problematizes any relationship between the wealth of a polity and the health of one. In what should be one of the world's richest countries, Nigeria's approach to federalism—states that cantonize identity groups—has haphazardly created a political environment in which the incentive structures of rentierist politics have in fact resulted in the "parcelization of sovereignty" that has undermined efforts to consolidate the postcolonial state there.[4] The approach of the Comprehensive Peace Agreement for Sudan—to demonstrate to the Southern Sudanese the advantages of autonomy and power-sharing within the Sudanese state before the final status vote—failed to find purchase with the people of what is now Africa's newest state. Conversely, schemes to engineer a Palestinian roadmap to a two-state peace via the endgame of gradated autonomy for the Palestinians (notably, the Oslo Accords) has led to a cul-de-sac where the ostensibly impossible—a one-state solution—now seems increasingly imaginable. Various "federalist" designs seeking to accommodate a trifurcated ethno-sectarian picture of the Iraqi polity[5] have, according to critics, created a de facto Kurdish state.

The jury is out on territorialized power-sharing but it will never render a definitive verdict. In the meantime, some observations are worth noting. As much as the problems of the postcolonial world can be attributed to the sudden "importation"[6] of a certain mode of Western European governmentality (i.e. the nation-state), similar questions can be asked about the routine prescription of territorialized power-sharing by the conflict resolution industry to meet its short-term needs (cessation of hostilities, erecting a neoliberal

---

[4] Michael Watts, "Blood Oil: The Anatomy of a Petro-Insurgency in the Niger Delta, Nigeria," in Andrea Behrends, Stephen P. Reyna, and Günther Schlee (eds.), *Crude Domination: An Anthropology of Oil* (New York: Berghahn, 2011), 67, citing Achille Mbembe, "At the Edge of the World," *Public Culture* 12/1 (2001): 259–84.

[5] For background, see Gareth Stansfield, *Iraqi Kurdistan: Political Development and Emergent Democracy*, Advances in Middle East and Islamic Studies (New York: Routledge Curzon, 2003).

[6] Bertrand Badie, *The Imported State: The Westernization of the Political Order*, trans. Claudia Royal (Stanford, CA: Stanford University Press, 2000). See also Robert H Jackson, *Quasi-States: Sovereignty, International Relations, and the Third World* (New York: Cambridge University Press, 1993).

political-economic order, the restoration of state–society relations). This question seems to have particular import given the fact that most models of territorial power-sharing are also drawn from the European experience of over five hundred years of state-building. Are there more culturally apposite forms of territorialized power-sharing to be found in the specific histories of the people in conflict rather than the annals of European state-making?

All the contributions to this volume make reference, whether directly or indirectly, to the tensions between cultural contestation in the Arab world and the dictates of the international system's state-based ontology. But among all the cases under examination here, the Western Sahara conflict initially presents itself as an interesting exception. The broad lines of difference structuring the dispute between Sahrawi nationalists and Morocco appear as if the conflict is both intra-ethnic and intra-religious. Rather than as a dispute based on linguistic, ethnic, or religious claims (or a combination of all three), one might be tempted to see the Western Sahara conflict as providing a unique space wherein more subtle lines of difference could be bridged through the identification of terms of shared historical and cultural reference. After all, the Moroccan state and the Western Sahara independence movement primarily identify themselves as Arab-dominated polities; both prioritize the Arabic language; and, like most Muslims in Africa, Moroccans and Sahrawis are Sunnis of the *Mālikī madhhab*. As a conflict that seemingly pits Arab against Arab and Sunni against Sunni, Western Sahara seems like the perfect site to test the idea that Arab problems require Arab solutions.

For several reasons, this chapter finds fault with this initial problematization of minority–majority conflicts in the Arab world, as well as the suggestion that the contested realities of the Western Sahara conflict can be neatly plotted into its abstract schema. By problematization, I mean the assertion of a problem–solution dyad where supposed Arab reluctance to confront minority issues is addressed by prescribing forms of power-sharing that are ostensibly more culturally legitimate than Western models.[7] As scholars have repeatedly underscored since Talal Asad's *Anthropology and the Colonial Encounter* and Edward Said's *Orientalism*,[8] the initial fault of this problematization rests in the reproduction of pragmatically untenable and politically irresponsible constructs such as the "Arab world," "Arab states," "Arab opinion," "the Arab street," etc.[9] These critiques are well known and are taken as the starting

[7] See David Campbell, *National Deconstruction: Violence, Identity, and Justice in Bosnia* (Minneapolis: University of Minnesota Press, 1998), pp. x–xi, citing Michel Foucault and Paul Rabinow, "Polemics, Politics and Problematizations," in Paul Rabinow (ed.), *The Foucault Reader* (New York: Pantheon Books, 1984).

[8] Talal Asad (ed.), *Anthropology and the Colonial Encounter* (London: Ithaca, 1973); and Edward W. Said, *Orientalism* (New York: Vintage, 1994).

[9] See also David Prochaska and Edmund Burke III (eds.), *Genealogies of Orientalism: History, Theory, Politics* (Lincoln: University of Nebraska Press, 2008); Diana K. Davis and Edmund

point for this examination. The critique launched here is an investigation into the problematic features of naming such things as "Arab solutions" to an "Arab problem" of minority relations in Southwest Asia and North Africa, as well as the nuanced ways in which Moroccan and Sahrawi nationalisms construct themselves. As this chapter will argue, both Moroccan and Sahrawi nationalisms are of recent invention. Ethno-histories cannot be treated as neutral historical artifacts. The haphazard deployment of ethno-history in the effort to "imagineer" solutions to contemporary conflicts not only reproduces a dangerous technique within colonial governmentality, whose disastrous lagged effects have become well understood in such cases as the Rwandan genocide, it also presumes the existence of an international politics that does not obtain. The structure of the international system itself—ostensibly declarative, in reality constitutive—places decisive constraints upon the ways in which parties to a conflict are allowed to re-imagine the institutional and territorial limits of sovereignty.

WESTERN SAHARA AND THE ARAB CONTEXT

Upon initial inspection, the Western Sahara conflict might appear to have interesting resonances with the problematization under examination here, that problematization being that if the broader Arab world seems antipathetic towards minority struggles, could an alternative framing of these struggles—particularly a framing that draws upon a more autochthonous lexicon of power-sharing—elicit a more positive response politically and socially? Such an approach might also lay the groundwork for more durable outcomes to seemingly intractable conflicts. This problematization, however, falters in the face of sustained interrogation. Subsequent sections of this chapter will analyze the Western Sahara conflict *vis-à-vis* Morocco's self-understanding as an ancient state and Sahrawi self-understanding as a nation. These sections will underscore the politicization of ethno-history so as to render the solution aspect of our problematization—i.e. the search for more culturally legitimate forms of territorial power-sharing—untenable. The purpose of this section is to unpack the initial diagnosis of the problematization and highlight its insufficiencies and contradictions.

Over the course of the past quarter century, the Morocco–Polisario struggle over Western Sahara has become mired in a UN peace process that lacks as

Burke (eds.), *Environmental Imaginaries of the Middle East and North Africa* (Athens, OH: Ohio University Press, 2011); and Michael E. Bonine, Abbas Amanat, and Michael Ezekiel Gasper (eds.), *Is There a Middle East? The Evolution of a Geopolitical Concept* (Stanford, CA: Stanford University Press, 2012).

much political imagination as it does political will. The latter is often attributed to the conflict's paucity of atrocious, "conscience shocking" violence and a related issue: the now two-decades-old ceasefire, which has produced a tolerable status quo for all the parties involved, the UN Security Council included. Part of the problem rests with the ethno-historical imaginations of the antagonists; the Kingdom of Morocco insists that, apart from the colonial interregnum of the first half of the twentieth century, it has had absolute sovereignty over Western Sahara for centuries. The view of most Sahrawi nationalists, claiming an ancient ethnic *habitus* of resistance to foreign domination,[10] can be summed up in Polisario's rallying cry: *Kūl al-watan aw al-shahīdah* (All the homeland or martyrdom).

The conflict was triggered in October 1975 when Morocco invaded the then Spanish administered colony.[11] Morocco's invasion deliberately aimed to prevent Spain from holding a referendum on independence in Western Sahara, as the International Court of Justice had recommended in its landmark opinion against the territorial designs of Morocco and Mauritania on the Spanish colony.[12] The apparent popularity of the Polisario independence movement in Western Sahara, which had formed in 1973 to fight Spanish rule, suggested that the population widely rejected the idea of joining with either Morocco or Mauritania. Fearing a colonial war with its neighbor to the south, Madrid opted to cut an illegal deal with Rabat and Nouakchott, and then promptly handed the territory over to them within four months.[13] With strong backing from Algeria, Morocco's regional adversary, as well as Libya, Polisario focused its efforts on fighting the new occupiers and escorting the large number of Sahrawi refugees fleeing the violence and instability. Approximately forty percent of the native Sahrawi population has since lived in exile as refugees in four camps near Tindouf, Algeria, where Polisario runs the *República Árabe Saharaui Democrática* (RASD, Saharan Arab Democratic Republic), a state-in-exile that has been recognized by over seventy governments and the African Union. Today roughly three-quarters of the territory is under Moroccan occupation (Mauritania withdrew in 1979), leaving two small areas under nominal Polisario control. The refugees in Algeria, meanwhile, now number over 120,000, while Sahrawi youth demonstrations in the occupied territory break out frequently, notably in 1999, 2005, and November 2010.

---

[10] Parroting this construction of Sahrawi identity, J. Mercer, "The Cycle of Invasion and Unification in the Western Sahara," *African Affairs* 75/301 (1976): 498–510.

[11] Jacob Andrew Mundy, "Neutrality or Complicity? The United States and the 1975 Moroccan Takeover of the Spanish Sahara," *Journal of North African Studies* 11/3 (2006): 275–306.

[12] Thomas M. Franck, "The Stealing of the Sahara," *American Journal of International Law* 70/4 (1976): 694–721.

[13] Hans Corell, "Letter dated 29 January 2002 from the Under-Secretary-General for Legal Affairs, the Legal Counsel, addressed to the President of the Security Council," UN Document S/2002/161.

It is believed that Moroccan settlers inside Western Sahara, whether of Arab or Amazigh origin, now outnumber the native Sahrawis by as much as two to one.

The war between Morocco and Polisario lasted until 1991, when the United Nations orchestrated a ceasefire to be followed by a referendum on independence organized by the *Mission des Nations Unies pour l'Organization d'un Référendum au Sahara Occidental* (MINURSO, UN Mission for the Referendum in Western Sahara). What followed was eight years of wrangling about the modalities of the vote, particularly the question of how to identify the native Sahrawi electorate. Once Rabat's efforts to pollute the electorate with Moroccans posing as Sahrawis became clear, Morocco decided that it was no longer willing to participate in a peace process where independence is an option.[14] In the decade since, the UN Security Council has pushed various mediators to find the seemingly non-existent middle ground between Western Sahara's right to a referendum on independence, as championed by Polisario and Algeria, and Morocco's insistence that its sovereignty over Western Sahara must first be recognized. In 2007, Morocco put forward a concrete autonomy proposal, which was quickly rejected by Polisario. Two UN mediators have convened a series of negotiations but little progress has been reported.

In the Arab world, the Western Sahara conflict is as obscure as it is in the broader agenda of the international community.[15] Though the dispute has had a profound effect upon North Africa since Morocco and Polisario first traded shots in late 1975, the conflict in Western Sahara ranks among the least-known struggles in the Arab world. The striking parallels with the Palestinian case—belligerent occupation, significant displacement of the native population, state-sponsored settlement by the foreign power—have been seemingly lost on broader Arab public opinion. It is, however, often represented as one of the few majority–minority conflicts in the region that is both Arab–Arab and Sunni–Sunni. Even in Algeria, which is Polisario's main backer, public outcry and organizing in support of Sahrawi rights is minimal and often state-managed. The failure of Polisario to receive stronger support from Arab opinion is not lost on the independence movement's leaders or Sahrawi

---

[14] Accounts of the failed UN referendum process: Charles Dunbar, "Saharan Stasis," *Middle East Journal* 54 (2000): 522–45; Adekeye Adebajo, *Selling Out the Sahara: The Tragic Tale of the UN Referendum*, Occasional Papers Series (Ithaca, NY: Institute for African Development, 2002); Erik Jensen, *Western Sahara: Anatomy of a Stalemate* (Boulder, CO: Lynne Rienner, 2005); and Anna Theofilopoulou, *The United Nations and Western Sahara: A Never Ending Affair* (Washington, DC: United States Institute for Peace, 2006).

[15] Even in scholarship, Western Sahara is an extremely neglected case even when it should be treated as seminal to the subject matter: e.g. Tozun Bahcheli, Barry Bartmann, and Henry Felix Srebrnik (eds.), *De Facto States: The Quest for Sovereignty* (New York: Routledge, 2004); and Nina Caspersen and Gareth R. V. Stansfield (eds.), *Unrecognized States in the International System* (New York: Routledge, 2011).

nationalists in general.[16] Western Sahara was even deliberately left off the founding agenda of the *Union du Maghreb Arabe* (UMA, Arab Maghreb Union, composed of Mauritania, Morocco, Algeria, Tunisia, and Libya), which helps account for its successful launch in the late 1980s. Now, however, Western Sahara helps account for its dismal lack of progress over the last two decades. One of the more striking features of the antagonism between Morocco and Algeria *vis-à-vis* Western Sahara is its selective application. Where the Western Sahara issue has disabled the UMA and fractured the AU, it has rarely been brought up by Morocco or Algeria in other places, such as the Barcelona Process (Euro-Med), launched by the European Union in 1995. Any simplistic picture of Morocco and Algeria constantly at each other's throats over Western Sahara should be tempered by an acknowledgment of the areas where they have strong mutual interests. Though their land borders have been closed for years, that has not stopped Algeria from exporting natural gas to Europe via a pipeline that transits through Morocco.[17]

As the question of Western Sahara has never been included in any regional public opinion polls, the only way to gauge Arab views on the issue is to look at a highly flawed source: the region's governments and institutions, including the media. Despite Polisario's attempt to represent the Sahrawi identity as primarily Arab, Western Saharan nationalism has not been strongly embraced in Arab political fora. Both the Arab League and the Organization of Islamic Cooperation (OIC) have remained antagonistic towards Polisario, though without formally endorsing Moroccan sovereignty over Western Sahara. Indeed, no state in the world has officially recognized Morocco as the *de jure* power in Western Sahara, though many have offered rhetorical support for Morocco's position generally or, more specifically, for Rabat's 2007 autonomy proposal to Polisario. Western Sahara's low profile in the Arab League has been related to the bloc's need to prioritize more important issues (i.e. the Palestinian cause[18]) and to maintain harmony amongst members (i.e. the now

---

[16] Lamine Bouhali, SADR's minister of defense, complained about the Arab League to an Algerian paper, *Le Jeune independent*: "During Hassan II's Green March on Western Sahara, the Arabs of Egypt and the Gulf as well as Saudi Arabia and even Sudan supported Morocco. They accused us of being Communists. Frankly, the problem of the Arabs is strange! Why this hostility? Why this hatred? Why this money designed to exterminate Saharans? Billions of dollars have been given to Morocco so it can provide itself with fighter planes, tanks, and so on. I cannot explain this frenzy." See BBC Worldwide Monitoring, "Western Saharan 'defence minister' says 'we are headed towards war' with Morocco,'" 22 May 2008 (retrieved via LexisNexis). On a similar note, a Sahrawi friend once insisted to me that when Western Sahara becomes independent, the Sahrawis will demand that RASD change its name to the Saharan *African* Democratic Republic. "What have the Arabs done for us?", she asked rhetorically.

[17] Yahia H. Zoubir, "In Search of Hegemony: The Western Sahara in Algerian–Moroccan Relations," *Journal of Algerian Studies* 2 (1997): 43–61.

[18] As an example of the priority of the Palestinian issue: a report from 1984 suggested that Syria was willing to offer aid to Polisario in its war against Morocco so that Algeria would not support divisions within the PLO (Judith Miller, "Battle within the PLO threatens a formal split," *New York Times*, 18 November 1984, 1, retrieved via LexisNexis).

shifting balance between the monarchies and the republics). The Arab League's apparent bias towards Morocco, however, is not an indication of a wholesale rejection of Sahrawi claims; in addition to Algeria, other Arab states—Mauritania, Libya, Syria, and, for what it is now worth, South Yemen—have all recognized the RASD at one point or another. Nor does any of this actually count as sufficient evidence of a regional unwillingness to accommodate minority rights. The question of whether or not the Arab League and, to a lesser extent, the OIC are reliable barometers of regional attitudes towards minority rights claims should be treated with as much caution as ever. If anything, the "Arab Spring" of 2011—which first manifested in Western Sahara in 2010 before protests broke out in Tunisia[19]—has elucidated the divide separating the populations and governments in North Africa and Southwest Asia. The simple point is that Arab non-recognition of the RASD cannot serve as an indicator of Arab attitudes towards the Sahrawis as a minority nor as an indicator of an antipathy towards minority struggles in the Arab world generally.

To say that the African Union is more sensitive to minority rights because it recognizes Western Sahara as a state, albeit occupied, is also an unwarranted reading of the situation. Rather, the African Union's primary concerns are *uti possidetis* (the sanctity of colonial borders) and self-determination (the right of colonies to choose independence), which are the principles grounding the existence of most African states but which Morocco has so blatantly violated in Western Sahara. Note the ambivalence in the Arab League's passive support for Morocco and the African Union's active support for Polisario. Nearly two-thirds of the Arab world's population resides in Africa (Mauritania to Egypt), and so the majority of Arabs and their governments ostensibly recognize RASD multilaterally, given their membership within the African Union, even if they do not recognize RASD bilaterally.[20] That the Western Sahara conflict could provoke almost contradictory reactions in two leading inter-governmental organizations is, from one point of view, nothing more than another banal example of international affairs' "organized hypocrisy."[21] From

---

[19] Jacob Andrew Mundy, "Western Sahara's 48 Hours of Rage," *Middle East Report* 257 (2011).

[20] Hence the debate between African and Arab states at the end of 2011 as to whether or not Morocco, rather than Mauritania (a state that recognizes RASD), should get the UN Security Council seat set aside for Arab states from Africa's allotment. In the end, Morocco won the vote. Regarding the "Arab-ness" of Northwest Africa, there is a growing awareness in the region that its peoples can no longer be simply bifurcated into an Arab majority and Amazigh minority groups as was the tendency given the Arab Nationalism that dominated the postcolonial regimes. Whatever the reason (cynical or not), political leaders in Morocco and Algeria now openly boast the Amazigh origin of all North Africans, suggesting that the days of casually referring to "Arab North Africa" might be coming to a close.

[21] Krasner, *Sovereignty: Organized Hypocrisy*.

another point of view, this ambivalence suggests that Western Sahara cannot serve as an index of Arab—or African—views toward minority struggles.

As is well known, the claim that Arab public opinion is antagonistic towards minority rights claims per se is seemingly undermined by the Palestinian issue, which consistently ranks among the top international concerns registered within Arab polities.[22] Perhaps more than any other global constituency, Arabs are generally more aware of the fact that Palestinians—*vis-à-vis* Jewish citizens of Israel—are not a minority by pure demography; indeed, the opposite is true. It is only by certain tactics of political geography aiming to cantonize them into three groups that Palestinians become minorities: Palestinian Israelis, Palestinians under occupation, and extra-territorial Palestinian refugees. The same recognition should be brought to bear on other cases as well. Minorities are not given; they are made through the machinations of politics, contingencies of history, forces of economic flow, the location of borders, and the allocation of territory. All of these processes are of course marked by unequal and uneven distributions and operations of power.

The Palestinian issue also highlights another important dynamic within the Arab world since the end of European control: the consistent and ceaseless manner in which Arab regimes have propagandized their subjects for the past half-century. One of the ways in which the Arab satellite television channel Al Jazeera has repeatedly provoked the ire of Moroccan officials[23] has been through the staging of bipartisan discussions about the question of Western Sahara—the kinds of discussion rarely found in the Moroccan media. This includes interviews with Polisario officials, such as its long-time leader, Mohammed Abdelaziz.[24] In 2005, the head of a major Moroccan publication suggested that his fellow citizens might have a different, less jingoistic attitude toward the question of Western Sahara if there was a more neutral airing of all the available facts. Five years later, his magazine was effectively destroyed by the Moroccan regime precisely because he attempted to stage a more honest national dialog on the issue.[25] If press freedom has a long way to go in

---

[22] Shibley Telhami, "The 2011 Arab Public Opinion Poll: Polling and Public Opinion, Middle East, The Arab Awakening and Middle East Unrest, Iran, Israel," *The Brookings Institution*, 21 November 2011. Available at <http://www.brookings.edu/reports/2011/1121_arab_public_opinion_telhami.aspx>, accessed September 2013.

[23] Most recently, Deutsche Presse-Agentur, "Morocco expels al-Jazeera over 'irresponsible' reporting," 29 October 2010, retrieved via LexisNexis.

[24] e.g. BBC Monitoring, "Al-Jazeera TV interviews Polisario leader on Western Saharan affairs," 17 June 2007, retrieved via LexisNexis.

[25] One of Morocco's most popular and provocative news magazines of the post-Hassan II era, *Le Journal* was forced to close its doors in 2010 due to financial troubles stemming largely from its controversial attempts to discuss the Western Sahara issue and the informal state boycott that ensued. See Reporters sans frontières, "Mise à mort du Journal Hebdomadaire: une semaine pour payer trois millions de dirhams de dommages et interest," 23 December 2006; and Human Rights Watch, "Morocco: Police Harass Two Outspoken Journalists," 9 June 2010.

Morocco and the broader Arab world, the question should instead be thus: Do Arabs not care about minorities or not know about them? The Palestinian issue could be the exception that proves the rule. Arab regimes support minority rights when those minorities are Arabs in non-Arab states but ignore or suppress minority issues when it affects the broader political project of Arab nationalism, hence the silence and reticence towards Kurds in the east and Imazighen in the west. With less overt state control of the political system and media, it is possible that a more transparent conversation about minority issues will commence in the Arab world. Intergovernmental institutions such as the Arab League might also begin to represent the views of the governed within its member states rather than the whims of the besieged governors. The basic point, however, remains: beliefs about and attitudes toward minority rights in the Arab world remain woefully underdetermined as a result of the intertwined and mutually reinforcing legacies of Western imperialism and despotic governance.

WHOSE PAST? THE INVENTION OF TRADITION IN NORTHWEST AFRICA

Having just raised serious questions about whether or not the problem of minority conflicts in the Arab world has been correctly diagnosed, a critique of the prescribed solution might seem unwarranted. But it is equally the objective of this chapter to question the idea of "Arab solutions" to minority conflicts as much as it is to question the initial framing of the problem. Whether or not Maghrebi histories provide an alternative to Western models of territorial power-sharing is dependent upon which histories one selects and, by implication, which histories one then ignores. Whose tradition are we going to adopt as our framework for a solution? The potency of this question rests in the acknowledgment that the Western Sahara conflict is rooted in two traditions, Moroccan and Sahrawi nationalisms, whose irreconcilability is the actual source of the conflict. In the following paragraphs, it will become clear that it is not Moroccan history that tempts us to seek within it traditions of power-sharing with the Sahrawis. It is the fact that Morocco now claims Western Sahara that produces the history to justify its irredentism. The contemporary and political character of the Western Sahara conflict—as opposed to its historical and ethnological interpretations—is rendered even more stark when one considers the fact that the Sahrawis share far more cultural and historical ties with the people of Mauritania.[26] If the Western Sahara conflict

---

[26] During a visit to the Moroccan occupied capital, Al-ʿAyun, in 2003, I met a Sahrawi student whose family seemed representative of the contemporary Sahrawi predicament. His uncle is a member of the Moroccan monarchy's Sahrawi Loyalist advisory body (*Conseil royal consultatif*

was between Polisario and Mauritania, it might then be possible to interpret the situation as "inter-tribal" or at least intra-ethnic. But since 1979 Mauritania has renounced all claims to Western Sahara and has maintained bilateral relations with the RASD. In its current configuration, the Western Sahara conflict is not merely about competing nationalisms, Moroccan and Sahrawi; more importantly, it is regional and geopolitical as well.[27]

The Moroccan state is traditional only in so far as an autochthonous façade has been grafted onto the technologies, techniques, and territories of rule implanted by Hispano-French colonialism. The ostensible basis of relations between the Moroccan state and its populations, including loyalist Sahrawis, is regulated within a modern postcolonial state apparatus largely inherited upon independence. Following the end of the protectorate, the Moroccan monarchy recoded some of its state agents and structures in a native vocabulary of an imagined *sharīfian* state that for centuries enabled and distended the power of successive *sulṭāns* throughout the lands of direct (*bilād al-makhzan*) and indirect (*bilād al-sibā*) sovereign control. In some contexts, the informal and formal structures that have underwritten the ability of the Moroccan monarchy to rule has been called the Makhzan (sometimes *makhzin* in Moroccan *Dārijah*). The mutations within the Makhzan, particularly its hybridization with European state structures grafted onto the Moroccan polity during forty years of Hispano-French colonialism, has arguably received less attention than the putative formal model of the historical—pre-colonial—Makhzan.[28] The recent edition of *The Historical Dictionary of Morocco*, a massive scholarly reference work, is a perfect example. Its entry for *al-Makhzan*, "the [Moroccan] government as a whole," discusses the historical development of the Makhzan as a coercive and extractive set of institutions but only up to colonialism (*c.*1912). Yet under French colonialism, the Makhzan was codified and territorialized alongside the colonial administrative regime, so that they operated in parallel. Following independence, the Monarchy adopted this system wholesale. Though the Makhzan continues to use some pre-colonial designations for its deputies (*walī, al-bāshā, al-ʿamīl, al-raʾīs al-dāʾirah, khalifah, qāʾid, qāʾid mumtaz, al-shaykh, al-muqaddam*),

---

pour les affaires sahariennes), his father was an important figure in Polisario, his sister is an RASD official, while other members of his family live in Mauritania and serve in its government.

[27] See Stephen Zunes and Jacob Andrew Mundy, *Western Sahara: War, Nationalism and Conflict Irresolution* (Syracuse, NY: Syracuse University Press, 2010), ch. 3.

[28] *Pace* Henry Munson, *Religion and Power in Morocco* (New Haven, CT: Yale University Press, 1993); and Abdellah Hammoudi, *Master and Disciple: The Cultural Foundations of Moroccan Authoritarianism* (Chicago, IL: University of Chicago Press, 1997). See also Edmund Burke, *Prelude to Protectorate in Morocco: Precolonial Protest and Resistance, 1860–1912* (Chicago, IL: University of Chicago Press, 1976); M. E. Combs-Schilling, *Sacred Performances: Islam, Sexuality, and Sacrifice* (New York: Columbia University Press, 1989); and David Montgomery Hart, *Qabila: Tribal Profiles and Tribe–State Relations in Morocco and on the Afghanistan-Pakistan Frontier* (Amsterdam: Het Spinhuis, 2001).

most of these are Arabic substitutions for common governmental posts in any modern state.[29]

It is not just the Moroccan regime that has historicized itself in this way; Western scholars have been willing to adopt these narratives of rule as well. In the Anglo-American tradition of anthropology, Morocco has been, and remains, a premier research site, a fact that has helped reinforce the idea of Morocco as a space of tradition.[30] Neighboring Algeria has been a comparably inhospitable terrain for ethnography since the end of French colonialism (Bourdieu being a notable exception), leading to its reproduction as a *political* space par excellence, particularly within the comparative political studies of rentier effects on hydrocarbon exporting states, wherein 1962 becomes year zero for a new Algerian polity.[31] One of the few scholars to offer a direct challenge to this tendency in Morocco studies is historian Edmund Burke III:

the contemporary Moroccan state is not the old Makhzan writ large. Whereas the latter was puny, the modern Moroccan state can deploy its power throughout the national territory, disciplining and orienting opinion, intervening in depth in the society where it chooses. Seen from this angle, the history of contemporary Morocco is characterized by a radical discontinuity with its precolonial past, and its culture is 'modern' and not 'traditional.' Modern in the sense that it is the result of a complex layering of heterogeneous cultural practices strongly influenced by the European Enlightenment but shaped also by participation in a global world economy and international system. The selective amnesia of scholars about the colonial auspices under which the Moroccan state made its transition to modernity is especially striking.[32]

Whether or not the past Makhzan would recognize the postcolonial self calls for speculation, but Burke's point is nevertheless well taken. To relegate the

---

[29] Thomas Kerlin Park and Aomar Boum, *Historical Dictionary of Morocco* (Lanham, MD: Scarecrow, 2006), 226–8.

[30] Ernest Gellner, *Saints of the Atlas* (London: Weidenfeld & Nicolson, 1969); John Waterbury, *The Commander of the Faithful: The Moroccan Political Élite—A Study in Segmented Politics* (London: Weidenfeld & Nicolson, 1970); Burke, *Prelude to Protectorate in Morocco*; Dale F. Eickelman, *Knowledge and Power in Morocco: The Education of a Twentieth-Century Notable* (Princeton, NJ: Princeton University Press, 1985); John P. Entelis, *Culture and Counterculture in Moroccan Politics* (Boulder, CO: Westview, 1989); and M. E. Combs-Schilling, "Sacred Performances: Islam, Sexuality, and Sacrifice," in Rahma Bourqia and Susan Gilson Miller (eds.), *The Shadow of the Sultan: Culture, Power, and Politics in Morocco* (Cambridge, MA: Harvard University Press, 1999).

[31] e.g. John P Entelis, *Algeria: The Revolution Institutionalized* (Boulder, CO: Westview, 1986); and Miriam R. Lowi, *Oil Wealth and the Poverty of Politics: Algeria Compared* (Cambridge: Cambridge University Press, 2009).

[32] Edmund Burke, "Theorizing the Histories of Colonialism and Nationalism in the Arab Maghrib," in Ali Abdullatif Ahmida (ed.), *Beyond Colonialism and Nationalism in the Maghrib: History, Culture, and Politics* (New York: Palgrave, 2000), 27–8.

Makhzan to the past is to ignore the fact that the colonial reformulation of the Moroccan state has produced something quite different from its predecessor.

Regardless of the historical reality of the imagined Moroccan polity prior to the establishment of French and Spanish protectorates during the first decade of the twentieth century, the Moroccan irredentist claim on the territory of Western Sahara is essentially a claim of affiliation and subordination between its peoples and the *Sulṭān*.[33] Morocco's case for sovereignty over Western Sahara and its peoples, as laid out in its arguments before the International Court of Justice in 1975, presents a monarchical model where there are two dramaturgical variations on the acknowledgment of his sovereignty. One, local leaders (*qāʾids*) and representatives of the crown (*khalīfahs*) regularly performed acts of allegiance (*al-bayaʿah*) directly to the *Sulṭān* in the *bilād al-makhzan*; two, everyone else made reference to his religious authority during prayers (*khuṭbah*) as the region's foremost spiritual leader (*amīr al-muʾ-minīn*) and as a direct descendant (*sharīf*) of the Prophet Muḥammad whether in the *bilād al-sibā* or *bilād al-makhzan*.[34] As noted above, this vocabulary of rule is not specific to relations between the Moroccan *sulṭān* (*malik* [king] after independence) and the Hassaniyyah-speaking populations that are now widely recognized as the Sahrawis. In general, this model is said to have actuated all state–society relations in precolonial Morocco for centuries, including all constituent groups within the mosaic of ethno-linguistic populations that have inhabited the territorially fluctuating entity called Morocco, minority and majority groups alike.

What seems to be occurring in most discussions of Morocco is a confusion between a state and a nation. Whether or not the semi-successive[35] Moroccan regimes were pre-Westphalian states or merely Arab and Berber empires before independence is debatable. And whether or not the greatest regime, in terms of alleged territorial control, *al-Murābiṭūn* (Almoravids), is "Moroccan" is easily contested as well.[36] According to the master narrative, all Moroccan regimes were alike in the fact that the people of Morocco recognized

---

[33] Abdeslam Maghraoui, "Ambiguities of Sovereignty: Morocco, The Hague and the Western Sahara Dispute," *Mediterranean Politics* 8/1 (2003): 113–26.

[34] The other main aspect of Morocco's case before The Hague in 1975 was "external" displays of sovereignty. That is, alleged indications of foreign recognition of Moroccan sovereignty over the areas of Western Sahara before 1885, mainly British and Spanish. As with the "internal" displays of sovereignty by the Moroccan monarch's alleged subjects in the nineteenth century, the ICJ likewise found the evidence unconvincing in the case of external recognitions of Moroccan sovereignty.

[35] There were often extended periods of "anarchy" between regimes and contested successions in Morocco.

[36] Though they founded Marrakesh in the eleventh century, the Murabituns' origins were among the nomadic pre-Arabized Imazighen of present-day Mauritania and former Spanish Sahara. The Murabituns' tri-polar empire also included capitals in Timbuktu and Spain, making them just as Malian or Andalusian/Spanish as Moroccan.

the Sultan's religious authority as "leader of the faithful" (*amīr al-mu'minīn*). The only commonality between "Moroccan" regimes, until colonialism, was a shared desire to accumulate power in areas that include the space we now call Morocco. This was done either through direct coercion (military campaigns) or indirectly through deputized proxies (Makhzan). Political scientist John Waterbury described the resulting historical pattern as a "stable system of violence." As *al-Sulṭān* collected taxes through military campaigns (often to punish insubordinate areas or to assert control over trans-Saharan trade and sub-Saharan slave markets), more taxes allowed for bigger armies. Larger armies could collect more taxes, and so on. In this way, the precolonial Moroccan state falls into the kind of pattern of state-building modeled by Charles Tilly.[37] We might consider all Moroccan regimes as state-like, at least in terms of their institutional behaviour. However, the presence of a state does not imply legitimacy in claimed areas of rule, it does not imply the existence of a polity, nor even awareness of the state's existence among all the alleged subjects.

We have very intricate histories of the Moroccan state: the history of loosely connected attempts to build a self-sustaining apparatus of control in the area we now call Morocco. Nations, however, are something quite different from states, though we often say "nation-state" to gloss over the difference. Nations imply a people; states, on the other hand, are the institutions that rule over them. States, furthermore, entail a territory over which the sovereign has a monopoly of violence. We are in the habit of seeing the world as cantonized into states, but much to the detriment of seeing the world in other ways. In the field of international relations, scholar John Agnew highlighted the pitfalls of this "territorial trap," when the basic ontological unit of a discipline—for him, nation-states—actually inhibits understanding.[38] Historiography, as well, suffers greatly when it accommodates the modern states, and inadvertently works to reify counter-temporally.[39]

---

[37] Charles Tilly, "War Making and State Making As Organized Crime," in Peter B. Evans, D. Rueschemeyer, and T. Skocpol (eds.), *Bringing the State Back In* (Cambridge: Cambridge University Press, 1985), 167–91.

[38] J. Agnew, "The Territorial Trap: The Geographical Assumptions of International Relations Theory," *Review of International Political Economy* 1/1 (1994): 53–80.

[39] Morocco, in its current form (i.e. its territorial extent), was established in a Franco-Spanish convention of 1912. At that point in time, Morocco began to take on the form of a modern nation-state, a favored unit of analysis for Western historiography. Yet whatever Morocco was before then, or how the people imagined themselves in all areas deemed "Morocco," is not problematized. The concept of Morocco as an identifiable space is defined "up time" (i.e. backwards), mirroring Anderson's nationalisms. Though "Morocco" is a historically formulated concept, whose meanings before 1912 and after 1956 are quite different, it is treated as ahistorical. Historians apply it to all periods partially out of convenience (i.e. to avoid convoluted discussions like this one), and partially out of chronic deference to state history. Like Lewis Carroll's Cheshire Cat, we have the logical impossibility of predicates without an object to hang on. We talk about Morocco before there is a Morocco to talk about.

Moroccan history has very little to do with the people that inhabited the areas now known as Morocco. It tells us very little about the kinds of lives they led, the ways they viewed themselves, or their relationship with the various sultans that claimed to rule over them. Even works in Moroccan historical anthropology—examining life outside the ruling elite—are so marked with this state bias that every quotidian act is (mis)interpreted as legitimating the Sultan's authority.[40] One might then suggest that a "people's history" of Morocco is lacking. Such a history, however, would still have to begin from the faulty premise of a Morocco before there is Morocco.

From Benedict Anderson we realize that, when it comes to nationalist histories, the present tells us much more about the past,[41] yet most Western scholars cling to the opposite in the case of Morocco. If anything, Moroccan history tells us much more about the way in which the postcolonial regime wants its subjects (and the world) to imagine Morocco. With the legitimacy of hereditary monarchies rooted in the past, it comes as no surprise that the past—a very particular version of it—is highlighted for maximal legitimacy. The monarchy in Morocco gains legitimacy not only by claiming descent from the Prophet Muhammad, but also from an astounding incumbency: a claim to regional authority dating back to shortly after the Islamic conquest of North Africa. Like most countries, the Moroccan state has formalized certain depictions of the past and then encoded them in the national pedagogy. No surprise that following independence from Spain and France, officials from the Interior Ministry wrote Morocco's most important historical textbooks for primary and secondary schools. The most telling claim of Moroccan state history is its belief that populations were subject whether they knew it or not. This tendency was recently manifest in the "Greater Morocco" claim launched by the Moroccan Independence Party (*Hizb al-Istiqlāl*) shortly before independence in 1956. Morocco, according to Moroccan nationalists, not only included the French and Spanish protectorates but also encompassed western Algeria, northern Mali, and all of Mauritania and Western Sahara. These areas were (and for some, still are) Moroccan by virtue of the fact that one Moroccan sultan or another claimed them.

Yet these claims to control contain another telling idiosyncrasy. For Moroccan state history, the Sultan's authority extended even to areas that explicitly rejected it. Central control over "Morocco" was always in a state of flux, oscillating between *bilād al-makhzan* (lands of control) and *bilād al-sibā* (lands of anarchy). Both nevertheless remained "Moroccan" even if the latter, for example, had not seen a sultan's deputy or been taxed for centuries. For the most part, Western scholars have failed to interrogate these elite narratives of

---

[40] Munson, *Religion and Power in Morocco*, 121–5.
[41] B. Anderson, *Imagined Communities: Reflections on the Origin and Spread of Nationalism* (New York: Verso, 1991), 205.

Moroccan history.[42] The political implications of endorsing such narratives are clear enough. Not only does it legitimate an authoritarian power structure that has been accused of gross and ongoing human rights violations since independence in 1956,[43] it also provides legitimacy to an irredentist narrative and thus a war of aggressive territorial expansion in the former Spanish Sahara. The concept of *bilād al-sibā* largely grounded Morocco's postcolonial claims on its neighbors.[44] Morocco's illegal occupation of Western Sahara is justified on this passive and indirect concept of authority. Holding a self-determination referendum, which would legitimize Morocco's claim over the territory, is considered out of the question. Western Sahara is Moroccan, even if the native Sahrawis, the African Union, the United Nations, and international law do not agree. Little wonder then that Sahrawi nationalists find little cultural legitimacy in Moroccan state narratives.[45]

WHOSE PRESENT? THE POLITICS OF NAMING
AND CLAIMING MINORITY RIGHTS
IN WESTERN SAHARA

Just as there is no authentic Moroccan tradition from which we can unearth culturally legitimate models of territorial power sharing *vis-à-vis* Western

---

[42] As anthropologist Combs-Schilling naively wrote, "the links between the central monarch and his people varied, yet can be summarized by two dominant forms of integrations. In the first, the link was administratively direct, and the regions involved were known as *bilad al-makhzan*, 'the lands of formal government.' In the second, the link was administratively indirect; it rested more on political influence than political control, political loyalty rather than political apparatus. The regions involved were known as *bilad al-siba*, 'the lands of dissidence,'" Combs-Schilling, *Sacred Performances*, 183.

[43] See Susan Slyomovics, *The Performance of Human Rights in Morocco* (Philadelphia, PA: University of Pennsylvania Press, 2005).

[44] Claims on Mali and Mauritania were abandoned by 1970; claims on western Algeria were abandoned though the final border between the two in the Sahara proved difficult to negotiate because of Moroccan irredentism and the lingering mistrust from the 1963 "Sand War."

[45] The obvious response to this conclusion is that Western notions of sovereignty and the liberal-Westphalian state are not compatible with Morocco's own "traditional" conceptions of sovereignty, which are founded in Islamic traditions. A recent defense of this thesis has come from Moroccan academic Abdeslam Maghraoui (Maghraoui, "Ambiguities of Sovereignty"). His article is a belated response to the International Court of Justice's 1975 rejection of Morocco's historical claim to Spanish/Western Sahara based on the premise that two different and ultimately incompatible notions of sovereignty, Moroccan and Western, were in play. What instantly renders Maghraoui's argument a non-starter is the fact that Morocco failed to prove sovereignty over Western Sahara before The Hague *using its own criteria and its own evidence*. The Court's opinion was indeed very clear: Western Sahara's right to self-determination trumped the weak claims of Morocco and the nearly non-existent claims of Mauritania. See International Court of Justice, *Western Sahara, Advisory Opinion* (The Hague: International Court of Justice, 16 October 1975).

Saharan nationalism, the political, contemporary, and still contested character of Sahrawi identity also needs to be underscored to understand the dynamics of this conflict. At the center of the Western Sahara dispute is not just a question of land but also of bodies and imaginations. After all, Western Saharan nationalism, the *raison d'être* of Polisario, necessarily requires the existence of a Western Saharan people. The concept of the Sahrawi is problematic in so far as the identity itself is still denied by some while a number of incompatible and contested definitions remain in circulation. Frequently the native people of Western Sahara are often seen as coterminous with the idea of the Sahrawi people. At the time of the Morocco–Polisario ceasefire in September 1991, when it was widely believed that a UN referendum on independence was just around the corner for Western Sahara, one young resident of the refugee camps near Tindouf, Algeria, stated flatly, "The Sahrawi people will vote massively in favor of independence."[46] A recent manifesto published by a group of dissident Sahrawi nationalists expressing their dissatisfaction with Polisario's leadership equated the "Sahrawi cause" (*la Causa sahraui/al-qaḍiyyah al-ṣahrawiyyah*) with the effort to establish an independent state in Western Sahara.[47] Yet it is not just Sahrawi nationalists who are guilty of conflating Sahrawis with Western Saharans. Spain's previous foreign minister, Trinidad Jimenez, was asked by the *ABC* newspaper to explain Madrid's current policy towards the Western Sahara question; she answered, "Spain has always had the same position on the Sahara and we have championed, within the UN framework, the Sahrawi people's right to self-determination."[48]

The problem with this view—using native Western Saharan and Sahrawi interchangeably—is that there are also people who can call themselves Sahrawi (on the basis of culture or blood) but who inhabit areas outside, yet adjacent to, the territory of the former Spanish Sahara. Observers and participants in the Western Sahara conflict rarely make the all-important distinction between Moroccan Sahrawis, Algerian Sahrawis, Mauritanian Sahrawis, and Western Sahrawis. As the UN referendum effort discovered in the 1990s, defining and identifying bona fide Sahrawis native to Western Sahara is easier said than done. All in all, it took the UN mission almost six years (1994–99) just to establish an electorate of some 86,000 voters for the referendum on independence.[49] It was partly due to the fact that both Morocco and Polisario had so vociferously contested the voter identification procedures, that the UN

---

[46] Boubker Belkadi, "Sahrawi refugees confident on Western Sahara referendum," *Agence France Presse*, 6 September 1991.

[47] "Manifiesto por la justicia, la decencia y la independencia total," Spain, 4 February 2011 (on file with author).

[48] BBC Monitoring, "Spanish minister discusses Palestinian state, ties with China, Gibraltar," 28 December 2010, text of report by Spanish newspaper *ABC* website, on 27 December 2010.

[49] See Dunbar, "Saharan Stasis"; and Jensen, *Western Sahara: Anatomy of a Stalemate*.

Secretariat and Security Council pushed for the abandonment of the referendum in February 2000.[50]

While it is important for the purposes of organizing a referendum in Western Sahara to make distinctions between Sahrawis native to lands other than Western Sahara, it must also be recognized that the idea of a Sahrawi people is very much rooted in the creation of the Spanish Sahara. In its most basic sense, the term *Ṣaḥrāwī* is the Arabic adjective for Saharan. The native or, more importantly, non-Spanish people of the Spanish Sahara, came to call themselves Sahrawis in the sense that they were Spanish Saharans by land but not Spanish by blood. So they simply called themselves Saharan or, in Arabic, Sahrawi.[51] It is primarily for this reason—the territorial and political uniqueness of Western Sahara's Spanish administration in a sea of French colonial hegemony—that the constitution of nationalist differences between Mauritanians and Sahrawis became possible despite sharing the same language and the same extended kinship networks. The presence of a significant Hassaniyyah-speaking population indigenous to southern Morocco might seem to provide some grounds for Moroccan–Sahrawi reconciliation if not for the fact that a significant percentage of Morocco's Sahrawi population were political and environmental refugees from Spanish Sahara in the 1950s and 1960s. The growing number of pro-independence activists who originate from southern Morocco also speaks to the complex nature of Western Saharan nationalism.

The situation is further complicated by three important factors. (1) The population that would come to see themselves as Sahrawis inhabited a broader area and maintained familial, cultural, and social linkages with populations in the adjacent colonial territories of French Morocco, southern Spanish Morocco, parts of French West Africa (later Mauritania and Mali), and French Algeria. Attempts to map the geographical distribution of the major Sahrawi social groups (sometimes called "confederations" or "tribes"), whose historical range includes the territory of Western Sahara, make this fact clear.[52] (2) Colonial repression, changes in the built environment, and droughts in the 1950s and 1960s greatly disrupted established patterns of Sahrawi life in and

---

[50] Theofilopoulou, *The United Nations and Western Sahara*.

[51] See Jacob Andrew Mundy, "Colonial Formations in Western Saharan National Identity," in Nabil Boudraa and Joseph Krause (eds.), *North African Mosaic: A Cultural Reappraisal of Ethnic and Religious Minorities* (Newcastle: Cambridge Scholars Press, 2007).

[52] Various efforts to map the geographical distributions of social groups in Western Sahara can be found in Juan Bautista Vilar, *El Sahara Español: Historia De Una Aventura Colonial* (Madrid: Sedmay Ediciones, 1977); Muhammad Ibn 'Azuz Hakim, *Al-Siyadah Al-Maghribiyyah Fi Al-Aqalim Al-Sahrawiyyah Min Khilal Al-Wath'iq Al-Makhaziniyyah* (Casablanca: Mu'assasat Bansharah, 1981); Maurice Barbier, *Le Conflit au Sahara Occidental* (Paris: L'Harmattan, 1982); John Damis, *Conflict in Northwest Africa: The Western Sahara Dispute* (Stanford, CA: Hoover Institution Press, 1983); José Ramón Diego Aguirre, *Historia Del Sahara Español: La Verdad De Una Traición* (Madrid: Kaydeda Ediciones, 1988).

around the Spanish-administered colony, driving many to seek refuge or opportunity in the neighboring French colonies turned independent states. (3) As a Non-Self-Governing territory according to the United Nations, the *native* people of Western Sahara—not all Sahrawis—have the right to independence. This right does not extend to the entire ethnic group but only to Sahrawis born within the boundaries of the former Spanish Sahara. For this reason, the architects of the referendum in Western Sahara had to make a fundamental yet problematic distinction. On the one hand, there are Sahrawis as a broader ethnic group, one that inhabits areas of southern Morocco, western Algeria, northern Mauritania, and all of Western Sahara. On the other hand, there are those ethnic Sahrawis who are exclusively native to Western Sahara. According to this logic, all (native) Western Saharans are Sahrawis but not all Sahrawis are native to Western Sahara. Identity, of course, does not obey such clean distinctions but such is the "arbitrary yet sacrosanct" norm of *uti possidetis* that, with few exceptions—West Papua, East Timor, and Western Sahara being the most egregious violations of that norm—guided the decolonization of a billion people in the twentieth century.[53] A major argument for maintaining colonial boundaries was to stave off the very kinds of irredentism that is at the heart of Morocco's claim to Western Sahara and the four decades of conflict that it has engendered.

Since the beginning of the conflict with Polisario, the Moroccan government has attempted (to date[54]) to portray the Western Sahara conflict as a dispute between Rabat and Algiers, and not a dispute between Morocco and the Sahrawis. In 1982, for example, then Moroccan chief of staff Colonel-Major Abdelaziz Benani made a clear reference to Algeria when he told the *New York Times*, "If there were no foreign interference in the region, there would be no war. If our neighboring countries wanted to stop this war, it would be easy for us to live in peace."[55] It was even suggested in 1983 that Morocco had made a significant compromise in the Western Sahara peace process when, in the midst of secret negotiations, Rabat accepted Polisario as the legitimate representative of the Sahrawi people.[56] However, that acceptance was indeed

---

[53] Thomas M. Franck, "Theory and Practice of Decolonization," in Richard Lawless and Laila Monahan (eds.), *War and Refugees: The Western Sahara Conflict* (New York: Pinter, 1987), 11; and George E. Joffé, "Self-Determination and Uti Possidetis: The Western Sahara and the 'Lost Provinces'," *Morocco* 1/1 (1996): 97–115.

[54] When asked recently if "the issue of the Sahrawi people [was] down to a problem between Morocco and Algeria," Morocco's current Foreign Minister, Taib Fassi Fihri, responded, "[. . .] I hope we can resolve this problem, and we believe that Algeria has the key to solving it" (BBC Monitoring, "Moroccan minister visits Portugal," 2 March 2011 (text of report by Portuguese newspaper *Publico* website on 24 February 2011)).

[55] Pranay B. Gupte, "Morocco, backed by US, Spurs Economic Buildup in West Sahara," *New York Times*, 4 May 1982, A16.

[56] James Dorsey, "Morocco and Algeria pave the way for an end to Saharan war," *Christian Science Monitor*, 28 March 1983, 7.

begrudging. In diplomatic circles, Morocco continues to question the international standing of Polisario as the legitimate representative of the people of Western Sahara[57] and denies the existence of RASD (hence its boycott of the African Union); meanwhile, on the ground in the occupied Western Sahara, Morocco has cultivated its own bodies to represent the Sahrawis, notably the Conseil royal consultatif pour les affaires sahariennes (CORCAS, the Royal Consultative Council for Saharan Affairs), which is often presented in international forums, including recent rounds of UN talks, as the legitimate counterpart to Polisario. Morocco would like to frame the Western Sahara conflict as an intra-ethnic dispute but only between Sahrawi loyalists and rebels. Polisario seeks to frame the conflict either as an international dispute between Morocco and RASD or as a problem of international law premised on Western Sahara's current standing as the last non-self-governing territory in Africa to achieve self-determination.

The most generic view of the Western Sahara conflict purveyed by the Moroccan government and the Moroccan population in general is that the Sahara question is a problem of separatism fueled by Algerian machinations. Polisario, according to this view, represents a small minority of renegade Moroccans, or even foreigners, funded and supported by Algeria seeking the illegitimate secession of Western Sahara from Morocco. This has been a motif in the Moroccan narrative since the early years of the war. A 1980 documentary on the war in Western Sahara featured an interview with the then Moroccan speaker of the Parliament, Dey Ould Sidi Baba, a Mauritanian who became a Moroccan citizen.[58] In the film, Baba insisted that Polisario was entirely composed of foreign fighters and that any discussion of the Sahrawi people constituted an attack on Morocco's sovereignty and an outrage against the people of Morocco.[59] Speaking in Washington, DC in 1982, the then Moroccan foreign minister, Mohammed Boucetta, described Polisario in 1982 as "a fiction armed by Libya and sheltered by Algeria." He then asked rhetorically, "What is the Polisario? No more than 10 people."[60]

Moroccan efforts to deny any demographic or geographical specificity to the territory of Western Sahara are also reflected in the long-standing designation of the territory as Morocco's "Southern Provinces," "Southern Regions,"

---

[57] Morocco's minister of communications recently said, "Le Maroc refuse de considérer que le Polisario serait le représentant unique et légitime des populations sahraouies" (quoted in *L'Expression*, "Manœuvre diabolique de Mohammed VI," 27 January 2011).

[58] See Abdellatif El Azizi, "Hommage. Âlem, diplomate et patriote," *Tel Quel* 192, <http://www.telquel-online.com/192/sujet3.shtml>, accessed September 2013.

[59] BBC Summary of World Broadcasts, "In Brief; Hungarian television film on the Western Sahara conflict," 14 January 1980.

[60] *New York Times*, "Moroccan plays down talks on U.S. use of military base," 21 May 1982, A6, accessed via LexisNexis.

or simply the "Moroccan Sahara."[61] The areas of Western Sahara under Moroccan control are currently divided into three large regions comprised of several provinces each.[62] The two northernmost regions overlap with southern Morocco. The international boundary that separates Western Sahara from Morocco exists neither on Moroccan maps nor on the ground in the border regions of the former Spanish Sahara. The most prominent material frontier inside Western Sahara today is the 2,500 km-long defensive barrier that Morocco constructed in the 1980s against Polisario attacks.

Given that Morocco does not see Western Sahara as a separate country and because the idea of a Sahrawi people is so closely tied to the nationalist project of Polisario, Rabat has understandably been reticent to give any recognition to the Sahrawi identity, even as a distinct ethno-linguistic grouping on a par with the Imazighen (Berber) groups in Morocco. One will frequently encounter within Moroccan political discourse the idea of Sahrawis as a geographical identity rather than a political or ethnic one—Saharan/Sahrawi as literally "of the Sahara." By this definition, Moroccan settlers, regardless of their ethnic background, whether speakers of Moroccan Dārijah or Tamazight, can actually become Sahrawi. Inversely, there is the assertion by one Moroccan sociologist that Sahrawis are becoming Moroccan by virtue of increasing rates of intermarriage between residents of the Moroccan Sahara and residents of Morocco proper. A closer look at the data, which fails to record any ethno-linguistic or political indicators (such as native or settler status in Western Sahara), reveals that the vast majority of these marriages are between peoples from Sahrawi-dominated areas in southern Morocco and Western Sahara.[63]

Others outright deny the existence of a Sahrawi people. In a recent intellectual defense of Rabat's Western Sahara policies, Abdelhamid El-Ouali, a Moroccan scholar of law and politics, charged that Spain created the "pseudo-Sahrawi nationalism" in 1973 and that the Sahrawis are a "so-called people"; El-Ouali even finds it necessary to place "Sahrawi people" in inverted commas.[64] The logic here is quite simple. If there is no Sahrawi people, there is no Sahrawi nation. If there is no Sahrawi nation, there can be no claim to Sahrawi self-determination, independence, and statehood. This tendency within the Moroccan elite discourse on Western Sahara holds some parallels with the Israeli views that reject the existence of a Palestinian people, perhaps most

[61] For early examples, see Associated Press, 22 March 1977; BBC Summary of World Broadcasts, "The Obasanjo-Traore visit to Morocco" (Rabat home service in Arabic, 12:00 GMT 6 May 1979), 9 May 1979.

[62] These are the southernmost Oued Ed-Dahab and Lagouira regions; the central-western Laâyoune, Boujdour, and Sakia El Hamra regions; and the northeastern Guelmim and Es Semara regions.

[63] Mohamed Cherkaoui, *Morocco and the Sahara: Social Bonds and Geopolitical Issues* (Oxford: Bardwell, 2007), 139–52.

[64] See Abdelhamid El-Ouali, *Saharan Conflict: Towards Territorial Autonomy As a Right to Democratic Self-Determination* (London: Stacey International, 2008).

infamously instantiated in Golda Meir's 1969 statement to the *Sunday Times*: "There were no such thing as Palestinians." More frightening is the fact that contestants in the 2012 United States Presidential race continue to echo Meir's assertion that there were only Arabs in Palestine, not Palestinians.

Elsewhere Moroccan views towards the ethnological status of the Sahrawis are more ambiguous. Sahrawis are often called *Ḥassānī*, in reference to their dialect of Arabic, Hassāniyyah, in the same way that speakers of Tarifit Berber of the north are called Rifi or Tashilhit-speakers of the south are called Shilhī. The 2007 autonomy proposal Morocco submitted to the United Nations includes a provision allowing for local control over "cultural affairs, including promotion of the Saharan Hassani cultural heritage." Yet the proposal also calls for the "Parliament of the Sahara autonomous Region" to have a number of seats exclusively for "members elected by the various Sahrawi tribes." While Morocco's proposal does not strictly define the meaning of the term "Sahrawi," it is likely limited to the "tribes" recognized by Spanish authorities and the UN referendum mission in Western Sahara as those groups with populations living inside the former Spanish Sahara in 1974. This is not the same as recognizing the Sahrawis as a people or a nation, a recognition that would help legitimate a claim of self-determination. Indeed, the Moroccan irredentist view is strongly in favor of the transnational language of minority rights. The Moroccan tendency to view the problem of Western Sahara as an "internal" one exacerbated by "foreign" intervention (i.e. Algeria and the United Nations) sees the minority rights framework as one that accepts or implies Moroccan sovereignty over Western Sahara. Moroccans tend to view Polisario's nationalist claims of self-determination as a foreign or imperialist discourse, one based on Western notions of sovereignty. In so far as the language of minority rights works within the parameters of a single sovereign state recognizing the rights of the minority, it is easy to see why the Moroccan government would prefer to treat the Sahara question within this framework.

As one might expect, Sahrawi nationalists tend to hold the converse view. The language of minority rights is objectionable in so far as it de-legitimates their struggle for an independent state. Sahrawi nationalists have not sought international legitimacy through an appropriation of the global lingua franca of minority or indigenous rights. Indeed, casting the question of Western Sahara as a problem of minority rights would likely be taken as an offense by many Sahrawi nationalists in so far as it assumes or implies Moroccan sovereignty over Western Sahara. Polisario's struggle to achieve independence for Western Sahara has largely been coded in the vocabulary of its inception in the early 1970s: national self-determination, third-world liberation, and the struggle against foreign domination—claims that co-constituted the international political milieu of late colonialism and the early postcolonial period. If there is any discourse of minority rights within the Western Saharan nationalist community, it tends to take one of two forms. First, there is the question of intra-ethnic domination (i.e. tribalism, residual slavery) that is still considered a problem amongst the Hassāniyyah-speaking populations of the westernmost Sahara, mainly Sahrawis and Mauritanians. Second, there is the question of the status of Moroccan settlers who will be allowed to remain behind in an independent Western Sahara. While these issues, particularly the former, are important questions related to the rights of minorities, it should be noted that Sahrawi nationalists view and address these issues within the framework of a struggle for independence and statehood, not as a question of better governance on the part of Morocco.

CONCLUSION

Though Western Sahara is supposed to serve as an unproblematic case in the search for culturally legitimate solutions to minority conflicts in the Arab world, to accomplish this would require the subordination of one people's narrative to another. This recognition should give pause to those, driven by their global cosmopolitanism, who seek culturally legitimate solutions to minority conflicts in the nonexistent terrain of historical consensus. This does not preclude Moroccan and Sahrawi nationalisms from reconstructing their pasts in order to create a common future. Though such an act might hold the appeal of more ethno-historical legitimacy than Western models of modern territorial power-sharing, it should be recognized that the manufacturing of such culturally legitimate narratives derives not from finding Sahrawi-Moroccan commonality in the past but from them deliberately making it.

The ethical danger of imagineering culturally legitimate forms of territorial power-sharing to end minority conflicts in the Arab world and beyond is not limited to quixotic naivety. The more important consideration is the entailed reproduction and reification of identities. Such processes bear a striking resemblance to the ways in which colonialism often attempted to use ethno-historical narratives to fashion new or replicate old colonial polities over which the metropole could then seemingly use its power more effectively, if often by ruling indirectly. Perhaps the greatest testament to the dangers of imagining cultural legitimacy and then socially engineering it came during the Rwandan genocide, wherein the effects of European ethnography and historiography manifested in an unspeakable horror.[65] The peoples of Africa's Great Lakes region continue to live with these devastating effects.

To situate the problem of Western Sahara entirely with the conflicting ethnological frames of the main actors is also to place geopolitical

---

[65] Mahmood Mamdani, *When Victims Become Killers: Colonialism, Nativism, and the Genocide in Rwanda* (Princeton, NJ: Princeton University Press, 2001).

considerations outside the frame. While the existence of conflicting Sahrawi and Moroccan nationalisms is likely a sufficient condition for the Western Saharan conflict, a necessary condition for its continued durability is the support rendered to Morocco by key allies on the UN Security Council, mainly France, though often the United States when push comes to shove. A more robust appreciation of the factors sustaining the Western Sahara conflict might suggest that it is the imagination of the conflict's more passive actors, rather than the antagonists themselves, that is in desperate need of a rethink. More broadly, it might be worth considering the limits of the political at the international level and not just the limits of the imaginable at the level of Morocco and Polisario. While the latter is well understood, the former's complicity in the maintenance of a variety of conflicts and disputes worldwide is never fully explicated. There is certainly no harm in asking Polisario and Morocco to engage in a conversation wherein one or the other (or both) might have to reconsider its or their conception of sovereignty. But what might prove equally helpful in the case of Western Sahara, and people in conflict more generally, is to ask the impossible question: is the international system willing to contemplate alternative notions of sovereignty as well? It is the international system, after all, that forces peoples to choose between seeking independence and seeking autonomy. Forcing peoples to make that choice is not merely a question of justice (why should the burden of re-imagining fall upon the shoulders of some but not all?), it is a measurement of the structural violence embedded within and produced by our international political reality.

7

The Role of the Amazigh Movement in the Processes of Political Reform in Postcolonial Algerian Society

Eva Pföstl

Based on aggregate measures such as the Freedom House or Polity 5 indices, one can easily conclude that Algeria represents a classic example of stable authoritarianism. However, Algeria's political life includes some features that suggest a different picture: with relatively free media and a vivid civil society the democracy discourse is omnipresent.

The two different faces of political life in Algeria raise both theoretical and methodological challenges: although a growing consensus that the "transition paradigm" has outlived its usefulness as a conceptual tool exists among scholars, an alternative theoretical framework has yet to emerge. Recent debates (and events) revolving around political opposition and protest mobilization offer promising possibilities in the search for such an overarching framework.

In the second half of the 1990s, a plethora of new politically relevant actors emerged in Algeria. The interplay of specific national as well as international factors—political liberalization, economic restructuring, civil war, the globalization of justice, and Algeria's increasing embeddedness in international treaties—facilitated the emergence of new contesting actors, challenging the regime. However, these developments did not, contrary to what would be expected based on transition experiences in Latin America and Eastern Europe, develop discernible democratization dynamics. No strong and coherent preferable alternative was able to emerge which could destabilize the regime until February 2011.

In this chapter, the author will discuss the role of the Algerian Berber/Amazigh[1] movement in the process of political reform in the authoritarian context of Algeria.

---

[1] Today, the term "Berber" is viewed by many Amazighs as pejorative and is increasingly being replaced by "Amazigh" (lit. "free man"; pl. "Imazighen"; f. sing. "Tamazight"). "Tamazight" also

In 2001, after popular unrest in the Amazigh-speaking region of Kabylia, the Citizen Movement under the direction of various Kabylian "Coordinations," grounded in local Amazigh specificities but with claims for engaged citizenship and grassroots consensual democracy, presented one of the greatest democratic challenges the postcolonial Algerian state had ever faced. After some initial success, the movement is now spent—internally divided and externally co-opted—and has been unable to generate a wide popular mobilization either beyond the region of Kabylia or within the region itself, which might have otherwise replicated and diffused the idea of a national citizen's movement for democracy.

The issues at the heart of the insurrection in Kabylia in 2001 have been similar and in some cases even identical to those that drove young North Africans onto the streets, giving rise to popular revolts that shook the Arab world in 2011: the unsolved question of national identity, high unemployment, mismanagement of public resources, and a popular sense that *la hogra* (literally "contempt," that is, the humiliation the people suffered at the hands of regime power-holders at every level who abused their authority with impunity) is the main element marking the relationship between the governing and the governed.

The interaction among several of these factors in combination with the political uproar in the countries directly bordering Algeria have the potential to upset the political status quo and to force the Algerian elite to develop new strategies and modify the political system. It will be argued that key to Algeria's political future is whether a different sort of nation-building on the basis of a democratic citizenship will be promoted.

This chapter is structured in the following way. The first section briefly analyzes why the awakening of a new, modern ethnic identity among Imazighen, who defined themselves traditionally in local tribal terms, gained prominence comparatively recently. The second section aims to understand why the new political horizon created in the uprising in Kabylia, which gave birth to one of the largest protest movements in Algeria's postcolonial history, failed to translate into systematic change. Following this background information, in the third section the author will examine the trajectory of the Citizen movement, analyzing why, after a quick rise, this new political force became an arena for regime manipulation and opposition maneuvering as well as a victim of internal struggles and flawed structures and, like all previous Algerian movements before it, lost to the Algerian state. The final section explores the potential transformative capacity of the Amazigh movement *vis-à-vis* the Algerian state and provides an assessment of a future role for the movement after the 2011 uprisings in the Arab world.

refers to the Berber language, both specifically to the variant spoken by the Middle Atlas Imazighen and today covering all berberophones.

THE RISE OF A MODERN IDENTITY

The awakening of a new, modern, self-conscious Berber-Amazigh identity for a people who defined themselves traditionally in local tribal terms, gained prominence comparatively recently.[2] As recently as forty years ago, the leading opinion of politicians and scholars was that no meaningful political distinctions between Arab and Imazighen existed. In the 1970s, Gellner wrote "the Berber sees himself as a member of his or her tribe, within an Islamically-conceived and permeated world and not as a member of a linguistically defined ethnic group, in a world in which Islam is but one thing among others" and dismissed the possibility that Imazighen might develop an encompassing ethnic identity beyond their particular tribal loyalties within an Islamic milieu.[3] Generalized Amazigh ethnicity was asserted to be virtually nonexistent by what Charles Micaud called a "remarkable consensus" of scholars proclaiming an "absence of a serious" Amazigh question.[4] The mere fact of Amazigh linguistic distinctiveness was seen as an insufficient basis to assume that such a divide translated into a particular social or political distinction. Furthermore, scholars were aware of the internal diversity, centuries of colonialist influence, and centuries of coexistence and amalgamation with other groups that have made the Imazighen a complex group.[5]

The question that then arises is: why did Amazigh identity subsequently become a major political issue in Algeria, demanding the recognition of the existence of the Amazigh people as a collective and of the cultural-historical Amazighité of North Africa? Some scholars argue that the revival of a separate Amazigh identity was promoted by Western efforts to bring about a new order

---

[2] Already by the beginning of the 20th century, manifestations of an Amazigh identity claim had seen the light. These are exemplified by the pioneering work of Amar ou Saïd Boulifa (1897, 1909, etc.), and the work of Jean Amrouche, "Les Chants berbères de Kabyliae" (1939), cited in S. Chaker, "Preface," in Karina Direche-Slimani, *Histoire de l'émigration en France au Kabyle en XXe siècle* (Paris: L'Harmattan, 1997); see also M. Willis, "The Politics of Berber (Amazigh) Identity: Algeria and Morocco Compared," in Y. H. Zoubir and H. Amira-Fernández (eds.), *North Africa: Politics, Region, and the Limits of Transformation* (New York: Routledge, 2008).

[3] E. A. Gellner and C. Micaud, *Arabs and Berbers: From Tribe to Nation in North Africa* (London: Lexington Books, 1972), 285–303.

[4] Gellner and Micaud, *Arabs and Berbers*, Conclusion. See also Hugh Roberts, "The Unforeseen Development of the Kabyle Question in Contemporary Algeria," *Government and Opposition* 17/3 (1982): 312–34.

[5] M. Brett and E. Fentress, *The Berbers* (Oxford: Blackwell, 1996); M. Shatzmiller (ed.), *Nationalism and Minority Identities in Islamic Societies* (Montreal: McGill-Queen's University Press, 2005); P. Silverstein, *Algeria in France: Transpolitics, Race and Nation* (Bloomington, IN: Indiana University Press, 2006); J. McDougall, *History and the Culture of Nationalism in Algeria* (Cambridge: Cambridge University Press, 2006); J. E. Goodman, *Berber Culture on the World Stage: From Village to Video* (Bloomington, IN: Indiana University Press, 2006); and J. K. E. Hoffman and S. Gilson Miller, *Berber and Others: Beyond Tribe and Nation in the Maghrib* (Bloomington, IN: Indiana University Press, 2010).

aimed at weakening and undermining Islam through the sponsorship and encouragement of a separate Amazigh identity.[6] Others have pointed out that Amazigh identity has been consistently understated, and situate the current awakening of a distinct Amazigh identity within a Fanonian narrative of liberation that begins in repression and alienation, then moves through consciousness and awakening to resistance and struggle, culminating in realization.[7] More recently, scholars such as K. E. Hoffman and S. Gilson Miller have argued that Amazigh activists are espousing an explicitly "culturalist" message that attempts to strengthen Amazigh identity throughout the entire Amazigh population.[8]

Ethnicity must be seen as a constantly changing orientation, shaped and reshaped by forces from inside and outside the group,[9] and new ways of Amazigh "imagining," in the sense used by Benedict Anderson,[10] among segments of their diverse community, and new forms of political and proto-political action have emerged. According to Bruce Maddy Weitzmann, Tamazighen, led by Algerian Kabyles, have taken on many of the attributes of a modern ethnic group: "a named unit of population with common ancestry myths and historical memories, elements of shared culture, some links with a historic territory and some measure of solidarity at least among [its] elites."[11]

IMAZIGHEN: AN AMBIGUOUS MINORITY

Modern Amazigh identity has multiple poles of identity, allegiance, and affinity which gave rise to an ambiguous relationship between Imazighen and the Algerian state.[12] The most important is language. Tamazight, the umbrella name for all Amazigh dialects, is spoken by approximately 20–25 percent of the population in Algeria. There are two primary Tamazight dialects in Algeria and four smaller ones.[13] Taqbaylit, from the Kabylia region,

---

[6] For example, the creation and expansion of Amazigh studies at French universities in the post-independence period. See S. Chaker, *Berbères aujourd'hui* (Paris: L'Harmattan, 1998).

[7] D. Scott, *Refashioning Futures: Criticism after Postcoloniality* (Princeton, NJ: Princeton University Press, 1999).

[8] Hoffman and Miller, *Berbers and Others*.

[9] See also C. Geertz, *The Interpretation of Cultures* (New York: Basic Books, 1973); J. Migdal, *State in Society* (Cambridge: Cambridge University Press, 2001).

[10] B. Anderson, *Imagined Communities: Reflections on the Origin and Spread of Nationalism*, rev. edn. (New York: Verso Books, 1991). See also Hoffman and Miller, *Berbers and Others*.

[11] B. Maddy-Weitzman, *The Berber Identity Movement and the Challenge to North African States* (Austin, TX: University of Texas Press, 2011), Introduction.

[12] H. Roberts, *The Battlefield Algeria 1988–2002* (London: Verso, 2003).

[13] Taqbaylit, from the Kabylia region, spoken by 5 million people; Chaoui, from the Aures region southeast of Kabylia, spoken by 2 million people; Tamzabit, the dialect of the 200,000 Ibadi Muslims of the Mzab valley in the south around Ghardaia; Znati, the dialect of 150,000

is by far the most dominant because of the large population and the proximity of the region to the political and economic epicenter, Algiers. Like Arab Algerians, almost all Imazighen are Sunni Muslims of the Malikite school with the exception of the Mazibis, who are Ibadi Muslims. Nearly all Algerians, whatever their mother tongue, have Amazigh ancestry and this fact of shared ancestry is widely known and acknowledged in Algeria.[14]

Another aspect of the ambiguous relationship between Imazighen and the Algerian state is related to the legacy of French imperialism, which produced a "psychological conditioning" of the Arab population—particularly Arab elites: French colonial ethnography had advanced the claim that Imazighen were inherently more civilized than Arabs and therefore more trustworthy, more industrious, more democratic, and thus fundamentally more European than Arabs.[15] The colonial policies that flowed from this are known as the "Berber Myth." However, French efforts to favor and form alliances with the Imazighen[16] appear to have been abject failures because in the war for independence (1954–62), Imazighen played an essential role in the struggle for independence at both the elite and mass levels.[17] Socially, economically, and culturally, however, the impact of French policies and the colonial experience per se were profound, and this legacy rendered any particularist assertion of Kabylian Amazigh identity extremely suspect in nationalist eyes.[18] However, this did not prevent a high rate of Amazigh state participation because Imazighen are not generally discriminated against in public life on the basis of their identity: a large number of Imazighen have played and continue to play important roles in key political and military positions.[19] Likewise, many of Algeria's most celebrated artists and intellectuals have been Imazighen.

---

persons in the Touat-Gourara area in the country's southwest; Tachenouit, in the Chenoua and Zaccar Mountains west of Algiers, spoken by 100,000; and Tamesheq, the dialect of Algeria's approximately 100,000 traditionally nomadic Tuaregs of the far south (more than a million Tuaregs live in adjacent Mali and Niger).

[14] J. Mundy, "The Failure of Transformative Minority Politics in Algeria," in M. U. Mbanaso and C. J. Korieh (eds.), *Minorities and the State in Africa* (Amherst, MA: Cambria, 2010).

[15] See Patrici Lorcin, *Imperial Identities: Stereotyping Prejudice and Race in Colonial Algeria* (London: I. B. Tauris, 1995).

[16] The French government elaborated the famous Berber Decree in 1930, which allowed rural areas to establish courts based on Amazigh customary law rather than Islamic law. See K. Brown, "The Impact of the Dahir Berbère in Salé," in Gellner and Micaud (eds.), *Arabs and Berbers*, 201–15.

[17] P. A. Silverstein, "The Kabyle Myth: The Production of Ethnicity in Colonial Algeria," in B. K. Axel (ed.), *From the Margins: Historical Anthropology and Its Futures* (Durham, NC: Duke University Press, 2002), 122–55.

[18] William B. Quandt, "The Berbers in the Algerian Political Elite," in Gellner and Micaud (eds.), *Arabs and Berbers*, 301.

[19] H. Roberts, "Towards an Understanding of the Kabyle Question in Contemporary Algeria," *Maghreb Review* 5 (1980): 115–24; and H. Roberts, "Co-opting Identity. The Manipulation of Berberism, the Frustration of Democratisation and the Generation of Violence in

There are also two main Kabylia-based political parties: the Socialist Forces Front (Front des Forces Socialistes, FFS) and the Rally for Culture and Democracy (Rassemblement pour la Culture et la Democratie, RCD). These political groups played a somewhat defensive role in Algeria's civil war (lasting from the early 1990s until 2002) in opposing both major forces of the conflict, the Algerian government and Algerian Islamist forces.

Indeed, in postcolonial Algeria, an ambivalent denial of the Amazigh dimension can be found. This is not because of a stable, permanent suppression of the "Amazigh dimension," but rather the Algerian state's Jacobin insistence on the "exclusively" Arab-Muslim identity of Algeria. The Algerian state never excluded Imazighen from power, but as Arab nationalism is central to the way in which the Algerians constructed their nation, Amazigh identity was recast as anathema to the ideal of national unity, and active repression of Amazigh culture was the result.

Competing narratives of Algerian nationalism and the construction of a repressed minority

In Algeria the "Amazigh Question" was a major front on which the nationalists battled to defend the "Arab" character of national identity. The Arabo-Islamic formulation of Algerian national identity was formulated in the motto, "Islam is my religion, Arabic is my language, and Algeria is my country," which later became the official slogan of the National Liberation Front (FLN) and of the Algerian state.[20] The historiographical production of Algerian salafist historians[21] directly attacked French scholarship underpinning the Berber Myth, which celebrated a Europeanized autochthonous population. They retained the Imazighen as a primordial national ancestor, but maintained that the Imazighen are Semites, even from Arab origins. Thus, the Arabs and Imazighen were a conjoined race, "brothers" that had been reunited with Arab conquests and the spread of Islam into North Africa.[22] Such a definition of Algerian identity abolished the contemporary relevance of Amazigh as an ethnic category, subsuming it under Arabness. As the Algerian Popular Party (PPA) emerged after World War II, these tensions over the Arab and Amazigh dimensions of national identity came to a head in the

Algeria," Working paper 7, LSE Crisis State Programme, London School of Economics Development Research Centre, London, 2001.

[20] S. Sadi, *Algérie, l'échec recommencé?* (Algiers: Édition Parenthèses, 1991).

[21] J. Wyrtzen, "Colonial Legacies, National Identity and Challenges for Multiculturalism in the Contemporary Maghreb," in M. Ennaji (ed.), *Multiculturalism and Democracy in North Africa* (New York: Routledge, forthcoming).

[22] J. McDougall, *History and the Culture of Nationalism in Algeria* (Cambridge: Cambridge University Press, 2006).

1948–49 "Berberist Crisis." The immediate context for this crisis was the determination of the Algerian national movement to cast Algerian identity in exclusively Arab and Muslim terms; thus, rejecting the concept of an *Algerian Algeria* in which cultural pluralism could be allowed as an operative sociopolitical force. Tensions over the parameters of Algerian identity continued to be expressed in the following years, but ultimately a firm conviction to consolidate a strong Arab-Muslim cultural hegemony prevailed within the FLN leadership that took power in 1962.[23] Algeria's first independent president, Ben Bella, proclaimed in 1962, "We are Arabs . . . ten millions of Arabs" in reference to Algeria's entire non-French population at the time. A year later, he declared Arabization a necessary condition for Algeria's development.[24] Although the Imazighen satisfied the prerequisites of Islamic faith and geographic residency, their use of Tamazight and their perceived non-Arab culture excluded them from national inclusion.

Belkacem Krim first made demands that the Amazigh culture be officially recognized during the war of liberation. However, shortly after independence from France in 1962, the leadership of this cause passed to the Kabylia-based rebellions of Hocine Ait Ahmed's Socialist Forces Front (Front des Forces Socialistes, FFS). In 1964 the FFS organized an uprising in Kabylia in October. The rebellion failed; the FFS was banned and its leader was exiled to continue the operation of the FFS from abroad.[25] Between 1966 and 1989, the party was an opposition in exile grounded among Kabylian migrants. It had a broad social appeal, focusing on questions of social justice rather than specific Amazigh identity. The FFS was associated with democratic pluralism and the early movement for human rights.[26]

In 1968 the Amazigh Cultural Movement (MCB) was created to petition for more democracy and cultural pluralism. Despite its efforts, the MCB met with little tangible success because of pressure exerted on it by security forces. As a result of the inhospitable political and cultural climate that prevailed under Boudmedienne, the torch of Amazigh activism passed to the large Amazigh community living and working in France. In Paris in 1967, the Amazigh Academy of Cultural Exchange and Research was established, and in 1972 the Amazigh Studies Group was founded. The main aims of these organizations

---

[23] M. Brett and E. Fentress, *The Berbers* (Oxford: Blackwell, 1996).

[24] For Algeria as for most ex-colonies, decolonization demanded "recovery" of the nation's language, because during the long period of French colonization, the Arabic language was marginalized. A 1938 law had gone so far as to declare Arabic a foreign language in Algeria. See G. Grandguillaume, *Arabisation et politique linguistique au Maghreb* (Paris: Maisonneuve & Larose, 1983); and K. Taleb-Ibrahimi, *Les Algériens et leurs langues* (Algiers: El Hikma, 1995).

[25] A. Heggoy, "The FFS, an Algerian Opposition to a One Party System," *African Historical Studies* 1/2 (1969): 121–40; A. Guenoun, *Chronologie du mouvement berbére* (Algiers: Casbah Éditions, 1999).

[26] Roberts, *Co-opting Identity*.

were to promote knowledge and understanding of Amazigh culture, traditions, and languages and to pressure Algiers and other Maghreb governments to grant Amazighs greater political, cultural, and linguistic freedoms—activities stigmatized by the state government as neocolonialist projects to divide and rule the postcolonies.[27]

The principal focus of Amazigh's dissatisfaction regarding Algeria's postcolonial nation-building project has been the unrivaled status of Arabic, constitutionally foreseen as Algeria's only official language. The main objective of forced Arabization in the educational system and government was not to repress spoken Tamazight, particularly its Kabylian variety Taqbaylit, but rather to target the reliance on French at all levels of society. Yet if Arabization was primarily intended to liberate the country from its reliance on the colonizer's language, it also created a growing sense of marginality among Kabyles, who had adopted French as a preferred second language during the colonial period.[28] Other points Amazigh activists focused on were the repressive state policy with regard to their culture: the 1967 banning of a secondary school play in Tamazight in Tizi Ouzou, the 1973 dissolution of the chair of Amazigh studies at the University of Algiers, and the 1978 cancellation of a concert by the popular Kabylian singer Lounis Ait Menguellet.[29]

The first rupture

The first rupture with the Algerian regime came in 1980 when the authorities banned a scheduled lecture on Amazigh poetry by Mouloud Mammeri, a well-known Amazigh writer and anthropologist at Tizi Ouzou University. This event would come to be known as the Amazigh Spring—an evocation of the cultural flowering in Prague in 1968.[30] While "Berber Studies" had flourished since the late 1960s and 1970s in the French academy, the "Berber Spring" inaugurated a period of political mobilization in Algeria around Amazigh identity. The Amazigh Spring had implications for Algeria as a whole because it marked the first major demonstration of popular dissent and dissatisfaction with the Algerian regime since independence. Facing an Islamist challenge and the ensuing civil war in the 1990s, the Algerian state attempted to defuse Amazigh demands by making cultural concessions including the establishment of an institute for Amazigh studies at the University of Tizi Ouzou in 1990, the broadcasting of nightly news in Tamazight in 1991, the introduction

---

[27] See further under "The Potential Transformative Power of the Amazigh Movement" on the role of diaspora.

[28] Roberts, *Towards an Understanding of the Kabyle Question in Contemporary Algeria.*

[29] Shatzmiller (ed.), *Nationalism and Minority Identities in Islamic Societies.*

[30] J. Ruedy, *Modern Algeria: The Origins and Development of a Nation* (Bloomington, IL: Indiana University Press, 2005).

of teaching Tamazight in amazighophone regions in 1995, and a clause in the constitutional revision of 1996 that recognized Amazigh identity as one of the constitutive elements of Algerian national identity alongside the already acknowledged Arab and Islamic components. In 1995, the Haut Commissariat de l'Amazighite was founded, the first governmental institution for Amazigh culture with the main objective of facilitating the teaching of Tamazight as one of Algeria's "national" languages. In 1996, a constitutional referendum passed a three-pillar construction of the Algerian nation: Islamness, Arabness, and Amazighness. However, Amazigh activists were disappointed that Tamazight would not be recognized as an "official" administrative language. A clear sign that the Kabylian population was far from pleased came in mid 1998. The mysterious assassination of a leading Kabylian singer provoked a wave of protest and the typical state overreaction with the killing of several demonstrators. Still the ongoing civil war with violent confrontation between Islamists and the security forces in Algeria overshadowed almost all other political expressions.

THE RISE OF A NEW MOVEMENT

A renewed and more sustained period of popular unrest in Kabylia grew out of the clashes with the authorities in April 2001 during the annual commemoration of the events of spring 1980. The killing of an 18-year-old student, Massinissa Guermah, in the custody of the Gendarmerie enflamed the push for the Amazigh cause and mobilized additional people across a wider geographical area than the usual confines of the main cities in Kabylia. This event, combined with socioeconomic difficulties faced by people in the region and the impression of a detached, corrupt, and uncaring government, usually referred to simply as *la hogra*, or 'contempt', gave rise to violent confrontations with security forces and contributed to a space in which old grievances could be articulated in new forms.

The brutality with which the Gendarmerie Nationale responded had no precedent in the region since Independence and provoked an enormous trauma in Kabylian public opinion and a degree of international mobilization not seen at any other time during the entire history of the Algerian conflict.

This renowned uprising, dubbed the Black Spring, affected Algeria in three ways: it

1. parachuted new, politically relevant actors belonging to a generation hitherto strongly underrepresented into the political arena;
2. weakened the existing political party allegiances and led to the (re) appearance of more traditional forms of social and political organization;
3. forced the political elite to address the question of official national identity.

The uprising gave birth to a new movement, referred to as the "Kabyle citizens' movement" and as the "*Aruch*."[31] The former stressed a "contemporary democratic character and purpose," the latter a "traditional form of Kabyle self-organization."

The novelty of this movement was the local-level organization with the appeal to a particular idea of Amazigh tradition, which supplanted the regional and national scale of existing political parties.[32] Indeed, the structures that did emerge from this protest movement were founded firmly on the significance of territorially based organizations in Kabylia: *Inter-wilayas* (districts), *aarchs* (tribes), *daïras* (departments), and *communes* (CIADC), differing in genesis and internal structure and featuring a collective and generally young leadership. This explicitly territorial organization, based around a territorial unit from the pre-colonial period, represented according to some scholars "the need to reactivate the ancestral social organisation of Kabylia ranging from village committees to the *aarchs* [which] seems to unite a large consensus and was able to drive effectively the political mobilization."[33]

The politico-cultural significance of tradition as an important factor during this protest cycle is recognizable in the demands that were made to the Algerian state. However, the majority of the fifteen demands in the *El Kseur Platform* presented in June 2001 addressed socioeconomic or political mismanagement and nationwide grievances and did not deal with specifically Amazigh identity.[34] The first seven demands related to security and justice issues, stemming from the Gendarmerie's heavy-handed response to the Kabylia uprising. These included a demand for criminal proceedings against the responsible state agents; an amnesty for all imprisoned demonstrators and those awaiting trial; medical care; reparations for the families, including the granting of "martyr" status; and the termination of the state inquiry launched by President Bouteflika. The last eight demands focused mainly on socioeconomic issues. The most ambitious and also most controversial called for a withdrawal of the Gendarmerie from Kabylia (Art. 4) and the subordination of the presidency and the security services to democratically elected bodies (Art. 11). The only concrete demand relating specifically to Amazigh cultural

---

[31] International Crisis Group (ICG) Middle East/North Africa Report, *Algeria: Unrest and Impasse in Kabylia*, 15 (2003).

[32] M. Salhi, *Élite entre modernisation et retraditionalisation: Les acteurs de la contestation politique et identitaire en Kabylie*, 1980–2001, in CREAD-ARCAASD, *Élite et société dans le monde arabe: Le cas de l'Algérie et de l'Egypt* (Algiers: Casbah Éditions, 2002).

[33] Especially for the emigrant community the notion of the *aarch* became an important tool to re-imagine their identity and contributed to the myths that feed the culture of the diaspora. M. Collyer, "The Reinvention of Political Community in a Transnational Setting: Framing the Kabyle Citizens' Movement," *Ethnic and Racial Studies* 31/4 (2008): 687–707.

[34] ICG, *Algeria*.

heritage was the request for the recognition of Tamazight as an official language (Art. 8).

The failure of the Coordinations

In the month after the riots of 2001, new politics seemed to be emerging from the Kabylian crucible. The grand demonstrations of May and June 2001, followed by the electoral boycotts of 2002, were displays of the Coordinations' power, grounded in the submerged network of Kabylian society.[35] For a brief period the movement presented the greatest democratic challenge the post-colonial Algerian state had faced. Yet, this opportunity was not used to create a new political space with a new vision of the state.

After an initial success, the Coordinations were now a spent force—internally divided and externally co-opted—and were unable to generate a wide popular mobilization either beyond the Amazigh-speaking region of Kabylia, or within the region itself, which might have otherwise replicated and diffused the idea of a national citizens' movement for democracy. Almost none of the *El Kseur Platform* demands came to fruition. Some concessions obtained from the government were more symbolic than substantial. The rest are still trapped in an intractable negotiation process. Like every Algerian political movement before it, the Coordinations lost to the *pouvoir*.[36]

Closer examination of the movement reveals a deeply fractured political project with some revolutionary aspects as well as banally reformist or pathetically rent-seeking ones. From its inception, the movement clearly situated itself outside the framework of the regime and its institutions, that is, the formal political sphere based on party-political competition and the "voluntary sector" of legally recognized associations.[37] The spontaneous structures which did develop were founded firmly on the significance of territorially based organizations in Kabylia. The way in which Arush linkages determined and simultaneously circumscribed their political options and capacities severely limited the movement's ability to pursue its aims or deal effectively with the problems it confronted. Much of the modus operandi proved inadequate for the larger goal of transforming the whole of Algerian society. The almost complete exclusion of women from the protest movement was one such example.[38]

Examining the political demands represented by the El Kseur Platform under the banner of values and identity mainly revealed struggles of power and resources. In this sense, the strategy of Coordinations mirrored typical

---

[35] ICG, *Algeria*.   [36] Mundy, "The Failure."
[37] I. Werenfels, *Managing Instability in Algeria. Elites and Political Change since 1995* (New York: Routledge, 2007).
[38] S. Boukir, "Femmes dans les aarchs," *Passarelles* 24 (2002).

sociocultural perceptions and values of political practices. The Coordinations used their power in the same way that other Algerian interest groups had always used theirs: to get a piece of the pie. In fact, many demands presented at the El Kseur Platform would have translated into revenue for the Coordinations constituents. There are obvious points regarding reparations, the granting of "martyr" status,[39] and unemployment benefits. The struggle for the official recognition of Tamazight could also be interpreted as a fight against the complete Arabization of the formerly French-speaking civil administration, where dominant positions were held by Imazighen. Furthermore, the elevation of Tamazight as an official language would bring a new source of revenue, especially in the education sector, and a new network of power.

The Algerian state further weakened the Coordinations: it employed a *divide et impera* strategy against this new movement that consisted of three pillars: coercion, repression, and co-optation, a practice that still forms a key tactic of control.[40] The regime used violence to deter and repress the demonstrations, and the imprisonment of activists was central to the state's triumph. Furthermore, the state benefited from pre-existing divisions in the Kabylian polity. With the FFS and RCD already splitting political and generational sympathies in Kabylia, the appearance of the Coordinations as a new political actor gave rise to a tripartite system, and this was successfully managed by the *pouvoir* to prevent a coherent alliance of contesting actors.[41] Whereas the moderate faction of the movement focused on demands relating to the whole of Algeria, the government pursued a strategy of depicting the unrest in Kabylia as being an exclusively Kabylian affair, orchestrated essentially by the radical elements of the movement, driven by a dangerous ambition for autonomy and secession as well as personal political motives. Thus, the Algerian regime has largely managed to "ethnicize" the unrest and thus limit it to the regional level. In doing this, however, the government had to acknowledge the identity dimension and make concessions on that level, notably in the demonopolization of the Arabic language. In April 2002 the Amazigh language Tamazight was embodied in the Constitution as the second "national" language. Critics noted that Tamazight was already a constitutionally recognized language—the El Kseur Platform demanded Tamazight's elevation to an "official" language on a par with Arabic. In the autumn of 2003, Tamazight was introduced in the national school curricula from fourth grade onward as an optional course, limited, however, to schools in the Kabylia region.

---

[39] P. A. Silverstein, "Martyrs and Patriots: Ethnic, National and Transnational Dimensions of Kabyle Politics," *Journal of North African Studies* 8/1 (2003): 87–111.
[40] L. Martinez, *The Algerian Civil War* (London: Hurst, 2000).   [41] ICG, *Algeria.*

POTENTIAL TRANSFORMATIVE POWER
OF THE AMAZIGH MOVEMENT

Having outlined the trajectory of this protest movement and shown how a new political force became an arena of regime manipulation and opposition maneuvering as well as a victim of its own internal structures, it seems clear that while the ability of the movement to engage in resource mobilization has been proven, its capacity to sustain and transform the Algerian state remains an open question. Still, the development of Amazigh issues presents a series of challenges to the Algerian state.

An important factor relates to the future political evolution of the Amazigh movement. Analyzing the events of spring 1980 in Kabylia, a scholar concluded: "The relevant opposition is not: Kabylia vs. the nation-state but: Kabylia vs. the regime power. This is a very different matter."[42] This holds true also for the Black Spring of 2001 when protests were focused against the failures of the Algerian regime rather than the Algerian state. To be sure, moderate claims of the Imazighen pose a current threat neither to the territorial integrity of the Algerian state nor to ruling elites, which themselves contain important Amazigh components. The moderate faction of the movement would like to see it become a vehicle for general democratization and development of Algerian society. This stance explains the national scope of the two main parties in the region, the FFS and RCD. Those two parties, with an exclusively Amazigh base and leadership, have never admitted exclusive ethnic ideological orientations. Their discourse has always focused on national issues. Their leaders' attempts to de-ethnicize the Amazigh questions reflects the ambiguity of the social and political situation in Algeria. Amazighs in Algeria are attached to their national identity, and they have restricted their demands to preserving their culture and identity and implementing Western-style democracy. This stance also explains the presence of demands relating to the whole of Algeria in the El Kseur Platform. However, questions exist regarding whether the movement might evolve in a more radical direction. Some radical Amazigh militants are driven by an ambition for autonomy or even independence for Kabylia rather than general reform for Algerian society. In June 2001 the Movement for Autonomy in Kabylia, led by Ferhat Mehenni, was established. This development was interpreted as a move from civic nationalism to ethnic nationalism.[43]

A further development with a potential effect on system stability regards the relationship between the Amazigh movement and the Islamist movement. The Islamist movement defines itself through religion and anti-modern ideology

---

[42] Willis, "The Politics of Berber (Amazigh) Identity."

[43] A. Layachi, "The Berbers in Algeria: Politicized Ethnicity and Ethnicized Politics," in Shatzmiller (ed.), *Nationalism and Minority Identities in Islamic Societies*, 165.

and rejects the secular aspects of Arab nationalism, whereas the Amazigh movement defines itself by culture—although most Imazighen also consider themselves Muslims. Tensions have existed at times and from the Islamist point of view are especially related to three elements: (1) the issue regarding the "battle" of the national language(s) of the state: Islamists consider the Arabic language essential to the maintenance of the Islamic identity; (2) the endorsement of secular democracy. By "secular democracy," the Imazighen refer not only to a separation of religion and state or democratically elected bodies, but also to a "project of society" designed to replace "retrograde" ways of thinking and acting with "forward-looking" mentalities and behaviors;[44] and (3) the so-called Western neocolonial agendas, particularly considering the close links and educational background of many Imazighen, especially in France. It should, however, be stressed that the relationship between the two movements is not one of total animosity. The Islamist movement in the Maghreb is deferential toward the politics of Amazigh; this is evidenced by the conciliatory literature published by Maghrebian Islamist thinkers. Hassan al-Banna, the founder of the Muslim Brotherhood, was one of the first Islamists to comment on Amazigh issues, and the Moroccan Islamist Abdessalam Yassine published in 1997 *Dialog with an Amazigh Friend.*[45] On a political level, in 1995, shared concerns about issues of justice, reform, and democracy led the FFS to collaborate with representatives of the dissolved FIS alongside other opposition parties to sign a common document—the Rome platform—specifying the principles that could serve as the basis of peace talks with the Algerian government.[46] Significantly, the document also called for the recognition of Tamazight and the relegalization of the FIS. The two movements were also demographically similar, both drawing from the same constituency of mainly young men disenchanted by Algeria's high unemployment rate, severe housing shortages, and failed education system. According to some scholars, the Amazigh and Islamist movements share the characteristics of having the capacity to mobilize a large number of people in favor of major reforms in Algeria.[47]

The ethnic dimension of the Amazigh issue and its strong links with Europe ensure powerful support from Western countries. Indeed the link with Europe is important because a disproportionate part of the large expatriated Maghreb community is originally amazighophone. One of the consequences of the Berber Myth on contemporary politics was the French government's preference for Amazigh populations, opening wide avenues for Kabylian emigration

---

[44] Goodman, *Berber Culture on the World Stage*, 12.

[45] For a discussion see Maddy-Weitzman, *The Berber Identity Movement and the Challenge to North African States*, Introduction.

[46] W. B. Quandt, *Between Ballots and Bullets* (Washington, DC: The Brooking Institution, 1998).

[47] Willis, "The Politics of Berber (Amazigh) Identity."

to France and the establishment of a permanent connection between the two regions. In the first half of the twentieth century, as many as 80 percent of the self-designated "Beur" militants were of Kabylian origin.[48] There are currently an estimated 2.5 million Algerians and Moroccans of Amazigh origin in Europe, more than half of them in France, and the rest mainly in the Netherlands, Belgium, Spain, and Italy.

During the 1960s and 1970s, the significant, relatively wealthy and educated diaspora community facilitated the development of several Amazigh organizations in France that would provide important sites for the formulation and dissemination of discourses of Amazigh identity. Unlike later associations in France, which would target primarily the growing diaspora community, these early organizations were also oriented to Kabyles in Algeria. The first association, the Amazigh Academy of Cultural Exchange and Research, was founded in 1967 by a small group of Kabyle writers, artists, and intellectuals. It sought to situate Amazigh culture through a metadiscourse of human rights and universality that emphasized the similarities between Imazighen and other minorities. Having little popular impact, in 1969 one of its founders, Mohand Arab Bessaoud, took charge of the association, changed its name to Académie Berbère Agraw Imazighene, reorienting it toward a specifically political struggle for Amazigh linguistic and cultural rights in Algeria. It was the first organization to call explicitly for making Tamazight an official and national language. The association tended to promote an extremist and by many accounts racist (anti-Arabic) discourse which did not appeal to the growing number of university-educated Kabyles. In 1972 some of these left the Académie Berbère Agraw Imazighene, which would continue to exist until 1976, and formed a new group at Vincennes University in Paris: the Berber Studies Group. Unlike the Académie Berbère Agraw Imazighene, which had been legally constituted as an autonomous association of foreigners in France under the French law of 1901, the Berber Study Group took a particularly academic form: members of the group developed a script for Tamazight, standardized the language, produced dictionaries and translations, and conducted research into pre-Arabic civilizations in the Maghreb. The suppression of Amazighness in Algeria and its simultaneous rehabilitation in France served, according to some scholars, to codify and reinforce an Arab/Amazigh dichotomy in nearly the same terms as the colonial Berber Myth.[49] Others have seen the continuing development of Kabylian culture and transnational activism, especially the cultural flourishing of Amazigh music and poetry in France, as an opportunity that would not have existed without significant emigration and which would not have

---

[48] M. Khellil, *L'exil Kabyle: Essai d'analyse du vécu de migrants* (Paris: L'Harmattan, 2000).
[49] Silverstein, *Algeria in France*.

occurred in the hostile climate of Algeria.[50] In 2001, the events of the Black Spring provoked a degree of international mobilization not seen at any other time during the entire history of the Algerian conflict. Demonstrations in solidarity with the people of Kabylia were also held in Europe, especially in France, and in the US.[51] However, during this period the potential impact of diaspora on affairs within the Algerian state was limited. As underlined by Collyer, the great emphasis on territorial legitimacy was one of the key elements that emerged during this protest phase and resulted in a dramatic loss of autonomy within the diaspora. Once the protests within Kabylia had come to an end, the diaspora was not able to offer any new dynamic to the movement. This represents a chief difference from earlier periods of Kabylian diaspora activism, when in the 1960s and 1970s the Amazigh community in France played a central role in defining the modern understanding of Kabylian culture.

To this day the Amazigh diaspora has been seen by the Algerian state as an untrustworthy actor, and not regarded as a partner in the efforts to achieve a sustainable peace in Algeria. On the contrary, the political activities of the diaspora were stigmatized by the state government as neocolonialist projects to divide and rule the country and perceived as a security threat. For the first years of Algerian independence the FLN therefore paid great attention to developments of political activism in France and developed sophisticated surveillance methods.[52] Any attempt to challenge the mono-ethnic vision of the Algerian state was not tolerated from within Algeria and was strongly resisted by the state's operations in the diaspora. Today, the enhanced possibilities for transnational communication, mobilization, and action as well as the upsurge in domestic and international security concerns after 9/11 and the Arab Spring 2011 have heightened awareness of the role of diasporas.[53] Diasporas have the potential to act as bridges or mediators between their home and host countries and to transmit the values of pluralism and democracy. Overall, the Amazigh discourse is profoundly sympathetic to Western liberal-humanist values. It presents an interesting facet of civil society,[54] in that it is neither

---

[50] The invention of the modern Kabyle folksong by expatriate recording artists in France played a significant role in the spread of Amazigh collective consciousness. See Goodman, *Berber Culture on the World Stage.*

[51] There is some disagreement as to whether these events represented a concerted, coordinated international attempt to influence the Algerian government, or if it was simply a coincidence that different emigrant communities across the world chose to express their outrage more or less spontaneously in similar ways on similar days.

[52] M. Collyer, "Transnational Political Participation of Algerians in France: Extra-territorial Civil Society versus Transnational Governmentality," *Political Geography* 25 (2006): 836–49.

[53] See E. Østergaard-Nielsen, *Diasporas and Conflict Resolution—Part of the Problem or Part of the Solution?* Copenhagen, DIIS Brief, March 2006; R. Bauböck and T. Faist (eds.), *Diaspora and Transnationalism: Concepts, Theories and Methods* (Amsterdam: Amsterdam University Press, 2010).

[54] F. Cochrane, "Civil Society Beyond the State: The Impact of Diaspora Communities on Peace Building," *Global Media Journal: Mediterranean Edition* 2/2 (2007): 19–29.

wholly external nor internal, but somewhere between the two, making choices, as we have seen, based on a diverse array of options and the political opportunity structures available in the homeland.[55] This unique position therefore anchors the diaspora organization as a key part of civil society activism which can play a number of roles in conflict and in attempts to build peace within divided societies. However, their continuing labeling as "spoilers" or "extremists" with the concomitant isolation policy can be, especially in a period of transition to democracy, counterproductive and can end up in radicalizing and marginalizing crucial factors.[56]

With a political change in Algeria, a part of the Algerian diaspora could be expected to return in the near future. The decisive question would be if they would get involved in business primarily or whether they would develop an interest in entering into politics. Will the Amazigh diasporas have the ability to play a positive role in the transformative process by undertaking and promoting activities that aim at the sustainable transformation of structural conflict factors and patterns in all relevant social, economic, and political spheres? The Amazigh diaspora can become a credible actor if it engages critically with its own stereotypes and if it explores new grounds in terms of new networks and strategic alliances that transcend ethnic boundaries. The success of the Amazigh diaspora in the transformative process of Algeria depends not only on its capacity to mobilize its own constituency and on the access it has to power centers, especially in Europe, but also on how willing it is to assess its own strengths and weaknesses.

Contemporary processes of globalization combined with new ways of Amazigh imagining, in the sense used by Benedict Anderson,[57] have stimulated and reinforced a transnational consciousness of a specific Amazigh ethnopolitical identity with wider repercussions for Algeria, the neighboring states, and its relations with the rest of the world. The Amazigh Culture Movement, a transnational phenomenon of ethnocultural assertion, cuts across national boundaries: backed by and intertwined with elements of the Amazigh diaspora, Amazighism has not only become part of the larger political spectrum in two of North Africa's leading countries, Algeria and Morocco, but has also begun to reverberate in Libya, Niger, and Mali. The wider movement does not limit itself to promoting cultural and language rights for Imazighen and Tamazight speakers in each of the North African states. It also challenges the "Arab" character of North Africa with an explicitly

---

[55] As Adamson rightly points out, "the relationship of the diaspora to the homeland is defined by the desire for transformation, contestation and political change" (F. B. Adamson, "Mobilizing for the Transformation of Home: Political Identities and Transnational Practices," in N. Al-Ali and K. Koser (eds.), *New Approaches to Migration? Transnational Communities and the Transformation of Home* (London: Routledge, 2002).

[56] Bauböck and Faist (eds.), *Diaspora and Transnationalism*.

[57] Anderson, *Imagined Communities*.

Amazigh conception of the region, which it calls Tamazgha.[58] New media are opening paths for protesters of power. The internet, blogs, and the mushrooming of channels outside state authority, symbols par excellence of the contemporary global information world, have enabled activists all over the world to communicate and have become an additional element in the construction of the "imagined" Amazigh community worldwide. Indeed, it is quite a change from the 1980s when the events in Kabylia were a product of a particular experience in this specific region, rather than an experience known to Algeria's wider Amazigh population or even worldwide.

These challenges reveal the potentially transformative power of the Amazigh Movement. Likewise, any attempt by the Algerian *pouvoir* to underestimate this potential or repress the Amazigh movement could have negative consequences for future peace and stability in the country.

CONCLUSION: A NEW FUTURE FOR THE AMAZIGH MOVEMENT?

The issues at the heart of the insurrection in Kabylia in 2001 have been similar and in some cases even identical to those that drove young North Africans onto the streets, giving rise to the popular revolts shaking the Arab world in 2011: the unsolved question of national identity, high unemployment, mismanagement of public resources, and a popular sense that *la hogra* is the main element marking the relationship between the governing and the governed.

The interaction among several of these factors in combination with the political uproar in the countries directly bordering Algeria have the potential to upset the political status quo and to force the elite to develop new strategies and modify the political system. This situation could, seen in the short term, push nationalist reformers to adopt reforms that embrace wider participation and increase political competition for "self-interested strategic compliance,"[59] even if they have no immediate normative commitment to democracy. Yet, the question of democracy in Algeria requires thinking in terms of an extended time-frame.[60] At the same time, experiences with democratization in Latin

---

[58] See also the proclamation by the Tuareg of the new state of Azawad on 6 April 2013, <http://www.aljazeera.com/news/africa/2012/04/20124644412359539.html>, accessed September 2013.

[59] A. Przeworski, *Democracy and the Market: Political and Economic Reforms in Eastern Europe and Latin America* (Cambridge: Cambridge University Press, 1991).

[60] D. A. Rustow argued that one generation was probably the minimum period of transition because democracy involved "the emergence of new social groups and formation of new habits." See D. A. Rustow, "Transition to Democracy: Toward a Dynamic Model," *Comparative Politics* 2 (1970): 337–63 at 337.

America, Africa, Asia, and Southeastern Europe have questioned the very notion of democracy being the necessary outcome of transitions from authoritarianism.[61] The Algerian political system may indeed over time gradually incorporate more and more of what Dahl calls institutional guarantees for democracy, notably free and fair elections, freedom to join and form organizations, freedom of expression, alternative sources of information, and representative institutions for making government policies.[62]

Key to Algeria's political future is whether, beginning with the task of restructuring Algerian society, policies and mechanisms of transitional justice and reconciliation will be adopted. Since the late 1980s it is widely assumed that transitional justice can serve as an instrument to consolidate democratic transition.[63] By transitional justice, I mean an instrument of broad social transformation that rests on the assumption that societies need to confront past abuses in order to come to terms with their history and move on. Indeed, transitional justice has both backward- and forward-looking aspects. It affirms that governments must build institutions that will seek justice for past transgressions, while showing their commitment to good governance in the future.

Algeria experienced already a sort of "transitional justice" after the civil war by promulgating different laws, whether the 1995 "Rahma" (pardon) law, the 1999 "Civil Concord" or the 2006 "Charter of Peace and National Reconciliation."[64] The Charter provides amnesty to armed rebels, exonerates state security forces, and grants some compensation to victims and their families. However, the Charter was not based on a public debate, nor does it include a truth-seeking mechanism or investigation into abuses or measures to reform state institutions in order to prevent repetition of past violations. Not surprisingly the Charter was essentially doomed to failure.[65]

In order to make preparation for the future peace and stability of the country, especially with regard to ethnic animosity, in my view only a process of transitional justice based on the "nation-building dimension," as indicated by Kymlicka, can "help to reshape identities, and in particular, to weaken those aspects of people's identities that were the source of violence and

---

[61] See M. Ottaway, *Democracy Challenged: The Rise of Semi-Authoritarianism* (Washington, DC: Carnegie Endowment for International Peace, 2003); and D. Brumberg and L. Diamond, "Introduction," in D. Brumberg and L. Diamond (eds.), *Islam and Democracy in the Middle East* (Baltimore: Johns Hopkins University Press, 2003).

[62] R. Dahl, *Polyarchy: Participation and Opposition* (New Haven, CT: Yale University Press, 1971).

[63] See Paige Arthur (ed.), *Identities in Transition* (Cambridge: Cambridge University Press, 2011).

[64] For broader debates about transitional justice in the region, see the Chatham House report on "Transitional Justice and the Arab Spring" (February 2012).

[65] See R. Tlemcani, *Algeria Under Bouteflika* (Washington, DC: Carnegie Endowment for International Peace, 2008).

conflict, and to replace them with a strengthened sense of shared identity related to common membership in the national political community."[66]

In the Algerian case, transitional justice can serve the nation-building dimension, because the national identity is already seen, by Imazighen among others, as an inclusive one. Imazighen, despite their political conscious-ness, are remarkably loyal and dedicated to the concept of Algerian nationalism and the national (nation-state) identity is powerful and also "authentic" as the basis for a sense of identity and belonging. The power of national identity derives not just from the hegemonic nature of the state ideology, but also from the "vernacular communitarism" reflecting the "nested relationship" between the Imazighen and the nation-state.[67]

The ethnic conflict is driven by the state's rigid and culturally homogeneous ideal of Algerian culture, citizenship, and national identity. National citizen-ship (as opposed to legal citizenship) has become synonymous with Arabism. This definition inherently casts Amazigh culture as non-nationalist and alien, frames Amazigh identity as anathema to state and social solidarity, and was the underlying cause of human rights violations against the Amazigh. Algeria, like most postcolonial states, objects to the very idea of empowering national minorities. After independence from France in 1962 it was widely expected that the new state would successfully incorporate and assimilate Imazighen under the rubric of homogeneous "national" identity, based on common Islamic faith, the Arab language, the legacy of the struggle for independence, and a pan-Arabic ideology. This view is complemented by the widespread depiction of Algerian nationalism as reactive, first against French colonial domination and more recently, against dominant Western neocolonialism or the dominant influence of "Western values." There is also a related argu-ment, that the authoritarian and rentierist tendencies of the Algerian elite concern its intent on prioritizing their self-interest over the interests of the society they govern.[68] While the Algerian *pouvoir* has taken some initiatives in support of Amazigh rights, public authorities continue to perceive cultural and ethnic differences as a threat to the Algerian regime and the existing order and as a security concern and pursue practices of deliberate discrimination and persecution. These contradictory attitudes by the Algerian *pouvoir* con-tribute to a growing sense of cultural and linguistic alienation and exacerbate feelings of exclusion among Amazigh, complicating national integration. Combined with poverty and *la hogra* this provides a potent mix. Indeed, it is precisely for these reasons that a transitional justice process is needed in Algeria.

---

[66] W. Kymlicka, "Transitional Justice, Federalism and the Accommodation of Minority Nationalism," in Arthur (ed.), *Identities in Transition*.
[67] See D. Miller, *Citizenship and Nationalism* (Cambridge: Polity, 2000).
[68] Werenfels, *Managing Instability in Algeria*.

Algeria will become a peaceful country only if all citizens come to share a sense of identification with their political community. This is difficult to achieve with the insistence on an "exclusively" Arab-Muslim Algerian identity. Nation-building of this sort has been the cause of the historic injustices toward Amazigh.

A transitional justice process in Algeria is needed to promote a different sort of nation-building, one that is not "monocultural," hence accommodating Amazigh identities. Imazighen must be included in the nation not just as undifferentiated individual Algerian citizens, but also collectively, as a constituent component of the nation, pursuing a project which Kymlicka calls "citizenization."[69] As we have seen, there is a potential that identity could become mobilized in ways that, especially in a period of transition, could destabilize the country. It is therefore important to determine whether it is possible to accommodate such a minority nationalism in a way that is compatible with democratic stability.

A first step to inform Algeria's commitment to transitional justice relates to a model of constructing relations of democratic citizenship. In my view this model has two main features:

1. the involvement of the Amazigh movement in a transitional justice process of nation-building;

2. the adoption of a model of "multination and multilingual federalism."

Recent history shows us that transitional justice processes are frequently top-down—led either by international organizations and institutions or through state-centric approaches, often at the expense of local civil society. Too often these processes are conducted without concern for the people affected: they become a modern form of the *mission civilizatrice*, relying on coercive bargaining mechanisms more than on an inclusive dialog between parties.[70] Indeed, any transitional justice process that does not take into consideration civil society and its expressions at all levels (local and international) is unlikely to be sustainable.[71]

The ability of the Amazigh movement to be not only objectively effective but also perceived as a legitimate tool in the transitional justice process will be affected by the movement's recognition of the mistakes and failures of the past. Critical engagement with its own strengths, weaknesses, and stereotypes,

---

[69] Kymlicka, "Transitional Justice, Federalism and the Accommodation of Minority Nationalism."

[70] C. Yordan, "Towards Deliberative Peace: A Habermassian Critique of Contemporary Peace Operations," *Journal of International Relations and Development* 12 (2009): 58–89.

[71] The strategy of "communicative action" proposed by Habermas and Putnam's definition of social capital can make an interesting conceptual contribution here. See J. Habermas, *Further Reflections on the Public Sphere*, in Craig Claxon (ed.), *Habermas and the Public Sphere* (Cambridge, MA: MIT, 1993); and R. Putnam, *Bowling Alone: The Collapse and Revival of American Community* (London: Simon & Schuster, 2001).

and exploration of new ground in terms of new networks and strategic alliances that transcend ethnic boundaries, are necessary. The movement will need to break explicitly with nondemocratic and nonrepresentative approaches, agendas, and forms of activism as a precondition of an effective strategy of alliances with other democratic forces, regionally and nationally. Moreover, the movement will need to place less emphasis on mobilizing activities in ways that have tended to transgress the movement's own nonviolent principles and alienate public opinion, and invest in more imaginative activities that stimulate public debate.

A major role of the movement could be seen in the promotion, by a process of transitional justice, of a model of governance within a larger democratic constitutional order that all citizens can endorse and identify with. In the Western experience, the model of multination and multilingual federalism is increasingly seen as the best solution for managing ethno-national diversity, and for facilitating and promoting democracy. This model has two key features: (1) the creation of a federal or quasi-federal sub-unit in which the minority group form a local majority, and so can exercise meaningful forms of self-government, and (2) the recognition of the group's language as an official state language, at least within their federal sub-unit, and perhaps throughout the country as a whole.[72] Given the positive experiences with multination federalism,[73] this model is now perceived as an advanced form of government and could be a promising model for Algeria also. The question that arises is how transitional justice can contribute to the definition of such a new model of citizenship in Algeria. Will a model of multination citizenship be adopted voluntarily, without violence or international pressure? Only thus can it be seen as a model for a new democratic citizenship. There are no examples of a process of transitional justice accompanying the adoption of a model of multination federalism in the Western states, and even if there were they would probably not be helpful, because of the different circumstances.[74] As pointed out by Kymlicka,[75] it is generally assumed that models of multination citizenship are unlikely to be adopted, where there are either security concerns or the absence of human rights guarantees.

States all over the world are unlikely to accord a form of multination federalism to minorities that are perceived as disloyal, and therefore a threat

---

[72] W. Kymlicka, *Multicultural Odysseys: Navigating the New International Politics of Diversity* (Oxford: Oxford University Press, 2007).

[73] For an evaluation of the models of multinational federal states see W. Norman, *Negotiating Nationalism: Nations-Building, Federalism and Secession in the Multinational State* (Oxford: Oxford University Press, 2006).

[74] Spain and Northern Ireland are considered as "post-transition." See Kymlicka, "Transitional Justice, Federalism and the Accommodation of Minority Nationalism."

[75] W. Kymlicka, "Multination Federalism," in B. He, B. Galligan, and T. Inoguchi (eds.), *Federalism in Asia* (Cheltenham: Edward Elgar, 2007).

to state security. In Western democracies this is hardly an issue with regard to national minorities and indigenous people, but in Algeria, as already underlined, public authorities continue to perceive cultural and ethnic differences as a security concern. Indeed, if relations between the Algerian state and the Imazighen are seen only in this perspective, it reduces the scope to voice minority demands and the likelihood that those demands will be taken into consideration.

It is important, however, to reiterate that the Amazigh agenda operates within the existing state framework, while seeking to institute a liberal, democratic, multicultural order in which their own cultural identity can be developed unhindered. Despite their political consciousness, the Imazighen are remarkably loyal and dedicated to the concept of Algerian nationalism. The Amazigh requests of linguistic and cultural autonomy hardly appear to be inherently dangerous, or threatening to the cohesion or legitimacy of the state.

The second condition relates to the fact that states are normally unwilling to accept minority self-governments if they were seen as carriers of illiberal political cultures. This fear persists regarding the Amazigh question, especially in Kabylia regarding gender equality. However, there is the hope and expectation of what Nancy Rosenblum calls the "liberal expectancy":[76] the hope that democratic values will grow over time. Overall, the Amazigh discourse is profoundly sympathetic to Western liberal-democratic values, and it can be assumed that restricting individual freedom in the name of cultural authenticity will not be supported.

Algerian history has been strongly marked by violence and war. There is a historically rooted credo that only armed struggle and popular insurrection rather than negotiations will lead to political change and to this day it has undermined potential democratization dynamics.[77] In a state and a society that have just emerged from civil war and that are still struggling to cope with its effects, a process of reshaping and redefining the meaning of collective identities has already begun and will surely be fraught with difficulties. If the Algerian *pouvoir* wants what W. Zartman called "re-contracting"[78] or redefining its relations with its society, the Amazigh movement with its agenda of a more inclusive, more tolerant society of diversity, substantially related to broader issues of governance and justice, should not be underestimated as a force to reckon with in the future.

---

[76] N. Rosenblum, *Membership and Morals: The Personal Uses of Pluralism in America* (Princeton, NJ: Princeton University Press, 1988).

[77] L. Martinez, *The Algerian Civil War 1990–1998* (London: Hurst, 2000).

[78] W. Zartman and W. Mark Habeeb (eds.), *Polity and Society in Contemporary North Africa* (Boulder, CO: Westview, 1993).

8

The Gulf's Servant Class

Nicholas McGeehan

INTRODUCTION

Migrant workers in the Gulf Cooperative Council (GCC) states of Saudi Arabia, the United Arab Emirates, Kuwait, Qatar, Bahrain, and Oman do not fit the typical model of a minority, in the sense that they are non-indigenous economic migrants who would lay no claim to any common religion, culture, language, or ethnicity. Yet at the same time they are a clearly identifiable group in Gulf societies, and their exploitation and abuse is a consequence of their membership of this group. This chapter focuses on the migrant workers of the United Arab Emirates (UAE), whose mistreatment has been better documented than workers in the other GCC states.

The chapter has two central aims: to describe and characterize the system that regulates the employment of migrant workers in the UAE, and to posit theories on the underlying reasons for their exploitation. It presents the well-documented mistreatment of migrant workers as a corollary of a regulatory system whose effect, if not purpose, is a power relationship of profound inequality between migrant workers and national and expatriate employers, and argues that this facilitates one of the most extreme forms of human domination, slavery. With reference to the history of slavery in the region and its social significance to the ruling elite, it suggests that a slavery analysis can do far more than provide a legal characterization of the system.

The first section describes the *de jure* and de facto control mechanisms that regulate the employment of migrant workers, and while it does not describe their mistreatment and abuse—this having been amply documented in the media and in NGO reports—it must necessarily present a certain body of evidence in order to prove that this mistreatment is the corollary of systematic exploitation. With reference to recent case law from human rights law and international criminal law, it briefly explains why the system of regulation can be characterized as facilitating the trafficking and the enslavement, respectively, of migrant workers. The second section addresses the UAE's ruling elite. The two issues that are invariably overlooked in discussions on migrant workers are the ruling elite's prominent role in the private sector, and its skill in deflecting criticism. The UAE may have embraced Western neoliberalism, but while it is astute enough to appreciate the importance of presenting itself as a progressive state, its actions reveal it to be staunchly opposed to liberal democratic concepts such as human rights and multiculturalism. The third section of the chapter is an attempt to identify whether or not pre-existing prejudices or ideologies provide a justification for the abuse of migrant workers. It describes slavery's sociocultural significance in the region, and argues that it is the honorific value of slavery that best explains the abuse of domestic workers, and the elite's tolerance of servitude that places the systematic exploitation of the general migrant worker population into context.

A SYSTEM OF EXPLOITATION

The GCC states are dependent on migrant labor to varying degrees. Whereas Saudi Arabia and Oman, countries in which non-nationals comprise approximately 20 percent of the total population, would merely find it extremely difficult to cope in the absence of their migrant workforces, the United Arab Emirates, where non-nationals comprise 80 percent of the population, would grind to an immediate halt, as in all probability would Qatar, Kuwait, and Bahrain.[1] Without the labor of Indians, Pakistanis, Sri Lankans, Bangladeshis, Nepalese, and Filipinos, no shops would open, there would be no taxis on the street, and most importantly, no oil would flow. A conservative estimate would put the number of migrant workers in the region at 10 million,[2] yet despite the crucial role they play in sustaining the economies of the Gulf states, they have been excluded from their societies. The treatment of non-citizen workers in the United Arab Emirates, who constitute approximately 80 percent of an estimated population of 5 million,[3] varies enormously. There are three distinct classes of non-citizens in the UAE: a cosmopolitan professional class; a class of

---

[1] Precise figures and demographic breakdowns are not available. Figures here are taken from CIA World Factbook available at <https://www.cia.gov/library/publications/the-world-factbook>, accessed September 2013.

[2] The total population of the region is well over 40 million. See also Population Reference Bureau Country Statistics available at <www.prb.org>.

[3] No precise data exists on the population of the United Arab Emirates. The Population Reference Bureau estimates it to be 5.4 million. Statistics available at <www.prb.org>. The CIA's estimate is 5.1 million, available at <https://www.cia.gov/library/publications/the-world-factbook/geos/ae.html>, accessed September 2013.

predominantly Indian and Iranian entrepreneurs;[4] and a class of predominantly South Asian unskilled and semi-skilled workers. For the purposes of brevity this class of the laborforce, which includes female domestic workers, will simply be referred to as "migrant workers," as distinct from wealthier expatriates and Emirati nationals.

The legal framework that regulates both the ownership of businesses and the employment of non-citizen labor is known as the *kafala*, or sponsorship system.[5] Syed Ali has described this system as "the most basic principle underlying relations between citizens, expatriates and the state."[6] All businesses outside a country's free trade zones must, by law, be majority-owned by an Emirati national, known as a "kafeel" or sponsor. Emirati nationals therefore own the majority of all local businesses,[7] but rarely take any part in their running, leaving this to their expatriate partners. It has been claimed that the system allows Emirati nationals to extract money from their expatriates and that this has a trickle-down effect on migrant workers. One businessman described the exploitation of expatriates as "one of the core reasons for the low wage [and] poor living conditions and exploitation of unskilled [and] semi-skilled non-white collar workers."[8] Noha's recent study of Dubai's Indian entrepreneurial class offers a more nuanced analysis: "Foreign elites are complicit with the state in producing social and economic hierarchies that benefit both citizens and elite expatriates while maintaining a structure of labor migration that significantly disadvantages the majority of foreign residents living in the United Arab Emirates."[9] There is obviously exploitative potential in the relationship between national and expatriate business partners, even though there is no data to support any assertion that financial exploitation of expatriates is the norm; however, it is the exploitation of migrant workers that is the focus of this chapter and in that regard it is more often than not expatriates who are directly responsible. One of the ways in which UAE law facilitates this exploitation is through a system of sponsorship-based employment. Human Rights Watch describe its impact on migrant workers thus:

A foreign worker's legal ability to enter, live and work in the UAE depends on a single employer. If a foreign construction worker in the UAE quits, his employer will request

---

[4] Neha Vora, "Unofficial Citizens: Indian Entrepreneurs and the State-Effect in Dubai, United Arab Emirates," *International Labor and Working-Class History* 79 (2011): 122–39.

[5] Vora, "Unofficial Citizens," 126. The ownership of businesses is regulated by the Commercial Companies Law, whereas the sponsorship of employees appears to be regulated by Ministerial decree since it forms no part of domestic labor law.

[6] Syed Ali, *Dubai: Gilded Cage* (New Haven, CT: Yale University Press, 2010), 27.

[7] In practice there are legal and non-legal ways to get around the 51 percent rule and certain sectors in Dubai, for example, are controlled by merchants of various nationalities (Vora, "Unofficial Citizens," 127).

[8] Email from expatriate businessman "RK" to Mafiwasta, 11 July 2011, copy on file with author.

[9] Vora, "Unofficial Citizens," 123.

the Ministry of Labor to cancel his labor card; a foreign worker who remains in the UAE more than two months after his labor card is cancelled will be fined. The employer will then take the worker's passport to the Ministry of Interior, which upon being shown the cancelled labor card will cancel the foreign worker's visa, stamp his passport with a six month ban on returning to the UAE, and arrange for his deportation to his home country.[10]

Workers who abscond without the consent of their sponsor are deported and handed a one-year ban from returning to the UAE, and sponsors who fail to report absconding workers face a fine of 50,000 dirhams ($13,624).[11] The system for female migrant domestic workers is only different in the sense that they are employed by families, not by businesses. There is no prescribed minimum income for Emirati sponsors, who are eligible to employ up to three domestic workers at a time.[12] In 2010 the government announced a recent relaxation of the rules on cordially terminated employment,[13] but it is not clear if this applies to domestic workers and the *kafala* system continues to prevent workers transferring their sponsorship from abusive employers, who can simply report any perceived troublemakers as having absconded, thereby making the employee liable for deportation. Precisely how many thousands of migrant workers are living in the UAE without proper documentation as a result of the *kafala* system is unclear, but domestic workers abscond in huge numbers,[14] and according to a BBC report from January 2011, migrant workers living rough outside of labor camps on the streets of Dubai are so numerous that they are collectively referred to as the "khalli walli," which loosely translates as "the forgotten about."[15] Given that the *kafala* system also regulates the employment of professional expatriates, the abuses endured by migrant workers cannot be attributed solely to the effect of sponsorship-based employment, or indeed the prohibition on trade unions. Further control is exerted over migrant workers via three powerful de facto control mechanisms: the customary confiscation of passports, the customary imposition of debt, and the systematic denial of access to domestic remedies.

---

[10] Bill Van Esveld, *"The Island of Happiness": Exploitation of Migrant Workers on Saadiyat Island, Abu Dhabi* (Human Rights Watch, May 2009), 27.

[11] Van Esveld, *"The Island of Happiness,"* 28.

[12] See P. Bindhulakshmi, "Gender Mobility and State Response: Indian Domestic Workers in the UAE," in S. Irudaya Rajan (ed.), *Governance and Labour Migration: India Migration Report* (New Delhi: Routledge, 2010).

[13] Paul Holdsworth, "Sponsorship Rules for Foreign Workers to be Eased in the UAE," *Gulf Jobs Market*, 19 December 2010.

[14] In 2000, local authorities reported that nearly 12,000 domestic workers had absconded from their employers. Riba Sabban, "Migrant Women in The United Arab Emirates: The Case of Female Domestic Workers," GENPROM Working Paper No. 10, at 41. See also Ali, *Dubai*, 95–9.

[15] "Conditions of Dubai's Immigrant Workers Highlighted," *BBC News*, aired 20 January 2011.

Despite having been ruled illegal by a Dubai Court in 2001,[16] the confiscation of migrant workers' passports is customary practice. Every migrant worker interviewed by Human Rights Watch, in Dubai in 2006 and in Abu Dhabi in 2009, and all of those questioned by BBC journalists in its 2009 investigations had had their passports confiscated on arrival in the UAE.[17] In a 2007 amnesty for individuals labeled "illegal migrants," 40,000 passports were handed in to the Indian consulate, not by private firms, but by the UAE authorities.[18] Where debt is concerned, migrant workers in the UAE typically borrow between $2,000 and $4,000 dollars from a recruitment agent in the sending country to secure employment in the UAE.[19] UAE law prohibits companies from dealing with recruitment agents who impose these fees,[20] which are ostensibly to cover visa and travel costs and an agent fee, but there has been no attempt to enforce the law, only the announcement of a further layer of regulations.[21] Employers in the UAE increase the exploitative potential of the original debt by paying wages far lower than were agreed, holding wages in arrears for months at a time, and deducting wages indiscriminately.[22] A worker on the prestigious Sadiyaat Island project in Abu Dhabi described a common predicament:

I took out a loan at five per cent interest to pay the agency, and also sold my cows and took out a mortgage. The agency said we'd get a basic salary of 600 dirhams [$163], but that it would be up to 1,500 dirhams a month with overtime. But we haven't been paid yet and have been working on the island for two and a half months. The company hasn't set up any bank accounts. They say our first payment is going to be in cash. We were supposed to be paid today. We found out we're getting 520 dirhams [$141] basic salary and only 700 dirhams [$190] with overtime.[23]

The enforcement of labor laws protecting migrant workers' rights is such an infrequent occurrence that it would be more precise to describe labor law in the UAE as a set of voluntary standards. Ministerial decrees, such as the draft labor law of 2007 and the restriction on summer working hours, are

---

[16] Ruling by Dubai Court of Cassation, Case # 268 (2001), 27 October 2001.

[17] Van Esveld, *"The Island of Happiness,"* 27; Hadi Ghaemi, *Building Towers, Cheating Workers: Exploitation of Migrant Workers in The United Arab Emirates* (Human Rights Watch, November 2006); and "Slumdogs and Millionaires," *BBC Panorama*, aired 6 April 2009. See also Vora's comment that "I did get several opportunities to speak to South Asians who worked as taxicab drivers, retail shop employees, craftsmen, deliverymen, grocery store employees, domestic workers, and low-level office workers. In every case, the person I spoke to was not in physical possession of his or her passport" ("Unofficial Citizens," 133).

[18] Subramani Dharmarajan, "Amnesty: Many Passports Unclaimed," *Gulf News*, 23 August 2007.

[19] Van Esveld, *"The Island of Happiness,"* 27; and P. Bindhulakshmi, "Gender Mobility and State Response."

[20] Van Esveld, *"The Island of Happiness,"* 2.

[21] See "Labour Recruitment to the UAE," *Migrant Forum Asia*, 6 January 2011.

[22] Van Esveld, *"The Island of Happiness,"* 53.

[23] Van Esveld, *"The Island of Happiness,"* 51.

invariably announced in the immediate aftermath of well-publicized criticism, such as Human Rights Watch's 2006 report on construction workers in Dubai. The draft labor law of 2007 was never implemented, and no companies were ever fined for making their employees work in temperatures over 40 degrees, despite widespread flouting of the law.[24] The Ministry of Labor's passive approach to workers' rights contrasts markedly with its approach to employers, whose interests it guards swiftly with little regard for due process. In 2007 a large-scale protest of workers complaining about low wages led to the immediate deportation of 180 workers.[25] The Minister of Labor ordered that 250 work permits be issued to the company free of charge to replace the deported workers. He stated: "This is being done to compensate the company," who claimed to have lost 4 million dirhams as a result of the protest.[26]

The combined effect of the UAE's *de jure* and de facto mechanisms is a power relationship of profound inequality between migrant employees and expatriate and national employers. From a legal perspective, recent case law from highly respected courts of international human rights law and international criminal law provides authoritative support for the argument that the mutually reinforcing acts and omissions which regulate the employment of the UAE's migrant workers facilitate a violation of international prohibitions on trafficking and enslavement respectively.

In view of the fact that migrant workers' recruitment is characterized by deception and their labor is extracted by *de jure* and de facto coercive mechanisms, there is prima facie evidence both to support the classification of migrant workers as trafficking, and to extend the scope of criminal liability to employers as well as recruiters.[27] Moreover, recent jurisprudence from the European Court of Human Rights would suggest that it is the state itself which ought to bear responsibility for its facilitation of trafficking offenses.[28] In 2010 the European Court asserted jurisdiction over trafficking cases on the basis that it is an offense which invokes state responsibilities deriving from the

---

[24] David Keane and Nicholas McGeehan, "Enforcing Migrant Workers' Rights in the United Arab Emirates," *International Journal on Minority and Group Rights* 15 (2008): 81–115 at 86.

[25] Sunita Menon and Wafa Issa, "First Batch of 60 Workers Deported for Violent Protest," *Gulf News*, 15 March 2007.

[26] Sunita Menon and Wafa Issa, "Over 200 Workers to be Deported for Violence," *Gulf News*, 15 March 2007.

[27] Where migrant workers are concerned, trafficking in persons can be described as the coercive or physical transport into exploitation. There is a lack of clarity over the scope of the norm but experts such as Anne Gallagher argue that the internationally accepted definition of trafficking in persons as provided in Article 3 of the UN Trafficking Protocol can be interpreted in such a way for its scope to cover "owners and managers, supervisors, and controllers of any place of exploitation such as a brothel, farm, boat, factory, medical facility, or household" (Anne Gallagher, *The International Law of Human Trafficking* (Cambridge: Cambridge University Press, 2010), 30).

[28] *Rantsev* v. *Cyprus and Russia*, ECHR judgment of 7 January 2010.

prohibition on slavery, servitude and forced labor.[29] It found Cyprus to be in violation of these obligations on the basis that a specific visa regime for female cabaret artistes "did not afford . . . practical and effective protection against trafficking and exploitation."[30] Control over Cyprus's artistes was exercised by a combination of factors almost identical to those employed in the UAE: illegally imposed debt, the confiscation of passports,[31] and a sponsorship-based visa system which could be used to threaten workers with either deportation or "illegal" immigrant status.[32] Applying the Court's line of reasoning to the UAE's migrant workers it can reasonably be argued that, in effect if not purpose, the UAE's regulation of that sector of its workforce facilitates the trafficking and exploitation of approximately 4 million foreign workers. The same could be said of Kuwait, Bahrain, Qatar, Saudi Arabia, and Oman. Moreover, if we accept that slavery's global legal prohibition did not result in its eradication, and that it is no longer a practice which is effected by the legal ownership of an individual,[33] but by other factors that facilitate similar powers to legal ownership, then there is a compelling argument that the UAE and the wider region is a crucible for modern-day slavery. In 2001, the International Tribunal for the Former Yugoslavia offered this characterization of enslavement:[34]

indications of enslavement include elements of control and ownership; the restriction or control of an individual's autonomy, freedom of choice or freedom of movement; and, often, the accruing of some gain to the perpetrator. The consent or free will of the victim is absent. It is often rendered impossible or irrelevant by, for example, the threat or use of force or other forms of coercion; the fear of violence, deception or false promises; the abuse of power; the victim's position of vulnerability; detention or captivity, psychological oppression or socio-economic conditions. Further indications of enslavement include exploitation; the exaction of forced or compulsory labour or

[29] *Rantsev* v. *Cyprus and Russia*, para 282, "The Court concludes that trafficking itself, within the meaning of Article 3(a) of the Palermo Protocol and Article 4(a) of the Anti-Trafficking Convention, falls within the scope of Article 4 of the Convention."

[30] *Rantsev* v. *Cyprus and Russia*, para 293.

[31] *Rantsev* v. *Cyprus and Russia*, para 85. Quoting from the report of the Cypriot Ombudsman.

[32] *Rantsev* v. *Cyprus and Russia*, para 292. The Court described the practice of requiring cabaret owners and managers to lodge a bank guarantee to cover potential future costs as "particularly troubling."

[33] Slavery has never been defined purely in terms of ownership. Article 1 of the 1926 League of Nations Slavery Convention defines it thus: "the status or condition of a person over whom any or all of the powers attaching to ownership are exercised." 1926 Slavery Convention or the Convention to Suppress the Slave Trade and Slavery, 60 LNTS. 253, entered into force 9 March 1927. See Nicholas McGeehan, "Misunderstood and Neglected: The Marginalisation of Slavery in International Law," forthcoming in the *International Journal of Human Rights Law*, available online May 2011.

[34] Enslavement, as defined in Article 7(1)(c) of the Rome Statute of the International Criminal Court, is substantively identical to the definition of slavery in the 1926 Slavery Convention.

service, often without remuneration and often, though not necessarily, involving physical hardship.[35]

Many of these indications of enslavement can be found in the UAE: migrant workers' recruitment is characterized by deception, and employers habitually use threats or force against them; their socioeconomic vulnerability is compounded by the illegitimate imposition of debt and the routine denial of access to mechanisms of redress; and they are denied the right to leave their employer and cannot leave the country.

There is no need to delve further into the sometimes confusing legal distinctions between trafficking and slavery.[36] It suffices to say that both relate to a deprivation of the fundamental right to liberty. In assessing the scope for a more multicultural, democratic UAE, it is important to appreciate not only the gravity of the ongoing exploitation, but the government's autocratic nature and its vested interest in maintaining the status quo.

THE REPRESSIVE CORPORATIST STATE

The notion that the UAE is in some way a model of progress for the region is misguided, but it is one which the UAE works very hard to cultivate, and with no little success.[37] On 9 March 2011, 160 Emirati nationals submitted a petition to the authorities, described by one commentator as "one of the gentlest pleas for political reform in recent history."[38] It resulted in the arrest of many of its signatories, including Ahmed Mansoor, a blogger and a member of the Human Rights Watch advisory committee, and Nasser bin Ghaith, an Emirati economist and lecturer at the Abu Dhabi branch of the University of Paris-Sorbonne, and the dissolution of two of the country's oldest civil society organizations, the Jurists' Association and the Teachers' Association.[39] In an op-ed piece entitled "Trouble Making is No Human Right," Khalaf Al Habtoor, an Emirati construction billionaire, described the

---

[35] *Prosecutor* v. *Kunarac et al.* (Trial Judgment) IT-96-23-T & IT-96-23/1-T (22 February 2001), para 542.

[36] According to Patricia Sellers, the view that trafficking "should be definitively viewed by the same rubric of slave trading" that was outlawed by the 1926 Slavery Convention should not be controversial. Patricia Sellers, "Wartime Female Slavery: Enslavement?" *Cornell International Law Journal* 44 (2011): 115–43 at 125. Jean Allain offers an alternative perspective. Jean Allain, "Rantsev v Cyprus and Russia: The European Court of Human Rights and Trafficking as Slavery," *Human Rights Law Review* 10/3 (2010): 546–57 at 553.

[37] Thomas Friedman has described Dubai as "precisely the sort of decent, modernizing model we should be trying to nurture in the Arab-Muslim world" and "where we should want the Arab world to go." "Dubai and Dunces," *New York Times*, 15 March 2006.

[38] Anna Louie Sussman, "Repression in the United Arab Emirates," *The Nation*, 1 June 2011.

[39] Sussman, "Repression in the United Arab Emirates."

protesters as "malcontents" and stated that "the UAE authorities had every right to stop them in their tracks."[40] In 2009, Bill Clinton described Dubai as "the only country [*sic*] with huge amounts of imported workers that's actually passed legislation to give these immigrant workers a better deal in the Middle East."[41] The reality is that, despite years of criticism and an increased awareness of the problem, the UAE has successfully resisted calls for substantive change to its labor system. When the Pulitzer Prize-winning website PolitiFact.com subjected Bill Clinton's comments to some basic fact-checking, their initial assessment of "barely true" was updated to "mostly false" in July 2011.[42] The UAE has assumed human rights obligations but its failure to respect the basic legal principle of *pacta sunt servanda,* which obliges states parties to adhere to their obligations in good faith,[43] is evident in its recent dealings with the UN Committees on Racial Discrimination (CERD) and the UN Committee on Discrimination Against Women (CEDAW).[44] In 2009 and 2010, the UAE was required to report to the CERD and CEDAW Committees respectively. Both Committees delivered detailed recommendations to the UAE on migrant workers,[45] and requested that the UAE provide written information on their progress within one year. The CEDAW Committee in particular took a remarkably aggressive stance and issued detailed recommendations on migrant domestic workers and on the need to introduce comprehensive measures to tackle violence against women, including the provision of shelters.[46] The UAE has not submitted follow-up information to either committee, or implemented any policies which are likely to improve conditions for migrant workers. On the contrary, their most recent actions suggest the violations of workers' rights may become more serious. In March 2010, the UN Special Rapporteur on Human Rights Defenders submitted a complaint to the UAE, voicing its concerns over the UAE's harassment and deportation of the

---

[40] Khalaf Al Habtoor, "Trouble Making is No Human Right," *Gulf News,* 11 May 2011.

[41] "This Week Interview with Bill Clinton," *ABC News,* aired 18 April 2010.

[42] "Clinton Says UAE only Middle East Country to Pass Laws to Address Plight of Migrant Workers," PolitiFact.com, 20 April 2010.

[43] Article 26 of the Vienna Convention of the Law of Treaties states that "Every treaty in force is binding upon the parties and must be performed by them in good faith."

[44] All six GCC states have ratified the Convention on the Elimination of All Forms of Racial Discrimination, the Convention on the Elimination of Discrimination Against Women and the Convention on the Rights of the Child, although only Bahrain and Kuwait have ratified the two general human rights treaties, the International Covenant on Civil and Political Rights and the International Covenant on Economic, Social and Cultural Rights. For a full record of ratifications, signatures and accessions see the United Nations Treaty Collection online at <http://treaties.un.org/Pages/Treaties.aspx?id=4&subid=A&lang=en>, accessed September 2013.

[45] CERD, "Concluding Observations of the Committee on the Elimination of Racial Discrimination: United Arab Emirates," CEDAW/C/ARE/CO/17, 21 September 2009. In its concluding observations, the Committee outlined three issues as being of particular concern: the living and working conditions of non-citizen contract workers; the situation of domestic foreign workers; and the situation of stateless *bidoon* in the country.

[46] CERD, "Concluding Observations," paras 27, 37, 57.

director of the country's only independent shelter for victims of domestic violence. The UAE's response was that it had issued a warrant for her arrest.[47] In May 2011 it was revealed that the UAE has hired Erik Prince, founder of the private security firm Blackwater, to recruit an 800-strong private security force, which, according to reports, will be used to quell revolt in labor camps.[48]

Historian Suzanne Miers has written extensively about how states throughout the twentieth century played what she calls "the anti-slavery game" by humanitarian posturing which acts as "a smokescreen to deflect public criticism and avoid action."[49] In the twenty-first century, the UAE is one of the leading proponents of this art. To take one notable example, the International Labour Organization and the UAE held discussions on the introduction of trade unions as far back as 2005, when the undersecretary of the UAE Ministry of Labor said that the UAE could expect to have trade unions "very soon," and the then regional director of the ILO told local media that trade unions will be established in the UAE even though they may pose challenges to residents.[50] Six years later, there is no sign of trade unions. The ILO's conciliatory approach and focus on technical assistance has thus far rendered it almost entirely ineffective in the face of a government that knows that it can appease critics simply by effecting an earnest desire to reform. In a similar, but more worrying, vein, the UAE has been able to portray itself as an active partner in the global anti-trafficking crusade. Despite there being clear grounds to label the country a global hub of human trafficking and a crucible for modern-day slavery, the United Nations Global Initiative to Fight Trafficking was set up by money provided by the UAE, which makes it one of the main funders of a global anti-trafficking initiative being run by the ILO, UNICEF, the UN Office of Drugs and Crime, the International Office of Migration, and the Organization of Security and Cooperation in Europe.[51]

The UAE embraces the language of human rights and forges links with its institutions, while simultaneously violating its fundamental principles and it will continue to do so for as long as the public relations benefits of the former outweigh the cost of the latter. It is typically overlooked that the individuals who stand to profit most from the labor of migrant workers are the members of the country's ruling elite. The country's two biggest developers, Nakheel

---

[47] 2011 Report of the Special Rapporteur on the Situation of Human Rights Defenders, Margaret Sekaggya, A/HRC/16/44/Add.1, 28 February 2011, pp. 323–4.

[48] Mark Mazzetti, "Secret Desert Force Set Up By Blackwater's Founder," *New York Times*, 14 May 2011.

[49] Suzanne Miers, *Slavery in the Twentieth Century: The Evolution of a Global Problem* (Lanham, MD: AltaMira, 2003), Preface.

[50] *Gulf News*, 4 April 2005. Original article is no longer available online. A link to the same story is provided at Emirates Economist Blog, <http://emirateseconomist.blogspot.com/2005_04_01_archive.html>, accessed September 2013.

[51] See UN.GIFT.HUB at <http://www.ungift.org/knowledgehub/en/about/index.html>, accessed September 2013.

and Emaar, are part-owned by the government of Dubai, and a family's position within the ruling elite is predicated on its wealth, which comes either from oil or other business interests, such as construction.[52] In Naomi Klein's depiction of the growth of what she calls the corporatist state, *The Shock Doctrine*, she describes the conflicts of interest that characterized the administration of George W. Bush as "the whirling revolving door between government and industry."[53] In the UAE there is no door at all, let alone a revolving one. The government is industry, and those responsible for devising and enforcing the country's labor laws are the CEOs of the largest and most profitable firms. As such, it would be credulous in the extreme to believe that only the *de jure* control mechanisms described in the previous section reflect state policy. In view of the vast private business interests of the ruling elite and its unaccountable executive power, it might be more appropriate to characterize the UAE as a sovereign corporation, whose commitment to human rights constitutes little more than a branding exercise.[54]

THE GULF'S SERVANT CLASS

The final section of this chapter addresses the underlying reasons for the exploitation of migrant workers. To what extent do issues of race and gender impact on the discrimination endured by migrant workers or can this issue be reduced to a simple case of exploitative economic oppression in a country where neoliberal policies are complemented by autocratic rule?

There are indications that the regulation of migrant workers is engendering apartheid-style racialist sentiment in Emirati society.[55] When presented with the findings of unsanitary conditions in his company's labor camps, the Irish CEO of a large construction company, which worked on the prestigious Burj Khalifa, responded: "We try from the very outset to train the men in all aspects of cleanliness and hygiene but it is very difficult to change the habits that they unfortunately bring with them from their countries of origin."[56] An Iraqi

---

[52] Keane and McGeehan, "Enforcing Migrant Workers' Rights in the United Arab Emirates," 113.

[53] Naomi Klein, *The Shock Doctrine* (Harmondsworth: Penguin, 2007), 314.

[54] This is not intended as an analogy. In June 2009 the UAE prime minister set up the office of "Brand Dubai" whose purpose is to "enhance Dubai's image as an Arab city of international spirit and sensibility." Neeraj Gangal, "Sheikh Mohammed Creates 'Brand Dubai' Office," *Arabian BUSINESS.COM*, 13 June 2009.

[55] See Mafiwasta, "Country Shadow Report to the Committee on the Elimination of Racial Discrimination: The United Arab Emirates," CEDAW Shadow Report, October 2009.

[56] Email from Tom Barry, CEO Arabtec Construction to Andrew Bell, Producer, BBC Northern Ireland. No date specified, in response to original email from Andrew Bell to Tom Barry sent 17 March 2009, copy on file with author.

couple, interviewed by journalist Ghaith Abdul-Ahad, stated that they would never use the metro being built in the country if it wasn't segregated: "We will never sit next to Indians and Pakistanis with their smell."[57] There are echoes in both of these statements of what Randall Packard has described in the context of 1920s South Africa as a "generalized association of unsanitary behaviour with race."[58] A comparative analysis with the genesis of the South African Bantustan system would make for a fascinating study,[59] but it would be wrong to attribute the exploitation of migrant workers to their race. Race does not constitute a barrier to one's entry into the upper echelons of Emirati society and Dubai in particular is home to an established Indian elite.[60] Wealth is the principle determinant of status in the UAE, and the basis for discrimination is not nationality, ethnicity, or religion, but poverty. The absence of any minimum wage structure in the United Arab Emirates and the extreme poverty of neighboring south Asian states has created a situation whereby sending states effectively compete for the Gulf's business. The most attractive sending states are those whose workers will accept the lowest wages, and whose governments' dependence on remittances makes them least likely to cause a fuss when its citizens are mistreated. The result in the UAE is an economic stratification of society along clear ethnic lines, whereby a Filipino maid has a higher status than an Indian maid, and Nepalese construction workers undercut Sri Lankans. Racial discrimination against migrant workers is endemic, but it is inextricably linked to economic and social status and, in the case of male workers, it is compounded by their physical segregation in labor camps. That is to say that it is not the cause of their exploitation, but a by-product of that exploitation.

The exploitation of male migrant workers in labor-intensive sectors such as construction would, on the face of it, appear to be a case of exploitative economic oppression. Unlike the stateless *bidoon*,[61] who are denied citizenship and access to the well-paid public sector jobs available to nationals under the program of Emiritization,[62] migrant workers are intrinsic to the economic well-being of the UAE. The welfare of many citizens and expatriates depends directly upon the effort of migrant workers, and the country as a

---

[57] Ghaith Abdul-Ahad, "We Need Slaves to Build Monuments," *The Guardian*, 8 October 2008.

[58] Randall M. Packard, *White Plague, Black Labor* (Berkeley and Los Angeles, CA: University of California Press, 1989), 194.

[59] For a discussion on the links between segregation and racial discrimination in South Africa see Paul Maylam, *South Africa's Racial Past* (Aldershot: Ashgate, 2001).

[60] Ali, *Dubai*, 110–34.

[61] CERD (see this chapter n. 45), para 18: "the Committee remains concerned at the legal situation of some 'Bidoun', notably regarding their status as stateless persons and at allegations of discrimination they face on the labour market."

[62] The Emiritization program is a government initiative designed to get UAE nationals into skilled employment. See <www.emiritisation.org>, accessed September 2013.

whole would cease to function without their labor.[63] Indeed, in the sense that the *kafala* system defines one's relation to labor and the means of production, it might be said that it provides a legal basis for a globalized variant of the Marxist class structure. The argument is fairly persuasive in the case of migrant workers employed by businesses under the *kafala* system: migrant workers constitute the proletariat of Gulf society, toiling for the benefit of the expatriates and the nationals, who in this rudimentary class analysis would comprise the bourgeoisie and the landowners respectively. While this approach is consonant with the sovereign corporation analogy and Mike Davis's description of Dubai as "the apotheosis of the neoliberal values of contemporary capitalism,"[64] it fails to explain the disproportionate abuse endured by domestic workers, which has no economic value and cannot simply be attributed to the gender bias of migration. Where this exclusively female subset of the general migrant population is concerned, the most persuasive explanation for their mistreatment is not race, class, or gender, but the persistent legacy of domestic slavery in the region. The work of historians and anthropologists offers an important insight into the significance of slavery in the region, which not only explains the non-economic exploitation of domestic workers but provides important sociohistorical context to the economic exploitation of the general migrant worker population.

According to Albert Hourani "changes in economic life and social customs, as well as Ottoman, Egyptian and British actions against the slave trade" had largely brought an end to domestic slavery in the Arab-Muslim world by 1914.[65] Slavery historian Suzanne Miers has argued that British actions against the slave trade were largely ineffective in South Arabia and the Persian Gulf, a region she describes as "the Achilles' heel" in Britain's antislavery campaign, and where chattel slavery existed "on a considerable scale" until the 1930s.[66]

There is compelling evidence to suggest that domestic slavery is a persistent presence in the Gulf peninsula, and that it is perpetuated by the ruling elite for whom it retains significant honorific value. In his seminal work *Slavery and Social Death*, Orlando Patterson describes how in many societies the primary purpose of keeping slaves was their honorific value, and how in timocratic societies, which is to say those in which honor and pride were "excessively developed," this honorific value took on an increased significance.[67] In the "highly timocratic" Arab-Muslim world, "perhaps more than in any other part of the pre-modern world, slavery was not only a state of dishonour, but one in which a major function of the institution was to support the dignitas of the

---

[63] Erik Olin Wright, *Class Counts* (Cambridge: Cambridge University Press, 1997), 11.

[64] Mike Davis, "Fear and Money in Dubai," *New Left Review* 41 (2006): 47–68.

[65] Albert Hourani, *A History of The Arab Peoples* (London: Faber & Faber, 1991), 298.

[66] Miers, *Slavery in the Twentieth Century*, 166.

[67] Orlando Patterson, *Slavery and Social Death* (Cambridge, MA: Harvard University Press, 1982), 77–105.

master."[68] Although Patterson concedes that slavery persists in the contemporary world, he largely approaches slavery as a historical institution. This approach chimes with the conventional wisdom that in this era of human rights, slaveholding societies do not and cannot exist. If slavery exists in the twenty-first century, so goes the narrative, it is the preserve of transnational organized criminals.[69] It would be unwise to characterize the Arabian Gulf as a slaveholding society, but there is evidence that the ruling elite continue to attach honorific value to domestic slavery.

In 2010, after a UK court convicted a Saudi Prince of murdering his "manservant" in a London hotel, a Saudi scholar described the murder victim as:

one of thousands of black Saudis who are modern-day slaves of the ruling family, serving them in any capacity, including sexually. The culture of slavery pervades the country and while slavery was officially banned in 1964, it continued in practice, especially inside the walls of thousands of princely palaces. Members of the princes' inner circle are popularly called khawee, "minion". Essentially, they are subordinates who are there for the service or the amusement of a prince with an inflated sense of self-importance.[70]

In a lesser known case from 2008, several members of the ruling Al-Nahyan family of Abu Dhabi were arrested on trafficking charges in Brussels after seventeen female members of their personal staff escaped from the 5-star Conrad Hilton Hotel, the fourth floor of which they had occupied in its entirety for eight months, and sought the protection of the police.[71] Frederick Cooper's description of the Arab elite in nineteenth-century plantations of East Africa provides a striking sociohistorical context to these recent events.

Economic success per se did not define their status, although it was an important component of it. What defined the upper stratum of society is best described by a term still used by Arabs and Swahili today, *heshima*—meaning literally, "respect" ... In both Oman and Zanzibar, *heshima* meant having a retinue of slaves, and that was expensive.[72]

There has been no attempt here to suggest that all migrant workers in the UAE, or even a majority of them, exist in a condition of slavery. However, in a region where slavery's honorific value has been just as important as its economic value, it is the link between slavery and social status that best explains the presence of so many domestic workers and their mistreatment. Furthermore, in view of the fact that the ruling elite is responsible for devising

---

[68] Patterson, *Slavery and Social Death*, 92.

[69] The UN Trafficking Protocol is not an instrument of human rights law but optional protocol to the UN Convention Against Transnational Organized Crime.

[70] Ali Al-Ahmed, "Justice, even for Princes," *The Guardian*, 20 October 2010.

[71] Bruno Waterfield, "Women 'Enslaved' by Arab Royals," *The Telegraph* (London), 2 July 2008.

[72] Frederick Cooper, *Plantation Slavery on the East Coast of Africa* (London: Heinemann, 1997), 77.

and enforcing the country's labor laws, a labor system that tends towards enslavement, to the economic benefit of that elite, ought not to be regarded as anomalous or surprising.

CONCLUSION

The abuse of migrant workers in the UAE is the result of a set of mutually reinforcing acts and omissions which, when fully exploited by employers, leaves workers in a state of almost complete powerlessness. In overseeing this system, the UAE has not simply "abdicated its responsibility for worker well-being,"[73] it has created the conditions required for slavery to flourish. This is not an activist's attempt to hitch the normative and rhetorical power of slavery to his particular cause, but a dispassionate legal analysis, supported by judgments of respected courts of international law. The characterization of the UAE as a duplicitous state, whose ruling elite have an almost complete disregard for the rights of the workers upon whom their economy and personal wealth depends, may be perceived by some as an unduly cynical assessment, but the UAE's actions over recent years have provided ample evidence of its lack of good faith.

In the context of a volume on minority rights and multiculturalism, this analysis would suggest that to invoke terms such as citizenship, belonging, or loyalty in relation to migrant workers is somewhat premature. These are notions that may have resonance within the expatriate population, indeed Neha Vora has described Indian expatriates as "unofficial citizens of the UAE,"[74] but to apply them to migrant workers is to underestimate the gravity of their exploitation and to imply that they occupy a level of status in Emirati society. It is also to underestimate the state's resistance to reform and its contempt for notions of rights in general, whether individual human rights or minority group rights.

---

[73] Vora, "Unofficial Citizens," 137.   [74] Vora, "Unofficial Citizens," 137.

9

Hobbesian Citizenship: How the Palestinians Became a Minority in Israel*

Hassan Jabareen

INTRODUCTION

The literature that discusses the status of the Arab Palestinian citizens of Israel has never reached the crucial foundational questions of: (1) how, when, and why this group joined the Israeli polity; (2) what were the historical conditions of their incorporation into this polity; and (3) whether the terms of this incorporation, the foundation of their citizenship, still effect their legal status and rights today. This chapter deals with these questions, the answers to which will reveal one of the most unique historical circumstances that has occurred in the last three centuries concerning a defeated group joining a victorious new polity. This group is the first and only Arab group in modern history that has become a homeland minority; they did not become so by choice or consent or any international treaty but by the force of arms. Further, as a result of the establishment of Israel, they directly experienced the Nakba, the most cata-strophic tragedy in the history of the Palestinian people. Notably, the Arabs rejected the UN Partition Plan of Palestine in 1947 because they refused to divide their homeland and to compel a large number of Arab natives to become a minority subjected to a foreign Western group (just as the Zionist

* I wish to give special thanks to Will Kymlicka, Eva Pföstl, and Paul Kahn for their helpful insights and comments on an earlier draft of this chapter. I first introduced the ideas expressed here at a conference on "Multiculturalism and Minority Rights in the Arab World" held in Rome in 2011. I also wish to thank the Schell Center of Yale Law School for granting me a Robina Fellowship, which allowed me to write the article that has become this chapter. I also extend sincere appreciation to the participants in a Schell Center workshop where I introduced this earlier draft, especially Kiel Brennan-Marquez, Tom Dannenbaum, and Itamar Mann-Kanowitz. My thanks also go to Aeyal Gross, Amal Jamal, Darryl Li, Barak Medina, Adi Ophir, Ilan Pappe, Amnon Raz-Krakotzkin, Yehuda Shenhav, and Sawsan Zaher. And finally, this chapter would not have been written without the support—intellectually and personally—of my wife Rina.

leadership rejected the notion that Jews should live as a minority within a Palestinian Arab majority).

This chapter will focus on two key historical moments: the elections for and the initial legal acts of the first Knesset in 1949–50 and the post-1992 debates on constitutional reform. However, before turning to the three questions already posed, and to these events, it is important to address an important problem of perspective in the existing literature. It is common for Israeli legal scholars to argue that even if Arab citizens are marginalized in some respect by Israel's self-conception as a "Jewish and democratic state," this is no different from the status of minorities in many other Western states, and that Israel is, in this sense, similar to any Westphalian state.[1] This literature justifies demographic domination to ensure a Jewish majority by relying on liberal multiculturalist theories, which recognize the special rights of groups such as the Native Americans to control their membership policy.[2] Others point to some European countries, which are said to have adopted policies of ethnic hegemony.[3] Gavison, for example, claims that just as the hegemony of Christian culture in the United States does not negate American democracy, Israeli recognition for Jewish group rights does not negate the democratic aspects of Israel.[4]

This argument for the "normality" of Israel depends also on drawing a sharp distinction between Israeli rule within the Green Line and its control of the Palestinian territories occupied in 1967 (West Bank and Gaza, hereafter "the OPT" (Occupied Palestinian Territory)). The commentators' description of rule within the OPT as a colonial or occupation regime implicitly supports the conceptualization of the Green Line as a democratic nation-state. Palestinians living in the OPT, unlike those residing within the Green Line, are denied one of the most fundamental citizenship rights in a democracy: the right to elect and to be elected. These perspectives rely strongly on Artistotle's idea, "A citizen is . . . one who has a share both in ruling and being ruled," and

---

[1] The former Chief Justice of the Israeli Supreme Court, Aharon Barak, stated that this combination of Jewish and democratic values "makes Israel, Israel, just as there are values that make France, France and England, England." Aharon Barak, *A Judge in a Democratic Society* (Princeton, NJ: Princeton University Press, 2008), 80.

[2] Chaim Gans, *A Just Zionism: On the Morality of the Jewish State* (Oxford: Oxford University Press, 2008), 122–5, and Na'ama Carmi, "Immigration Policy: Between Demographic Considerations and Preservation of Culture," *Law & Ethics of Human Rights* 2/1 (2008). See my comments to Na'ama Carmi's paper delivered at an International Conference on "Demography and Human Rights," held by the Ramat Gan Law School in January 2007, available at <http://www.clb.ac.il/workshops/2007/articles/jabareen.pdf>, accessed September 2013.

[3] Alexander Yakobson and Amnon Rubenstein, *Israel and the Family of Nations: The Jewish Nation-State and Human Rights* (New York: Routledge, 2008).

[4] Ruth Gavison, "Can Israel be both Jewish and Democratic?" Van Leer Institute, Jerusalem, 1999 (Hebrew).

citizens claim the right "to take it in turns to exercise authority."[5] Even progressive international scholars such as Seyla Benhabib suggest that Israel is a pre-Westphalian state in so far as it still occupies the OPT, but for its Jewish population and its Palestinian citizens living within the Green Line it is a Westphalian state that exhibits strong features of a liberal social democracy.[6]

In short, within both the Israeli and the international literature, there is a tendency to say that the definition of Israel as a "Jewish and democratic state" fits more or less the general pattern of Western nation-states. Arab citizens may not be accorded group rights, since Israel is not a bi-national state, but their individual rights are guaranteed. Jewish citizens may be accorded certain ethnic privileges but these are seen as needed to express the self-determination of the Jewish people.

I will dispute the picture of Israel as a "normal" Westphalian state, and argue instead that even within the Green Line Arabs are governed by a *colonial form of citizenship*. If the Palestinian citizens enjoy individual rights, as portrayed by Israeli scholars, and the principle of anti-discrimination is about being neutral toward individual belonging and one's identity, how can Israeli law be neutral toward the identity of Israeli-Palestinians when Palestinians in the OPT are defined as "enemy aliens" or when it negates the right of return of Palestinian refugees based on their Palestinian national identity? Can we speak about equal rights for Palestinians in Israel by neglecting the fact that the high politics of Israel denies the Nakba and its consequences? How can we speak about democratic citizenship based on the Aristotelian idea when the Arab members of Knesset have never shared the right to rule by being part of the government? What sort of citizenship is it when both Jews and Arabs agree that Palestinian citizens should not serve in the army, even though military service is a main source of equal individual rights and citizenship?

To understand the nature of Palestinian citizenship in Israel, we need to challenge the popular perception that they enjoy equal individual rights. The reality is that perceptions of national loyalty—of who is a friend and who is an enemy—have profound effects on both individual and group rights. Carl Schmitt calls this the *Political*—the persistent tendency of states to reduce political relations to those between friend and enemy.[7] It is true that homeland minorities in the West were typically incorporated involuntarily into larger polities and have also suffered at various points in their history from the *political*, but they have since passed through a process of "citizenization" and

---

[5] Aristotle, *The Politics*, trans. T. A. Sinclair (London: Penguin, 1981), bk. III ch. 13, pp. 131, 115.

[6] Seyla Benhabib, "Democracy, Demography, and Sovereignty," *Law & Ethics of Human Rights* 2/1 (2008): 8–39 at 30.

[7] Carl Schmitt, *The Concept of the Political* (Chicago, IL: University of Chicago Press, 1996), 26.

decolonization.[8] The language of rights based on reciprocity—duties, rights, and loyalty—is accepted in majority–minority relations in Western European countries since it is not based on Hobbesian fear. In Paul Kahn's words, it is a debate between friends and not motivated by the *political*.[9] This account explains why the original national attachment of these groups to a nearby kin-state is not a serious factor of debate.[10]

Some scholars such as Yakobson and Rubenstein note that Israel's initial process of state formation is not that different from many Western countries, which caused tragedies to the natives. However, having noted this point of comparison, they do not go on to ask whether the citizenship of the Palestinians has undergone a process of decolonization or "citizenization." The lack of such an inquiry might be explained by the idea that raising colonial discourse will delegitimize the right for self-determination of the dominant group. But describing citizenship as colonial does not entail that rulers are foreigners who lack rights of self-determination; as Kymlicka puts it, "what matters is simply the facts of domination and vulnerability" and not the identity of the oppressors, whether they are foreign long-distance colonizing settlers or internal groups.[11] Mamdani expresses a similar opinion regarding colonial citizenship when he argues that the issue is examining the historical formation of citizenship and its development as a form of the state, and not the ideology, justifications, morality, or identity of the rulers.[12] Here I define "colonial citizenship" as a form of citizenship based on ethnic hierarchy, which is built on institutional discrimination that leads to vulnerability, domination, and control on matters that make the citizen a citizen. The ethnic hierarchy creates separate and unequal tracks in the exercise of fundamental rights and duties, which usually belong to citizens and not to aliens, such as the right to vote and to be elected.[13] Since equality between citizens is the basis and presumption of reciprocity, this language of rights—rights, duties, and loyalty—leads in crucial cases under colonial citizenship to a trap or a contradiction.

---

[8] According to Kymlicka, this process involved three stages. The first stage consisted in the decolonization of citizenship, which repudiated ideologies of group hierarchy; the second stage was a civil rights movement against racial segregation; and the third stage involved a struggle for minority rights and multiculturalism. Will Kymlicka, *Multicultural Odysseys* (Oxford: Oxford University Press, 2007), 91.

[9] P. W. Kahn, *Putting Liberalism in its Place* (Princeton, NJ: Princeton University Press, 2005), ch. 6.

[10] These historical developments are relevant mostly to homeland minorities since many Western countries still view some refugees and immigrant groups such as Muslims and Arabs as potential enemies.

[11] Kymlicka, *Multicultural Odysseys*, 280.

[12] Mahmood Mamdani, *Citizen and Subject: Contemporary Africa and the Legacy of Late Colonialism* (Princeton, NJ: Princeton University Press, 1996), 28.

[13] Linda K. Kerber, "The Meaning of Citizenship," *Journal of American History* 84 (1997): 833–54 at 834.

The first section of this chapter tracks the historical moments during 1949–50 of making the Palestinians a minority in Israel: how they were introduced to the new polity; how their citizenship was created, constrained, and shaped; what were the terms of loyalty; and how these terms shaped their language of rights. I will call these the "Hobbesian moments" of the Palestinians. Hobbes distinguished two political communities in relation to the sovereign: the first is the founding community that created the sovereign because of fear of the state of nature, and the second is the conquered, occupied, and defeated community that unconditionally surrenders to this sovereign because of fear of being killed by him.[14] This latter idea captures the Hobbesian citizenship offered to (and accepted by) Palestinians in their participation in the first election in 1949. As this chapter indicates, the Palestinians joined the Israeli polity when they began to use the language of rights as *Israelis* in 1949 and not when they were conquered in 1948 or when the Citizenship Law was enacted in 1952.

The second section explores the period after the Israeli constitutional revolution in 1992. This new constitutionalism is portrayed as turning Israel into a more "normal" state, and strengthening the principle of equality. I will argue that while the Palestinians started to assert their equal citizenship rights by creating distance from their humiliating rights talk established during the Hobbesian moments in 1949–50, the law attempted to reaffirm the original terms of their Hobbesian citizenship. The terms set down during the Hobbesian moments reappear, often through the new constitutional values of the "Jewish and democratic state," to limit individual rights and to reaffirm the terms of the *surrender*. Despite the strength of the right of freedom of speech and the intensive use of the language of rights, the *political* is still the dominant consideration in deciding the scope of Arab citizenship. I conclude that the story of Palestinian citizenship gives us a better understanding of the sources of the ideas of Israeli legal philosophy, the politics of surrender and partitioning, and the limits of theories of liberal constitutionalism.

THE HOBBESIAN MOMENTS OF 1949–50

The terms of citizenship for Arabs in Israel remain heavily shaped by decisions that were made in the earliest days of Israel's establishment. The Provisional State Council (PSC) was established on the day of the reading of Israel's Declaration of the Establishment of the State, 14 May 1948. The PSC functioned as a temporary legislature until the national election for the first

---

[14] Thomas Hobbes, *Leviathan* (Oxford: Oxford University Press, 1998).

Knesset on 25 January 1949.[15] In addition to the PSC, the Provisional Government (PG) was established and it appointed David Ben Gurion to serve as the temporary prime minister and the minister of defense. In Hobbes's words, this is the sovereign, which was established by the first political community. In this period the Jewish forces occupied more territory than had been designated for the Jewish State under the UN Partition Plan, General Assembly Resolution 181. Hundreds of thousands of Palestinians were forced, directly or indirectly, to leave their homeland and to become refugees for the first time in their history. Only about 160,000 Palestinians remained and they came under the control of Israel.[16] Many of the internally displaced moved to the Nazareth area in the north, which was designated for the Arab State under the Partition Plan but which also came under Israel's military control.

The debates held in the PG and PSC indicate that the main purpose of the first national election in Israel was to gain international legitimacy for the new state. The PG discussed the significance of immediate elections in its meeting on 8 August 1948 and here, the foreign minister argued that the election was very important to ease the acceptance of Israel as a new member of the UN: "if we will not have an election, our image in the world will be different and we cannot insist on our rights."[17] Ben Gurion supported this argument and added that, "if we will be a member of the UN, we are a sovereign state."[18] Ben Gurion made it clear that the election was important internationally, despite the fact that internally it was very risky to have an election at this time.[19]

The UN Partition Resolution set the terms for the new state's international legitimacy, relying on Westphalian constitutional premises. Accordingly, citizenship should be territorial in that all residents living within each of the defined territorial borders of the two states would be treated equally. The ethnic name of each state—the Arab State and the Jewish State—did not affect the principles of equal rights. In its session held on 3 November 1948, the PG decided that the elections could take place without deciding who were citizens: Israel had no citizenship law. At the time, Israeli official definitions distinguished "The State of Israel" from the terms "occupied territories" or "administrative territories." The former term referred to territory designated by the UN Partition Resolution to the Jewish State, while the second term referred to territory under the control of the Israeli army but designated as belonging to

---

[15] See the Knesset's website, "The Provisional State Council," available at <http://www.knesset.gov.il/review/ReviewPage3.aspx?kns=0&lng=3>, accessed September 2013.

[16] Ilan Pappe, *A History of Modern Palestine: One Land, Two Peoples* (Cambridge: Cambridge University Press, 2004).

[17] Israel State Archives, Protocol of the Provisional Government (PG), 8 August 1948, p. 28 (Hebrew).

[18] Israel State Archives, Protocol of the PG, p. 24.

[19] Israel State Archives, Protocol of the PG, p. 28.

the Arab State, such as the Nazareth area.[20] Israeli officials and even the Supreme Court used this distinction until the early 1960s. Ben Gurion explained the governmental policy before the PSC: "It is not wise to declare that we will not return the occupied territories and it is not wise to declare that we will return them."[21] During a discussion of the Election Ordinance, Ben Gurion suggested that it define "the State of Israel" to include "areas under the Israeli government's control," by which he meant to include the "occupied territories." Mr. Bechor-Shalom Sheetrit, the Minister of Minority Affairs, was the only member to object to Ben Gurion's suggestion: "Can anyone imagine that the UK would let her colonies' subjects participate in [the UK] parliament's election... It is absurd from an international law perspective... to grant this right to the Nazareth area."[22] The government ignored his objection. In fact, the relevant law that should apply in these occupied territories is the Hague Regulations, which regulate the customary laws of war and occupation. Accordingly, the occupying power is not allowed to demand loyalty and to ask the occupied inhabitants to swear allegiance to it.[23] Nonetheless, this law does not prohibit voluntarily accepting participation in the national elections of the occupying power. This sort of acceptance, however, has consequences as it indirectly accepts as binding the citizenship law of the occupying power. Exercising the right to elect and to be elected is about exercising active citizenship, which involves claims of rights, duties, and loyalty.

In November 1948 the PG decided to conduct a census of the population. Registration by the census-takers would give each person an identity card for the election. The army conducted the census under a curfew.[24] The Arab population had a strong interest in being registered in order to be counted as "present" and not to be deported as "infiltrators," an Israeli term referring to the 1948 Palestinian refugees who tried to return to their homes.[25] The results

---

[20] The term "administrative territories" belongs to Article 55 of the Laws and Customs of War on Land, The Hague Regulations of 1907 (hereafter the Hague Regulations), which provide that: "The occupying State shall be regarded only as an administrator and usufructuary... It must safeguard the capital of these properties, and administer them in accordance with the rules of usufruct." Israel later used the legal term "administrative territories" to refer to the West Bank, Gaza, and the Golan Heights after the occupation in 1967. In the 1980s the term was replaced by "The Territories."

[21] Israel State Archives, Protocol of the PSC, 17 June 1948, p. 33.

[22] Israel State Archives, Protocol of the PG, 12 December 1948.

[23] See Article 45 of the Hague Regulations.

[24] Anat Leibler and Daniel Breslau, "The Uncounted: Citizenship and Exclusion in the Israeli Census of 1948," *Ethnic and Racial Studies* 28/5 (2005): 880–902.

[25] According to Supreme Court rulings, the identity cards and the registration were not a guarantee of later registration as a citizen nor did it prevent deportation; thus, the purpose of the registration by the census was only for statistical reasons. See HCJ 155/53, *Kiwan* v. *Minister of Defense et al.* Isr SC 8, 301.

of the census indicated that the majority of eligible Arab voters lived in the occupied territory.[26]

The PG introduced progressive Westphalian terms for the first election based on actual residency in the territory, with no ethnic discrimination. In fact, in the eyes of many members of the PSC, the terms of the election were almost *anti-Zionist*. The majority wanted to grant the right to vote to Jewish fighters who were deported from Palestine by the British Mandate and put under arrest in Cyprus. The PSC felt that excluding the fighters from the vote would send a negative message to the people, especially during wartime. Nonetheless, the PG convinced the PSC members to change their position and the minister of transportation put the Westphalian territorial argument strongly: "We must be constrained to the territorial wall and a State is a territorial concept. If we do so we will stand on our rights here."[27]

This commitment to Westphalian concepts for the election is striking, given that Israel's Declaration of the Establishment of the State is based on extra-territorial concepts and notions that contradict the theory of *jus soli*. But as noted above, the UN Partition Plan emphasized the principle of territorial equality and more importantly, the territorial conception of the electorate provided a safe way to exclude the hundreds of thousands of Palestinian refugees from the election. Ben Gurion explained this plainly before the PSC:[28]

The world, the states, international public opinion and the UN might ask us, and we will not have an answer: why did you grant the right to participate in the election for some thousands in Cyprus...but you did not care for the rights of hundreds of thousands who lived in the country but were forced to leave [Palestinian refugees]? If Jews who are abroad have the right to vote, why won't the Arabs who were here but who now are also abroad have the same right? Isn't it an extreme discrimination?... every one of us wants our prisoners and soldiers abroad including the Cyprus group to participate in the election but the state's interest is stronger than our sentiments toward them... in order to give legitimacy to the first national election that constitutes the state of Israel...the election must be clean and make no one delegitimize its legality.[29]

We see here that Israel's purported commitment to providing equal voting rights to Jews and the Arabs living under one authority is grounded in a deeper commitment to *exclude* Palestinian refugees. It is a fantasy to suppose that this

---

[26] The PG's protocol of 17 November 1948 noted the figures thus: the Jewish population numbered about 720,000, and of that amount, 450,000–480,000 would be eligible to vote. The Arab population numbered *only* about 68,600, and of them, 30,000–35,000 would be eligible to vote; 66 percent of them lived in the "occupied territories." The number of Arabs noted in the PG protocol is very low in comparison to the number of Arabs estimated to have remained as of May 1948 (160,000).

[27] Israel State Archives, Protocol of the PSC, 28 October 1948, p. 22.

[28] Israel State Archives, Protocol of the PSC, 11 November 1948, p. 8.

[29] Israel State Archives, Protocol of the PSC, 28 October 1948, p. 20.

sort of ethnic hierarchy can be liberal toward the insiders and colonial toward the outsiders, given that the "outsiders" (the refugees) and the "insiders" (the Palestinians who remained) belong to the same people, with the same original claims to territorial belonging. In reality, despite the appearance of Westphalian territorial equality in voting rights, ethnic hierarchy and domination applied to insiders as well as outsiders. This explains why the Palestinians who remained went to vote while they were under military control and even prohibited from electoral campaigning within their society. In a speech before the PSC two weeks before the elections the minister of the interior acknowledged that the Arab population of the "occupied territories" is quiet and peaceful, but said that any election propaganda would be prohibited because it might fall into the enemy's hands.[30] After a historical review, he also concluded: "This is the first time in modern history that a population under a belligerent situation will exercise the right to elect and to be elected."[31] He added that when a national minority in Europe belongs to an enemy nation with active hostility, they boycott the state's election, but Israel is creating a historical, unique precedent.

We can see here, at this moment of creating Arab citizenship, three constitutive constraints. First, the issue of demography was already visibly at hand. In demographic terms, in order to build a Jewish State based on popular sovereignty, the state must create by force a minimal Palestinian population. Second, the security constraints placed on the Palestinians under Israeli control were not a matter of whether they themselves constituted a physical threat; it was already a matter of their belonging to one people, the enemy. Third, the factors of demography and security had already created two different laws for the voters in the first election.

Despite these constraints—demography, security, and differential laws—the new state viewed Arab participation in the election as vital to its interests. Arguably, the Arab vote had the power to legitimize Israel internationally as a democratic state and not as a colonial or apartheid regime. Equality between Arabs and Jews in voting would diminish the distinction between natives, occupiers, and settlers. Ben Gurion expressed this sentiment indirectly before the PG stressing that, unlike France, which did not need elections for its legitimacy since the French people had inhabited France's territory for many years, Israel needs this legitimacy. Moreover, the Arab vote would contribute to legitimating the de facto borders of the new state, which later became known as the Green Line. If the population of a region agrees to elect and to be elected for a parliament, they express their free will to accept the state's sovereignty.

This then is the conception of citizenship that Arabs were initially offered by the Israeli state—namely, a conception in which the appearance of

---

[30] Israel State Archives, Protocol of the PSC, 6 January 1949, pp. 14–18.
[31] Israel State Archives, Protocol of the PSC, 6 January 1949, pp. 14–18.

Westphalian equality based on territorial belonging is underpinned and undermined by a deeper friend–enemy dynamic tied to the exclusion of Palestinian refugees. Let us return to the situation of the Palestinians during the period between May 1948 and the first election in January 1949. At this time, the Palestinian people faced the most unimaginable national catastrophe in their history, called "the Nakba." The word "Nakba" in Arabic refers to "the catastrophe of the ages." Not only did the Palestinians who remained become for the first time a numerical minority under foreign control and belong to a defeated nation, but also they lost their leaders, elites, cities, and contact with their relatives, friends, the rest of their people, and the Arab nation. Movement between their villages was prohibited as they were put under military curfews and closure. Local and national communication in Arabic no longer existed. The Israeli forces demolished hundreds of Arab villages.[32] About one-quarter of this group moved inside other Arab villages as internally displaced persons and were not allowed to return to their original villages despite the fact that they had become citizens of Israel. In short, the language, the spaces, the geography, and the people totally changed during this short period. The picture of Europe in 1945 as portrayed by Tony Judt in his book *Postwar*, regarding the total destruction, the mass displacement, the movement of these refugees, and the loss of families and properties, is not far from the scene experienced by the Palestinians who remained in their homeland in 1948–49.[33]

Despite the tragedy of the Nakba, and even before the signing of the ceasefire agreement between Israel and its Arab neighbors' countries, the Palestinians who remained took part in the first parliamentary elections in Israel on 25 January 1949. Their participation rate was very high: 79.3 percent. The majority of the Arab vote, 51 percent, was given to the Arab list named "The Nazareth Democratic List," which subsequently sent two Arab members to the first Knesset. The name of the list carried the name "Nazareth," the symbolic city of the "occupied territory," and its list was totally controlled by the political party led by Ben Gurion. The second party, Maki ("The Communist List"), got 22 percent of the Arab vote; it sent one Arab member and two Jewish members to the first Knesset.[34]

---

[32] Jiryis noted that from May 1948 and during 1949, "Arabs were attacked, their property was confiscated, and they were forcefully expelled." Sabri Jiryis, *The Arabs in Israel*, trans. Inea Bushnaq (New York: Monthly Review Press, 1976), 15; and Tom Segev, *1949: The First Israelis* (New York: Henry Holt, Reprint Edition, 1998), 52.

[33] Tony Judt, *Postwar: A History of Europe since 1945* (New York: Penguin, 2005).

[34] Three Arabs were elected to the Knesset in 1949 among 120 members of parliament. The two members of the Nazareth List were: (1) Sief Adin Zoabi, the chair of the list, who served as an MK until 1977. He is an Arab Muslim from Nazareth and over time he became known among the Palestinians as a symbol of collaboration; and (2) Amin Jarjoura, an Arab Christian from Nazareth, who worked as a lawyer during the British Mandate. He served only one term and is not known today in Arab politics. The third Arab MK was Tawfeeq Tubi, an Arab Christian from

Arab participation in the 1949 election can be viewed as an act of deep self-exclusion from the politics of the Arab nation and the rest of the Palestinian people. Some of the activists among the remaining Palestinians tried quietly to advocate for a boycott of the election, since the situation was not stable, and it was too early to treat Israel as a political reality. The Palestinian leadership in the Diaspora and on Cairo radio called on the "insiders" not to surrender and to boycott the election in order not to legitimize the "colonial Zionist entity"; they promised that the case would soon be brought before the UN.[35] By participating, Arab insiders deviated from the long-standing political identity and the self-perception of the Arab nation and the Palestinian people. The Arab League and the Palestinian leadership opposed the UN Partition Plan, in part, because of their refusal to accept that Arabs would be a minority in their homeland. This refusal derived from the Palestinians' self-identification as natives.[36] The concept of nativity was strong enough for the Arab leadership to reject any partition of Palestine.[37] Conversely, the Zionist leadership rejected the idea of one state for all of Palestine because they did not want to be a minority among the Palestinian majority.[38]

Participation in the first election in Israel made the Palestinians who remained a minority. Their experience is totally different from that of other Arabs who were occupied by Israel in 1967 and later annexed to Israel, such as the Syrian Druze in the Golan Heights and the Palestinians of Jerusalem.[39] Undoubtedly, the acceptance of the Palestinians as being an "Israeli minority" created distance between them and their nation, which also contributed to

---

Haifa, who was only 27 years old when he was first elected to the Knesset; he served as an MK for forty-three years, from 1949 to 1992.

[35] See Atallah Said Copty (ed.), *Memoirs of a Palestinian Lawyer: Hanna Deep Naqara, Lawyer of the Land and the People* (Washington, DC: Institute for Palestine Studies, 2011), 235–40 (Arabic).

[36] John Strawson, *Partitioning Palestine* (London: Pluto, 2010).

[37] See Ilan Pappe, *The Ethnic Cleansing of Palestine* (Oxford: One World, 2006), 31–5; Walid Khalidi, "Revisiting the UNGA Partition Resolution," *Journal of Palestine Studies* 27/1 (1997): 5–21 at 16–17.

[38] As Khalidi notes: "At the time, one of the arguments frequently raised by the Jews against a unitary state in Palestine had been the unfairness of Arab majoritarian rule over the Jewish minority. Commenting on this argument, the Pakistani delegate at the UN, Zafrulla Khan, remarked: 'If it is unfair that 33 percent of the population of Palestine (the Jews in the proposed unitary state) should be subject to 67 percent of the population, is it less unfair that 46 percent of the population (the Arabs in the proposed Jewish state) should be subject to 54 percent?'" (Khalidi, "Revisiting the UNGA Partition Resolution," 17).

[39] While Israel annexed the Golan in 1981 and tried to impose Israeli citizenship on the inhabitants, they protested against this move by staging a long general strike. They have refused to participate in any Israeli election, municipal or national, and they continue to define themselves as an occupied population. Similarly, the Palestinians in East Jerusalem who are defined by Israel as Israeli residents still refuse to participate in the local election for the Jerusalem municipality. See Bashar Tarabieh, "Education, Control and Resistance in the Golan Heights," *Middle East Report* 194 (1995): 43–7.

their exclusion from the politics of the Arab states and later from the PLO. In some ways they lost having any actual kin-state or any Arab entity to raise the issue of their status before any international forum.

If participation in the first election is a moment of exclusion of the Palestinian refugees as well as a divorce between the "Israeli Arab minority" and their Arab nation, it is also a moment of "inclusion" of this group into the Israeli polity, a new framework introduced in one of the most celebratory moments in the Zionist movement's history. The Knesset held its opening celebration and its first working session in the Jewish Agency's Office on 14 February 1949. After the singing of Hativka, Israel's national anthem, only two speeches were delivered on this day. The first president of Israel, Chaim Weizmann, gave the celebratory Zionist and patriotic speech. The second speech was not delivered by the founder of the state and its prime minister, Ben Gurion, or by the leader of the opposition, Menachem Begin, or any other Jewish political leader: it was given by the Arab MK, Mr. Amin Jarjoura, in Arabic in the first working session of the Knesset. His full speech was translated into Hebrew and covered by the media as one of the celebratory moments of the new era.[40] Without a doubt, if the first election was introduced as a Westphalian moment based on the idea of a "state for all its citizens," so the opening session of the first Knesset, with an Arab MK speaking in Arabic wearing his Turkish *tarbush*, is a scene of a multicultural democracy at its climax. As Ben Gurion put it, in his first speech before the Knesset, this is the first time that the two peoples meet equally.

MK Jarjoura's speech is a landmark text. It is the first speech to introduce the universal civil rights talk of the Arabs in Israel in that it emphasized their desire for justice and liberty. But it also introduced the constraints of a patriotic Zionist framework, the dominant paradigm among the Arabs in Israel for a very long time. MK Jarjoura opened his speech by stating that:

It is a great day and a very historical one in which the *Yishuv* [Hebrew term indicating the Jewish entity before the establishment of the State of Israel] is celebrating this Knesset's opening [session] . . . I am using this opportunity to send to you on behalf of my colleagues and myself on the list, loyalty greetings on this great day . . . the eyes of the Arab citizens of Israel are looking forward to this Knesset which relies on justice and the interest of all.[41]

MK Jarjoura emphasized his hope that the state will be based on "equality and justice" between all citizens. But above all, he had to express strong loyalty to, and pride in, the new state. MK Jarjoura defined the Arabs not as "Israeli

---

[40] See coverage in the *Historical Jewish Press*, 16 February 1949 (Israel State Archives); newspapers *Davar*, 16 February 1949, 1; *Ha'aretz*, 16 February 1949; and *Al-Yum*, 16 February 1949.

[41] Protocol of the Knesset, First Session, 14 February 1949 (Hebrew).

Arabs," an infamous term used by the government, or the "Palestinian national minority" but as "Arab citizens of Israel." He was the first political leader to officially use this term, which is still dominant today. While he repeatedly spoke about equality and justice, he did not give any clues, even implicitly, about the tragedy of his people, although he delivered his speech during the climax of the Nakba.

MK Tawfeeq Tubi of *Maki* delivered his first speech during the Knesset's second session.[42] Throughout the years and until his retirement from the Knesset in 1992, MK Tubi became the most prominent nationalist leader among the Palestinians in Israel. In his speech, he expressed loyalty and welcomed the establishment of the new state, and in line with the position of the Soviet Union, he then heavily attacked the Arab leaders for not accepting the Partition Plan, and thus bringing on the tragedy of the Nakba. In addition, he also criticized the military actions against the Palestinians in Israel. Ben Gurion delivered his first speech during the Knesset's third session.[43] He welcomed the speeches of MK Jarjoura and MK Tubi, but he also strongly attacked MK Tubi for his pre-1948 national activities against the Zionist Movement in Palestine. Ben Gurion's first speech in the Knesset is the starting point of the de-legitimization rhetoric against the elected Arab leadership in Israel, which continues until this day.

If the PSC and PG made efforts to hold the first election in accordance with Westphalian territorial concepts, the first elected Knesset undertook four legal acts that totally negated the territorial concept and instituted the "colonial citizenship" of the Palestinians in Israel. The first law enacted was the Defense Service Law—1949, which imposes a duty on every Israeli citizen to serve in the military.[44] During the Knesset debate in 1950, MK Tubi demanded that the law be applied to Arab citizens. He explained that the Arabs' exemption from the military is a discriminatory act. Ben Gurion rejected this demand.[45] Both positions are problematic in ways that reveal the contradiction at the heart of Arab citizenship. MK Tubi's position tried to emphasize the Westphalian concept of a "state for all its citizens" but at the same time he asked the Arabs to be in the army that controls them and that is still fighting against their people. Ben Gurion's position is anti-Westphalian because it is based on the politics of the "friend–enemy" distinction. Whether or not it is morally justified to draft the Arabs, this law indirectly made the Israeli army a Jewish army. The characterization and structure of an army are the most significant elements in examining the relationship between sovereignty, citizenship, and

---

[42] Protocol of the Knesset, Second Session of the First Knesset.

[43] Protocol of the Knesset, Third Session of the First Knesset.

[44] The law in English is available at: <http://www.israellawresourcecenter.org/israellaws/fulltext/defenceservicelaw.htm>, accessed September 2013.

[45] Knesset Reporter, ch. 3, session held on 16 January 1950, pp. 534–5.

domination. As Hobbes put it, "And therefore, whosoever is made general of an army, he that hath the sovereign power is always generalissimo."[46] This "ethnic sacrifice" among the Israeli Jewish community has contributed strongly to the strength of the *Political* as well as the perception of "owning" the state as a Jewish state.

The second legal act was to leave the Emergency Regulations fully intact, especially those of the British Mandate, which were adopted by the PG. The Knesset did not decide to cancel, amend, or change these regulations. These regulations imposed a harsh military regime on the Palestinians in Israel, which lasted until 1966. With this omission, the military was accorded total discretion in setting curfews, imposing limits on freedom of movement, and ordering administrative detention, deportations, home arrest, internal exile, property demolitions, land confiscation, etc.[47] The military regime treated the Arabs in Israel as "enemy aliens."[48] Thus, an elected body did confirm the most radical laws used against Arab citizens even today.

The third legal act was the passage of the Absentees' Property Law—1950, which stipulates that an "absentee," *inter alia*, is someone who left his place of residence in Palestine after the UN Partition Resolution and thus, his property was transferred to the state.[49] In addition to the Palestinian refugees who left or were expelled from the homeland, Palestinians in Israel also found themselves defined as "absentees" and had their property expropriated by the state. For example, thousands of internally displaced persons who were forced to leave their villages and move to the Nazareth area and who voted in the first election are characterized as "present absentees." The government considered these individuals as citizens for the purpose of the election, although they lived in the "occupied territories," yet they were also designated as absentees from Israel because they lived in the "occupied territories."

The fourth legal act was the enactment of the Law of Return—1950, which stipulates that any Jew, including his or her non-Jewish family members, is entitled to immigrate to Israel and automatically receive citizenship. Section 4 of the Law of Return creates a stark contrast *vis-à-vis* the status of the Palestinian refugees by stating that any Jew who immigrated or who was born in this country before or after this law was passed will have the same status as someone who has immigrated under this law. This section made Jews "non-absentees" and always present. When this law was enacted, there was

---

[46] Hobbes, *Leviathan*, 111.

[47] See Jiryis, *The Arabs in Israel*, 9–16.

[48] This act violated the Laws of War of the 1907 Hague Regulations, which prohibit limiting the rights of civilians who are not involved in armed conflict. See Michael Kagan, "Destructive Ambiguity: Enemy Nationals and the Legal Enabling of Ethnic Conflict in the Middle East," *Columbia Human Rights Law Review* 38 (2007): 263–319 at 292–7.

[49] The English version of the law is available at: <http://unispal.un.org/UNISPAL.NSF/0/E0B719E95E3B494885256F9A005AB90A>, accessed September 2013.

still no citizenship law in place governing the status of Palestinians in Israel. Notably, Palestinians who were registered in the census and who had participated in the Knesset election in 1949 tried to use their identity cards and the fact that they participated in the election in order to fight deportation; however, the Supreme Court decided that an identity card is not a guarantee of status but is valid only for statistical purposes.[50] The Citizenship Law would be enacted only in 1952, and it adopts similar concepts to that of the Absentee Property Law.

These four laws together negated the façade of territorial citizenship and form the basis of colonial citizenship. On the one hand, the military regime and the Absentee Property Law were applied unequally to Arabs and Jews and created different legal regimes inside the same territory. On the other hand, the Law of Return enshrined a conception of citizenship based on ethnic extra-territorial belonging. If the 1949 election tried to distinguish "insider" Jews and Arabs from "outsider" Jews and Arabs based on territorial residence, these new laws came to prove otherwise. The linkage between the rights of the insiders and the outsiders is very strong. They imposed similar burdens on all native Palestinians, both refugees and those who remained, and conversely endowed benefits on all Jews in the world regardless of any territorial test. In this way, these legal acts created an apartheid regime in terms of citizenship and property with the additional component of force and domination over the Palestinians by an ethnic Jewish army. These laws, including the emergency regulations, are still valid today.

Despite this discrimination, the two Arab members of the Nazareth List voted for the Absentees' Property Law and the three Arab MKs voted for the Law of Return in 1950. They simply voted against themselves and to be excluded. If we agree with Dworkin that no one with self-respect would agree to be excluded, this vote is the climax of the Palestinians' humiliation, regardless of any reasons that may justify these laws.[51]

---

[50] HCJ 155/53, *Kiwan v. Minister of Defense et al.* Isr SC 8, 301. J. Cheshin noted that "an identity card is not a talisman against expulsion from the country . . . does not accord special rights, except for the right to receive an ID" (at 304).

[51] Ronald Dworkin, *A Matter of Principle* (Cambridge, MA: Harvard University Press, 1985), 502–6. Statman argues that individuals' self-worth is shaped to a large extent by what others think about them and how they are treated. Individuals cannot bestow self-respect on themselves; they need the other. "Humiliation takes advantage of this fact and seeks to injure self-respect by sending painful messages of subordination, rejection and exclusion . . . This vulnerability to humiliation is the flip side of the human urge for social inclusion and recognition." Daniel Statman, "Humiliation, Dignity and Self-respect," *Philosophical Psychology* 13/4 (2000): 523–40 at 535–6. One of the reasons that the national leader MK Tawfeeq Tubi did not write his memoirs, which could also be the history of the Arabs in Israel, is that he felt ashamed by his actions in 1949–50, as noted in this chapter. This information was brought to my attention by the General Secretary of Hadash (formerly Maki), Ayman Odeh.

In sum, despite the superficial appearance of normal Westphalian citizen-ship, citizenship rights for Arabs were subjected to Israeli patriotic Zionist conditions. These conditions include: (1) the expression of loyalty to the new state as a sovereign and legitimate entity; (2) the expression of loyalty to the new state's basic Zionist values; (3) the self-negation of the Palestinians' national identity and the Nakba, including the exclusion of the refugees and the historical injustice that occurred in the period of the state's foundation.

Hobbes stated that a defeated population, for fear of death, will authorize all the actions of the sovereign "that hath their lives and liberty in his power."[52] The defeated group's surrender should be unconditional and it should be signified as a relationship between the master and his servant. This "dominion is then acquired to the victor when the vanquished, to avoid the present stroke of death, covenanteth, either in express words or by other sufficient signs of the will, that so long as his life and the liberty of his body is allowed him, the victor shall have the use thereof at his pleasure."[53] Arabs' participation in the first election, alongside the Arab MKs' first speeches in the Knesset and their voting for exclusionary laws during this first Knesset, all together indicate an act of unconditional surrender, which I call the "Hobbesian moment" of Palestinian citizenship. The terms of this citizenship are Hobbesian in that they are based on surrender and humiliation. This citizenship was not ac-quired by free men and women but by a defeated people who were controlled, humiliated and filled with fear of expulsion.[54] Their only concern was to remain, to save their family life, and not to be deported.[55]

The Israeli government needed their vote for international legitimacy; a boycott of the election would have cast Israel as an occupying power. This put the Palestinians in an impossible situation. Hanna Naqara, the first Palestinian national cause lawyer who became known as "the lawyer of the land and the people," mentioned in his memoir a speech that he delivered in 1949 before a small Arab group to convince them to participate in the first election. His main argument was that Zionist parties would interpret a boycott as evidence that the Palestinians are a fifth column, a group that listens to its leadership abroad and rejects the "new reality." He emphasized that a boycott will give Zionist parties "a new reason to hit and attack again the last remaining Arab natives in this country." He added further that if we show indifference toward the election, the Zionist parties will say to the Jewish community, "you see how the Arabs behave, they don't want to live with us, they don't want to recognize

---

[52] Hobbes, *Leviathan*, 122.   [53] Hobbes, *Leviathan*, 124.

[54] Tom Segev noted that in 1949, the remaining Palestinians were "still dazed by the defeat. They were a frightened, leaderless people; they caused no danger to state security" (Segev, *1949: The First Israelis*, 52).

[55] Of course some Arab activists or small groups were interested in participating either because of their relationship with the new polity or because of other ideological reasons but their power could not explain the mass participation without the strong element of fear.

the State of Israel, and they are still bound to their leadership."[56] An elderly Arab man told me that some Arab cars on Election Day in Nazareth in 1949 flew white flags, exactly as the villagers put white flags on their homes to signify surrender at the moment of the Israeli occupation. Participation in the election, declarations of loyalty and support for exclusionary laws were all, as Hobbes put it, good signs of unconditional surrender to the sovereign.

THE RISE OF CONSTITUTIONALISM AND NATIONALISM IN THE 1990s AND SINCE

The 1990s marked a moment of optimism around the world for the prospects of liberal constitutionalism and minority rights. Internationally, the UN General Assembly adopted the Declaration on the Rights of Persons Belonging to National or Ethnic, Religious and Linguistic Minorities in 1992; the literature on liberal multiculturalism proliferated; the Apartheid regime fell in South Africa; and liberal constitutionalism spread as "the Enlightenment hope in written constitutions is sweeping the world."[57] Many countries adopted new constitutions through reconciliation processes with the active participation of groups historically discriminated against.[58] In these and other ways, older colonial and Hobbesian forms of citizenship were challenged and transcended in many countries, replaced with more inclusive and democratic citizenship.

Versions of these trends were also visible in Israel. In 1992 the Knesset enacted two Basic Laws—The Basic Law: Human Dignity and Liberty and The Basic Law: Freedom of Occupation. Unlike constitution-making processes elsewhere, these basic laws were not enacted through the active participation of the national minority, processes of reconciliation, or by recognizing historical injustices.[59] While most recent constitutions include the words, "We, the people of..." to refer to the whole political community with its diversity, Israel was instead defined for the first time in law as a "Jewish and democratic state." Nevertheless, these Basic Laws contain constitutional protections for certain civil liberties. The Israeli Supreme Court, under the leadership of Chief Justice Aharon Barak, strengthened the rhetoric of civil and human rights, and

---

[56] Copty, *Memoirs of a Palestinian Lawyer*, 238–9.

[57] Bruce Ackerman, "The Rise of World Constitutionalism," *Virginia Law Review* 83 (1997): 771–97 at 772.

[58] Yash Ghai and Guido Galli, *Constitution Building Processes and Democratization* (The International Institute for Democracy and Electoral Assistance, 2006), 5.

[59] See Aeyal Gross, "The Constitution, Reconciliation, and Transitional Justice: Lessons from South Africa and Israel," *Stanford Journal of International Law* 40 (2004).

for the first time in Israel's legal history delivered landmark decisions in anti-discrimination cases brought by Palestinian citizens of Israel.[60]

Optimism was strengthened by the signing of the Oslo Accords in 1993 between Israel and its arch-enemy the Palestine Liberation Organization (PLO). Although the Oslo Accords did not relate in any way to the status of the Palestinian citizens of Israel—and maybe because of that—the new political changes locally and internationally strongly influenced their politics in the 1990s; it transformed their political imagination. The "two-state solution" was perceived as a viable and legitimate political track. In this framework, within the 1967 lines, Jews and Palestinians would constitute the legitimate citizens of the political community; the former constitutes the majority and the latter is a national minority. Based on this conceptualization, the Palestinians in Israel began to claim not only civil liberties but also group rights, and for the first time they began to refer to themselves as a "national minority."[61] This terminology is not obvious; the term "minority" was never used before in their political discourse and was perceived as disempowering.[62] By the 1990s, however, the Arab elites perceived this term as empowering due to the new international legal status of national minorities as well as the rise of multicultural politics worldwide. By conceiving of themselves as a permanent national minority, Palestinians in Israel now repositioned themselves to challenge the "essence" of the political community in order to determine "who is a citizen" and who is "politically *in*." Dr Azmi Bishara, the founder of a new Arab national party, Balad, coined the concept of "full identity, full citizenship."[63] This agenda became dominant politically among other Arab parties and it led

---

[60] See e.g. HCJ 6698/95, *Ka'adan et al.* v. *The Israel Land Administration et al.*, P.D. 54 (1) 258 (decision delivered 8 March 2000); HCJ 1113/99 *Adalah et al.* v. *Minister of Religious Affairs et al.*; HCJ 4112/99, *Adalah et al.* v. *The Municipalities of Tel Aviv-Jaffa et al.*

[61] Notably, Palestinian academics started to use the term "national minority" for the first time: e.g. Nadim Rouhana and As'ad Ghanem, "The Crisis of Minorities in Ethnic States: The Case of Palestinian Citizens of Israel," *International Journal of Middle East Studies* 30/3 (1998): 321–46; Amal Jamal, "The Ambiguities of Minority Patriotism: On Love for Homeland versus State among Palestinian Citizens of Israel," *Nationalism and Ethnic Politics* 10/3 (2004): 433–71.

[62] State officials used the term "minorities" but the phrase articulated by MK Jarjoura "the Arab citizens of Israel," was the dominant expression. The *Ittihad* Arabic-language newspaper of Maki did not use the term "minority"; instead it used "the Arab masses" or "the Arab citizens." The term did not appear in the Arabic literature and the former mayor of Nazareth, one of the strongest Arab national leaders, and a former MK of Maki, Tawfeeq Zayad, wrote in the 1950s in his poem: "But ... are we a minority? No ... and one million nos. We are here the majority. We are the nation who is ready for sacrifice to build its happiness ... in Egypt ... in Algeria ... in Iraq ..."

[63] See Ari Shavit, "Citizen Azmi," interview with Azmi Bishara, Ha'aretz, 29 May 1998, available at: <http://azmibishara.com/site/topics/article.asp?cu_no=1&item_no=249&version=1&template_id=294&parent_id=29>, accessed September 2013; and Amal Jamal, "The Vision of the 'Political Nation' and the Challenge of 'State of all its Citizens': Explorations in Azmi Bishara's Political Thought," *Alpayeem Journal* 30 (2006): 71–113 (Hebrew).

to challenging the definition of Israel as a Jewish state and to highlighting the claim for a "state for all of its citizens."

This new liberal climate of the 1990s, and its hopes for a new form of citizenship, lasted a short time. It ended with one of the most shocking events for the Palestinian citizens—the October 2000 killings. On 29 September 2000, the head of the opposition, MK Ariel Sharon, decided to challenge the peace negotiations between the PLO and the Barak government by entering the Al Aqsa Mosque compound. During this "visit," many Palestinians were killed and injured by Israeli security forces. These acts marked the beginning of the Second *Intifada*. During protests against the killings, thirteen Palestinians were killed in Israel by the security forces. An official commission of inquiry was established and the Arab citizens cooperated actively with its work. In its report, the Commission emphasized that the police exceeded their power by violating their own open-fire regulations and that the police must stop treating Arab citizens as "enemies."[64] It also recommended that the Attorney General (AG) open criminal investigations against the police officers and commanders who were involved in the killings. However, in January 2008, the AG decided to close all of the files, explaining that the police opening fire was legal, likening the situation to a military battle, which justified the use of deadly force. In this way the AG treated civilian Palestinian demonstrators as "enemies" standing in a warlike confrontation.[65] The Arab leadership decided not to appeal to the Supreme Court against the AG's decision and instead to turn to the international community.

Another development taking place was a wave of new legislation directed against the citizenship status of Palestinians in Israel. In 2003 and 2007, the Knesset passed the most discriminatory laws since 1950, namely, amendments to the Citizenship Law, which banned Arab family unification in Israel. It prohibits family unification between Palestinian citizens of Israel with their spouses from the West Bank, Gaza, and "enemy states" (Iraq, Iran, Lebanon, and Syria). In two cases, the Supreme Court upheld these amendments by a six to five majority by accepting the AG's position that every "enemy alien" such as the Palestinian living in the OPT is a security threat.[66] The principle of "separate and unequal" creates more than ever a clear apartheid regime in citizenship (naturalization and family life).

---

[64] Report of the Official Commission of Inquiry, September 2003, available at: <http://elyon1.court.gov.il/heb/veadot/or/inside_index.htm>, accessed September 2013 (Hebrew).

[65] "Adalah: Mazuz's Decision to Close October 2000 Investigation is Racist and Inflammatory," *Adalah's Newsletter* 44 (January 2008).

[66] HCJ 7052/03, *Adalah et al.* v. *Minister of Interior et al.* (1) Isr LR 443 (2006), available in English at <http://elyon1.court.gov.il/files_eng/03/520/070/a47/03070520.a47.htm>, accessed September 2013. See also HCJ 466/07, *MK Zahava Galon—Meretz-Yahad et al.* v. *Attorney General et al.* (decision delivered 11 January 2012).

Yet another blow was the constitution-making process initiated by the Knesset in 2004, which continued for three years but was not completed. While the Arab MKs initially hesitated, they ultimately decided not to participate in the process for three main reasons. First, the Knesset did not suggest any terms of reference for national minority participation. Second, the drafts of the proposed constitution did not determine the borders of Israel and Arab MKs refused to be a part of legalizing the occupation of the OPT. Third, the drafts strongly emphasized the ethno-centric nature of the state.[67]

The Palestinian elites decided to take a different tack and to address the Israeli public directly, outside of the Parliament. In 2006 and 2007, several Palestinian institutions proposed their own future vision documents.[68] These documents mark the first time that the Arab national movement has articulated clearly their relationship with Israel as citizens, as well as their relationship to their Palestinian people and to their Arab nation. The common element of these "Arab documents" is that they emphasize: (1) the narrative of the Nakba as the constitutive element of the Palestinians' identity; (2) the claims for a democratic state that guarantees full equality between Arabs and Jews; (3) the demand to end the Israeli Occupation; and (4) a remedy for the historical injustice mainly in land matters and the recognition of the Right to Return of Palestinian refugees based on UN Resolution 194. They set forth provisions on citizenship, official languages, educational and cultural institutions, model mechanisms for the Arab minority's participation in parliamentary decision-making, and distributive and restorative justice.[69]

These documents show that Arab citizens, having embraced a language of rights, were deconstructing assumptions and identities inherited from the Hobbesian moments in 1949. In order to be "included" and not deported, they presented themselves in 1949–50 as if they had no connection to their Nakba and no belonging to the Arab nation. Now, in the name of "inclusion," they rejected their Hobbesian identity and instead articulated their historical claims with connection to the consequences of the Nakba. As an act of

---

[67] See e.g. Nadim Rouhana, "Constitution by Consensus: By Whose Consensus?" *Adalah's Newsletter* 7 (November 2004); Jonathan Cooke, "Israel Constitutional Committee Faces a Double Bind," *Adalah's Newsletter* 7 (November 2004); and Hassan Jabareen, "Collective Rights and Reconciliation in the Constitutional Process: The Case of Israel," *Adalah's Newsletter* 12 (April 2005).

[68] There are three documents: the "Democratic Constitution" prepared by Adalah, the Legal Center for Arab Minority Rights in Israel; the "Future Vision" document put forward by the National Committee of Arab Mayors in Israel, and the "Haifa Declaration" led by Mada al-Carmel. Available at <http://www.adalah.org/newsletter/eng/mar07/thabet.php>, accessed September 2013.

[69] The only Arab political group that expressed serious opposition to these documents was the extra-parliamentary Islamic movement led by Sheikh Raed Salah. They claimed that no one authorized these Palestinian groups to articulate a vision on behalf of Arab citizens, and also objected to the documents' liberal, secular spirit as well as to the two-state solution.

surrender, their claim to civil rights in 1949–50 was subordinated to the superiority of Zionist values. Now their claims for equal rights reject Zionist superiority. Their new language of rights puts a strong emphasis on the need for a remedy as a homeland minority for the historical injustice to them.[70] All of this does not mean that their struggle started only in the 1990s or that they were unaware of their national Palestinian identity. In the past, their struggle focused on how to survive, but in the 1990s it shifted to how to live. The *articulation* of rights language is always attached to the group's politics; when your existence is at stake, it takes one form, and when you seek better ways of life, it takes on another form.

In asserting their own national rights, the Arab citizens did not attempt to delegitimize the rights of the Israeli Jewish community. The total loss of the Palestinian entity in 1948 led the Palestinians to surrender to the use of the Hebrew language, and through the years they became bilingual. Outside the Jewish community, they are the only Hebrew speakers in the world. Now, they demand that Israel become a bilingual state based on mutual respect and equality. In addition, and very importantly, the Arab documents recognized clearly the right of self-determination of Israeli Jews through the claim for a bi-national state. These documents are the first and only "official" Arab statements in the history of the Arab nation to recognize this right.[71]

The Palestinian elites believed, from a Habermasian perspective, that the Arab documents would open a constructive dialog with the Jewish Israeli elites, but they were wrong. Israeli officials, politicians, and academics lashed out with hostility toward the documents, which they perceived to be an attempt to delegitimize the existence of the state as Jewish.[72] This criticism reached a climax when the director of the General Security Services (GSS) declared that the Arab citizens of the state constituted a "strategic threat" and

---

[70] The first time that the term "homeland minority" was used in Israel regarding the Palestinians was in my article in *Mishpat Umimshal (University of Haifa, Faculty of Law)* 6/1 (July 2001): 53–86 (Hebrew). A shorter version appears in English as "The Future of Arab Citizenship in Israel: Jewish-Zionist Time in a Place with no Palestinian Memory," in Daniel Levy and Yfaat Weiss (eds.), *Challenging Ethnic Citizenship* (New York: Berghahn Books, 2002), 196–220.

[71] The Israeli treaties with Egypt, the PLO, and Jordan recognize the right of Israel to exist as a sovereign state but they do not refer to questions of the essence of the state. There is no serious debate in the Arab world regarding these questions.

[72] For example, Shlomo Avineri, a professor of political science at the Hebrew University, who represents the mainstream academic position, emphasized that, "Adalah's proposal is a very clear and sophisticated mechanism for disestablishing Israel as a Jewish state" (quoted by Dan Izenberg, "The Future Vision of the Palestinian Arabs in Israel," *Jerusalem Post*, 4 April 2007). See also Rory McCarthy, "Israeli group calls for increased rights for Arabs," *The Guardian*, 28 February 2007, quoting Avineri on the Democratic Constitution: "It is an Arab nationalist programme and its aim is to de-legitimize Israel as a Jewish state. This document is not going to end discrimination. It is counter-productive and will create the exact opposite effect—an extreme response from the Israeli right-wing."

that the GSS intends to "disrupt activities of any groups that seek to change the character of Israel as a Jewish and democratic state even if they use democratic means."[73]

All of these developments—the response to the Or Commission, the discriminatory citizenship law, the exclusionary constitutional process, and the response to the Arab documents—indicate two important points. First, they reveal the deep linkage between the status of Palestinian citizens of Israel and the rest of their people. October 2000 and the AG's response, as well as the Arab MKs' refusal to take part in the Knesset's constitution-making process, are connected to matters belonging to the Occupation, while the Citizenship Law and the Arab documents belong to categories of "enemy aliens," the Nakba and demography. Second, they reveal the deep limits on the extent to which the terms of citizenship could be renegotiated. It seems clear that Israeli officials and the Israeli Jewish public do not accept that the terms of Arab citizenship include the right to challenge discriminatory laws that are based on Zionist values and the identification with the Nakba narrative, even if these actions are done peacefully and democratically.

What is the source of these hostile positions? I argue that these positions are constituted by the law that sets forth the scope of the constitutional values of the "Jewish and democratic" state, as they were decided by the Supreme Court. I will also explain that these Court decisions attempt to reaffirm the terms of the Hobbesian moments.[74]

The elections law is the best example by which to explain the status of the Arabs in the "Jewish and democratic" state. Article 7A of the Basic Law: The Knesset authorizes the Central Election Committee (CEC), which is composed of representatives of the Knesset parties, to disqualify any political party list from running in the elections if its agenda either negates Israel as a Jewish and democratic state, incites racism, or supports a terror organization. In 2003, the AG and right-wing MKs disqualified MK Azmi Bishara and his political list from running in the Knesset elections.[75] On review before the Supreme Court, the AG's representative argued that the principle of "a state for all of its citizens," the central plank of the party's platform, negates Israel as a Jewish

---

[73] See Yoav Stern, "Arab leaders air public relations campaign against Shin Bet," *Haaretz*, 6 April 2007; "Not a matter for the Shin Bet," *Haaretz* Editorial, 28 May 2007; Yitzhak Laor, a non-Zionist intellectual, criticized the Shin Bet in "Democracy for Jews only," *Haaretz*, 30 May 2007.

[74] Trubek's analysis is relevant here when he emphasizes that the Law has constitutive power to influence the consciousness of the public including the relations with others; David Trubek, "Where the Action Is: Critical Legal Studies and Empiricism," *Stanford Law Review* 36 (1984): 575–622 at 604. See also Robert Gordon, "Critical Legal Histories," *Stanford Law Review* 36 (1984): 57–125 at 57.

[75] (Election Confirmation) EC 11280/02, *The Central Elections Committee for the 16th Knesset* v. *MK Ahmad Tibi et al.* PD 57 (4) 1 (decision delivered on 15 May 2003).

and democratic state.[76] The Court, in a seven to four decision, voted to overturn the decision to disqualify. The majority canceled the decision based on procedural grounds and articulated the standard for disqualification. In order to disqualify a party, the state must provide evidence to demonstrate its central activities actively oppose the following: a Jewish demographic majority in Israel; the Law of Return; Hebrew as the primary language; and the Jewish symbols, national holidays, Jewish law, and heritage as part of the cultural life of the state. In this case, Barak decided that the AG provided insufficient evidence. The four justices in the minority decided that the mere contradiction between the Jewishness of the state and the notion of full equality based on a "state for all its citizens" is sufficient by itself to disqualify.

The majority decision could be read as a victory for liberal constitutionalism, especially as the Israeli public shares the AG's view that the mere principle of a civic state negates the Jewishness of the state. However, here again we need to situate this case in the broader context of Hobbesian citizenship. As the Palestinians' citizenship was conditioned on their acceptance of the Zionist narrative in 1949, the Court in the Bishara case, close to fifty-five years later in 2003, reaffirmed these conditions. But unlike the Hobbesian moments where the Arabs affirmatively expressed their loyalty to the state, in Bishara they are asked to do so passively. As the majority expressed it, no one can demand that Bishara work with the Jewish Agency to encourage Jewish immigration but he should not propose bills in the Knesset to cancel the Law of Return.

The appearance of Arab politicians before the Elections Committee or the Court to prove that they are not anti-Zionist and that there is not enough evidence to show that they struggle strongly and actively for full equality has become an act of humiliation as well as de-legitimization for the Arab MKs in almost every election.[77] In fact, this process of de-legitimization started with Ben Gurion's first speech in the Knesset against MK Tubi. It is rarely used against right-wing parties that incite to racism by advocating actively for the transfer of Arab citizens or against ultra-orthodox Jewish religious parties that are not only anti-Zionist but also negate the democratic values of the state by

---

[76] Then Attorney General Elyakim Rubinstein (now a Supreme Court justice) wrote in 2002: "The Israeli Arabs are full citizens of the state as a fundamental right... At the same time we have to struggle against every attempt to remove from Israel its character as a Jewish and democratic state. Whoever calls to turn the character of the state into 'the state for all its citizens' intends to remove the Jewish identity of Israel. Our duty is to struggle strongly against that without compromise." See Elyakim Rubinstein, "Government Advisory Opinion and the Rule of Law: Assignments and Complication in a Jewish, Democratic and Polarized State," *Mahkare Mishpat* 17/1 (2002), at 7, 14 (Hebrew).

[77] See e.g. Adalah, "Elections Q & A: The 2013 Israeli Elections and Arab Parliamentarians," 11 December 2012, available at: <http://adalah.org/Public/files/English/International_Advocacy/Arab-MKs/Questions-and-Answers-Israeli-Elections-Arab-Parliamentarians-2012.pdf>, accessed September 2013.

seeking a state based on *Halacha* (Jewish religious law). The irony is that these groups consistently vote for the disqualification of Arab parties.

We see here a clear double standard. There is no political will to apply disqualification tests to Jewish parties that sit in the governmental coalition. Indeed, the Court has already decided that a political party that advocates the transfer of Arab citizens is legitimate.[78] The voters of one society, Jewish Israelis, have free party platforms and the voters of the other society, Palestinian citizens, may only advocate limited party platforms. If an Israeli Jewish political party advocates for the transfer of Arab citizens, or for "Greater Israel," or for a *Halacha* state, they will be allowed to run for the Knesset. But if an Arab political party that advocates actively in the Knesset for full equal citizenship, for the right of return, for a one-state solution, or for a state based on the UN Partition Plan, or an Islamic Movement with an Islamic agenda, such as the one led by Sheikh Salah, were to run for election, it might be disqualified. If Arab participation in the 1949 election was limited for security reasons, now it is restricted on ideological grounds based on the constitutional values of "Jewish and democratic."

This suggests that the new Israeli constitutionalism—including its doctrine of a "Jewish and democratic State"—has left untouched the basic terms of Hobbesian citizenship. These constitutional innovations were done on the initiative of liberals with good intentions. However, as Kahn argues, law is what it is determined to be by an authorized decision, not by the intentions of its original drafters or through its neutral language,[79] and it is right-wing politicians who have driven the development of the "Jewish and democratic state" doctrine. To take just one example, in 2011, right-wing politicians in the Knesset enacted the "Nakba Law," which aims to limit the freedom of expression of any association funded by the state against challenges to the values of the state as "Jewish and democratic" or commemoration of Nakba Day. This law attempts to regulate love and sadness, happiness and tragedies.

Baruch Kimmerling is one of the few Israeli scholars to suggest that the two Basic Laws enacted in 1992, "are among the most problematic, ethnocentric

---

[78] In Civil Appeal 7504/95, *Yasine v. The Registrar of Political Parties*, the Supreme Court ruled that a political party that advocates for the voluntary transfer of Arab citizens of the state should be registered as a legitimate party. However, in 1985 the Supreme Court confirmed the CEC's decision to disqualify the political party led by Meir Kahane as one that "incites to racism" since it advocated strongly for ethnic segregation between Arabs and Jews in all fields such as workplaces, universities, marriage, beaches, etc. To use the analogy and differentiation between petty Apartheid and grand Apartheid of South Africa, these cases indicate that the Court is ready to disqualify a Jewish party as racist if it advocates for petty Apartheid, like Kahane, but not for grand Apartheid, like Lieberman, who seeks to transfer Arab citizens to the OPT in order to maintain a Jewish majority in Israel.

[79] Paul Kahn, *Political Theology: Four New Chapters on the Concept of Sovereignty* (New York: Columbia University Press, 2011), 73–90.

and discriminatory in the Israeli codex."[80] But it is important to emphasize that Israel did not become an ethno-national state just in 1992; its ethnic constitutional values existed long before and without being written in law books. For example, when the first Arab nationalist group, the Al-Ard Movement, attempted to run for the Knesset in 1965 based on a platform that included the demand for full equality, support for the Right to Return and for anti-colonial movements in the Arab world, the Supreme Court disqualified it from participation based on security reasoning.[81] At the time, there was no written law authorizing such disqualification. In a dissenting opinion, Justice Cohen found that no evidence was introduced to indicate that the Al-Ard Movement constituted a threat to national security and that the disqualification is against the principle of the rule of law. But the majority upheld the disqualification by ruling that the mere existence of Israel is the highest constitutional value and there is no need for a written law to confirm it. Chief Justice Agranat added that the fact of the Jewishness of the state is a constitutional axiom. Challenging this dominant ethnic ideology was perceived by the Court as a security threat, just as the head of GSS perceived the "Arab documents" in 2007 as a security threat.

All of this suggests that, following Schmitt, we need to distinguish "the Constitution" from "constitutional law"—and to distinguish "the People" from "citizens"—and to recognize that the latter term is always subordinate to the former. As Schmitt famously stated: "The concept of the state presupposes the concept of the *Political*."[82] A political community is a group that defines itself based on who is its enemy and the willingness of its members to make sacrifices. This shared identity of the *Political* group does not rely upon legal norms,[83] and being a citizen by itself does not make one belong to the political community. Schmitt argues that the political character of the state refers to the founding *People* who produce the Constitution and thus the Constitution, which includes the identity of the polity, and its substantive principles, must prevail and take precedence over constitutional law, since it expresses the will of the *People* and its identity.[84] Based on this analysis, the scope of "We, the People," as understood by Schmitt, does not refer to "We, the Citizens" but to a founding particular *People* who are attached to the *political* and its friend–enemy dynamic.

The *Bishara* case illustrates this logic. It interprets the sovereign as related to the founding people: Israel is a Jewish state and not a Jewish–Arab state. It is a

---

[80] Baruch Kimmerling, "Jurisdiction in an Immigrant–Settler Society: The 'Jewish and Democratic State'," *Comparative Political Studies* 35 (2002) 1119–44 at 1141.

[81] (Elections Appeal) EA 1/65, *Yardor v. the Chair of the Electoral Committee of the 6th Knesset*, 19(3) P.D. 365.

[82] Schmitt, *The Concept of the Political*, 19.

[83] Schmitt, *The Concept of the Political*, 26–7 and 38.

[84] Carl Schmitt, *Constitutional Theory* (Duke, NC: Duke University Press, 2008), chs. 1 and 2.

state for a *particular people* who founded it, who fought for its establishment, who sacrificed its young men and women through bloody war for its existence, and who were willing to kill and be killed for the cause of the people. The finality of the 1948 War is not for negotiation or legality. When the Court in the *Al-Ard* case referred to "high, unwritten constitutional values," it meant not only the state's mere existence but also its foundational identity of and for a *particular people*.

In Schmitt's terms, we can say that the constitutional reforms of 1992 may have changed "constitutional law" in Israel, but they have not changed "the Constitution" or the definition of the People and did not lead to a decolonization process or to any "new beginning." More generally, it has not changed the fundamental political imagination of Jewish Israelis, or the requirement of Arabs to accept this political imagination as a condition of participation. To be accepted, the Arabs had to negate their original identity as Palestinians and welcome the state's identity as it appears in the Declaration of the Establishment of the State. This offer of conditional citizenship by Israeli Jews—and its acceptance by Arabs—has been the foundation of Israel's imagined democracy. The disqualification cases reveal this logic: while Arabs are not permitted to challenge the Zionist narrative by demanding a state for all their citizens, their participation is nonetheless permitted, and indeed essential, to shore up the image of Israel as a just Westphalian state. If in the past the terms of surrender appeared through the military regime, now they appear through demands for loyalty to the constitutional values of "Jewish and democratic." If we agree that the acceptance of Zionist values during the Hobbesian moments was an act of humiliation, then we can understand that asking for loyalty from the Arabs to these values is also a humiliation, regardless of the respect afforded to the right of self-determination of Israeli Jews.

Relying on Kahn's analysis, we can summarize that the law applied to Arab electoral participation is different from the others. Despite the fact that the Court in this period dismissed all of the disqualification cases against Arab political parties and their candidates, this law conditions Arab MKs' entrance to the Knesset on ideological terms; it limits their rights actively to challenge the legality of Zionist laws and it restricts their right to rule in turn, as they have never been a part of the governmental coalition. The exercise of this fundamental individual right and its consequences is based on an unwritten track: *separate and unequal.*

These cases concern fundamental individual rights and not questions of group rights. The *Political* works strongly against the individual rights of Arab citizens not because they are perceived as an enemy in its strict Schmittian sense, and not because they constitute a real security threat, but because of their national belonging. This Palestinian national belonging carries with it the Nakba, the "refugeeness," and the Occupation. The Arabs in Israel are an unarmed group and they do not fight. An enemy does not sit in the Parliament or as a Justice on the bench of the Supreme Court. Yet the *Political* was behind the Attorney General's closing of the October 2000 killings files, and also behind the family unification laws and the Absentee Property Law that treats internally displaced Arab citizens as "present absentees."

The language of rights works in the liberal nation-state to ensure that the relationship between citizens is based on friendship and not enmity or an ethnic or hierarchical relationship. What is striking in Israel, however, is that neither side has expressed interest in the most basic *starting point* of rights and duties—namely, the right to rule and to be ruled in return. Arab MKs have been in the Knesset since 1949 but have never asked (or been invited) to join a government coalition. Both sides agree that Arab citizens should not serve in the military, a fundamental aspect for equal citizenship. Arab MKs chose not to participate in a constitution-making process, which is essential to any democratic relationship between the minority and the majority. In one of the crucial cases for Palestinian citizens, the October 2000 killings, they chose not to go to court to challenge the AG's decision to close all the files.

None of this is "normal." A minority in a nation-state seeks to be part of the government, to lead the army, and to struggle for their rights through the state's institutions. While there are cases in nation-states where minorities do not claim rights and duties, like the Amish in the US who avoid participating in public schools or courts, these cases are owing to religious reasons. In the case of the Palestinians in Israel, the reason is different; it is because of the *Political*, national hierarchy, domination, and control. The political behavior is more similar to that of an occupier–occupied relationship or a colonial citizenship than to that of citizens in a democratic nation-state.[85]

CONCLUSION

The politics of the foundation of Palestinian citizenship still strongly shape Israeli law and its legal philosophy. The Nakba is central to this politics. Israeli legal scholars do not reach the Nakba in their analysis of citizenship. A Westphalian decision was taken once in Israeli history, in 1949, to introduce Israel as a state for all its citizens. The Israeli legal philosophy sees only this

---

[85] Lately the two groups are debating whether Arab citizens should do national civil service instead of serving in the army. I wrote elsewhere in Hebrew about this debate. Here, I will argue that instead of inquiring into the first question—why the Arabs do not serve in the army—they moved to the second question of why they do not instead do civil service. The answer to the first question will tell us that the character of the legal regime reveals the problematic of the second question since it relies on *imagined* equal rights and duties between the citizens based on the notion of the right to rule and to be ruled in turn. To note, reciprocity presupposed legal structure based on equality between citizens which does not exist here.

decision without its context. Based on this imaginary perception, the "Arab minority" was always a part of the Knesset and has always participated equally. In this sense, the Arab vote creates the perception of Israel as a democratic state and without this participation, Israel is an apartheid state. This might explain why this philosophy imagines the borders of the "Jewish-democratic state" as the area in which Arab citizens vote, and why it portrays the Palestinian citizenship as though it is born as democratic and continues to be such without passing any process or stage of colonization or decolonization.

Contrary to the dominant perception, it is not accurate to say that Israel upholds individual rights. The track of *separate and unequal* works strongly against Arab citizens in terms of the four fundamental rights and duties that make a citizen a citizen: citizenship (family life and naturalization), the franchise, land rights, and the army. The power of the *Political* allows us to think also about the politics of partition and division. In all the cases mentioned in this chapter we noticed the strong linkage between the rights of the "insiders" and the "outsiders." The attempt to show that the legal status of one Palestinian group has nothing to do with the other is false. How the Arabs introduced themselves to the Israeli polity through the Hobbesian moments has also contributed strongly to the politics of partitioning.[86]

The politics of surrender and the concept of the finality of war still shape Israeli law and its legal philosophy. This old concept of war, as Whitman puts it is, "a kind of trial with a kind of verdict," where the loser accepts the finality of the war and its consequences.[87] This finality is not a matter of legality or negotiation. Accordingly, there will be no return of the refugees and no Jewish–Arab state. It is thus no wonder that the Israeli government demands that the Palestinian leadership recognize Israel as a Jewish state.[88] But the evolution of the Palestinians' language of rights teaches us that they accept the fact that they lost the war but they do not accept the surrender including the terms of the war's finality.[89]

---

[86] To understand the power of the Hobbesian moments, let us imagine their absence. Suppose that the Arabs living within the Green Line behaved like the Arab Druze of the Golan Heights and never participated in Israeli elections. How then can one imagine Israel as a democracy? Could the PLO have signed the Oslo Accords without referring to them when these Palestinians also declared that they are under occupation? Could any Arab country agree to adopt a two-state solution when part of the "occupied people" live within the Green Line? What would the status of the UN Partition Plan be? Could any Israeli liberal scholar speak then about a "Jewish and democratic state" within the Green Line?

[87] James Q. Whitman, *The Verdict of Battle* (Cambridge, MA: Harvard University Press, 2012), 3.

[88] Hassan Jabareen, "Why Palestinians can't recognize a 'Jewish state'," *Ha'aretz*, 2 September 2011.

[89] Many Israeli scholars are unaware as to the adoption of the politics of surrender and the concept of finality of the war. Yakobson, for example, blames the Palestinian citizens for using the Nakba narrative and not adopting instead the first speech of MK Tubi in 1949, in which he blamed the Arab leaders for the Nakba. Yakobson is not aware that Tubi himself felt ashamed

This concept of war and the idea of surrender contradict the basic principles of modern international law, including the laws of war.[90] It is an anachronistic concept today to consolidate war victory and the dominance of a particular group in any constitution.[91] In this sense, the constitutional values of the "Jewish and democratic state" are the continuation of the war by other means.

In my view, the story of Arab citizenship in Israel reveals the limits not just of Israeli constitutionalism, but also of liberal constitutionalism more generally. Many prominent liberal scholars argue that constitutional guarantees of political participation are fundamental for creating civic relations amongst citizens. Rawls and Dworkin view the right of participation in elections as fundamental for guaranteeing individual rights and civil liberties.[92] Minow argues that using the language of rights will help in building a common identity between groups, and Mouffe contends that representation will minimize relations of enmity.[93] But this literature avoids the role of the *Political* and the power of ethnicity. Today Palestinians have strong rights of freedom of expression, and the exercise of these rights is greater than in the past. No one was arrested for initiating and supporting the Arab documents. There are no limitations on their right to use the international arena. There is no criminal law that prohibits the expression of non-Zionist views. However, it is apparent that the more that Palestinian citizens use their "rights talk," the greater the antagonism between the two communities. When they are less assertive of their rights, the resentment is much less; when they assert their rights forcefully, racist laws are enacted. Exercising the right to vote and sitting in the Knesset since 1949 has not led Arabs to exercise the right to rule and to be ruled in turn. Despite this participation, domination still runs very deep. The colonial citizenship that existed during the Hobbesian moments is still valid.

and humiliated by this speech. Gans is one of the most liberal Israeli philosophers, and he argues that the political solution should be based on two states delineated by the 1949 borders; no right of return to the Green Line; and since Palestinian citizens belong to the enemy, and for defense, Israel must keep its Jewish domination in security and demography. Gans portrays the Hobbesian state and relies on the principle of finality of war. But all Hobbes's philosophy is about eradicating mutual fear by an agreed contract between the parties, which either Gans does not grasp or he assumed that the Palestinians would accept their inferior status. See Alexander Yakobson, "Speech for the Nakba Day," *Ha'aretz*, 24 May 2012 (Hebrew); Gans, *A Just Zionism*.

[90] Whitman, *The Verdict of Battle*, 260.

[91] As Ghai and Galli emphasize, "Unlike older, classic constitutions, perhaps, constitutions today do not necessarily reflect existing national polities or power relationships, consolidating the victory and dominance of a particular class or ethnic group" ("Constitution Building Processes and Democratization," 13).

[92] John Rawls, *A Theory of Justice* (Cambridge, MA: Belknap, 1971); and Ronald Dworkin, "Liberal Community," *California Left Review* 77 (1989): 479–504.

[93] Martha Minow, "Interpreting Rights: An Essay for Robert Cover," *Yale Law Journal* 96 (1986–87), 1860–915; and Chantal Mouffe, *The Democratic Paradox* (London: Verso, 2000).

Kymlicka explains that a dominant group's acceptance of minorities' claims requires the existence of reliable human rights protections and the de-securitization of ethnic relations.[94] Drawing an analogy from Kymlicka's work will lead us to suggest that we need a process of reconciliation in which to speak first of all about the equal rights of the two peoples in Palestine in the absence of the politics of surrender and division. This process must treat seriously and equally the rights of self-determination of the two nationalities, Israeli Jews and the Palestinians, as well as the civil and political rights of individuals who belong to these peoples.[95] Only then will we be able to discuss political regional arrangements, be it one state, two states, three states, or some other alternative model.

[94] Kymlicka, *Multicultural Odysseys*, 182–5.

[95] To date there is no serious debate in the Arab world, except among the Palestinians, regarding the right of self-determination of Israeli Jews. The dominant position in the Arab world still refers to Israeli Jews as a religious group and not as a nationality entitled to national self-determination.

10

The Federalization of Iraq and the Break-up of Sudan*

Brendan O'Leary

Iraq and Sudan have been important places that respectively mark the northern and southern frontiers of the Arab-majority world. Their postcolonial histories may be read as experiments in the willingness of "Arab nation-states" to accommodate national and ethnic differences. The differing fate of federalism in the two countries, so far, is not owed exclusively or even primarily to inherent differences between the Kurds and the South Sudanese. Indeed, there is no basis for claiming that the latter were somehow inherently more inclined to secession than the former. To understand the differing fate of federalism in the two places up to 2011 we must also examine differences in the Arab majority in the two countries, in their conceptions of nationhood, their internal cleavages, and their security outlooks. Exploring the two cases may illuminate the variety and contingency of Arab states' responses to their national and ethnic minorities, and the factors that underpin accommodation.

The title of this chapter, "The Federalization of Iraq and the Break-up of Sudan," may be rephrased as the question, "Why has Sudan broken up, whereas Iraq *may* remain intact?" The question matters because the survival of Iraq's federation matters, and not just because of whatever views one holds on US foreign policy. The break-up of Sudan, currently in incomplete and messy progress, also matters, and not just for the peoples directly affected, but for federalists and secessionists everywhere. First, however, I must explain why I am addressing these questions. The arguments here did not originate in methodological design. I have lived in Sudan because my father worked there

* Katharine Adeney, Ali Dinar, David Edgerton, Bernie Grofman, George Jones, Will Kymlicka, Ian S. Lustick, John McGarry, Jack Nagel, Khaled Salih, Heather Sharkey, Rudy Sil, Gareth Stansfield, Jessica Staunton, and the editors of *Government and Opposition* commented usefully on this chapter, a revised version of the Leonard Schapiro lecture: Brendan O'Leary, "The Federalization of Iraq and the Break-up of Sudan: The Leonard Schapiro Lecture," *Government and Opposition* 47/4 (2012): 481–516.

for the United Nations (1969–76). I have also spent significant time in Iraq. In the spring of 2004 I advised the Kurdistan Region during the making of the Transitional Administrative Law of Iraq, and again during the making of Iraq's Constitution in the summer of 2005.[1] Related advisory work continued intermittently until spring 2009, when I became the Senior Adviser on Power-Sharing to the Standby Team of the Mediation Support Unit of the United Nations. During my UN secondment I had two Sudanese engagements. In one I was loaned to Chatham House to facilitate dialog between the Sudanese People's Liberation Movement (SPLM), which had run the government of South Sudan since the Comprehensive Peace Agreement of 2005, and the National Congress Party (NCP), which had been in power in Khartoum, alone or in coalition, in disguise or in the open, albeit with a name change, since the *coup d'état* led by Omar Hassan Ahmed al-Bashir in 1989. Among my tasks was to make impartial presentations in Juba and Khartoum on how power-sharing might be organized to make unity more attractive, one of the options on which the South Sudanese were scheduled to vote in a referendum in January 2011. Another task was to address how peaceful secessions work, the other option in the referendum. In December 2009 I participated with some of the same politicians and their officials in a three-day seminar organized in South Africa to craft realistic scenarios for what Sudan would be like after January 2011. We discussed boundaries, security, the ownership of natural resources, including oil and water, citizenship rights, nomads and settled farmers, and public debt—the issues that still animate the governments and armed forces of Sudan and South Sudan. My second engagement, in 2010, took me to Doha, Qatar, where the African Union, the UN, and the government of Qatar were mediating another peace process between the government of Sudan and rebel movements from Darfur: my task was to assist in the drafting of power-sharing proposals regarding the Darfur region, the states of Darfur, and arrangements within Sudan's federal government.

These engagements, not a formal political science agenda, inspired my question, yet what follows is influenced by my discipline. Having worked with Kurdistan's leaders when they wanted to make Iraq a workable federation I was impressed by their decision not to press their claims to a formal right of secession, even though Iraq has brought Kurdish people a history of coercive assimilation, territorial gerrymandering, ethnic expulsions, and partial genocide. Why did Kurdish leaders not behave as a range of organizations and persons, including the International Crisis Group, still suggest they are *really* behaving? Why are their leaders not overt secessionists? Why have they not behaved more like the South Sudanese these last five years? Having worked with the UN to encourage North–South negotiations, and within the

---

[1] The Kurdistan Regional Government bought out my time from my university.

negotiations over Darfur, I was equally impressed by the apparent determination of the Khartoum regime not to do what was required to hold its state
together. Its leaders mostly seemed to prefer "down-sizing" to further constitutional or power-sharing concessions, at least to the South. Why? Conversely,
why were so few South Sudanese willing to pursue the conviction of their late
leader John Garang that unity could be made attractive?

LONG-RUN PARALLELS

Let me first observe six remarkable long-term parallels in the histories of
Sudan and Iraq that have not to my knowledge been systematically noted
before. They serve to show the compelling reasons why both the Kurds and the
South Sudanese should have been equally ardent secessionists in the decade
that has just passed.

1. Sudan and Iraq are both postcolonial states with common imperial formations and
heritages; in each case three historically distinct entities were coerced into precarious
unities by British imperialist successors to the Ottomans.

The places that became Iraq and Sudan were subjected to both Ottoman *and*
British imperialism, with the important caveat that the British and the Ottomans, later the Egyptians, allegedly co-governed the Sudan in a condominium
(1898–1956) that has no parallel in the history of Iraq. It was, however, a
distinction without a significant difference, because British governor-generals
administered Sudan with British military officers and colonial district officers;
Egyptians served mostly as the infantry.[2]

Modern Iraq was invented by the British conquerors of World War I, who
combined the Ottoman *vilayats* of Basra, Baghdad, and Mosul, which had
never before been governed as one jurisdiction. Modern Sudan was created
though Kitchener's conquest of the Mahdist state in 1898, and the subsequent
conquest of the Darfur sultanate in 1916. Sudan's formation, however, is more
like Iraq's than often realized, because it too is a British-manufactured trinity
(see Fig. 1). Its first component was the core of the brief Mahdist state,
itself built on Turkish/Ottoman Nubia, in turn built on the demesne of the
Funj or Sennar sultanate.[3] Its second, South Sudan, was partially conquered

---

[2] See e.g. R. O. Collins and R. L. Tignor, *Egypt & the Sudan* (Englewood Cliffs, NJ: Prentice-
Hall, 1967); see also R. A. Lobban Jr., *Global Security Watch: Sudan* (Santa Barbara, CA: Praeger,
2010), 26. Egyptian nationalists, colonized colonizers, regularly displayed racist and colonialist
attitudes toward all Sudanese (see E. M. Troutt Powell, *A Different Shade of Colonialism: Egypt,
Great Britain, and the Mastery of the Sudan* (Berkeley, CA: University of California Press, 2003),
passim). That helps explain why their projects for the unity of the Nile valley failed.
[3] See R. S. O'Fahey and J. Spaulding, *Kingdoms of the Sudan* (London: Methuen, 1974).

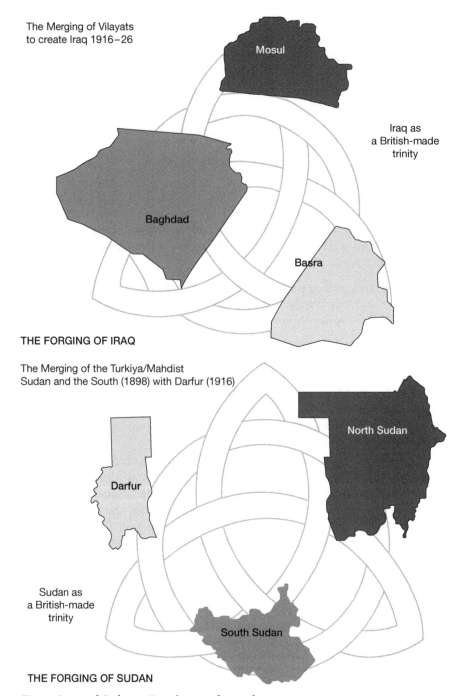

The Merging of Vilayats
to create Iraq 1916–26

Mosul

Iraq as
a British-made
trinity

Baghdad

Basra

THE FORGING OF IRAQ

The Merging of the Turkiya/Mahdist
Sudan and the South (1898) with Darfur (1916)

North Sudan

Darfur

Sudan as
a British-made
trinity

South Sudan

THE FORGING OF SUDAN

Fig. 1. Iraq and Sudan as British-manufactured trinities.

very late in the "Turkiyya," and fully reconquered by the British after 1904.[4] Sudan's third part, Darfur, was added during World War I after Sultan Ali Dinar's unwise decision to join the war as an ally of the Germans.[5]

To baptize these new "three-in-one" entities the British used old Arabic names, but inaccurately. Among the medieval Arab geographers, *al-Iraq al-Arabi* described what is now Shi'ite-dominated southern Iraq, the Ottoman *vilayat* of Basra. *Al-Jazeera* referred to what is now central and central north-western Iraq, later partially absorbed into Baghdad *vilayat*; today much of it is known with loose respect for geometry as "the Sunni Arab triangle." Kurdistan was Kurdistan until the late Ottoman reformers partitioned it, and incorpor-ated its southern portion into Mosul *vilayat*.[6] In short, the British used an old name of part of the future state, Iraq, for the entirety of the new entity, to the permanent irritation of the Kurds. Their imperial purpose was to unify the Arabs of Iraq against the Turks.

Whereas the original uses of *Iraq* specified a more restricted space than its current borders, the British used the Arabic word "Sudan," from *Bilad al-Sudan,* or "Land of the Blacks," far more narrowly than in its original usage, to demarcate what became Sudan from Egypt. "Sudan" was a medieval Arab geographers' term for the belt of "Black Africa" beneath Arab-majority north Africa, i.e. for the wide swathe of sub-Saharan Africa from the west to the east coast of the continent (Senegal and Ethiopia were encompassed). Different speakers used *Sudan* for subsets of this space: the Egyptians and the British used it for the eastern territories, while today's Mali was called *Soudan* by French imperialists.[7] The original extension did not encompass many ethnic groups now called "Sudanese." Northern Arabs initially used *Sudani,* meaning "black," in a derogatory fashion to refer to allegedly inferior, non-Muslim, Southern peoples, i.e. the enslaveable. Sudanese nationalists, however, later

---

[4] The "Turkiyya" is the name Sudanese give to the Ottoman administration established after 1821 by the Albanian-born Muhammed Ali, but Egyptians as well as the Turkish-speaking elite were enthusiastic participants in the conquest and colonization of the Sudan. In what later became South Sudan, Ali's grandson, Ismai'il Pasha, the Ottoman viceroy of Egypt, took the lead in supplying European and Egyptian traders and adventurers, and in establishing an adminis-tration in the late 1860s and early 1870s. R. O. Collins, *The Southern Sudan in Historical Perspective* (New Brunswick, NJ: Transaction, 2006), 19ff.

[5] Darfur had been an independent sultanate, until partially conquered in late Ottoman times, and later by Mahdist forces, but 'Ali Dinar recovered its independent sultanate for a brief interval (1898–1916). R. S. O'Fahey, *The Darfur Sultanate: A History* (New York: Columbia University Press, 2008).

[6] For discussions see A. Northedge, "*Al-Iraqi al-Arabi*: Iraq's Greatest Region in the Pre-Modern Period," in R. Visser and G. Stansfield (eds.), *An Iraq of Its Regions? Cornerstones of a Federal Democracy* (New York: Columbia University Press, 2008), 151–66; R. Schofield, "Bor-ders, Regions and Time: Defining the Iraqi Territorial State," in Visser and Stansfield (eds.), *An Iraq of Its Regions?*, 167–204; and C. Catherwood, *Winston's Folly: Imperialism and the Creation of Modern Iraq* (London: Constable, 2004).

[7] See H. J. Sharkey, *Living With Colonialism: Nationalism and Culture in the Anglo-Egyptian Sudan* (Berkeley, CA: University of California Press, 2003), 17 and 125.

subverted *Sudanese*, embraced the concept, and made Sudan stand for a larger entity that included all northern Sudanese.

Iraq and Sudan later saw some joint investment in the new national ideas embedded in their colonial and post-independence names. Arabs, Sunni, or Shi'ite Muslim, or Christian, secularized or otherwise, came to share an Iraqi identity, though they may have deeply differed on all else that matters in politics. More strikingly, the Northern and Southern Sudanese, though undergoing divorce, will both retain the names of Sudan and Sudanese. The secessionist state, however, has had to concede the right of the title to the name to the rump, according to precedents in international law.[8] That is why the world's newest state is called the Republic of South Sudan.

In neither Iraq nor Sudan was allegiance to the state or its professedly national identity ever uniform or ubiquitous, and both became spectacular examples of state- and nation-building failures. Darfur resembles Kurdistan in some respects because it was predominantly but not exclusively Muslim on incorporation into the British Empire. Historically religiously syncretic and tolerant, both Darfur and Kurdistan had prior sultanates or principalities, and in each case they were the last of the three historic territories brought into the new British-manufactured composite. Identification with the original place-name remained very strong for the largest ethnic group in these cases: Kurdistan means a place abounding in Kurds; and Dar-Fur means the land of the Fur.[9] It is not important here to decide, as if it were easy, whether the Kurds or the Fur were historically one or many, what matters is that Kurds and the Fur remained culturally and linguistically distinct from the largest Arab-speaking group (as did many other minorities in both countries and in these regions). Darfur had been conquered in 1872 by a slave-trading adventurer at the end of the Ottoman Turkiyya (1821–84), but regained its independence from the Mahdist state until conquered by the British in World War I. Ottoman and British "pacification" of the Kurds was an unfinished business when Iraq became independent. Kurdistan, Darfur,[10] and South Sudan retained their local languages and customs and, through indirect colonial rule, some of their traditional elites survived into modernity. Indeed, landed aristocracies emerged or were made from those who were previously tribal leaders.

In the twentieth century neither Iraq nor Sudan accomplished the collective amnesia that Ernest Renan thought necessary for nation-building.[11] That is

---

[8] Marc Weller, Professor of International Law at Cambridge, gave this advice to the SPLM in Juba in the summer of 2009.

[9] See the 1911 entry for Kurdistan in the *Encyclopedia of Islam*; on the Darfur sultanate see O'Fahey, *The Darfur Sultanate*.

[10] See A. M. Lesch, *The Sudan: Contested National Identities* (Bloomington, IL: Indiana University Press, 1998), 18.

[11] See E. Renan, "What is a Nation?" in A. Zimmern (ed.), *Modern Political Doctrines* (London: Oxford University Press, 1939), 186–205. For appreciative criticism see E. Gellner,

not just because people are still dying today who were born in autonomous Darfur, or in Mosul *vilayat*, before Sudan and Iraq took their recent shapes. The failure to create inclusive, complementary, and forward-looking Sudanese or Iraqi national identities reflects far more than insufficient time, and was overdetermined.

2. Iraq and Sudan are both postcolonial majority Arabic-speaking states at the outer extremities of the Arab-majority world.

On any ethnographic description, at its northern and eastern extremities *al-Iraq al-Arabi,* Arab Iraq, fades into places dominated by Kurdish, Turkish, and Iranian cultures and peoples. To its immediate north, Muslim Arab Iraq overlooks a range of religious and minority micro-nationalities among what are now called "the disputed territories," notably Assyrian, Chaldean, and Syriac Christians, and Sunni and Shi'ite Turkomen. Being proud, situated at linguistic, ethnic, and sectarian frontiers, and fearful of acculturation, may lead a group to redouble its commitment to its own identifications. Nationalists at the center of postcolonial Iraq determined to make an Iraqi nation through Arabization, at least in language, and indeed to take Iraq into a wider "pan-Arab" nation.[12] In the Baathist dream, full unification of all Arab (or Arabic-speaking?) lands was envisaged.[13] Neither the pan-Arabist nor the Iraqi national formula had any place for Kurds, unless they ceased to be Kurds, or were left aside with anomalous and asymmetric autonomy. Sunni Arabs were especially tempted by pan-Arabism because the rest of the Arab and Arabic-speaking world is predominantly Sunni Muslim. Shi'ite Arabs, by contrast, were much more disposed toward an Iraq-first or an Iraq-alone identity: sharing Shi'ite Islam with their eastern neighbors did not make them Persians.

Colonial Sudan's southeastern, southern, and western extremities faded into non-Arab, non-Arabic speaking, Christian, and polytheist Africa. Here too Sunni Arab leaders displayed arrogant insecurities when they came to

---

"Nationalism and the Two Forms of Cohesion in Complex Societies," in *Culture, Identity and Politics* (Cambridge: Cambridge University Press, 1987), 6–28.

[12] For pan-Arabism among the ex-Ottoman officers who governed Hashemite Iraq and its influence on British imperial policy see the work of Leonard Schapiro's colleague, Eli Kedourie, "Pan-Arabism and British Policy," in *The Chatham House Version and Other Middle-Eastern Studies* (Hanover, NH: University Press of New England, 1984), 213–35. See also M. Eppel, "The Elite, the Effendiyya, and the Growth of Nationalism and Pan-Arabism in Hashemite Iraq, 1921–1958," *International Journal of Middle East Studies* 30 (1998): 227–50 at 227–43.

[13] See M. Mufti, *Sovereign Creations: Pan-Arabism and Political Order in Syria and Iraq* (Ithaca, NY: Cornell University Press, 1996), *passim*; and S. Haim, "The Party of the Arab Ba'th: Constitution," in S. Kedourie (ed.), *Arab Nationalism: An Anthology* (Berkeley: University of California Press, 1962), 233–41. For a good illustration of pan-Arabist thinking see Nicholas Ziadeh, "Arabism [1950]," in E. Kedourie (ed.), *Nationalism in Asia and Africa* (London: Weidenfeld & Nicolson, 1971), 294–303.

power after independence. North Sudan's "Arab" as opposed to "Arabized" status remains a live historical and political question. Are Arabized Nubians Arabs? That is, are Sudan's self-defined Arabs of Arabian ethnic stock?[14] That the North has been distinctly and mostly Arabic speaking for several centuries no one denies, though Sudanese Arabic is said to be "creolized," and "Juba Arabic" is a separate vernacular. Predominantly Islamized and Arabized northern Sudan was certainly distinct from the uniformly non-Muslim South in 1956 when Sudan became independent. Many Sudanese nationalists blamed British imperial strategy, codified in the Closed Districts Order of 1922, for sealing off South Sudan from Islamic evangelism, and from the Arabic language.[15] The parliamentary and military rulers of postcolonial Sudan tried to rectify what they saw as the British artificial blockage of progress through Arabization and Islamization. These programs, however, met unexpected but profound resistance. Cultural and ethnic Arabization, emanating from the North, even failed to absorb all Darfuri Muslims as co-nationals, though Arabic is the language of educated Darfuris; and many of the diverse peoples of the Nuba mountains also resisted Arabization and Islamization.

"Arab Muslims" constituted majorities according to census evidence in both Sudan and Iraq, but they were internally disunited. The northern Muslims of Sudan have had infamous intra-Sunni (including intra-Sufi) sectarian divisions, though never yet as violently deep as those between Sunnis and Shi'ites in Iraq.[16] The respective ethnic majorities of both Iraq and Sudan states confronted territorially concentrated minorities, either with histories of autonomy, or of aspirations to sovereignty, notably in Kurdistan, South Sudan—and Darfur. Centralists intermittently tried to homogenize these peripheries—they said, "develop," "modernize," or "civilize"—often under the influence of pan-Arabist doctrine. The Arabist centralizers had Islamicists, Islamists, and pan-Islamists among their ranks, or as their critical supporters, or as their successors. These centralists faced *continuous* resistance from at least one-fifth of the population: in Iraq from the valleys, plains, and mountains of Kurdistan, and in Sudan, from beneath the *Sudd*. In their most capacious

---

[14] The British imperialist official Harold MacMichael collected the genealogies of the tribes, but treated accounts of the Arab origins of Sudanese tribes as "parables"; see *A History of the Arabs in the Sudan: And Some Account of the People who Preceded Them and of the Tribes Inhabiting Darfur* (Cambridge: Cambridge University Press, 2011 (1922)), i and ii. See also A. A. Ibrahim, "Breaking the Pen of Harold MacMichael: The Ja'aliyyin Identity Revisited," *International Journal of African Historical Studies* 21/2 (1988): 217–31; and Sharkey, *Living With Colonialism*, 17 and 125.

[15] Arab merchants were obliged to move or return to the North, an expulsion defended as the paternalist defense of the southerners.

[16] See G. Warburg, *Islam, Sectarianism and Politics in the Sudan Since the Mahdiyya* (Madison, WI: University of Wisconsin Press, 2003); and M. Burr and R. O. Collins, *Revolutionary Sudan: Hasan al-Turabi and the Islamist State, 1989–2000* (Leiden: Brill, 2003).

definitions, the Kurdistan Region and South Sudan encompassed nearly a third of the relevant host's habitable land. Since 2003 both Sudan and Iraq have faced fresh armed resistance, but from within a different fifth of their populations, from the non-Arabized of Darfur in Sudan, and from the central Sunni Arab triangle in Iraq, whose elites had recently been displaced from power. That introduces another parallel.

3. From independence until 2005 both states were dominated at elite level by a group from one ethnic group from one part of the country.

The founders of the Justice and Equality Movement's *Black Book,* published in 2000,[17] used official Sudanese sources to show what all knew, namely that after independence the country had been dominated, especially in its public sector, by people from three northern riverine tribes, the Shaygiyya, the Ja'aliyan, and Danagla, representing less than 5.5 percent of the population. They have dominated presidential and ministerial offices, and lower-tier official positions, and ensured that resource-allocation disproportionally favored part of the North at the expense of the rest of the country—including Darfur and the West, and the East, not just the South.[18] Some detect the shadow of ancient Nubia behind this dominance.[19]

Hanna Batatu, in work first published in 1978, showed the extent to which Sunni Arabs, concentrated in the center, west, and west-north-west of Iraq, dominated the army, the political class, senior officialdom, and the landowner class from the formation of the British mandate in 1920. The ascendancy of Sunni Arabs partly flowed from an original network of ex-Ottoman military officers, who came to power with the British-sponsored Hashemite monarchy.[20] Subsequently, of the fifteen members of the Baathist Revolutionary

---

[17] See J. Flint, "Darfur's Armed Movements," in A. de Waal (ed.), *Darfur: A New History of a Long War* (London: Zed Books, 2007), 150–1.

[18] The *Black Book: Imbalance of Power and Wealth in Sudan* perhaps moves too quickly from evidence of overrepresentation to assumptions about resource-allocation, but the ratios between revenues raised and expenditures incurred in Sudan's regions, and child mortality and educational attainment data, confirm the book's potent accusations. "The data support the claims made in the Black Book that the Sudan has been governed to benefit those regions disproportionately at the expense of all others—who account for 80 percent of the population, or around 25 million people," A. Cobham, "Causes of Conflict in Sudan: Testing the Black Book," *European Journal of Development Research* 17/3 (2005): 462–80.

[19] See Lobban, *Global Security Watch,* 26.

[20] See H. Batatu, *The Old Social Classes and the Revolutionary Movements of Iraq: A Study of Iraq's Old Landed and Commercial Classes and of its Communists, Ba'thists and Free Officers.* 3rd edn. (Princeton, NJ: Princeton University Press, 2004), first published in 1978, especially bk. 1 pt. II ch. 10, "The Crown and the ex-Sharifian Officers." "Under the monarchy, no fewer than 44.8 percent of all appointments to the premiership and 21.7 percent of all appointments to the post of minister of interior and minister of defense went to ex-Sharifian officers," p. 1115. The subtleties of Batatu's analyses are necessarily erased above, notably, his tracing of the growth of a Shi'ite Arab bourgeoisie before 1958 (partly because of their historic exclusion from politics under the Ottomans), and of a Kurdish landlord class. Like many, however, he radically

Command Council between 1968 and 1979, fourteen were Sunni Arabs; the other, carefully footnoted Batatu, was an "Arabized Kurd."[21] The ascendancy of the Baathists after 1968, under first Hasan al-Bakr and then Saddam Hussein, reorientated dominance *within* the Sunni Arabs of Iraq, bringing the "country cousins" from Tikrit into a preeminence rather like that of the three Sudanese riverine tribes, and eventually led to an almost risible patrimonialism among Saddam's immediate relations.[22] Nominally the Baath were secular and inclusive, but over time, direct and indirect discrimination against Kurds and Shi'ite Arabs deepened. When the Baathists' secular commitments were more than nominal some Christian Arabs were incorporated in the dominant power elite.

4. The two countries had similar political trajectories after the Egyptian revolution that brought Nasser to power: authoritarian nationalism, state socialism, petro-statism, centralization, militarism, and civil wars.

Swept up in the enthusiasms of Nasserism,[23] Iraq and Sudan were deeply influenced by republican Arab nationalism, as a program for government and as a mentality that encouraged the coercive nationalizing of minorities. Both countries developed strong pan-Arabist orientations in foreign policy, notably in their support for Palestine, the PLO, and later for Marxist and then Islamist Palestinian insurgents. Yet they were pragmatic toward the Arab monarchies, and took Saudi money, investments, and mosques when expedient, and fought domestic and foreign wars with Saudi resources. Both countries' Arabists were torn between doing what was required to build their states as nation-states, and their wider orientation toward the Arab world. They were influenced by, yet deeply wary and jealous of, Nasser's Egypt. Sudan's northern Arabs in the Umma party had sought Sudan's independence early in opposition to Egypt's project for "unity of the Nile valley," though the Unionist party, as its name suggests, had aspired to an Arabized Nile. Iraq's Baathists supported union with Egypt and Syria, and put this aspiration on the Iraqi flag. Yet al-Bakr and Saddam pointedly avoided delivering the cherished unification. Sudan's Socialist Union similarly foresaw unity with Egypt and Libya, but by the 1980s both the Sudanese and Iraqi regimes regarded Egypt as having betrayed

---

underestimated Sunni–Shi'ite divisions, see e.g. p. 1131, and badly mistook the likely trajectories of class and ethnic politics.

[21] Batatu, *The Old Social Classes*, 1090–2, table 58–3.

[22] There are sobering yet sometimes funny tales of abuse of power by Saddam's family, e.g. A. Bashir, *The Insider: Trapped in Saddam's Brutal Regime* (London: Abacus, 2005).

[23] For lucid discussions of Nasserism's repercussions see F. Ajami, *The Arab Predicament: Arab Political Thought and Practice since 1967* (Cambridge: Cambridge University Press, 1999); and F. Ajami, *The Dream Palace of the Arabs: A Generation's Odyssey* (New York: Vintage, 1999).

pan-Arabism to the Zionists, and Sudan and Libya were frequently at war through proxies in Chad and Darfur.

Both countries followed the Egyptian template of free officer movements. General Abdul Karim Qasim overthrew the Iraqi monarchy in a bloody coup d'état in July 1958, as the head of a Free Officers Movement. Colonel Gaafar Muhammad al-Numairi came to power in May 1969 in a peaceful coup d'état, also leading a Free Officers Movement. Some of his officer training had been in Egypt. The wily Numairi outmaneuvered Sudan's Mahdists and communists, and proved more ruthless than they had been when they had chances to remove him. He crushed the Ansar of the Mahdists, created a one-party state under the Sudan Socialist Union, negotiated autonomy with the South, and initially proclaimed a secular state. He remained in power until 1985, constantly reinventing himself and his regime first as socialist and then capitalist, first as pro-Soviet and then pro-American, first as secular and then as the divine instrument of Sharia law—sketching himself as a Sunni imam version of a Grand Ayatollah, yet without any of the preparatory credentials in Islamic law. His remarkable about-turns bear comparison with Saddam's later oscillations between 1991 and 2003. Both men had proclaimed themselves secular, turned on their domestic communists and Islamists, and then proclaimed themselves Islamists when their regimes were endangered.

Qasim had neither Numairi's political antennae nor his ruthlessness; he sentenced to death those who conspired against him, but did not execute them. Nor did Qasim have Numairi's amazing good luck. He died in a hail of bullets. Numairi, having been deposed, was allowed to return from exile, entertain running for office, and die in his bed in Khartoum. In 1968 Hasan al-Bakr was more like Numairi, a nationalist soldier who largely created an authoritarian socialist party from office. Al-Bakr's Baathists, like Numairi, made tactical alliances with communists, and strategic alliances with the Soviet Union, only later to switch cold war alliances—Numairi more completely. Numairi and the early Baathists were also *state* socialists, with the emphasis on the state component, socializing domestic and foreign private enterprises. Later Numairi and his Islamist successors, and the Baathists under Saddam, embraced privatization with the zeal of converts, or corrupters.

Both Iraq and Sudan became *petro-states*, facilitating authoritarianism and corruption, and their governments exploited their revenues to increase rather than reduce ethnic and religious antagonisms. This coincidence is not an endorsement of the strong version of the "resource-curse" thesis, which asserts direct causation between natural-resources-based revenues and the absence of democracy; and directly links "lootable resources" to civil wars.[24] Iraq was

[24] See M. Ross, "A Closer Look at Oil, Diamonds, and Civil War," *Annual Review of Political Science* 9 (2006): 265–300; M. Ross, "How Do Natural Resources Influence Civil War? Evidence From Thirteen Cases," *International Organization* 58/1 (2004): 34–67; and P. Collier and

authoritarian, indeed a landlords' regime, before its oil wealth came significantly on-stream, and patrimonial modes of corruption and patronage were inscribed in its formation.[25] At independence in 1932, Iraq was already under the de facto control of army officers and a minority of Sunni Arabs, who would neglect the interests of Kurds and Shi'ite Arabs, and at worst deliberately exclude them from patronage and equal citizenship. The preeminence and political interventionism of the military under the Hashemite monarchy, carrying out coups between 1936 and 1941, as well as the bloody execution of the royal family by the Free Officers in 1958, owed more to Arab nationalism than it did to Iraqi oil wealth.[26] Though in 1956 Sudan was perhaps better prepared than Iraq for democratic government at its independence—at least in the North—it too quickly became authoritarian. Long periods of military rule were punctuated by very brief parliamentary interludes (1956–58, 1964–65, and, on a very generous coding, since 2010). Authoritarianism manifested itself long before Sudan's oil wealth was known, or fully developed—oil has flowed for export only since 1999.

In both countries the first armed conflict between the major estranged periphery and the center preceded extensive knowledge of the scale of oil deposits—in Kurdistan in the 1920s, and in South Sudan in the 1950s. The peripheries initiated revolt because their leaders rejected the new state that excluded them, not because they initially hoped to head petro-states in their own right. In both cases Arab and British politicians misled the periphery about their prospects of autonomy or of federal status before independence was official. In any case, oil infrastructure and pipelines are not very lootable, and following the historical record is a better guide to causality in conflict than Paul Collier's regressions. In both cases, the political centers *became* additionally motivated to keep these peripheral zones within their ownership and control after they appreciated the significance of their major oil deposits. That explains why successive Baghdad regimes were determined to deny the Kurds control over Kirkuk governorate and city, and why successive Khartoum regimes denied the South control over its oil resources, and tried to prevent the return of Abyei to the South (from which the British had removed it after 1905). These motivations help explain why Iraqi and Sudanese regimes

A. Hoeffler, "Greed and Grievance in Civil War," *Oxford Economic Papers* 56/4 (2004): 563–95. For some critical responses see M. Heiberg, B. O'Leary, and J. Tirman (eds.), *Terror, Insurgency and the State: Ending Protracted Conflicts* (Philadelphia, PA: University of Pennsylvania Press, 2007), introduction and conclusion.

[25] See C. Tripp, *A History of Iraq* (rev. edn., Cambridge: Cambridge University Press, 2007), *passim*.

[26] See R. S. Simon, *Iraq Between the Two World Wars: The Militarist Origins of Tyranny* (New York: Columbia University Press, 2004); and K. Salih, *State-Making, Nation-Building and the Military: Iraq 1941–1958* (Göteborg: Department of Political Science Göteborg University, 1996).

orchestrated ethnic expulsions in oil-rich regions, and why they seek to minimize the territories of Kurdistan and South Sudan.

Their colonial heritages, overinflated militaries, and preferences for state socialist development projects led both countries to hyper-centralize. Khartoum, Omdurman, and Khartoum North have merged as a megalopolis, surrounded by a "black satellite belt," comprised largely of refugees from Sudan's internal wars. The CIA Worldfact Book reports Khartoum city as having just over 5 of Sudan's more than 40 million people; it reports Baghdad city as having 5.75 of Iraq's 30.3 million people. Another measure of population centralization is the state level in Sudan or the governorate level in Iraq. In the 1990s Sudan was Africa's largest country until the secession of the South, and even then was over a quarter of the size of the United States. It was estimated that up to two-thirds of Sudan's population lived within 300 kilometers of Khartoum, while the 2008 census reported over 7 million people within Khartoum State. The greater Khartoum area therefore encompasses nearly one-fifth of Sudan's population. Baghdad governorate, despite the Sunni and Shi'ite Arab civil war, encompasses about one-quarter of Iraq's population.

Alongside Kitchener at the conquest of Sudan in 1898 rode a young journalist, who wrote in the spirit of Gibbon, Montesquieu, and the theory of Oriental despotism,

The degree may vary with time and place, but the political supremacy of an army always leads to *the formation of a great centralized capital, to the consequent impoverishment of the provinces*, to the degradation of the peaceful inhabitants through *oppression and want*, to the *ruin of commerce*, the *decay of learning*, and the *ultimate demoralization even of the military order* through overbearing pride and sensual indulgence.[27]

Winston Churchill was describing the Ottoman and Mahdist worlds, but his description serves just as well for Iraq and Sudan in recent times. The exceptions to centralization, namely, the autonomy pacts with Kurdistan and South Sudan, and Numairi's brief experiments with administrative decentralization, proved short-lived.

Unsurprisingly both Sudan and Iraq became deeply repressive toward both ideological and ethnic minorities. Partly in consequence they have had among the longest wars between center and periphery in the annals of postcolonialism. The Anya-Nya guerrilla organization fought the North from Sudan's independence in 1956 until 1972, building on the mutiny of the Equatoria

---

[27] W. S. Churchill, *The River War: An Account of the Reconquest of the Sudan* (Kindle edn., original 1902), location 1814. On the theory of Oriental despotism see B. O'Leary, *The Asiatic Mode of Production: Oriental Despotism, Historical Materialism and Indian History* (New York: Blackwell, 1989), ch. 2.

Corps in 1955. From 1983 until 2002 the SPLA fought successive Khartoum governments, led by Colonel John Garang. North–South war filled most years between 1956 and 2011, and the period since 2002 may be read as an armed truce, tempered by violations. In the North–South wars, the highest estimated human death-toll from combat, collateral damage, war crimes, and war-induced famine and disease reaches 2 million.[28] After 1963 Darfur was the site of a thirty-year cross-border and inter-regime war of bewildering complexity, involving Libya and Chad and Darfur-based organizations and proxies, a war about which internationals cared little, and for which there seem to be no reliable death-estimates.[29] Since 2003 Darfur has often been aflame. In the anglophone world, and according to the prosecutor of the ICC, that is because the Khartoum regime has deliberately deployed its army and encouraged nomadic Arab militias in a racist and partially genocidal war against the Fur, the Zhagawa, and the Masalit.[30] The Khartoum government, by contrast, argues that it is engaged in a counter-insurgency war of state preservation against terrorists with foreign sponsors, and that the current Darfur conflict was originally a version of the age-old conflict between nomads and settled farmers, now aggravated by climate change.[31] Khartoum's reported death-toll of 10,000 is very much less than the UN's estimate of 300,000. A minority of scholars and credible legal advocates and policy-makers have debated the veracity of the charge of genocide,[32] but no one credible denies extensive war crimes and crimes against humanity. The internal wars in and around

---

[28] Benjamin Valentino in his study of *Final Solutions: Mass Killings and Genocide in the 20th Century* (Ithaca, NY: Cornell University Press, 2004), 83, table 5, reports that between 250,000 and 500,000 were killed in the suppression of the South Sudanese between 1956 and 1971, and that between 1 million and 1.5 million were killed between 1983 and 2002.

[29] See M. Burr and R. O. Collins, *Africa's Thirty Years War: Libya, Chad, and the Sudan, 1963–1993* (Boulder, CO: Westview, 1999).

[30] See J. Flint, *Darfur Destroyed: Ethnic Cleansing by Government and Militia Forces in Western Sudan* (New York: Human Rights Watch, 2004); M. Vehnämäki, "Darfur Scorched: Looming Genocide in Western Sudan," *Journal of Genocide Research* 8/1 (2006): 51–82; J. Hagan and A. Polloni, "Death in Darfur," *Science* 313 (2006): 1578–9; J. Hagan and W. Rymond-Richmond, *Darfur and the Crime of Genocide* (Cambridge: Cambridge University Press, 2009); S. M. Hassan and E. R. Carina (eds.), *Darfur and the Crisis of Governance in Sudan: A Critical Reader* (Ithaca, NY: Cornell University Press, 2010); A. Haggar, "The Origins of the Janjawid," in A. De Waal (ed.), *War in Darfur and the Search for Peace* (Cambridge, MA: Harvard University Press, 2007); A. De Waal and G. H. Stanton, "Should President Omar al-Bashir of Sudan be Charged and Arrested by the International Criminal Court? An Exchange of Views," *Genocide Studies and Prevention* 4/3 (2009): 329–53.

[31] Earlier conflict in Darfur certainly had these traits; see A. De Waal, *Famine that Kills: Darfur, Sudan, 1984–1985* (Oxford: Oxford University Press, 1989).

[32] See G. Prunier, *Darfur: The Ambiguous Genocide* (London: Hurst, 2005); N. Kasfir, "Sudan's Darfur: Is It Genocide?," *Current History* 104/682 (2005): 195–202; M. Mamdani, *Saviors and Survivors: Darfur, Politics, and the War on Terror* (New York: Pantheon, 2010); and De Waal and Stanton, "Should President Omar al-Bashir of Sudan be Charged . . . ?" The principal US writer making the argument of genocide has been Eric Reeves, *A Long Day's Dying: Critical Moments in the Darfur Genocide* (Toronto: The Key Publishing House, 2007).

Darfur and the North–South wars are, however, merely the biggest wars in Sudan's modern history. A full picture would recount the conflicts in the early 1990s within the Nuba mountains and Blue Nile state, the insurrection led by the Beja Congress in Eastern Sudan after 2005, and the current rebellions in south Kordofan and Blue Nile.

Under the Baathists Iraq too had an almost unbroken record of repression and internal wars on a horrendous scale, though it is unfair to the Baathists to imply there was no previous history of armed antagonism in republican or monarchical Iraq. Masoud Barzani, the current president of the Kurdistan Region, in his memoir of his father Mustafa Barzani, recounts two "Barzan revolts" in Iraq, in 1931–2 and 1943–5.[33] After providing the military leadership of the Mahabad Republic in Iranian Kurdistan, Mustafa Barzani and his mostly Barzan Kurds went into exile in the Soviet Union, but returned to Iraq after the overthrow of the monarchy in 1958, and resumed conflict with Baghdad governments in 1961. Leaving brief truces, briefer negotiations, and a short-run autonomy agreement dishonored by the Baath to one side, General Barzani spent the rest of his life leading the Peshmerga against Baghdad armies. In the end he was defeated by the sudden collective reversal of US, Iranian, and Israeli support in 1975, and his mistaken decision not to return to guerrilla warfare. After his death in Washington in 1979 his sons assumed the leadership of the Kurdistan Democratic Party, and together with a rival organization, the Patriotic Union of Kurdistan, led by Jalal Talabani, intermittently fought Saddam's regime, with and without Iranian support, until 1992. The price paid by the Kurdish people was extremely high. Extraordinary repression, brutal Arabization, coercive displacement, the bulldozing of nearly 4,000 Kurdish villages, the forced urbanization, and mass incarceration of Kurdish civilians in detention centers, the deployment of chemical weapons, notably in Halabja, all succeeded one another in escalating horror. The genocidal Anfal campaign climaxed the repression: the KRG estimates 182,000 men, women, and children were killed.[34] The defeat of Saddam Hussein in Gulf War 1 did not immediately relieve the misery of the Kurds. They paid for their US-encouraged revolt by being assaulted by Saddam's helicopter gunships. A mass exodus to Turkey and Iran was only reversed after

[33] See M. Barzani, *Mustafa Barzani and the Kurdish Liberation Movement, with an introduction by Ahmed Ferhadi* (New York: Palgrave Macmillan, 2003).

[34] See the contributions of P. W. Galbraith and others to reports of the United States Senate Foreign Relations Committee, especially *Chemical Weapons Use in Kurdistan* (1988), *Kurdistan in the Time of Saddam Hussein* (1991), and *Saddam's Documents* (1992); see also Galbraith's memoir, *The End of Iraq: How American Incompetence Created a War Without End* (New York: Simon & Schuster, 2006), chs. 3–8. For secondary sources see B. O'Leary, J. McGarry, and K. Salih (eds.), *The Future of Kurdistan in Iraq* (Philadelphia, PA: University of Pennsylvania Press, 2005), preface and ch. 1. In his study of twentieth-century mass killings and genocide, Valentino reports that between 65,000 and 265,000 people died in the suppression of Kurdish rebellions between 1961 and 1991 (Valentino, *Final Solutions*, 83, table 5).

the implementation of no-fly zones by guilt-ridden administrations in the US, the UK, and France. Baathist-organized mass repression of the Shi'ite Arabs was even more ferocious in 1991. Up to 300,000 Shi'ites may have perished in the repression of their intifada, and Peter Sluglett[35] estimates that nearly the same number perished in the assaults on the lands of the Marsh Arabs and the southern governorates in the late 1990s.[36]

5. Regimes in both countries have been geopolitically insecure and have aggravated their "bad neighborhoods."

Sudan had nine neighbors until 2011 (Central African Republic, Chad, Democratic Republic of the Congo, Egypt, Eritrea, Ethiopia, Kenya, Libya, and Uganda), whereas Iraq has six (Iran, Jordan, Kuwait, Saudi Arabia, Syria, and Turkey). These neighbors mostly have bleak records, at least regarding their democratic credentials. Neither Iraq nor Sudan is likely to benefit soon from the hypotheses of democratic peace theory, though for Sudan, Kenya, Egypt, and Tanzania now show some democratic promise, as do Turkey and Jordan among Iraq's neighbors. In both Iraq and Sudan, insurgencies and coup attempts were externally aided, often with bases, as well as arms and funds. Libya, Uganda, Ethiopia, Eritrea, and Chad at various junctures supported either the South Sudanese rebels or Arab militias. Iran has supported Kurdish and Shi'ite rebels, while Saudi Arabia, Jordan, and Syria recently turned blind eyes to the passage of Sunni jihadists. Turkey has two military bases in Kurdistan of doubtful legality, and periodically pursues its own domestic counter-insurgency through attacks on the dwindling platoons of the Kurdish guerrilla force of the PKK (the Party of Kurdistan's Workers) who have bases in the inaccessible Qandil mountains.

Sudan and Iraq were sinners internationally as well as being sinned against. Both interfered in their neighbors' politics. Under al-Turbi's influence in the 1990s the Khartoum regime sponsored al-Qaeda, and Pan-Islamist Congresses—called the terrorists' "Davos in the desert." Those close to Turabi tried to assassinate Hosnī Mubārak in Addis Ababa, and colluded in the bombing of US embassies in East Africa. The truly major external aggression was Saddam's invasion of Iran, quietly supported by the Western powers and Saudi Arabia. It led to perhaps one million deaths, and to Saddam's subsequent attempted annexation of Kuwait to recoup his war debts. In short, both countries have had bad neighborhoods, conducive neither to stability, nor to

---

[35] M. Farouk-Sluglett and P. Sluglett, *Iraq Since 1958: From Revolution to Dictatorship* (London: I. B. Tauris, 2003).

[36] Another parallel that merits further investigation is the use made of tribes, and tribal militias, to conduct counter-insurgency in both Iraq and Sudan. Baghdad regimes, under the monarchy, the republic, and the Baath, exploited traditional fears of the Barzan Kurds, supporting what Kurdish nationalists call the *jash*. Khartoum governments have systematically armed and supported Arab tribal militias in Darfur, and against the South Sudanese.

foreign trade and investment, let alone to democratization or the peaceable management of domestic ethnic and religious tensions. These neighborhoods partly explain periodic hyper-centralization in Baghdad and Khartoum and the military's dominance in politics. The two countries' immediate geopolitical neighborhood has had independent causal force: no additional words about past Soviet or current US and Chinese policies toward either country, or Israel's history of support for the South Sudanese and the Kurds, are required to code these neighborhoods as tough.

6. Within relatively recent memory both countries experienced autonomy and power-sharing settlements for their major disaffected peripheral regions, which failed.

In March 1970 Mustafa Barzani, for the Kurdistan Democratic Party, and Saddam Hussein, then vice president of Iraq, negotiated an agreement, which recognized a Kurdistan Region (with its final boundaries to be determined), to which was delegated extensive autonomy in language, education, policing, and local government. It was also agreed that the KDP would nominate ministers to serve in the Baghdad cabinet. Iraq would be a bi-national state, and Kurdish an official language. The Baathists soon started to renege when it became plain that using fresh and fair census returns would deliver Kirkuk and other disputed territories to the Kurdistan Region. Barzani resumed armed struggle in 1974, rejecting the Baathist legislation of the agreement, confident that he would enjoy the support of the US, Iran, and Israel.[37] He was wrong: all three powers reversed their positions when the Shah of Iran and Saddam cut a deal in Algiers in 1975. The betrayal and crushing of the Kurds led to Henry Kissinger's infamous defense that covert action "should not be confused with missionary work."[38] After the defeat of Barzani, the Baathists kept a puppet legislature in Erbil, redrew the boundaries of the Northern governorates, and gerrymandered Kirkuk governorate, by reducing its size by half, subtracting and transferring Kurdish majority districts, and adding Arab-majority districts from and to other governorates respectively (see Fig. 2). These manipulations were reinforced by racist Arabization programs, inducing southern Shi'ite Arab settlers into Kirkuk, expelling large numbers of Kurds and Turkomen, and attempting the coercive assimilation of the

---

[37] For a stimulating account that focuses too much on Barzani's allegedly naive conduct, and not enough on Iranian, US, or Baathist duplicity, see D. McDowall, *A Modern History of the Kurds*, 3rd edn. (London: I. B. Tauris, 2004), 327–40.

[38] He made the remarks to the Pike Commission. One current researcher argues that declassified documents and other contemporaneous evidence suggest that Kissinger was angry at the Shah's betrayal of the Kurds: <http://blogs.lse.ac.uk/mec/2011/11/07/are-all-leaks-good-the-pike-committee-report-kissinger-and-the-distortion-of-events/>, accessed September 2013.

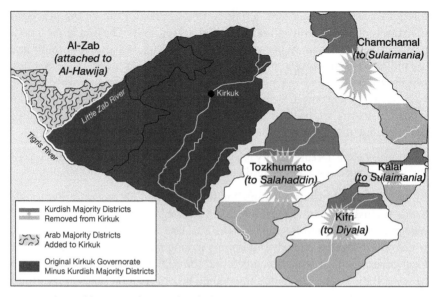

Fig. 2. The Saddam-mandering of Kirkuk.

remainder. An autonomy experiment with some promise ended in cynical boundary manipulations, and ethnic expulsions.[39]

Much the same happened in South Sudan, almost step by step. In March 1972, at Addis Ababa, President Numairi's regime signed an agreement with the delegate of Major General Joseph Lagu of the Southern Sudan Liberation Front and Anya-Nya, creating a South Sudan Region, with its own legislature and executive, and with the right to use its preferred official language, English.[40] Southerners were to hold cabinet offices and senior positions in the Sudan army. As with the initial Kurdistan agreement, the Addis negotiators left the final boundaries of the region to subsequent determination: Article 3 (iii) specified that areas that "were culturally and geographically a part of the Southern complex" might have the chance to join South Sudan after a referendum. The South Sudan autonomy agreement lasted almost a full decade, and had a genuinely promising start, though nothing was done to resolve the boundary of the "southern complex." Like Kurdistan, South Sudan had its internal divisions, often rooted in the tribal past. It had much deeper

---

[39] The expulsion of Kurds from Kirkuk had a precedent: from 1971 the Baath expelled 50,000 Fayli (Shi'ite) Kurds to Iran on the spurious grounds that they were Iranian citizens, even though they had lived in Iraq, including Baghdad, since Ottoman times.

[40] The run-up to the Addis Ababa Agreement may be found in R. O. Collins, *The Southern Sudan in Historical Perspective* (New Brunswick, NJ: Transaction, 2006), 67–98.

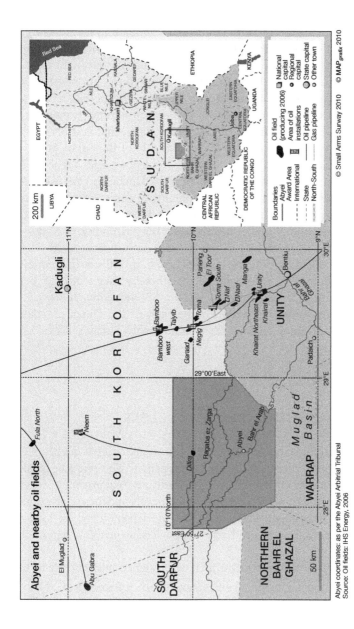

Fig. 3. Sudan's Kirkuk.

internal ethnic divisions, and lacked any extensive experience of self-administration let alone self-government. When Numairi started to tack toward
Islamists after 1977 he decided to take advantage of the array of internal
Southern divisions, tribal, regional, and personality-based. He first partitioned
the South into three provinces, before unilaterally abrogating the Addis Ababa
Agreement in September 1983, at the same time as he formally imposed
shariah law throughout Sudan. Numairi and his successors sought to crush
the new southern armed forces that emerged in response, but never experienced a victory like that of Baghdad over Barzani. In another remarkable
parallel, Numairi's Islamist successors encouraged ethnic expulsions in
Abyei,[41] in southern Kordofan, and in Blue Nile states, that is in those parts
of the "Southern complex" expected to become part of the South under the
1972 Addis Ababa agreement.

Abyei, shown in Fig. 3, is the homeland of Ngok Dinka, and the traditional
grazing land of the Misseriya Arabs. It contains Sudan's largest oilfield in
production, the most promising of other fields in production, and others
unproven and promising. Whether it ends under the jurisdiction of Khartoum
or Juba is therefore of material and not just ethnic importance. Abyei was
transferred to Kordofan, outside the colonial South, in 1905, at the request of
many Dinka tribal leaders, who believed that thereby they would be better
secured against the incessant raids of slavers. Subsequently, however, the
educated Dinka and now the overwhelming bulk of the Dinka population
aspire to be part of South Sudan. Abyei is therefore Sudan's Kirkuk; and
Kirkuk is Iraq's Abyei.

SHORT-RUN PARALLELS

These long-run parallels should reinforce my present-centered question: why
is Sudan breaking up, whereas Iraq *may* hold together? The evidence presented strongly suggests that the Kurds of the Kurdistan Region should want to
secede from Iraq at least as vehemently as the South Sudanese have wanted
to establish an independent sovereign state. Moreover, these six long-run
parallels are matched by powerful recent parallels, which can be sketched
more briefly.

In 2005 potentially transformative texts were signed and ratified in both
countries, with the aid but not at the diktat of US diplomats. In 2005 the
government of Sudan and the SPLM/SPLA signed a Comprehensive Peace

---

[41] For a useful if dated discussion of the Ngok Dinka, the Misseriya Arabs, and Abyei see
F. M. Deng, *War of Visions: Conflict of Identities in the Sudan* (Washington, DC: Brookings
Institution, 1995), ch. 7.

Agreement (CPA). The CPA was then embedded in an Interim Constitution. It ended the long war and gave the Khartoum government six years to make good its commitments to make unity attractive. A power-sharing government was established. Proportionality principles were applied both to an interim legislature and a freshly freely elected legislature, and in the composition of the cabinet, civil service, public bodies, and the military. The government of South Sudan was granted far-reaching autonomy and veto rights, and its president was to be first vice president of Sudan or the president—depending on election outcomes. Power-sharing was to be matched by wealth-sharing. An agreed formula would apply to the allocation of oil revenues. Disputed Abyei would have the right to join South Sudan in a referendum on the same day in January 2011 that South Sudan would vote either to endorse the newly attractive power-sharing formula or to secede. Separate security systems would be preserved, pending the referendum, but joint forces and separate forces would patrol the disputed territories.

Baghdad–Kurdish relations underwent a similar textual transformation. In August 2005 the Iraqi National Assembly agreed on a draft Constitution, subsequently ratified in a high-turnout referendum in October by four out of five of Iraq's voters, by fifteen of its eighteen provinces, and by over 95 percent of Kurds in three provinces, as well as by the Kurdish-led majority in Kirkuk. A power-sharing transitional collective presidency was established for one term. Proportionality rules were to apply to the permanent legislature—with special protections for micro-minorities—and these have so far ensured multi-party coalition federal governments. The Kurdistan Region has far-reaching federal autonomy, and veto rights over future constitutional change. The first president under the new order was a Kurd, Jalal Talabani. Power-sharing was matched by a wealth-sharing formula. Revenues from existing oilfields, to be jointly managed by regions, provinces, and the federal government, were to be allocated across Iraq's regions and provinces, on a per capita basis, with some qualifications.[42] Newly exploited oilfields, by contrast, were to be owned by their regions and governorates, but federation-wide revenue-sharing for-mulae were not precluded and have been proposed by the Kurds. Disputed Kirkuk, and other adjacent territories, were to have their Baathist distortions rectified, and their status resolved through a referendum, which would let their peoples decide whether they wished to join the Kurdistan Region.

After the signing of the CPA, at least until the death of John Garang in a helicopter crash in July 2005, but also afterwards, external expert opinion considered the break-up of Iraq more likely than the break-up of Sudan.

---

[42] See B. O'Leary, "Federalizing Natural Resources," in M. E. Bouillon, D. M. Malone, and B. Rowswell (eds.), *Iraq: Preventing a New Generation of Conflict* (Boulder, CO: Lynne Rienner, 2007), 189–201; and B. O'Leary, *How to Get Out of Iraq with Integrity* (Philadelphia, PA: University of Pennsylvania Press, 2009).

Garang was expected to deploy his prestige and capabilities to mobilize a coalition of all the peripheries against the chastened Islamists with whom he would share power in Khartoum, and he was expected, by many, to have a good chance of winning any free contest for the presidency. After his death many key SPLM figures in the North, notably General Secretary Pagun Amum, sought to keep Garang's agenda of transforming Sudan as a whole into a secular, multi-ethnic, pluralist democratic federation. By contrast, before and after the making of the new Constitution, post-Saddam Iraq was descending into a ferocious intra-Arab civil war, in which numerous Sunni Arab and Baathist organizations initiated sectarian war against the Shi'ite Arab-led government and civilians, only to receive far more than they had bargained for. In 2006 one of my colleagues in Kurdistan's constitutional advisory team, Peter Galbraith, published a book with the title *The End of Iraq*. His prediction was widely believed throughout Europe, North America, and the countries of the Arab League. People expected the Kurds to leave a burning ship, not to help put out the fires (as they did when they lent troops to try to restore order in Baghdad in 2006–07). Recent history therefore strengthens our puzzle: if the Kurds and South Sudanese obtained similar agreements in 2005, and if Iraq's Arabs had an internal civil war after 2003 at least as violent as the civil war in Darfur after 2003, then why has Kurdistan remained within Iraq while South Sudan has left Sudan?

The answer does not simply lie in the respective texts of the constitutions, though that has to be part of the story. The CPA established that a referendum in January 2011 would give South Sudan the right to choose secession. If Kurds had demanded such a referendum, and successfully scheduled it within Iraq's constitution, then they too might have been voting for secession in January 2011. Kurdish leaders, however, chose not to try to place the right of secession squarely within the text of Iraq's Constitution, though they did insist, at the initiative of President Barzani, that the Preamble would define Iraq as "a voluntary union of land and people," thereby implicitly giving Kurdistan the right to determine whether the voluntary contract is broken in future. Instead, the Kurds traded. Rather than an explicit right of self-determination within Iraq's Constitution, they achieved their key negotiating objectives: extraordinary regional status; control over regional security; control over regional natural resources; regional legal supremacy in all but the very limited exclusive powers to be held by the federal government; and a process, including a referendum, that promised to bring Kirkuk and other disputed territories into the Kurdistan Region. Kurds sought the practicalities of maximum feasible statehood within Iraq rather than formal independence.

The question is, why? Textualism does not tell all. At any recent juncture when they controlled the bulk of the region, i.e. any time after Gulf War 1, the Kurdish leadership could have held a referendum favoring secession, and would likely have won comprehensive endorsement from their voters. They can still do so in future. John Garang, by contrast with Barzani, was obliged to place the right to secession in the CPA in 2005 to keep his coalition together. Garang, by contrast with Barzani, strongly believed in and hoped to maneuver to make a success of "attractive unity," i.e. to create a power-sharing Sudan under his leadership. His death was certainly contingent. Had Garang survived his helicopter crash, would the SPLM have advocated a vote for unity in January 2011? Would the SPLM's leaders have done more to ensure that unity was made attractive between 2005 and 2011?

The puzzling difference in South Sudanese and Kurdish behavior is not resolved by pointing to the religious compositions of the two potentially secessionist regions, and their respective centers. Some think it natural that Christian and traditionalist South Sudan should secede from the Islamic North, whereas Muslim Kurds would be happier within predominantly Muslim Iraq. They are mistaken; Kurdistan is not staying within Iraq because most Kurds share Sunni Islam with Sunni Arabs. Most Kurds reject the puritanical, indeed fanatical and exclusionary forms of Islam currently in favor among Sunni Arabs; they embrace tolerant and privatist Sufi traditions, and affiliate with a different Islamic jurisprudential school. More important, the political practice and dispositions of Sunni Arabs have made Kurds very tempted to secede from Iraq. Sunni Arabs have more often displayed racist contempt toward Kurds than have Shi'ite Arabs. A Sunni Arab-led Baathist regime and a predominantly Sunni-Arab-officered army genocidally assaulted Kurdistan. Most Sunni Arabs largely remain inveterate centralists, as well as unrepentant for complicity in the crimes of Baathism.[43] It was Saddam's primary victims, Kurds and Shi'ite Arabs, who primarily made the Constitution of 2005. They did not do so because they had convergent views on Islam.[44] It is true that the Khartoum Islamist regime's insistence on keeping the shariah in the North helped cement the argument for the secession of South Sudan, but the Kurds have not stayed within Iraq because most of them are Muslim.

Nor is the puzzle resolved through focusing on culture, ethnicity, or language. Kurdistan is more homogeneous, culturally, ethnically, and linguistically than South Sudan, and therefore might be expected to be more cohesive in its opposition to Baghdad than South Sudan has been toward Khartoum. One cannot even make much of the Kurdish civil war between 1994 and 1998 when the Kurds had internationally unrecognized autonomy, but spoiled their prospects through inter-party fighting. The reason that emphasis is misplaced is because during the same decade the SPLM split, and there was a nasty

---

[43] Change may be on its way: some Sunni Arabs are currently embracing federalism, and the creation of Sunni Arab region(s) with the powers of Kurdistan, precisely because they realize that they are unlikely to dislodge Shi'ite Arabs from their new ascendancy in Baghdad.

[44] Through the careful delimitation of federal powers in the Constitution, regions, not federal Baghdad governments, regulate religious affairs, so Kurds have blocked the vista of a Shi'ite theocracy.

Dinka- and Nuer-based civil war in South Sudan that Khartoum was able to exploit. The legacies of both internal civil wars underpinned fragilities in both South Sudanese and Kurdish movements, and therefore cannot account for the different dispositions of their leaders toward secession.

Is the resolution of the puzzle found in the fact that the Constitution of Iraq has worked better than the Comprehensive Peace Agreement? That may be part of the answer, but it is incomplete. Kurdistan has flourished since 2003, expanding its economy, and attracting extensive inward investment. It has had two free elections to the region's new assembly, won by coalitions led by the two historic rivals, the KDP and the PUK, who have alternated the premiership. The KDP has led the Regional Government in Erbil, with Masoud Barzani as president; the PUK, under Jalal Talabani, has led for Kurdistan in Baghdad. Moreover, three elections to Iraq's Parliament have not, so far, produced a dominant Arab party or bloc determined to overthrow Kurdistan's autonomy. Kurds have held the foreign ministry as well as the presidency. They have played kingmakers, removing one prime minister, Jaffri, and twice put Maliki into the premiership, despite deep reservations on the second occasion—and current regrets. The Peshmerga are completing their unification as the Kurdistan Regional Guard and would put up stiff resistance to any incursions by the new Baghdad army. These facts suggest that Kurds are at last benefiting from membership of Iraq, on their own terms.

Granted, not everything is running smoothly. The new Baghdad governments have denied or sought to block Kurdistan's exercise of its rights over natural resources, especially its rights to issue its own contracts and control its own oil and gas exports. There has been no resolution of Kirkuk and the disputed territories, and the scheduled date has passed by which a referendum was to have been held. Within the KRG, the PUK has fractured, and a populist Goran party in Sulaimania raucously opposes both the KDP and the PUK. Arab centralists have reemerged willing to repeat the betrayals of the monarchy and the Baathists and overturn solemn constitutional commitments to the Kurds. Prime Minister Maliki has shown strongly authoritarian proclivities. Arab Iraq once again has a very large army, and a range of semi-incorporated militias. Yet Kurdistan's leaders have remained patient.

In Sudan the death of Garang froze the transformative dynamics that might otherwise have flowed from the CPA. After his death, both the NCP and the SPLM warily preferred to consolidate power in their respective zones before reluctantly holding much-delayed elections in April 2010, less than ten months before the scheduled referendum, partly because of disputes over the 2008 census results, which suggested that the South's electoral share of power in a united Sudan would be significantly less than under previous assumptions. Neither the elections in the South nor those in the North were fully competitive, free, or fair. The SPLM's mandate of 93 percent in the South undoubtedly reflected genuine strong majority support. The NCP's 68 percent, though proportionally lower, looked highly inflated, partly because of boycotts by traditional Northern parties, and in Darfur, but economic growth and oil-based prosperity in the North meant that the incumbents would have done well in a more open and fair contest.

The aspiration of Garang to lead a multi-regional and multi-ethnic democratic opposition to power throughout Sudan may have been a fantasy. The 2008 census results, the official electoral performance of the NCP in the North, and the unwillingness of Arabs or the Arabized to vote for the SPLM in 2010 all suggest as much. The SPLM did not even push the international community to require Khartoum to oversee a fully free and fair election in the North in 2010, so we do not know what might have happened had the NCP faced the real prospect of regime change through a fully fair electoral contest. The SPLM preferred to keep its bargain with the devil it knew, i.e. to keep the referendum as a route to freedom, rather than risk a new Northern parliamentary coalition in the North betraying its promises to the South—as had happened in 1964 and 1986. Yet, like Iraq's Constitution, the CPA was not completely dishonored. Some of the commitments made by the North in the CPA were followed up: the South did receive its promised share of oil revenues under credible monitoring, and the security pact held, despite multiple crises. The referendum, begrudgingly, was allowed to proceed. In sum, neither the Constitution of Iraq nor the CPA has been faithfully implemented to the letter and spirit by Baghdad or Khartoum, but they were partially implemented, and much more than many expected.

Another possible resolution to the puzzle is the existence of greater party and social pluralism within the Kurdistan Region by comparison with the utter dominance of the SPLM in South Sudan. Surely South Sudan was far more unified behind secession than the Kurdistan Region? That, however, is too quick a conclusion, even if we leave aside the fact that the elections and the constitutional referendum in the Kurdistan Region were freer and fairer, and better internationally scrutinized. From 2005 Kurdish public sentiment was at least as intensely in favor of secession as that of the South Sudanese. In an unofficial civil society referendum held in Kurdistan on the same day as the October 2005 referendum to endorse the Iraqi Constitution, eleven out of twelve of those asked, in a very high turnout, endorsed independence for Kurdistan as their preferred option. The same respondents were simultaneously endorsing the Constitution of Iraq which had just been negotiated by their leaders.

These facts prove that a largely united leadership in the South followed or confirmed its public's secessionist sentiment, whereas a coalition of Kurdish leaders have successfully persuaded its public to back them in a federalist strategy—even though the Kurdish leaders and their public prefer independence in their hearts as much as the South Sudanese. In short, we must ask why the respective leaderships made the decisions they did during and after 2005.

The answer lies in the strategic assessments and choices made by the Kurdish and South Sudanese leaders in their differing geopolitical neighborhoods, and their different assessments of their respective Arab-majority centers. The answer is also to be found in the strategic choices of those with whom they negotiated.

South Sudan had a more facilitative external environment for secession. The SPLM had support, through time, albeit with variation, from Eritrea, Ethiopia, Kenya, and Uganda. Its precursors did too. Sudan's ambassador to Jordan, Mohamed Osman Saeed, indiscreetly said in November 2010 that after secession the North, "will gain a good neighbor and will be relieved from three lousy neighbors."[45] He did not name the lousy, but since the break-up, Sudan has no borders with Uganda, Kenya, or the Democratic Republic of the Congo. Predominantly Christian eastern black Africa has favored an independent South Sudan as a buffer against Islamic and Islamist North Sudan, and in 1991 Eritrea and Ethiopia had set a regional precedent for a secessionist referendum. Kenya, Uganda, and Ethiopia believe that they can have good security, trading, and energy pipeline relations with South Sudan. Together with a visibly more reluctant South Africa, these black African powers obliged the African Union to accept the agreement made in the CPA. Some African diplomats rationalized South Sudan's future independence as a belated act of self-determination for what had been a separately administered British colonial domain, but that was not the legal basis on which South Sudan's independence rested: it was founded on the North's consent.

The SPLM's leaders after August 2005 determined that their dead leader's vision of transforming the Arab-majority center of Sudan was unachievable. They believed the predominantly Arab and Muslim North was obdurately unwilling to make a pluralist federation work. In 2009 in presentations and dialogs in Khartoum in which I participated before several of the dominant players in the NCP, the DUP, and the Umma parties, NCP leaders persistently ruled out what some called "the Nigerian option,"[46] i.e. secularizing the federation and confining the shariah law to Muslim-majority states. The other Northern party representatives remained silent. The NCP preferred, in short, to downsize Sudan, and to pursue its own political and religious agenda within a reduced state, rather than to make a fully pluralist accommodation with the South and non-Muslims. No better evidence for this view can be found than President Bashir's declaration at a rally in the eastern city of Gederaf in December 2010, a few weeks before the referendum, "If South

---

[45] *Al-Arab Al-Youm*, Jordan, cited in the *Sudan Tribune*, Khartoum, 30 November 2010.

[46] As part of a Chatham House mediation effort I presented the Nigerian model as an alternative in Khartoum in 2009, to absolute opposition from NCP representatives. For brief Sudan–Nigerian comparisons see R. Cockett, *Sudan: Darfur and the Failure of an African State* (New Haven, CT: Yale University Press, 2010), 291–4.

Sudan secedes, we will change the constitution and at that time there will be no time to speak of diversity of culture and ethnicity . . . Sharia and Islam will be the main source for the constitution, Islam the official religion and Arabic the official language."[47] In Sudan, the South's potential federalists became committed secessionists because they (correctly) estimated that they faced a central power unwilling to make the necessary accommodations to make unity attractive, even though South Sudan faces a far tougher path to economic development than an independent Kurdistan Region, and even though the failure to resolve Abyei retains the potential to create a new war.

The KRG's geopolitical milieu, by contrast, is less hospitable for secession. Turkey, Iran, and Syria have historically fiercely opposed Kurdish secessionism, though they have often exploited Kurdish rebel movements in contests with Baghdad governments. The US has opposed Kurdish secessionism in Iraq, both in deference to its Turkish ally, and because since 1980 it has usually sought a strong Iraq to balance against Iran. Bluntly put, the US was nominally neutral but actively favored South Sudan's secession because it weakened what it regarded as a potentially disruptive Islamist government. By contrast, US ambassadors sweet-talked Kurds, but strongly opposed their secession from Iraq because Washington feared both strengthening Islamist Iran and aggravating Turkey.

For some, this comparative difference between the neighborhoods of the Kurds and the South Sudanese, and the strikingly different US postures toward both regions, is all that is needed to resolve the puzzling difference between Kurdish and South Sudanese conduct after 2005. It is necessary, but not sufficient. Kurds are not wholly the prisoners of their neighbors, nor are they the dependent clients of the US. They are active agents, and their assessment of their Arab-majority center, and their own "grand strategy," based on hard-won knowledge of their region, mattered.[48] Their grand strategy amounts to a defense-in-depth of dramatic federal autonomy within Iraq. It is intended to prevent Iraq from again becoming an over-centralized rentier state, which led them to detention centers and mass executions, and to build the substance of independence and successful economic and political development without having the formal sovereign pleasures of South Sudan. Extensive autonomy and power-sharing are being defended internally through alliances within Iraq (based on vigilant and revisable judgments of shared interests with particular Shi'ite, Sunni, and secular Arab parties and tribes). The task is made easier by the deep divisions between Shi'ite and Sunni Arabs,

---

[47] *Reuters*, Khartoum, 19 December 2010.

[48] "Strategy" exists in all human interactions; "grand strategy" refers to the overall political, military, economic, and cultural goals of a state and the alliances and instruments chosen to protect them in different domains. The Roman and Byzantine Empires had grand strategies but so, I argue, may a regional government.

and through the Kurdistan Region's control over its own security. Proportional representation and multi-party coalitions, for now, have prevented any unified centralizing Arabist bloc from emerging—though the possibility cannot be excluded.

The Kurds' best hope of a principled Arab partner lay in their constitution-making alliance with the Supreme Council for the Islamic Revolution in Iraq (SCIRI; now the Islamic Supreme Council in Iraq, ISCI). ISCI is dominated by the leading Shi'ite family of the Hakims, who in 2005 were ardent champions of a southern region modeled on Kurdistan. But ISCI has been badly damaged, both by its poor performance in running southern governorates, and by Iranian sabotage of what they had initially established as their front organization. ISCI has now quietly revised its postures and made alliances of convenience with the Sadrists. The weakening of ISCI has obliged Kurds to be pragmatic in their deals with Arab parties.

Externally, Kurds have pursued constructive diplomatic and external relations with the US, the EU, and East Asia, and their oil and gas companies, all made feasible under their new constitutional rights. They have especially pursued an active "*Westpolitik*"[49] with Turkey, and, more quietly, détente with Iran, to create commercial and political alliances, and to entrench recognition of the KRG's constitutional rights. To attract inward investment the KRG has provided the laws of a mature capitalist legal order. To protect the KRG's revenue interests, its people, and their environment, its policy-makers took care in the drafting of the Region's Oil and Gas Law. The KRG prioritized its own law only after the failure of the federal Iraqi cabinet and parliament to progress a draft law of February 2007. The KRG's strategy has been to build a credible base of inward investment, from which it could then negotiate more productively with its federal partners in Baghdad, both on Iraq-wide revenue-sharing, and on production, marketing, and exporting. It has had obvious successes, though the jury remains out. The KRG is prioritizing resolving disputes over oil and gas because these are central to its budget, its economic development, and funding the Peshmerga, while it is prepared for a much slower pace of change on resolving the disputed territories.

Relations with Turkey have shown zigzags, but the overall trajectory has been positive. It is Turkey itself which has truly zigzagged. Initially shocked by the US decision to enforce regime change in Iraq, Turkey feared that the removal of the Baath would lead to an independent Kurdistan, and revive the PKK. Some of its "deep state" special operatives, intent on the assassination of Iraqi Kurdish politicians, were arrested by American soldiers. But Turkey's Justice and Development (AKP) government (and some of its military) have

---

[49] The analogy is with West German Chancellor Brandt's "*Ostpolitik*," which promoted constructive change through rapprochement with East Germany and its neighbors.

rethought their positions, in private and in public. They realized that the Turkomen minority is insufficiently weighty to provide leverage in the new Iraq, especially within Kirkuk. More significantly, they realized the advantages of building constructive interdependence with what they now are prepared to call the Kurdistan Region (rather than Northern Iraq). The KRG recognizes that its relations with Ankara are easier if they fit Turkey's energy ambitions, and its ethnic politics. Turkey's ambitions include being the transit hub for Caucasian, Caspian Sea, and Iraqi oil and gas to Europe, a development the EU welcomes to lessen its dependence on Russia. Ceyhan on the Mediterranean has long been an export route for the Kirkuk oilfields, but has had reduced volumes since the Gulf War of 1991. Turkey's policy-makers realize that the Shi'ite leaders in the Baghdad federal government, formally or informally, have prioritized the redevelopment of Iraq's southern oilfields. This, in turn, has made Turkey's policy-makers better disposed toward the KRG, not only a champion of its own new fields, and of export through Turkey, but also of repair and renewal of the Kirkuk oilfields. The KRG has also promised to be an effective agency for Turkey in achieving the peaceful dissolution of the PKK within Turkey, though that requires Turkey to complete its improved treatment of its own Kurds. In short, newly constitutionalized Kurdish nationalism within Iraq is—at least potentially—allying with newly democratized soft Islam in Turkey. Both are affected by the fact that Kurdish votes matter, and are potentially pivotal, in Iraq and in Turkey.

The federalization of Iraq, by comparison with the break-up of Sudan, is therefore not merely a realist tale of comparative state neighborhoods, or of the impact of US power and preferences. It is also a tale of the greater democratization of Iraq—and Turkey—and regime transformation compared with Sudan. The enhanced potential electoral pivotality of Kurds in Iraq and Turkey has been decisive in shaping KRG grand strategy, a pivotality that the South Sudanese were much less likely to command in a united Sudan once the 2008 census results were reported. Kurdish strategic adaptation, to remake both Iraq and Turkey in their interests, is the key and little-understood part of the federalization of Iraq. The Southern Sudanese strategic reappraisal of Garang's vision after the census returns, and its freshly critical evaluation of the dispositions of northern parties, is the key and insufficiently understood part of the break-up of Sudan.

These arguments help explain why Kurdish leaders, for now, are committed to the federalization of Iraq, whereas the South Sudanese are committed to independence. Their negotiating partners also mattered. Key North Sudanese were downsizers. They preferred a smaller and more homogeneous Sudan to the compromises required by a pluralist federation. They may also have miscalculated their bargaining power with a newly independent South Sudan, believing that they could easily extract enough rent from their pipelines to make good most of their revenue-losses. The Arabs of Iraq, by contrast, have not been downsizers, so far, but that is not too difficult to explain. Sunni Arabs want to keep the Kurds in Iraq because a Kurdless Iraq would have a very large Shi'ite majority. The Shi'ite Arabs want to keep the Kurds in Iraq to balance against the Sunni Arabs. Each bloc of Arabs is reluctant fully to make the concessions that Kurdistan wants, but someone usually breaks from their ranks to make short-run deals with the Kurds. Democratic rules may make this a sustainable game.

No comment has been made on whether the South Sudanese or the Kurds are making the right choices given their interests, and their appraisals of their geopolitical environments. Nor has it been suggested that the federalization of Iraq is secure, or that the secession of South Sudan will proceed smoothly. An explanation has, however, been presented, which accounts for why Kurdish and South Sudanese leaders rationally chose different strategies during and after 2005, even though both of them led mass publics that longed for independence from states that had never earned their allegiance, and had never done enough to deserve it.

Twinned comparisons are not large-N studies. Of what general significance is this comparison for political science? First, it suggests that precolonial and colonial pasts matter: the colonial and postcolonial eras did not erase the prospects of all restoration projects, old polities or regions can resurrect. Second, even when faced with a clear but weakened domestic adversary, secessionists and autonomists have to overcome huge collective action problems and usually a regional and global order hostile to their preferences. Third, autonomy, federal or otherwise, need not lead to secession: nationalists are strategists, and may settle for less than their optimum. Fourth, nationalists' projects are facilitated when they are faced with "downsizing" centers. Explaining secessions should focus therefore on what accounts for the development of downsizing mentalities. Lastly, democratization may enhance the credibility of federalism as a settlement for the historically excluded, and their parties, but it will only convincingly do so when the group in question obtains pivotality.

The South Sudanese leaders judged the prospects of democratization under the Arab majority in Sudan to be dim, but it was their assessment of their own likely lack of pivotality in any democratic and federal future that decisively shaped their decision to seek independence rather than to try to make a new Sudan. The South Sudanese also had low expectations of the democratic opposition to Bashir in the North. During 1964–69 and 1986–89, when Sudan had had parliamentary democracy, the precursors of the Northern Opposition had not delivered either on South Sudan's autonomy or on repeal of Sudan-wide shariah law. Indeed some within the SPLA feared that the Northern opposition might outflank Bashir, and attack him for making concessions to the South Sudanese: after all, they had not been parties to the making of the CPA. Kurds' confidence in the credibility of the democratic commitments of their Arab partners has always been low, but, by contrast, they know, for now, that the Arabs of Iraq are sufficiently divided to give pivotality to Kurdish voters and leaders, provided they remain sufficiently united. But the Kurdish leadership has taken out insurance. They hope that détente with Turkey will help them if they ever need to make a fresh international case for secession, e.g. after the installation of a new Arab dictatorship in Baghdad, or after successive Arab-led governments have breached the constitutional commitments they made in 2005. As I revised this chapter for publication it looked increasingly plausible that the insurance policy would soon be cashed.

11

How Does the Arab World Perceive Multiculturalism and Treat its Minorities? The Assyro-Chaldeans of Iraq as a Case Study

Joseph Yacoub

INTRODUCTION: THE RENEWAL OF ARAB POLITICAL DISCOURSE

The themes of multiculturalism and minorities are both important and highly topical in the Arab world, especially at a time when the world is going through unprecedented changes in the areas of democracy, civil liberties, and human rights. The major transformations and changes occurring in the Arab world, from the Gulf to the Atlantic (Tunisia, Egypt, Libya, Yemen, Syria, Bahrain, Jordan, Oman . . .) involve a total change in its customary ways of perceiving, analyzing, and dealing with the world.[1]

Indeed, we are witnessing the emergence of a new Arab political discourse based on sovereign peoples and the common will, freedom from external interference, the principle of a common citizenship transcending particular affiliation (ethnic or religious), coupled this time with a constitutional state, democracy, civil liberties, equality and non-discrimination, the concept of dignity, non-violence, an awareness of individual rights, social justice (the right to work as a fundamental human right . . .), and ethics in governance. There is also a preference for a parliamentary system with limitations on the powers of rulers.

---

[1] Cf. Joseph Yacoub, "Un discours politique renouvelé," *La Croix*, 4 March 2011.

In terms of ideas, a political philosophy of law is emerging. It is introducing and combining duly authorized substantive law, democratically determined by society and through popular representation, with the principles of natural law inherent to people by virtue of their humanity, and that goes beyond contingencies. It thus combines human nature and individual empowerment; history and the individuality of peoples. As such, this discourse is humanist and universal, and creates a people-centered dynamic.

While this change in political thinking is unprecedented, it must be stressed that over the past two decades—as the upshot of territories being conquered to the detriment of certain states—the Arab world has embarked upon a period designed to give birth to political and social democracy. These trends are now becoming visible and are reflected in practice.

In recent times, access to information has been evolving. The number of meetings on the need for political reforms increased, and these were widely reported by the media and satellite channels such as *Al Jazeera*, which thereby introduced the values and rules of democracy, gradually inserting them into society's mores. There was very broad discussion on the content of democracy, secularism, the nature and functions of a modern civic state, the need for a social pact between government and governed, separation of powers, citizenship, the status and role of civil society and the status of women, the need for a contemporary analysis and interpretation of shariah, self-government in earthly matters, the right to be different, the condemnation of social exclusion, and, lastly, the independence of the judiciary. This discussion expressed support for democracy and the rules of politics, and was preoccupied with constitutions that limit the authority of those in power. It also focused on guaranteeing the fundamental rights of citizens, individually and collectively, and respecting the rights of ethnic, cultural, and religious minorities within Arab national entities.

In so doing, the Arab world has revived a tradition of humanist and progressive thought and attempts at secularization that have marked its history. Of course, the Arab world has always known nationalist, rationalist, and religious movements (both Muslim and Christian) advocating liberation and freedom from bondage. The revolutions under way belong—both naturally and logically—to this tradition.

At the moment, people are waiting to see how events progress. The stakes are high and the actions taken will have a tremendous impact on how the Arab world rethinks nationalism, reforms its constitutional bodies, amends its legislation, deals with its past, and revises its history and religious textbooks, all with a view to introducing political pluralism, cultural diversity, and a common citizenship, and to enhancing the status of its ethnic, linguistic, and religious minorities.

MULTICULTURALISM IS A REALITY
IN THE ARAB WORLD

In its geography and history, and in its ethnic and cultural anthropology, the Arab world is multiple and complex. There are clearly common features and points of convergence, as well as differences, among Arab countries. The Arab world, united by language, history, religion, culture, and a common destiny, is made up of a plurality of ethnic, national, cultural, linguistic, sectarian, and religious affiliations, all of whose origins are distant and ties often tangled.

It is the heir to multinational empires, and a pluralism of identities, religions, cultures, and legal systems. It acknowledges their communities and bodies of customary law (Assyrian, Babylonian, Byzantine, Arab, and Ottoman Empires).

Long opposed to any identity-based recognition, the Arab world has been anxious about the concerns of ethnic, cultural, and religious minorities ever since the establishment of rigid and ultra-centralized nation-states following World War I. The once impregnable fortress was now caught up in—and at times destabilized by—issues long denied.

This vast geographical grouping has always been at a crossroads of peoples and religions—a center of civilization in which the past is still very present. One need only examine its history to realize that it is neither uniform nor monolithic, and that it encompasses populations who were often marginalized by the dominant historiography or unfairly treated by government policies. Still, these are indigenous populations, native to these lands since ancient times, dating back to the Mesopotamians, the Syrians, the Phoenicians, the Canaanites, the Berbers, and others.

Take the example of Iraq. Alongside the Arabs and Kurds (in the northern part of the country), there are Mandaeans (or Sabeans), Assyro-Chaldeans, Yazidis, Turkmen, Armenians, Bajalans, Chabaks, Kakaïs (or Sarlis), nomadic tribes, Jews (once numerous), Circassians, Chechens, Persanophones, and others. Their belonging to a minority community is theoretically recognized and some communities are mentioned in the Iraqi Constitution, adopted in 2005, which states that the country has multiple nationalities, religions, and faiths. Since countries may be composed of several different categories of minorities, the situation differs from country to country, according to the various ideologies and political regimes. The treatment of minorities can vary within a country, and some communities are spread across several states (the Kurds and Assyro-Chaldeans are examples). Treatment varies, from recognition of the community and the faith (as in Lebanon) to the absence of religious freedom (as in the case of Christians in Saudi Arabia).

Present in several countries (Syria, Iraq, Turkey, Iran), the Kurds, whose history dates back to the Medes and ancient Mesopotamia, have all the features of a nation, yet are deprived of a state (except in Iraq where they enjoy considerable autonomy).

It is true that the Arab world is nationalistic. This reflects its history and its struggle against colonial domination. It is proud of its nationality and its identity. That said, there are several visions of nationalism, ranging from exclusive to soft nationalism.

Here is an example. In 1946, Abd al-Rahman Azzam, an Egyptian, and the first Secretary General of the League of Arab States (1945–52), made the following remarks on the subject of Arab identity. These remarks, which had a prophetic tone, involved the succession of civilizations that have marked the history of this world:

I think everything that is happening now in the world is simply the groundwork for a new message, and I have faith in God who created us in this land, who made us the heirs of the Pharaohs, Babylonians, Phoenicians, Chaldeans, Carthaginians, Aramaeans and later the Arabs, who bequeathed us a legacy of the great religions preached by Moses, Jesus and Mohammad, and who has long put us to the test to cleanse us. I have faith in the message of this new nation, the nation of the future . . .[2]

Addressing the Arabs, he exhorts them, saying:

O Arabs (. . .) you are the heirs of religions and civilizations dating back to the dawn of history. May endurance and tolerance be your predominant qualities, as they were among your fathers.[3]

Unfortunately, this pluralist conception did not prevail.

WHAT IS THE STATUS OF MULTICULTURALISM AND MINORITIES IN THE ARAB WORLD?

As for the recognition accorded multiculturalism, in reality there is a tremendous struggle to convert it into practice, and when this does occur it is often following conflict. It is interesting in this regard to observe the evolution of constitutions in some Arab countries that have undergone a transition from highly unitary or even exclusive nation-states to the kind that recognize diversity.

Arab states are a long way off from considering the practical elements of multiculturalism management. And in cases where these elements do capture

---

[2] Cited by Anouar Abdel-Malek, *La Pensée politique arabe contemporaine* (Paris: Éditions du Seuil, coll. Politique, 1970), 215–16. English trans., *Contemporary Arab Political Thought*, trans. Marco Pallis (London: Zed Books, 1984).

[3] Cited by Abdel-Malek, *La Pensée politique arabe contemporaine*, 216.

the attention of government, their concretization remains shaky or stagnates at an unacceptable level, which gives rise to the questions: Is there adequate legislation in this area? Do minorities have political representation? What is the influence of civil society and minority advocacy groups? What is the status of freedom of conscience and religion?

On another level, international bodies (the UN, UNESCO) have adopted standards on cultural diversity and minorities that commit the Arab countries, most of whom have subscribed to these standards. For its part, the Arab League adopted an Arab Charter on Human Rights on 23 May 2004, at the Tunis Summit. The Charter contains several clauses on multiculturalism and minorities, which will be analyzed in detail.

There can be no doubt that nationalism has been a constant in the history of the Arab world. Yet it is a restrictive nationalism, and this has resulted in the marginalization or exclusion of communities ethnically and linguistically non-Arab, such as the Kurds, the Berbers, and the Assyro-Chaldeans. But when one observes the Arab realities of the past two decades, there has been a gradual— be it timid—shift away from an exclusive nationalism that admitted of no exception toward a less rigid nationalism.

This raises questions of a philosophical, anthropological, and political nature. There are seemingly theoretical and conceptual difficulties in recon-ciling the absolute and the relative, or in squaring Arab universalism with the distinctive cultural and national characteristics of the peoples and communi-ties that make up its universe. When it comes to recognizing pluralities, there are theoretical weaknesses. Moreover, issues of ethnic, national, and cultural diversity are immediately politicized, which often distorts the way they are understood. The Arab geopolitical context and the positioning of foreign powers do not favor calm interpretation of these problems.

On the other hand, there is sometimes an excess of nationalism, fostered by authoritarian regimes, as if the Arab world feared for its unity and cohesion were it to recognize its diversity. It must also be said that this issue is politically manipulated by the authorities, who do not hesitate to use it for their own purposes.

Hence the importance of rethinking the concepts underlying the social organization in this part of the world and reconsidering the way they are being employed. These concepts include: the nation-state; forms of govern-ment (unitary, federal, multi-ethnic, multi-country); the will to live together and the unity of the body politic; integration and assimilation; equality and non-discrimination; preferential treatment and affirmative action; secularism; common citizenship; self-government and the right to self-determination; the teaching of history and teaching about religions.

A number of these concepts are found in the Arab Charter on Human Rights, which we will now analyze.

THE ARAB CHARTER ON HUMAN RIGHTS, MULTICULTURALISM, AND MINORITY RIGHTS

Adopted on 23 May 2004[4] at the Tunis Summit of the League of Arab States, the Arab Charter on Human Rights came into force on 16 March 2008 under Article 49, which required ratification by seven states (these were Jordan, Bahrain, Libya, Algeria, United Arab Emirates, Palestine, and Yemen). Two other countries, Qatar and Saudi Arabia, ratified it later. The Charter consists of a Preamble and fifty-three articles, some of which are dense and lengthy.

Despite its many theoretical shortcomings, the Charter contains several provisions on human rights, cultural pluralism, and minorities, even if the wording is sometimes cautious and despite the discrepancies between the way it is applied and reality. It pays tribute to the Arab nation and the monotheistic religions and civilizations that have succeeded one another within its geographical territory, incorporates human rights, accepts allegiance to universal principles, and recognizes fundamental human rights instruments. The Charter supports human freedom and dignity, the rule of law, and the right of peoples to self-determination. It condemns all forms of discrimination, and enshrines the right to equality before the law, the right to participate in public affairs, minority rights, and freedom of thought, belief and religion. It is worth examining several of these provisions in detail, starting with the Preamble.

The Preamble is original and from the very beginning conveys the spirit of the Charter, stating "In Praise of the Arab nation and the monotheistic religions." In the Preamble, we find a striking reference to the Arab nation—which is exclusive in character—and recognition of the differences within it, though this is limited to religious differences. It proclaims the pride of belonging to the Arab nation, the dignity of man, belief in the monotheistic religions, the inclusion of human rights, the rule of law, and adherence to universal values and principles. It states:

Proceeding from the faith of the Arab nation in the dignity of man that God has honoured since the inception of the world and in the fact that the Arab homeland is the cradle of religions and civilizations whose lofty values have enshrined the right of man to a life of dignity based on freedom, justice and equality.[5]

According to the Preamble, this involves "giving concrete expression to the eternal principles of brotherhood, equality and tolerance among human beings—principles enshrined in Islam and other divine religions." It says we

---

[4] Following the revision of the 1994 Charter; composed of forty-three items.

[5] For the text of the Charter, see *Travaux et Jours*, 80, Université Saint-Joseph de Beyrouth (Spring–Summer 2008): 185–207. The same issue contains two analytical articles on the Charter: Ahmed Mahiou, "La Charte arabe des droits de l'homme," 209–37; and Nabil Maamari, "La Charte arabe des droits de l'homme de 2004," 239–56.

are "proud of the humanitarian values and principles the Arab nation has developed over its long history, and that have helped significantly in disseminating science between East and West, making religion the focal point of the world and the preferred destination for those seeking knowledge and wisdom."

The Preamble also proclaims "faith in the unity of the Arab homeland" and defends "the right of nations to self-determination, and to preserve their wealth and grow." It also affirms "the rule of law" and its contribution "to the protection of human rights considered in terms of their universality and complementarity." It is certain that "human enjoyment of freedom, justice and equal opportunity is the yardstick by which one should measure the value of any society." The text "reaffirms" the principles of the UN Charter, the Universal Declaration of Human Rights, and the provisions of two international covenants on human rights (1966), and claims to "take into account" the Cairo Declaration on Human Rights in Islam.[6]

Let us turn now to the content of the Charter. The Charter proclaims individual and collective rights and the right of peoples to self-determination, and establishes civil, political, economic, social, and cultural rights. In particular, it aspires to reconcile national identity and human rights, universal values, and the cultural characteristics specific to the Arab world.

The first Article is innovative in this regard, and merits special attention. It says that the Charter aims to achieve the following objectives "within the framework of the national identity of Arab States and the feeling of belonging to a common civilization":

(a) "Making human rights central to national concerns in Arab States (. . .)" and converting them into policies;

(b) "Fostering among individuals in Arab States a pride of identity and loyalty to their country, and an attachment to the land, its history and the common concerns of its citizens, and taking measures to ensure that they are imbued with a culture of fraternity, tolerance and openness to others" in accordance with human rights;

(c) "Preparing new generations in Arab States for a free and responsible life in solidarity-based civil society founded on a balance between awareness of rights and respect for obligations and governed by the values of equality, tolerance and moderation";

(d) "Firmly rooting the principle that all human rights are universal, indivisible, interdependent and interrelated."

---

[6] The reference to the Cairo Declaration of Human Rights in Islam, which appeared in the 1994 Charter, though differently formulated, was not removed.

Article 2 establishes the right of peoples to self-determination and the right of resistance to foreign occupation. The self-determination of peoples, which is a collective right, becomes a prerequisite and a basis for the enjoyment of individual rights, as noted in the Declaration on the Granting of Independence to Colonial Countries and Peoples (1960), and Article I of the International Covenant on Civil and Political Rights adopted by the UN General Assembly in 1966. It adds, probably with Iraq in mind, that people "have a right to the protection of national sovereignty and territorial unity."

Article 3 concerns non-discrimination: Each state that is party to the Charter undertakes to ensure that all individuals within its jurisdiction are entitled to enjoy its rights and freedoms . . . without distinction (Art. 3). The Charter also enshrines the right to equality before the law (Art. 11), the right to liberty and security of all individuals (Art. 14), and the right to participate freely in public affairs (Art. 24).

For our purposes, a central question concerns the recognition of minority rights. It is in the Eastern traditions and Arab heritage to give a special status to non-Muslim communities (Christian and Jewish). This religious status can include the use of liturgical language and cultural elements if these facilitate the practice of the religion. Aside from a partial recognition of the cultural sphere, there is rarely recognition of minority rights other than those pertaining to the religious sphere. However, the question of minorities is more wide-ranging and extends beyond the religious field, as it involves the overall problem of identity and belonging. Consequently, it is concerned with Arab identity itself and examines relationships with others.

However, the Arab Charter develops this idea slightly. It explicitly recognizes the rights of persons belonging to minorities, which "can not be denied the right to enjoy their culture, use their language and practice the precepts of their religion" (Art. 25).[7] It adds that "the law regulates the exercise of these rights."[8]

As for the right to freedom of thought, belief, creed, and religion, it recognizes—both in what it expresses and in the freedom accorded parents—to "freely provide for the religious and moral education of their children"

---

[7] This article reminds us of clause 27 of the International Covenant on Civil and Political Rights, adopted by the UN General Assembly in 1966, which states: "In those States in which ethnic, religious or linguistic minorities exist, persons belonging to such minorities shall not be denied the right, in community with the other members of their group, to enjoy their own culture, to profess and practise their own religion, or to use their own language."

[8] Compare with the first version of the Arab Charter on Human Rights, dated 15 September 1994, which states, concerning minorities: "Minorities have the right to enjoy their culture and express their religion in worship and observance" (Art. 37). To compare the Arab Charters of 15 September 1994 and that of 23 May 2004, read Mohammed Amin Al-Midani, *Les Droits de l'homme et l'islam: Textes des organisations arabes et islamiques*, 2nd edn. (Strasbourg: Université de Strasbourg, 2010).

(Art. 30). The Charter guarantees the right to information and freedom of opinion and expression (Art. 32).

The Charter not only recognizes these rights but accords them priority. It says that nothing in this Charter shall be construed "so as to prejudice the rights and freedoms protected by the internal laws of participating States or set out in international or regional instruments on human rights that the participating States have adopted or ratified, including the rights of women, children and persons belonging to minorities" (Art. 43).

Accordingly, Arab countries are obliged to make domestic law conform to the requirements of the Charter:

> Participating States undertake, in cases where their legislation or other provisions in force do not guarantee effective implementation of the rights set out in this Charter, to take the legislative or other measures necessary for this purpose, and to do so in accordance with their constitutional procedures and the provisions of this Charter. (Art. 44)

It can be seen that the Arab Charter on Human Rights contains several elements for recognizing multiculturalism and minorities, and has made progress—at least theoretically—on the problematization of human rights. That said, it is far removed from the reality.

THE FUTURE OF THE ARAB CHARTER ON HUMAN RIGHTS

Given current changes in the Arab world, how should one interpret this Charter and what is its future? To understand the human rights situation in the Arab world, one needs to take into account several factors: the overall historical and geopolitical context; the status of the League of Arab States; the various attempts to amend its Charter and modernize this institution (since the 1980s),[9] including efforts in the area of human rights; the nature of Arab regimes and their often discordant policies; the dominant ideologies; the two versions (compared) of the Arab Charter on Human Rights; and the introduction of minorities.

---

[9] On the various attempts to amend the Charter of the Arab League, and on its modernization, see Abdelfattah Amor, "Rapport introductif," to *Le Problème de l'amendement du Pacte de la Ligue des Etats arabes*, symposium organized by the Centre d'Études, de Recherche et de Publication, Faculty of Law, Political Science and Economics, University of Tunis, 15–17 April 1981 (Tunis: CERP, 1982), 25–58 (in Arabic). See also Magdi Hamad, *La Ligue des Etats arabes: Introduction à l'avenir*, Le Monde de la connaissance 345, 2nd edn. (Kuwait: Conseil national de la culture, des arts et des lettres, 2007), 193–294 (in Arabic).

The status of the Arab League, the first regional organization, was approved on 22 March 1945. It made no mention of human rights or minorities, unlike the UN Charter, adopted in June of that year which did refer to human rights. The Preamble of the Charter of the Arab League declared a desire "to increase the close ties that bind the Arab States," to "cement and strengthen these ties . . . on the basis of respect for the independence and sovereignty" of the states and "direct their efforts towards the common good of all Arab countries, improve their lot, secure their future, help them realize their aspirations." "Within the framework of its rules and the conditions prevailing in each state," the League's objectives emphasized "close cooperation between member states" on economic and financial issues, communications, intellectual matters, issues of nationality . . . social issues, and health (Art. 2).

The idea of human rights had been in preparation since 1960. On 3 September 1968, the Arab League created an Arab Standing Committee on Human Rights. In December 1968, an Arab Regional Conference on Human Rights was held in Beirut. On 10 July 1971, the Committee presented a draft declaration (thirty-one items) to the League Council, initiated by a committee of experts. It was, however, unsuccessful.[10] Its first Article stated: "No discrimination as to race, colour, origin, religion, sex, wealth or political opinion may be allowed in the exercise of rights and freedoms included in this declaration."

In 1979, the Arab League headquarters was moved from Cairo to Tunis,[11] and a new general secretary was elected, Chadli Klibi, of Tunisia. Discussions then resumed on the need to amend the status of the Arab League and on human rights (10th Summit, Tunis, 22 November 1979). In June 1981, a first draft was drawn up by the secretariat of the Arab League and sent to member states. It even discussed issues such as democracy, social justice, and human rights.[12]

In March 1985, the Arab Standing Committee on Human Rights wrote a new draft of the Arab Charter, but that plan too was rejected by the League Council. In 1993, a new draft Charter was drawn up in Cairo by the same committee. On 15 September 1994, after twenty-three years of procrastination and delays, the 102nd meeting of the Council of the League of Arab States ended up adopting this draft as the Arab Charter on Human Rights. In its Preamble, the Arab governments confirmed their commitment to the 1948 Universal Declaration of Human Rights, the 1966 International Covenants on Human Rights, and the 1990 Cairo Declaration on Human Rights in Islam.

---

[10] See Boutros Boutros-Ghali, "La Ligue des Etats arabes," in Karel Vasak (ed.), *Les Dimensions internationales des droits de l'homme* (Paris: Bernan Associates, 1978), ii. 575–81; "Les minorités et les droits de l'homme en droit international" (in Arabic), in *Al Siassa al-Doualia* 39, Cairo, January 1975, pp. 10–20.

[11] Until 1989, following the rupture in 1978 of Egypt's relations with other Arab nations.

[12] See *Le Problème de l'amendement du Pacte de la Ligue des Etats arabes*, 311–15.

Nonetheless, this first Charter was the focus of numerous criticisms and it too would be revised to modernize it. Further meetings of the Arab Standing Committee on Human Rights took place in 2002, 2003, and in January 2004. It should be noted that since the 2001 Arab Summit in Amman, human rights have been included in League resolutions.The discussions of the Arab Standing Committee on Human Rights ultimately led to the adoption of the new version of the Arab Charter on Human Rights, which was approved on 23 May 2004 at the Summit of the League of Arab States, held in Tunis (remembered during the Summit of March 2010).

Why was there so much prevarication on human rights and so many delays? This group of disparate and discordant states seemed unable to develop common policies, especially in the field of human rights, and to put them into practice. States opposed the inclusion of human rights in their legislation since these were in sharp contrast with their own ideas and practices. Moreover, many Arab states that have signed and ratified international documents—though sometimes with reservations—are not even close to honoring their obligations. One is obliged to ask, do they really believe they need a Charter? Otherwise, why would the mechanisms for monitoring human rights be so deficient (Arts. 45–8 of the Charter)? Given the nature of the regimes in question, there is reason to doubt their sincerity.

Moreover, the current uprisings in the Arab world and the emergence of civil societies have highlighted the lack of democracy and the lack of goodwill on the part of certain governments; populations faced with dictatorial and despotic regimes are demanding respect for civil liberties and human rights.

Take the example of Syria, where the population—in revolt since 15 March 2011—has been fiercely repressed. In August 2011, the regime, facing a society vociferously demanding freedom, dignity, and democracy, responded cruelly—with repression, siege, and the invasion of cities such as Deraa, Hama, Latakia, and Deir-Ezzor. But when one reads the Syrian Constitution and compares it to the Arab Charter on Human Rights, there is a wide gulf between these two instruments. Consider this example: Syrian basic law sets up the Baath Party as the "leading party in society and in the State" (Art. 8), despite the fact that Article 24 of the Arab Charter protects the right to freely engage in political activity, to participate in the conduct of public affairs, to stand for office or to choose one's representatives in free and fair elections. It is understood that the declaration made in the Arab Charter precludes that made in the Syrian Constitution. Moreover, the Syrian opposition is calling for repeal of Article 8 of the Constitution.

In the face of the ruthless repression of its people by the Damascus regime,[13] Arab and international society began, as of August 2011, to change its

---

[13] See Cécile Hennion, "Assauts meurtriers du régime syrien contre les manifestants avant le Ramadan," *Le Monde*, 2 August 2011, p. 6. The Assyrian Democratic Organization (ADO), a

attitude.[14] It was a very bloody August,[15] with an assault by Syrian tanks against the city of Hama. The *Le Monde* headline of 9 August 2011 read: "Arab critics further isolate the Syrian regime."[16] Also, they were demanding an "immediate" end to the violence. On 14 August the Syrian regime continued the crackdown, and Damascus carried out a heavy offensive against protesters in the coastal city of Latakia, sending in warships and tanks.[17]

Nabil Al-Arabi, the new Secretary General of the Arab League,[18] called on Arab states to respond positively to the demands for change on the part of their populations, by complying with the Arab Charter on Human Rights, as well as with two documents entitled "Change and Modernization in the Arab World" and "The Pact, Harmony and Solidarity."[19]

Pressure on the Syrian regime mounted. On 8 August 2011, the Arab League called on Damascus to end the violence.[20] In an unprecedented move, King Abdullah of Saudi Arabia—in a statement issued 7 August 2011—strongly condemned the crackdown: "It is impossible for the Saudi kingdom to accept what is happening in Syria. These actions have no justification."[21] The UN Secretary General, Ban Ki-moon, called the violence of the repression "extremely shocking." Meanwhile, on 3 August 2011, the UN Security Council, breaking its silence, issued a statement that for the first time condemned the crackdown against the demonstrators, though it took no concrete action.[22] Faced with worsening repression, on 18 August Western countries made a direct call for the departure of President Bashar al-Asad.[23] On the same day, a report to the Security Council by the UN High Commissioner for Human Rights, Navi Pillay, on the atrocities committed by the Syrian regime, drew up a list of the brutal actions, which were equated with "crimes against humanity."[24] At an extraordinary meeting of 22–3 August, the

---

Syrian political party of the Assyrian community, issued a statement on 1 August 2011, strongly denouncing the repression of the Syrian people.

[14] See Alexandra Geneste, "Le bain de sang en Syrie pousse l'ONU à réagir," *Le Monde*, 3 August 2011, p. 4.

[15] The same month of August saw the fall of the Qaddafi regime.

[16] Article by Laure Stephan, p. 8.

[17] See *Dernières Nouvelles d'Alsace (DNA)*, Strasbourg, 15 August 2011, p. 3.

[18] Nabil Al-Arabi was elected head of the Arab League on 15 May 2011.

[19] See *Ashark Al-Awsat* (an Arab daily), London, 2 August 2011, p. 2.

[20] See Vincent Braun, "Syria. Bachar face aux rafales arabes," *La Libre Belgique*, Brussels, 9 August 2011, p. 11.

[21] Braun, "Syria. Bachar face aux rafales arabes," 11.

[22] See Alexandra Geneste, *Le Monde*, 5 August 2011, p. 6.

[23] See Nathalie Nougayrède with Sylvain Cypel and Jean-Pierre Stroobants, "Les Occidentaux réclament le départ de M. Al-Assad," *Le Monde*, 20 August 2011, p. 4. See also the editorial in *Le Monde*, on the same date, devoted to Syria: "Pressions sur Damas: mieux vaut tard que jamais," 1.

[24] See "La crise syrienne. Rapport accablant de l'ONU sur les exactions du regime," *Le Monde*, 20 August 2011, p. 5. See also Editorial: "Pressions sur Damas," 1.

UN Human Rights Council adopted a resolution[25] condemning the systematic violations of human rights and demanded an immediate cessation to the violence.[26]

For its part, the Arab League, at a ministerial meeting held in Cairo on Saturday, 27 August and devoted to the question of Syria, issued a statement in which delegates urged the Syrian regime to stop the shedding of blood, "before it's too late." The foreign ministers called on the Syrian regime to "respect the right of the Syrian people to live safely and with dignity" and "respect their legitimate aspirations for political, economic and social reform."[27] In his opening speech, the Secretary General of the Arab League, Nabil Al-Arabi, acknowledged the importance of the emerging Arab public opinion: "The Arab League is under pressure from Arab populations to make further efforts in the period ahead."

Clearly, the success of the Arab democratic revolutions is a prerequisite for respect for human rights; it could transform the League of Arab States and give human rights in these countries greater legitimacy and credibility, in line with international standards, both in theory and in practice. In addition, something extraordinary has occurred: since January 2011, human rights have become a dominant theme in the Arab media.

What then is the future of this charter? To explore this, we will consider a case study: the Assyro-Chaldean minority in Iraq.

CASE STUDY: THE ASSYRO-CHALDEANS OF IRAQ

Who are the Assyro-Chaldeans? Historically, culturally, linguistically, nationally, and in terms of their religion the Assyro-Chaldeans have always been a minority in Iraq. They are known and referred to under several names: Assyrians, Chaldeans, and Syriacs. Despite claims made in certain texts, they are practically deprived of full citizenship and often feel they have lost their identity.[28]

Since 2003, nearly a third of Assyro-Chaldeans have opted for exile for reasons of deteriorating safety, continuing instability, threats and intimidation,

---

[25] Thirty-three states voted in favor of the resolution, four voted against, and there were nine abstentions. Note that four Arab countries (Qatar, Kuwait, Saudi Arabia, and Jordan), members of the Council of Human Rights, were among the Member States who called for the holding of this session.

[26] See Agathe Duparc, "L'ONU stigmatise les atteintes aux droits de l'homme commises par le régime syrien," *Le Monde*, 24 August 2011, p. 8.

[27] See the website (in Arabic and English) of the Arab League: <http://www.arableagueonline. org>, accessed September 2013.

[28] See Joseph Yacoub, "Le statut constitutionnel des chrétiens d'Irak," *Proche-Orient Chrétien* 58/3–4, Jerusalem (2008): 277–91.

killings and assassinations, repeated aggression against places of worship, and the discrimination to which they are subjected in Baghdad, Mosul, Kirkuk, and elsewhere.[29]

Marginalized, underrepresented, and excluded from political participation, Christians are the victims of every type of harassment and must contend with very stressful conditions on a regular basis. Over thirty churches have been targeted by bomb attacks, often coordinated in several cities, such as the attacks of 1 August 2004, and that of Sunday, 29 January 2006. The year 2004 alone saw fourteen churches attacked. Priests have been kidnapped and murdered.

In 2010, Iraqi Christians were the target of several attacks. The most heinous was committed on 31 October in the Syriac Catholic Cathedral in Baghdad and killed forty-six people.[30] On 2 August 2011, a car bomb exploded outside the Syrian-Catholic Church of the Holy Family, in the northeastern Iraqi city of Kirkuk, wounding sixteen people, including women and children. Two other churches were also targeted.[31] The Assyrian Universal Alliance (AUA) issued a statement condemning the attack. On this occasion, its Executive Committee reiterated its demand for an autonomous Assyrian province in the province of Nineveh: "As Iraq's indigenous people, Assyrians continue their demand for the establishment of an Assyrian province on our ancestral lands as an integral part of the Federal Republic of Iraq and administrated by Assyrians under the jurisdiction of Iraq's central government, in which we will provide the security forces necessary to safeguard our people."[32]

The current situation is unusually dire, but the political history of the Assyro-Chaldeans has been anything but tranquil. It has alternated between periods of calm and periods of anxiety. In August 1933, when Iraq was an independent country under a monarchy, there was a massacre of Assyrians, followed by a wave of Arab nationalism, in which they suffered somewhat.

The Iraqi state is young. It came into being in 1921 under a League of Nations mandate entrusted to England. It was a monarchy from 1921 to 1958. The first Constitution of this country dates back to March 1925, giving approval to the established monarchy, which was predominantly Sunni— whence Shi'ite frustrations. The Constitution guarantees equality before the law irrespective of religion, language, and nationality (Art. 6), and freedom of religion and conscience for all Iraqis (Art. 13). It also says:

---

[29] See Preti Taneja, *Assimilation, Exodus, Eradication: Iraq's Minority Communities since 2003* (London: Minority Rights Group International, 2007), 8–11, 20–1.

[30] See "Situation des chrétiens," *Proche-Orient Chrétien* 60/3–4, Jerusalem (2010): 426–32.

[31] See François d'Alançon, "En Irak, un attentat vise une église à Kirkouk," *La Croix*, 3 August 2011, p. 6.

[32] See the website of the Assyrian Universal Alliance: <www.AUA.net>, accessed September 2013.

Islam is the official religion of the state, and observance of the rites of the various Islamic sects that exist in Iraq must be respected and may not suffer any hindrance. Absolute freedom of belief is guaranteed to all inhabitants of the country, as well as the freedom to practice religion according to their customs.

Until 1958, in accordance with Article 6.2 of the Election Law, Christians had four deputies, as well as ministers.[33] In fact, Article 37 of the Constitution stipulates "the electoral system applicable to deputies shall be determined by a special law providing for the principle of secret ballot and reflecting the equitable representation of non-Muslim minorities." Thus the Basic Law sought to give to Christian (and Jewish) minorities the right to be represented in the House of Deputies. In 1926, Baghdad enacted a so-called local-languages law, but it was poorly enforced.

Under the provisions of this first Constitution, which instituted a bicameral parliamentary system, the Chaldeans were represented in the Senate by their patriarch, who was appointed by the Palace (Emmanuel II Thomas, and later Joseph Ghanimé VII). This contrasted with the situation of the mountain Assyrians, who were denied any national representation on the pretext that they were not nationals (having come from Turkey) before the war of 1914.

In August 1933, under the same monarchy, the Assyrians were the victims of a massacre in which four thousand died. An exodus to Syria followed. Soon after World War II, there was an exodus of Christians from the north to the cities of Baghdad, Basra, and Kirkuk. They were seeking a better life.

During the period from 1970 to April 2003, the Assyrians were under strict control. The monarchy was overthrown and the Republic established on 14 July 1958, and a Constitution adopted later that year. Following the rise to power of the Baath Party in July 1968, religious freedom was upheld. Nonetheless, this freedom was controlled and, under pain of severe repression, could not be deployed to meddle in politics. Under Saddam Hussein, political activists were mercilessly pursued. Then, starting in 1991, the Iraqi regime changed direction. Drawing back on secularism, it made concessions to the Islamists. Alcohol was prohibited, despite the fact that Christians—and Christians alone—had the right to manufacture and sell it, be it at their peril.

To survive, the churches in Iraq played a mediating role. On the other hand, the churches had little freedom or room for maneuvre. So, to save their communities they were forced to deal with the political powers. However, without this strategy of constant compromise—including compromises that were perhaps less than sincere—Christians, it is said, might have long disappeared from Mesopotamia.

The Constitution in force until the fall of Baghdad on 9 April 2003 had been enacted on 17 July 1970, and enshrined the rule of Baath Arab nationalist

---

[33] One deputy in the province of Baghdad, two in the province of Mosul, and one in Basra.

ideology. From the perspective of the political regime, the real power was in the hands of the President of the Republic and the Council of Revolutionary Command (CRC), which was the highest authority in Iraq and performed a variety of functions (Arts. 37–46 and 57–60).

Citizens, said the Constitution pretentiously, are equal before the law, without discrimination based on sex, race, language, social origin, or religion (Art. 19). The Basic Law also required that the state guarantee freedom of religion, expression, and opinion, and that any racial, religious, or linguistic discrimination was prohibited: "Freedom of religion and belief and that of practising religious rites is guaranteed, provided that this does not contradict any provisions of the Constitution or laws, nor come into conflict with morality and public order" (Art. 25).

While proclaiming that Iraq is "part of the Arab nation" (Art. 5.a), it says that the Iraqi people consist—in theory—of two main ethnic groups: ethnic Arab and ethnic Kurdish (Art. 5.b) and *other nationalities*. Arabic is the official language, while Kurdish is the official language alongside Arabic in the Kurdish region (Art. 7). This region, in which the population consists mainly of Kurds, enjoys self-government (Art. 8), which was officially pro-claimed on 11 March 1970 and implemented in accordance with a law passed on 12 March 1974, in a highly conflictual geopolitical context. But there was a gulf between textual proclamation and reality, and the repression was fierce.

On 16 April 1972 the content of the constitutional term "other national-ities" was explained by way of the promulgation of Decree No. 251 by Iraq's Revolutionary Command Council. These nationalities included Assyrians, Chaldeans, and actual Syriacs, all of whose cultural rights and Arameo-Syriac identity were recognized—at least theoretically.

As a result, cultural, artistic, and media institutions emerged to promote the culture and language of these "other nationalities." From that point on, the Muhafazat (governorate) of Mosul has been called Nineveh, a reference to the name by which this region was known historically, while another governorate is called Babylon (in the centre of the country).

Of particular interest in this period were the founding of the Academy of the Syriac Language, the publication of works on religion and theology, the founding of unions of Syriac writers and artists, and the production of textbooks in the two written forms of Syriac (Eastern and Western). However, despite the publication of several textbooks, teaching the Syriac language was never allowed in either public schools or private schools, which were, more-over, nationalized. As for publications, they were automatically subjected to the filter of severe state censorship.

The Assyro-Chaldeans have produced a rich and diverse literature in Arabic, as well as in their other tongue, Aramaic, in the form of intellectual and literary works—both sacred and secular. These have included not only various versions of the Bible but also exegesis, liturgy, theology, translation, political thought, mysticism, spirituality, religious architecture, music, sacred art, linguistics, philosophy, poetry, and history. Since they were familiar with and even mastered Greek, the Assyrian-Chaldean and Syriac Christians transmitted Greek thought to the Arabs and helped introduce the concepts of logic and philosophy to the Arabic language.[34] The seventh to tenth centuries were decisive in this respect. The Abbasid period was probably the most prolific period for translation the world has ever known. During this period, the Bayt al-Hikma ("House of Wisdom"), an academy of sciences founded in Baghdad by Caliph al-Mamun (786–833), stood out by virtue of its many translators, the most illustrious of whom was Hunayn ibn Ishaq, who headed up the academy.

There are numerous Arab sources chronicling the major contribution made by these Christians to the Arab Golden Age. Of particular note are Ibn al-Nadim (Kitab al-Fahrist, 987, the primary source on this topic), al-Jahez, Ibn Abi Usaybia ('Uyun al-Anba fi Tabaqat al-Atibba, 1269), al-Massoudi (893–957), Yakut al-Hamawi (+ 1229) and Ahmad Amin.

As concerns the modern and contemporary periods, since 1850 Iraqi Christians have continued to play this role by actively participating in the Arab Renaissance as theorists, actors, and translators. Among the Iraqi authors who have played a crucial role, one could mention Thomas Audo, David Joseph, Eugene Manna, Afram Barsoum, Afram Rahmani, Boulos Behnam, Alphonse Mingana, Addai Scher, Gorguis Awad, Boulos Bédaré, Albert Abouna, Jacques Isaac, Youssif Habbi, Louis Sako, Isaac Saka, and Sarhad Jammo.

THE SITUATION AFTER APRIL 2003

On 9 April 2003 Baghdad fell and Saddam Hussein was toppled by US troops. It was a major turning point. Since then, the country has been embroiled in endless conflict and rivalry of a religious, sectarian, and ethnic nature, rather than moving toward a global, civic vision. In addition, there has been persecution of the Assyro-Chaldeans,[35] followed by an unprecedented exodus.

The Iraqi Parliament approved the text of the Constitution on 28 August 2005, and on 15 October of that year Iraqis voted on it.[36] It is particularly

---

[34] See the excellent work, *Les Syriaques transmetteurs de civilisations: L'Expérience du Bilad el-Sham à l'époque omeyyade*, in Arabic, French, and English. Syriac Heritage, Proceedings of Symposium IX, 2 vols. (Antelias-Lebanon: CERO–L'Harmattan, 2005): 295 and 359 respectively.

[35] See Joseph Yacoub, "La Marginalisation des chrétiens d'Irak," *Confluences Méditerranée* 66 (2008): 83–98.

[36] See Joseph Yacoub, "L'Irak est en miettes, sa Constitution aussi," *Le Monde*, 22 October 2005.

interesting to analyze how the Constitution raises the question of ethnic, cultural, and religious minorities. Its preamble refers to both the secular and religious heritage of Iraq, heir to Mesopotamia. It is said that Mesopotamia was the homeland of the apostles and prophets, the home of "pure Imams," and founders of the civilization that devised the first code of law, the Hammurabi Code. It also refers to a republican, federal, democratic and pluralistic society that shows respect for the law and the establishment of justice and equality; for women, children, and their rights; and for developing a culture of diversity.

The Iraqi state is defined as a federal (Art. 1), democratic, and resolutely parliamentary system of government, established in reaction against the former presidential system, which was extreme and dictatorial. Its federalism was adopted without debate, which explains why it is vague; there was no attempt to change people's attitudes for want of a federalist culture.

What nation-state identity would Iraq be assigned? The official name was the subject of many heated debates and much controversy. How was one going to refer to that state? Shi'ites favored a state referred to as Islamic, a designation that the Kurds and the laity rejected. The Sunni Arabs requested that it simply be called the Republic of Iraq. In the end, the name "Republic of Iraq" was adopted (Art. 1).

Concerning the national identity and its context, the Constitution initially stated that Iraq is "a part of the Islamic world" (Art. 3) and that only "the Arab people of Iraq" form part of the Arab nation (Art. 3). This clause angered Amr Moussa, the Secretary General of the Arab League, and was cause for concern for the Cooperation Council of Gulf Countries (CCGC). In an effort to appease Arab circles, this Article was amended on 14 September 2005 by deleting the clause that only "the Arab people of Iraq form part of the Arab nation," and replacing it with the following clause: "The Iraqi state is a founding and active member of the League of Arab States and is bound by its Charter" and a part of the Muslim world.

What about the "components" (the term used in the Constitution) forming the Iraqi people? Iraq is made up of different nationalities, religions, and denominations (Art. 3). As for languages, Arabic and Kurdish are the two official languages of the State (Art. 4). However, the Constitution guarantees the rights of those who speak Turkmen, Syriac, and Armenian in public and private institutions (Art. 4.1). Moreover, the Turkmen and Syriac languages are considered official languages in administrative areas where these linguistic communities have high concentrations (Art. 4.4).[37]

---

[37] The same article stipulates that each region (*iqlim*) or province (*mohavazat*) may use another indigenous language as a supplementary official language, if that proves to be the recommendation of the majority of its people, expressed through a referendum (Art. 4.5).

In addition, Article 125 says that the Constitution must guarantee the administrative, political, cultural, and educational rights of the various nationalities: Turkmen, Chaldeans, Assyrians, and all other segments of the population. These rights are set out by law.

But how does one define the concept of "components" and what is the relationship between the various elements and the unity of the Iraqi people? Does the country have a national and social fabric that transcends its differences? The Constitution does not really clarify this, though it does say "the Basic Law is the guarantor of the unity of Iraq" (Art. 1). There is obviously a lack of consistency.

The wording of these norms contains no vision of a unified Iraq, with sectarian, ethnic, regional, and religious characteristics outweighing national interest and public affairs. Moreover, as we shall see, the balance of power between the prerogatives of the provinces and those of the central government is poorly constructed, which weakens national policies and disrupts social harmony. Furthermore, the debate over this Constitution revealed the profound differences separating the communities. Also, there have been frequent calls for revising the Iraqi Constitution because of its vagueness, which weakens its credibility.

Like the term "components," another vague term, "constants" (suggesting an abiding feature), in this case based on religion, appears in the Constitution. Although the term was not defined, it referred to the tenets of Islam and their stable character. With this Constitution, from this point forward religion played an important political role. Thus, it forbids the passing of laws that are opposed to the "constants and precepts of Islam" (Art. 2), as well as to "the principles of democracy, human rights and fundamental freedoms in this Constitution." The Constitution guarantees "the Islamic identity of the majority of the Iraqi people." It also endorses the "religious rights to doctrinal freedom and the religious practices" of all individuals. Christians are mentioned by name, as are the Yezidis and Mandaeans (Sabeans).

Regarding the status of religion, the Transitional Administrative Law of 8 March 2004 had already endorsed this; Islam figures prominently here (Art. 7), and this status was confirmed in the new Constitution. Islam is "the official religion of the Iraqi state" and "the main source of legislation" (Art. 2). Furthermore, it says that the Federal Supreme Court will be made up of judges and experts in "Islamic jurisprudence" (Art. 92) and law. Its status is determined by law, and must be accepted by a two-thirds majority of Parliament. Among other things, it decides on the constitutionality of laws and interprets provisions of the Constitution. It is difficult to know what its choices will be, given the constitutional balancing between religious precepts, democracy, and human rights.

On the other hand, it says that the holy places have a legal personality due to their religious and civilizational nature. Accordingly, the Iraqi state guarantees and protects these places as "religious and civilizational entities" benefiting from complete freedom of religious worship (Art. 10). The text recognizes and guarantees religious freedom, practice, and belief: "Everyone has a right to be different, but without prejudice to the rights of others and public morals" (Art. 17).

Article 41 states that in matters of personal status, Iraqis are free to comply with the rules of their religions, faiths, beliefs, and choices. Every individual enjoys freedom of thought, conscience, and doctrine (Art. 42). The followers of all religions are free to practice their religious rites and manage their religious property and institutions (Art. 43). The Iraqi state ensures the safety of places of worship for Muslims, Christians, Yazidis, and Sabeans (Art. 43).

While they are in favor of secularism, the Assyro-Chaldeans understand, realistically, why Islam is specifically mentioned in the Constitution: the majority of the population is Muslim. But they do not accept sharia as the only source of legislation because in their view this would constitute a serious violation of religious freedom for non-Muslims, to whom Islamic law should not apply. In this connection, the spiritual leaders of Iraq's churches place emphasis on the Constitution's principles of citizenship, equality of opportunity, and freedom.

The Assyro-Chaldeans and the Iraqi churches have also issued petitions on religious freedom and women's rights, in which they defend secularism and view any constitutional Islamization of the country as "most alarming." When it comes to religion, they note that Iraq is diverse and that this diversity has always been recognized legally.

They start off by defending a secular and democratic state: "What we want is a democratic, civil, pluralistic and federal state, one separating religion and state, that is to say, one that does not politicize religion. Each fulfils its duties and acquires the right to please God and serve humankind." This was the position taken on 13 August 2005 and reiterated shortly thereafter by Shlemoun Warduni, auxiliary to the Chaldean Patriarch, Emmanuel II Delly. The Constitution, he added, must be based on citizenship without mentioning nationalities because "we are for the homeland and the homeland is for all of us." He went on as follows: "the strength and unity of Iraq resides in and is realized through this equality." If one really insists on mentioning the nationalities, then all of them should be mentioned: Arabs, Kurds, Chaldeans, Assyrians, Syriacs, and Turkmen . . . with a view to equality and without hegemony. Concerning religious rights, they have pleaded for freedom of belief and worship, as based on the Universal Declaration of Human Rights. Regarding the Islamic shariah and its possible inclusion as a source of legislation in the Basic Law (Art. 2), this has been conditioned by the fact that it did not restrict citizens to the "constants," in order that the Constitution, they said, might serve as a model of inclusiveness, and respect the laws of the other religions. Specific laws must be adopted for each religion with a view to coordinating the religious beliefs of all Iraqis, as well as guaranteeing the rights of women and disabled persons in accordance with their respective religions.

Immediately after the adoption of the Constitution, Assyro-Chaldean dignitaries also expressed reservations over Article 2 of the Constitution, noting its ambiguities and conveying their concerns in this regard.[38] Another important matter was that on 6 September 2005 the Council of Catholic Bishops of Iraq, chaired by the patriarch of the Chaldean Church, Emmanuel III Delly, issued a statement in which he reiterated his concerns about the multiple interpretations that might come into conflict with Article 2 of the Iraqi Constitution.

Despite the climate of insecurity and persecution, the Assyro-Chaldeans continue to brave the dangers and testify in Baghdad, Kirkuk, and Mosul, not to mention northern Iraq, which is under Kurdish jurisdiction and where they enjoy relative safety. What are they accomplishing despite the difficulties and obstacles? What positions and actions are their religious, civil, and political leaders taking in Iraqi affairs? Are they supporting a plan for Iraq that transcends ethnic and religious differences?

Within Kurdish autonomous institutions, they are represented in the Kurdish National Assembly and the state apparatus of the Kurdish entity (government and administration), to mention only two institutions. The most recent Kurdish regional elections were held on 25 July 2009, preceded on 24 June 2009 by the adoption by the Kurdish Parliament of a draft constitution for the Kurdish Region. Eleven seats are reserved for minorities, including five for the Assyro-Chaldeans.[39] The latter are active in the Kurdish region and have political parties, associations, research centres, cultural groups, publishing houses, schools (which teach Syriac), numerous publications, and several information media (press, radio, TV). There is a Syriac culture and arts directorate in the Kurdistan Region.

Iraqi parliamentary elections were held on 7 March 2010, electing five Christians including Yonadam Kanna, the Secretary General of the Assyrian Democratic Movement. Provincial elections were held on 31 January 2009 in fourteen out of eighteen Iraqi provinces.[40] The Chaldeo-Assyrian-Syriacs won the three seats reserved for them in Baghdad, Basra, and the province of Nineveh.

In addition, in March 2007 the Iraqi journal *al-Fikr al-Masihi* ("Christian Thought"),[41] published continuously since 1964, won the Gold Medal

---

[38] See statement of Mgr Paul Faraj Rahho, Archbishop of Mosul, to the Italian Catholic news agency Asia News, 30 August 2005. Mgr Rahho was killed on 13 March 2008, following his abduction in Mosul.

[39] See the website of the Kurdistan Regional Government: <www.krg.org>, accessed September 2013.

[40] See Joseph Yacoub, "Interview," *L'Avvenire* (an Italian daily), Milan, 1 February 2009.

[41] See its website: <alfikr-almasihi.com>, accessed September 2013.

awarded by the International Catholic Union of the Press (ICUP). This journal, whose editor is the Dominican Father Yousuf Thomas, is a mine of information and a melting pot of ideas, despite being beset by every imaginable impediment. Published in Arabic—with a summary in French—and appreciated by everyone, this publication has survived the worst crises in the history of Iraq. Reaching all levels of Iraqi society, *al-Fikr al-Masihi* has become a reference point for Christians, Muslims, and other religions. As for the Chaldean Patriarchate, it publishes a respected magazine, *Nagm Al-Mashriq* ("Star of the East").

In Kirkuk, 10,000 Chaldeo-Assyrian-Syriacs[42] pursue a multitude of activities despite the climate of insecurity.[43] This is a highly sensitive city whose ethno-demographic character was changed by Saddam Hussein (forced displacement of Kurds, Arabization, settlement of Arabs from the South), and whose status remains uncertain.[44]

In the media, the Assyro-Chaldeans are active in publication (books, journals, periodicals) and in audio-visual media (television, news agencies such as the Assyrian International News Agency, and several internet sites including one that is especially popular: <ankawa.com>).

Elsewhere, particularly in the south, in Basra, the Christian presence is dwindling due to the exodus, and only small Chaldean, Syriac, and Armenian communities remain there.

AN AUTONOMOUS ADMINISTRATIVE PROVINCE FOR THE ASSYRO-CHALDEANS?

On the other hand, since time immemorial the Assyro-Chaldeans have lived in dense concentrations on sections of land around Mosul, the overwhelmingly Arab capital of Nineveh province. For reasons of safety—and supported in this

---

[42] A dramatic decrease compared to 20,000 in 2003.

[43] The Chaldeans have four schools and two kindergartens, as well as programs in Syriac on television and radio. Two Christians represent the community on the Municipal Assembly.

[44] The city of Kirkuk, which is the capital of the province (*muhafazat*) of Taamim has a multi-ethnic composition: Kurds, Arabs (Sunni and Shia), Turkmen, Chaldeo-Assyrian-Syriacs, and Armenians. At one time, there were Jews. This is a historic city dating back to the Sumerians and Babylonians. Christianity there goes back to the first few centuries. This means that it has been very diverse. It abounds in castles and citadels, and is the location of the tomb of the prophet Daniel. It is an important cultural centre for Turkmen, who have been in the area since the twelfth century. It is located 255 km northeast of Baghdad, has fewer than one million inhabitants and is very rich in oil resources. Kurds claim it as their province: they view it as an integral part of Kurdistan—historically, geographically, and demographically. Arabs, Turkmen, and other minorities have strongly opposed this claim, fearing its Kurdization. From time to time, the city has experienced ethnic tensions, and security there has deteriorated markedly.

by its diasporas, particularly its US wing—part of the community is calling for the creation of its own territory, a geographical and administrative entity that would protect the Assyro-Chaldeans and their cultural and religious rights within a relatively homogeneous region (i.e. a safe haven). In fact, Assyro-Chaldean political groupings and associations have proposed a settlement plan of this type. Some are asking that their country be connected to Kurdistan, which, on its own behalf, is demanding lands in this same province (and in three others); however, the Arab population does not necessarily agree with these demands, which are controversial.[45]

In fact, the areas disputed by Arabs and Kurds belong to four different provinces (Nineveh, Al-Ta'mim, Diyala, Wasit) whose boundaries could be subject to change based on ethnic and religious affiliation. In addition to the city of Kirkuk (al-Ta'mim province), this involves the *Qadas* (districts) of Makhmour[46] (south of Mosul, predominantly Kurdish), Aqrah (north of Mosul, predominantly Kurdish), Mandali (Diyala province, predominantly Turkmen), Tall Afar (Nineveh province, predominantly Shi'ite Turkmen), Sinjar and Sheikhan (Nineveh province, predominantly Yezidi Kurds), the *qada* of Hawija (province of Kirkuk, predominantly Arab and whose population does not wish to be incorporated into Kurdistan), and Khanaqin (Diyala province, predominantly Shi'ite Kurds). The Kurds are also laying claim to the *qada* of Badra in the province of Wasit (Art. 2 of the draft Kurdish constitution).

What is the significance of the self-government plan and how should it be interpreted? To start, we need to clarify the status of the provinces in the Iraqi Constitution. As we have seen, with respect to local government, the Iraqi Constitution theoretically guarantees administrative, political, cultural, and educational rights to the different Iraqi nationalities, including the Assyro-Chaldeans: "This Constitution shall guarantee the administrative, political, cultural, and educational rights of the various nationalities, such as Turkmens, Chaldeans, Assyrians, and all other constituents, and this shall be regulated by law" (Art. 125). We can therefore say that the Assyro-Chaldeans are recognized as a nationality, together with its associated rights. So far, however, the measures taken in this regard have not conformed sufficiently to Article 125.

In addition, Section V (Chapter I, Arts. 116–21) of the Basic Law gives broad decentralization powers to the regions (*Iqlim*) and provinces (*Mohafazat*).[47] However, under Article 117.2, new regions (one or more provinces) can

[45] On this issue, see "Les Chrétiens d'Irak rêvent d'avoir d'un canton," *Al-Watan Al-Arabi* (Arabic weekly), Paris, 23 April 2008, pp. 28–9.

[46] Located on the border between the cities of Mosul, Arbil, and Kirkuk, this *qada* currently depends on Mosul, and consequently on the province of Nineveh. The majority of the population is Kurdish and seeks its incorporation into Kurdistan.

[47] Iraq is divided into eighteen provinces and one region, Kurdistan, which has three provinces: Dehok, Arbil, and Suleimanyié.

be formed and equipped with their own Constitution that establishes the structure of *Iqlim* powers: legislative, executive (including security forces), and judicial powers, and powers of representation in Iraqi embassies abroad to pursue cultural, social, and development matters (Arts. 120 and 121). Chapter 2 of Section 5 of the Constitution (Arts. 122–3) defines the powers of provinces that have not been formed into broad-based, decentralized regions.

But unlike the Kurds, who have three provinces in the north (Dehok, Arbil, and Suleimanyié) grouped into one region, namely, Iqlim Kurdistan (the Kurdistan Region, recognized by the Iraqi Constitution, Art. 117.1), and which gained self-government in 1992,[48] the Assyro-Chaldeans have no specific geographical province, let alone a region. The territory in which they are demographically dense is incorporated into Nineveh province, which has a large Arab majority. The rest of the population lives in settlements concentrated in the autonomous region of Kurdistan. Those who live in Baghdad are scattered over several neighborhoods. Others (far fewer) are found mostly in Kirkuk and Basra.

However, fear of ghettoization means that there is no general agreement concerning these plans.[49] In this regard, Pope Benedict XVI has repeatedly called for the protection of Iraq Christians and reiterated the Vatican's preference for "regional and negotiated resolution of the conflicts and crises troubling the region."[50] At the same time, he expressed his opposition to the plan for gathering Iraqi Christians into one region, the Nineveh Plain.[51] That said, not all Iraqi Christians are Catholic and opinions are divided on this issue.

While proposals for territorial autonomy are controversial, the more general concept of self-government has captured a lot of attention. The concept of self-government—not to be confused with independence—is resurfacing. After a long period in which it was of secondary importance, the concept has become central. Self-government is acquiring clarity and making positive intellectual and prescriptive progress. It is now accepted by international law, and has gradually become an everyday concept and norm.

In addition to equality, non-discrimination,[52] respect for the inherent dignity of every person, and differential treatment (affirmative action), it

---

[48] Self-government in Kurdistan has been a reality since 1992; it has been approved by the Iraqi Constitution (Arts. 117 and 141).

[49] See Louis Sako, "The plains of Nineveh, a trap for Iraqi Christians!," *Asia News*, Rome, 6 July 2007.

[50] *Le Monde*, 12 June 2007.

[51] See Isabelle de Gaulmyn, "Benoît XVI s'inquiéte des retombées de la politique américaine en Irak," *La Croix*, 11 June 2007.

[52] Article 14 of the Iraqi Constitution recognizes the equality of all Iraqis before the law regardless of gender, race, ethnicity, nationality, origin, colour, religion, faith, belief, opinion, or social or economic status.

would be appropriate to retain the possibility of self-administration—within the framework of existing states—when a minority has a dense presence inside a territory.

Indeed, there has been much discussion of the principle of equality and non-discrimination as advanced by the UN's Universal Declaration of Human Rights[53] and confirmed in all international treaties on human rights. As for differential treatment, it is embodied in different ways in different countries, political systems, cultures, and civilizations, including the United Kingdom, Canada, United States, India, and South Africa. Each of these countries uses specific measures to restore equality affected by social, ethnic, economic, cultural, and linguistic imbalances; it seeks to correct these inequities and thereby contribute to the common good.

As for the institutional content of self-government, its jurisdiction and its effects—and despite the traditional hostility of the Arab countries to such a plan—they vary from one country to another depending on their political system. Admittedly, in some cases minorities are given a personal right (*sui juris*). There are several categories of self-government, depending on the context and the specific case: sociocultural, administrative, regional, territorial, aboriginal self-government, and self-government for regions with special status due to their history, geography, or population density. The right to self-government implies an option given to minorities for self-determination within a state respectful of diversity; this in turn implies a sense of duty. Here, one might refer to it as "self-government/solidarity."

Of course, minorities have the right to self-government in all matters relating to their local affairs—affairs in which the institutional content and jurisdictional reach may vary. Clearly, a minority that is concentrated in one area, as are the Assyro-Chaldeans of northern Iraq, might benefit from self-government, whereas a dispersed minority might benefit from greater equality, non-discrimination, and differential treatment (affirmative action).

In this case, the right to self-government involves the right that should be granted to Assyro-Chaldeans for self-determination in a responsible way and as part of the *existing* state, provinces, and regions, and implemented with a sense of duty and respect for each other's diversity. Furthermore, it should be noted that this is not the first time there has been talk about self-government for the Assyro-Chaldeans: the plan has a history. The question has surfaced recurrently since 1919, when it was raised at the Peace Conference,[54] and then again in 1930, 1935, 1937, and 1945.

---

[53] See Articles 1 and 2 of this Declaration, adopted by the UN General Assembly on 10 December 1948.

[54] See Claire Weibel Yacoub, *Le Rêve brisé des Assyro-Chaldéens: L'introuvable autonomie* (Paris: Cerf, 2011), 113–82.

As we noted, Assyro-Chaldean groups are actively working for self-government. Some dream of having their own flag, their own government, and their own security forces. In 2011 a number of initiatives were taken and thirteen organizations called for self-government. A memorandum, released on 15 July 2011, was presented to the Iraqi and Kurdish authorities.[55] Previously, an assembly of these thirteen Chaldeo-Assyrian-Syriac organizations had published its political program, in which it set national targets, including the creation of an autonomous province in the districts (*quada*) and subdistricts (*nahya*) of Hamdanié, Tell-Keif, Baachika, Al Qush, and Bartelé, in association with the other national and religious groups living there, and in accordance with guarantees set out by the Iraqi Constitution.[56] It also requested activation of Article 35 of the Kurdish region's draft Constitution, which requires granting self-determination to the Assyro-Chaldeans following a referendum on the Constitution.[57]

Is an autonomous territory in the plain of Nineveh a viable option? This depends on what basis it would be created. Some discussions have centered on an autonomous province for Christians, others on a province for ethnic Assyrian-Chaldean-Syriacs. Thus, a few questions are in order. First, what would be its geographical and administrative nature: provincial, district, or borough? What would be its scope? Is it desirable to create a province based on a religion? This option can be ruled out, because it would contradict the secularism defended by Assyro-Chaldeans; it would have harmful consequences.

An ethnically based plan might be difficult to attain. Would it be binding a priori on the Iraqi Constitution? Also, to what extent would it be reconcilable with the unity of Iraq, which is the Mesopotamian homeland to which the Assyro-Chaldeans refer, and to which they are very attached? Thus, one must first define the concepts of unity and diversity and their relationship. Of course, a nation may be a melting-pot for several nationalities.

The other difficulty resides in the fact that the Assyro-Chaldeans are not the only minority living within the zone claimed in the Nineveh Valley (Hamdanié, Tell-Keif, Baachika, Al Qush, Bartelle ...); this region is also inhabited by Arab Muslims, Yezidis, Kurds, Mandaeans (Sabeans), and Chabaks. How would these minorities react, and what would be the reaction of the Arab majority that is in competition with the Kurds, who claim territory in the Province of Nineveh?

---

[55] See the website: <www.ankawa.com/forum/index.php>, accessed September 2013.

[56] See n. 55. This platform also calls for strengthening citizenship among the Iraqi people and the revision of education and teaching programs to bring them into line with the country's diversity.

[57] See n. 55.

On the other hand, their low numbers and the Arabic and Kurdish environments are such that they could not withstand the political inflexibility this type of plan would entail. The Kurds imposed their autonomy, which dates from 1992. As for the Arabs, most are opposed to self-government on the part of minorities and seem wary of political plans they describe as secessionist. In present circumstances, it is to be feared that such demands are likely to further isolate Assyrians, draw attention to their particular characteristics, and affect the national and social fabric of Iraq, already quite fragile. In addition, creating a new province (consisting of districts, subdistricts, and villages)[58] in Iraq is not easy, either legally or administratively.

In August 2011, the thirteen Assyro-Chaldean-Syriac organizations that had been brought together in the previously mentioned assembly embarked upon an important initiative with the Iraqi authorities to make known their plan for an autonomous province. On 16 August Osama Al-Noujeifi, the chairman of Parliament, and Khaled Al-Atteya, chairman of the governing parliamentary coalition (known as the "State of Law" parliamentary group) received a delegation. On this occasion, Iraqi officials praised the patriotism of Iraqi Christians, and made known their opposition to the division of the country and their commitment to its sovereignty and unity.[59] However, the chairman of the Iraqi Parliament insisted on the territorial unity of the province of Nineveh, and referred to it as the "red line."[60]

What then are the options? The question is now open, and merits careful reflection and a dispassionate, realistic approach. From the standpoint of self-government, the story is a painful one. It reminds us that whenever the Assyro-Chaldeans have claimed self-government, it was rejected out of hand and ruthlessly repressed, without any reaction from the international community.

That said, the Iraqi government is obliged to protect its citizens. The Iraqi Constitution contains positive measures in support of the Assyrian-Syriac-Chaldeans; these measures must be set in motion and put into practice. Article 125 of the Constitution recognizes the Assyro-Chaldeans and their national administrative, political, cultural, and educational rights. Similarly, Article 4 establishes the Syriac[61] language, among others, as an official language in administrative units where the Assyro-Chaldean community is highly concentrated.[62] Given these conditions, by strengthening specific details (in the form of law) of these legal norms, one can hope for a more acceptable outcome in terms of giving recognition to the Chaldeo-Assyrian-Syriacs.

---

[58] See Article 122 of the Iraqi Constitution, which determines the status of the provinces.
[59] See the website at n. 55.   [60] See the website at n. 55.
[61] As well as the Turkmen language.
[62] On 16 August 2011, the Iraqi Parliament adopted a new law concerning the Ministry of Education. Among other things, it involves the creation of a Department of Syriac Studies. See the website at n. 55.

CONCLUSION

Since becoming independent, Arab countries have failed to give consideration to any serious overall policy for minorities. There has been an inability to put the resources of these countries to their best use, since nationalism has always had an overriding influence. It is now crucial that the numerous minorities be fully recognized and obtain the right to equality and non-discrimination.

Change in the Arab world in the areas of democracy and liberation must now include multiculturalism and the concerns of minorities in its field of vision and its political and social space. To accomplish this, reforms are required, including the development of a political culture of multiculturalism and minority rights. One can only hope that the current changes portend a better tomorrow.

With regard to Iraq, we may conclude that its Constitution contains no citizen-centered plan and is not supported by any guiding political philosophy. Partisan, uncompromising considerations dominate. Nonetheless, if its Constitution is here to stay, it should at least be given a more constructive role—one able to reconcile unity and diversity.

Index